D0274978

ANDERSONIAN LIBRARY
WITHDRAWN
FROM
LIBRARY
STOCK
UNIVERSITY OF STRATHCLYDE

OXFORD MEDICAL PUBLICATIONS

Causal Relationships in Medicine

Causal Relationships in Medicine

A Practical System for Critical Appraisal

J. MARK ELWOOD

Professor and Chairman,
Department of Community Medicine and Epidemiology,
University of Nottingham

Oxford New York Melbourne
OXFORD UNIVERSITY PRESS
1988

Oxford University Press, Walton Street, Oxford OX2 6DP
Oxford New York Toronto
Delhi Bombay Calcutta Madras Karachi
Petaling Jaya Singapore Hong Kong Tokyo
Nairobi Dar es Salaam Cape Town
Melbourne Auckland
and associated companies in
Berlin Ibadan

Oxford is a trade mark of Oxford University Press

Published in the United States
by Oxford University Press, New York

British Library Cataloguing in Publication Data
Elwood, J. Mark
Causal relationships in medicine:
a practical system for critical appraisal
1. Medicine. Causal explanation
I. Title
610'.1
ISBN 0-19-261703-6

Library of Congress Cataloging in Publication Data
Elwood, J. Mark.
Causal relationships in medicine: a practical system for critical appraisal/J. Mark Elwood.
(Oxford medical publications)
Bibliography Includes index.
1. Epidemiology——Research——Methodology. 2. Causation.
I. Title. II. Series.
[DNLM: 1. Epidemiologic Methods. 2. Epidemiology. WA 950 E52c]
RA652.4.E48 1988 614.4'028——dc19 88-9921
ISBN 0-19-261703-6

Set by Colset Private Limited, Singapore
Printed in Great Britain
at the University Printing House, Oxford
by David Stanford
Printer to the University

To Candace,
Jeremy and Briana

Contents

Preface

The purpose of this book is to help readers to use their existing skills and knowledge more effectively. Physicians and other health workers have often a curious training: an extensive, even rigorous experience in one or more of the laboratory sciences, followed by a clinical apprenticeship and a style of practice which is neutral or even antagonistic to critical thinking. Then, faced with making decisions independently, they have to deal with a rapidly developing subject, with new ideas and new findings appearing regularly. Moreover, when health professionals have mastered the accepted norms of practice in their chosen field, they become aware of the limitations of current knowledge, and a perhaps long buried spirit of curiosity may emerge.

Questions in medical practice—and I include in this the work of medical scientists, nurses, health educators, and others—deal with the actions and fate of people in a real world. To deal with these questions, the health professional may have available a great deal of subject matter knowledge and practical experience, some basic scientific method, some half-remembered statistics, and so on; but usually lacks skill in how to apply these disparate items. The unhelpful and inaccurate impression is sometimes created that one's previous experience is of little help, and one must return to study new subjects in great depth. I believe that what is more important is some guidance on strategy, on the relevance of one's existing knowledge, and demonstrations of some new methods chosen to be practical, reasonably simple, and widely applicable; the latter because the next issue which arises may be quite different from the current one.

The approach I present here has developed in response to questions in the areas of aetiological research, early diagnosis and screening, randomized and non-randomized clinical trials, prognostic studies, health service issues, and the evaluation of health education and promotion. For any one of these, the specialist can find more comprehensive works; my objective in this book is to emphasize the aspects common to these issues.

The book should be useful to two groups of colleagues. The larger group are those who need to read, evaluate, and apply new findings in their own field, and students who need to sort and select material; they will find here a logical scheme which they can apply to new questions and new literature. For those who are engaged in or starting research themselves, the same skills are needed, and also I have selected some widely applicable analytical methods which are frequently used in current literature and yet are not often to be found in introductory courses or texts. The appendices should be a useful reference source for these; I am aware of no other source which brings together these methods and the statistical tables needed to interpret them. In this regard, I am well aware of the difficulty which statistical methods pose to many health professionals whose formal mathematical training perforce ended many years ago. Statistics is but one aspect of study design and interpretation. I would encourage those who are uncomfortable with statistics to use the rest of the book first—ignore chapter 7—as they will find that most of the relevant issues can be dealt with by logical and careful thinking, without more than basic arithmetic.

One always has a loftier purpose; mine is to attempt to bridge some gaps: between practising physicians and researchers, between medical investigators and those with other backgrounds, between those who are concerned with therapy and those concerned with prevention, and between those who study small numbers of subjects in a clinical setting and those who study larger numbers with a community orientation.

December 1987 J.M.E.
Nottingham

Acknowledgements

This book has grown irregularly through my teaching and research activities over the past ten years, and so has been influenced in uncountable ways by the guidance, stimulation, and questioning of my colleagues and students. It is impossible to mention all those who have helped me devèlop these ideas; they include my colleagues in the Department of Community Medicine and Epidemiology in Nottingham, those at my former base in the Cancer Control Agency of British Columbia, and those at the Department of Preventive and Social Medicine at the University of Otago, Dunedin whose hospitality and helpful advice during a sabbatical period has helped me to finish the work. I must specifically record my thanks to Jim Pearson, Andy Coldman, George Spears, and Professor David Skegg whose detailed comments on draft chapters have been most helpful; and to Pam Gillies, Julian Little, Richard Madeley and Richard Gallagher whose suggestions and encouragement have been most valuable. I have had wonderful support on secretarial and technical matters from Joyce Gilbert, Alison Langham, and Graham Widdowson in Nottingham, and from Eileen Moore and her colleagues in Dunedin. My wife and children have suffered considerably from lost evenings and weekends over a long period, and for their patience and good humour I will always be grateful.

I wish to thank the senior authors and publishers who have allowed me to reproduce material; in particular Professors Martin Vessey and Desmond Julian, and Dr Harry Ziel, and the publishers of the *Lancet* and the *New England Journal of Medicine* for the papers considered in Chapters 9, 10 and 11. The appendix of statistical tables helps make the book a complete text, and thanks are due to Dr G.H. Fisher and Hodder and Stoughton for statistical Tables 5 and 6, reproduced from *The new form statistical tables*. I am also grateful to the Literary Executor of the late Sir Ronald A. Fisher, F.R.S., to Dr Frank Yates, F.R.S. and to Longman Group Ltd., London, for permission to reprint Tables I, II, VIII4, from their book *Statistical Tables for Biological, Agricultural and Medical Research* (6th edition, 1974), reproduced as Tables 1–4. Appendix 2 includes material from a review article, used by permission of Dr Andy Coldman and the *Canadian Medical Association Journal*, originally published in that journal, Vol. 121, October 20, 1979.

Introduction

There is occasions and causes, why and wherefore in all things.

—William Shakespeare: Henry V, v; 1599

This book will present a system which should assist the reader to evaluate the results of studies in the health and medical fields, in terms of the extent to which those results support a cause and effect relationship. The method presented is one of many possible approaches, but over several years many practising physicians, nurses, health educators, medical students and other health care professionals have found it interesting and useful. It is a general method applicable to a wide range of issues, although of course for each issue expertise in the particular subject matter is essential.

The scheme is shown in Exhibit 1. We start with a discussion of the concept of causation (Chapter 1), and then discuss the types of study design which can be used to demonstrate causation (Chapter 2) and the way in which their key results can be expressed precisely and simply (Chapter 3). We then move to the central issue of the interpretation of the results of any one study. We consider how the subjects in a study should be chosen (Chapter 4), and then consider in turn each of the three non-causal explanations which have to be eliminated before a judgment of a causal explanation can be made. These are observation bias (Chapter 5), confounding (Chapter 6), and chance variation (Chapter 7). We can then consider whether the results show features which positively support causation (Chapter 8). From this approach, we can decide the extent to which the results of a particular study support a causal interpretation. The next step is to move beyond one particular study to see how the results of other studies of the same or different types affect our conclusions, and to what extent we feel the conclusion is valid outside the context of the particular study (Chapter 8). We then provide a review of these steps, and consider how this scheme for the evaluation of causal relationships can be applied to important issues within the reader's own field of interest. Chapters 9, 10, and 11 give examples of the application of the scheme to three studies of different designs: a cohort study, a case-control study, and a randomized clinical trial.

Most of this book can be understood without complex mathematics. Statistical issues are dealt with in Chapter 7, and the statistical methods of most value are summarized for reference in the appendices. Statistical questions form only one aspect of the evaluation of evidence. Readers who wish to ignore the mathematical parts of this book should feel free to do so, as the approach we present should be valuable even to readers who wish to leave the details of the statistical issues to others.

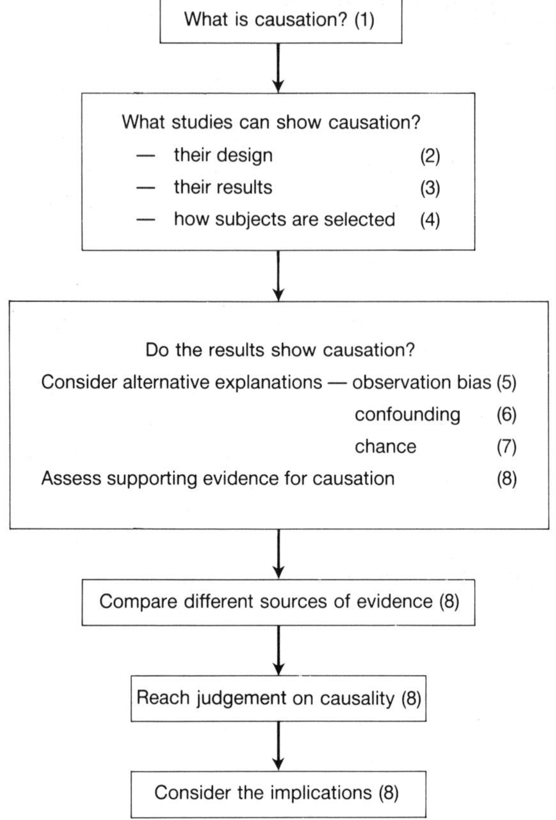

Exhibit 1. The assessment of causation. The overall strategy presented in the book for assessing the evidence for and against causality in a particular issue. Numbers indicate the relevant chapter

1. The importance of causal relationships in medicine

Intellectual progress is by no one trait so adequately characterized as by the development of the idea of causation.
—Herbert Spencer: The data of ethics, IV; 1879

The study of causal relationships is essential to medicine (Ex. 1.1). In the therapeutic situation, the decision to offer a treatment is based on the assumption that that treatment will *cause* an improvement in the patient's condition. The study of the aetiology of a disease involves determining which factors *cause* the disease to occur. In broader questions of the provision of health services, the decision to provide a certain type of health facility assumes that the existence of that facility will *cause* an improvement in the health of the community which it serves. It is the purpose of this work to explore the methods available to us to test whether relationships are in fact causal, and therefore to decide whether the assumptions behind decisions relating to therapy, aetiology, and health service management, are true or false.

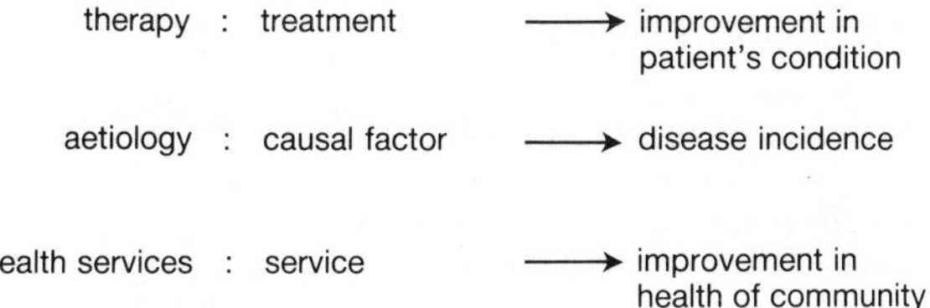

Ex. 1.1. The relevance of causal relationships in medicine. Decisions on therapy, aetiology or health services provision all make assumptions of cause and effect relationships

The nature of causation

To discuss causal relationships, we must have a definition of causation, and this definition will determine the means by which causation can be demonstrated or disproved. The concept of causation often brings to mind what is only an extreme and limiting situation, that is the situation where a certain event always and invariably follows another event. This is a familiar notion because it is regularly observed in the physical sciences. For example, Boyle's Law states that at a given temperature, the volume of a fixed mass of a gas is inversely proportional to its pressure. Thus under those circumstances of mass and temperature, a change in pressure will result invariably and

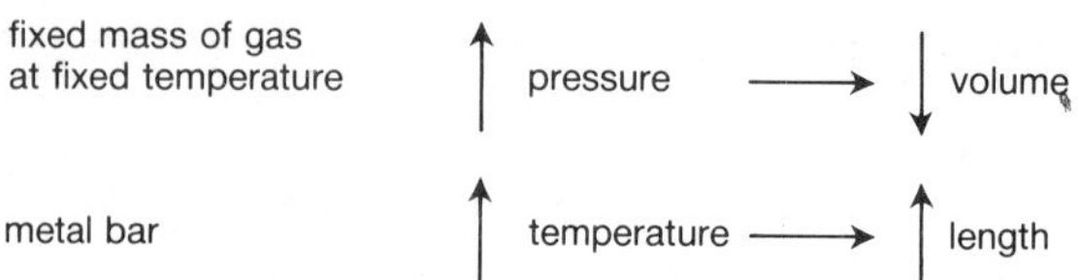

Ex. 1.2. Simple causal relationships. Causal relationships in the physical sciences are often simple, as in Boyle's Law relating pressure and volume of a gas, or the effect of heat on a metal bar. The causal agent is sufficient, the time relationship is short, and replication is easy

automatically in a corresponding change in volume (Ex. 1.2). The effect is instantaneous, can be replicated easily, and can be expressed as a simple mathematical relationship. There is therefore little difficulty in accepting the notion that a change in pressure causes a change in volume. Similarly there is little difficulty in the concept that applying heat to a metal bar causes it to expand; again there is an invariable and almost immediate relationship between the outcome, that is the change of length of the bar, and the exposure, that is the heat applied to the bar.

This type of causation has a number of special properties. The chief among them is that the causal agent is 'sufficient', in other words the operation of the one defined causal agent invariably produces the outcome. Second, the time relationship between the exposure and the outcome is very short. Third, because the situation can be modelled in an experiment, it can be replicated with ease under controlled conditions.

infection with mycobacterium tuberculosis ⟶ clinical tuberculosis

Ex. 1.3. Simple causal relationship? An apparently simple causal relationship in medicine. But while the causal agent is necessary, it is not sufficient and the time relationship is uncertain

Situations which are relevant to human health and disease are rarely as simple. In human health and disease not all causal agents are sufficient. For example, the disease tuberculosis is caused by infection of the human body by the tubercle bacillus (Ex. 1.3). However infection by the tubercle bacillus does not invariably lead to clinical tuberculosis. Only a small proportion of those who are infected by the bacillus develop clinical disease, and a number of other factors influence whether the disease develops, such as poor nutrition (Ex. 1.4). Thus a combination of tubercle bacillus infection and poor nutrition, with perhaps other factors, is required for clinical disease. We must consider both the tubercle bacillus and poor nutrition as causal factors.

The tubercle bacillus in this situation is a 'necessary' cause of the disease. We can now define two categories of causal factors. *Sufficient* causal factors, acting on their own, will invariably produce the outcome, while *necessary* causal factors are those without which the outcome cannot occur (Ex. 1.5). In the Boyle's Law situation, a change in pressure was both necessary and sufficient for a change in volume, given that the other circumstances were

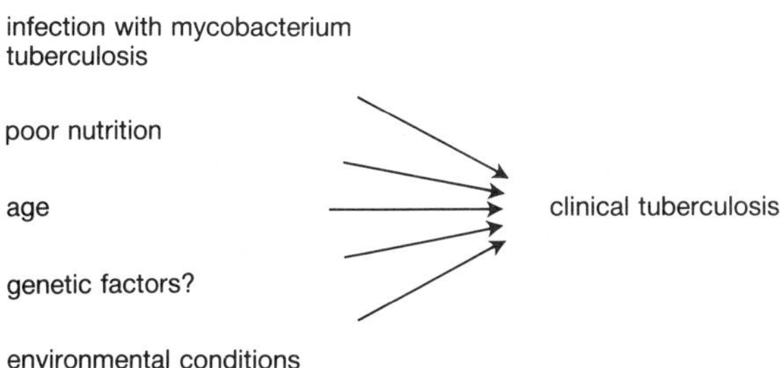

Ex. 1.4. Simple causal relationship? A somewhat more complete diagram of the causes of clinical tuberculosis

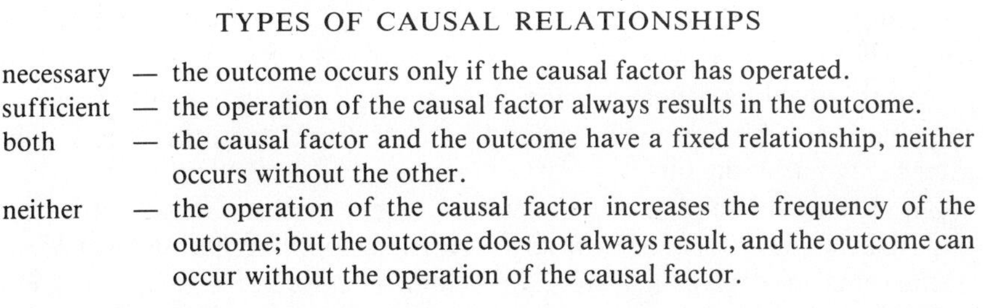

TYPES OF CAUSAL RELATIONSHIPS

necessary	— the outcome occurs only if the causal factor has operated.
sufficient	— the operation of the causal factor always results in the outcome.
both	— the causal factor and the outcome have a fixed relationship, neither occurs without the other.
neither	— the operation of the causal factor increases the frequency of the outcome; but the outcome does not always result, and the outcome can occur without the operation of the causal factor.

Ex. 1.5. The different types of causal relationships. The last category is by far the most important

fixed; in the metal bar example, heat was a sufficient but not a necessary cause; there are other ways of lengthening a metal bar.

Most situations in health and disease do not fulfil the criteria either for necessary or for sufficient causation. If an otherwise healthy patient is admitted to hospital with multiple fractures, and the patient had been hit by a bus just outside the hospital, most people would conclude that there was a causal relationship between being hit by the bus and having multiple fractures. But the relationship implies neither that the cause is sufficient nor that it is necessary. Not all people hit by buses have multiple fractures. Not all patients with multiple fractures have been hit by buses.

A frequent error of logic is to define causation in a way which describes only the limiting case of the necessary and sufficient cause. This leads to the conclusion that in most real situations causation cannot be demonstrated, and therefore decisions must be made without any method of separating real from spurious relationships.

We must use a concept of causation which is relevant to medical issues, and define a causal association in a way which is applicable to most real situations. The definition of cause we will use is: a factor is a cause of an event if its operation increases the frequency of the event (Ex. 1.6).

DEFINITION OF CAUSE

cause: a factor is a cause of an event if its operation increases the frequency of the event

Ex. 1.6. The general definition of cause. Necessary and sufficient causation are merely extremes within this definition

The opposite of a causal factor is, of course, a preventive factor, whose operation decreases the frequency of the outcome event. The concept of causality, and the evidence required to assess it, applies also to preventive and therapeutic issues.

Returning to the patient with multiple fractures, what led us to the decision that these were caused by having been hit by a bus? The main evidence is the immediate time relationship. We conclude from questioning the patient and witnesses that the patient was acting normally and did not have multiple fractures immediately before being hit by the bus, and we conclude from an examination of his current state that he had multiple fractures immediately after being hit by the bus.

Suppose we move to another situation, where a patient shows confusion and neurological signs which are consistent with a chronic subdural haematoma, and gives a history of being knocked down by a car some months previously. Can we assume a causal relationship in this case? Because the time relation is not so clear, we cannot easily make such a judgment, as other events which occurred before the clinical signs developed may have been causal. Suppose, however, we study a number of patients who have subdural haematomata, and we find that most of them give a history of a head injury. We should then be justified in suspecting that the apparent connection between the two events indicates a cause and effect relationship. However, we should realize that our method of recording a history of previous injury was deficient. We should expect that many patients who had had an injury would not be able to report it, and similarly many of the injuries reported might be expected as part of normal life. To go much further we should ask ourselves whether the frequency with which such events are experienced by patients with subdural haematomata is different from what we should expect; and then we should need to know what we should expect. We should need to determine the frequency of such injuries in similar people who did not have a subdural haematoma.

So, where the time relation is not clear, and the concepts of necessary and sufficient cause do not hold, we need a *quantitative* assessment of the relationship, based on observations not on one individual but on a number of individuals.

A direct test of causation

The most direct test of the quantitative definition of causation is therefore to have two groups of individuals, who are very similar in all relevant characteristics, and apply to one group the putative causative factor. 'Relevant' characteristics are those factors, other than the one under study, which affect the frequency of the outcome event. If a causal relationship exists, the frequency with which the defined outcome is observed will be higher in the group exposed to the putative causal factor than it will be in the other group. A study design which uses this approach is the randomized trial; that is, the assignment of the treatment for each subject is made by a random or chance procedure (Ex. 1.7).

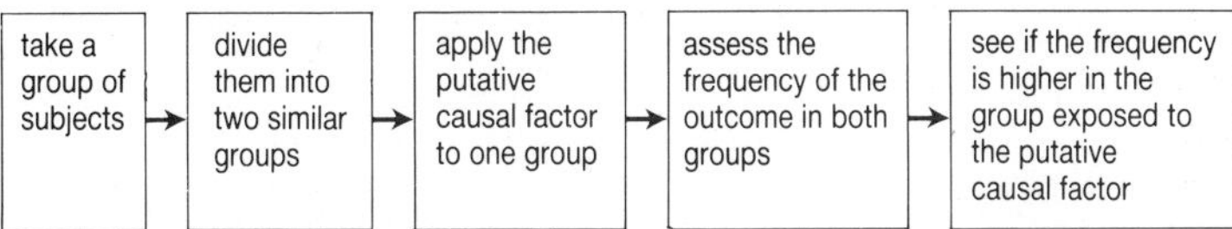

Ex. 1.7. One way to test causation. When applied to therapy for patients, this is the randomized clinical trial. It is also the basic controlled experiment of biology and other sciences

Randomized trials were used first in agricultural science, where, for example, fertilizers were applied to plots of soil and identical untreated plots were used for comparison; subsequently, crop yields were measured. The causal relationship between fertilizer application and crop yield was seen in the difference in crop yield between treated and untreated plots. The application of this technique to medicine dates from the late 1940s; a trial of therapy for tuberculosis is often regarded as the first such study (Ex. 1.8). The method has been used most extensively in trials of methods of therapy, where the methods compared are generally similar, for example the choice between giving one drug and giving a different drug. The ways in which randomization contributes to the study design will be discussed in later chapters; at present it is useful to note the two main features. Because the groups receiving each of the treatments being compared are selected by a chance assignment, they are likely to be similar to each other in regard to any factors (other than the treatment) which influence the outcome; so differences in the outcome will be easier to interpret. Because the different groups are being treated and assessed at the same time, it is often possible to design the study so that neither the subjects nor the investigators are aware of which treatment has been given, and this 'double-blind' method will allow the observations of outcome to be made in the same way for all subjects.

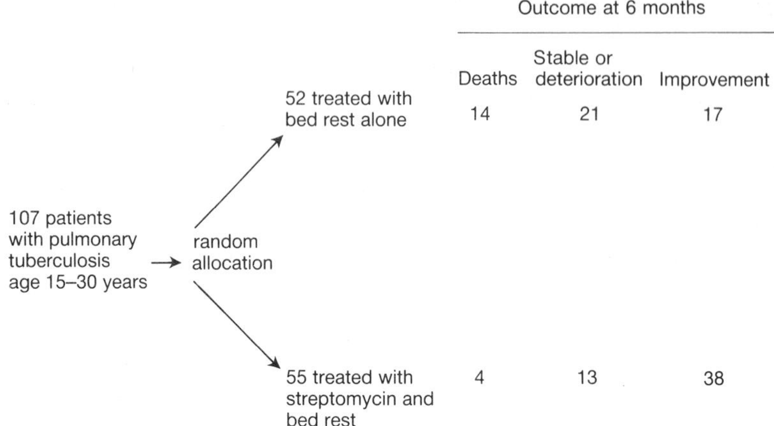

Ex. 1.8. A trial of chemotherapy for advanced pulmonary tuberculosis, which was organized by the British Medical Research Council and which began in 1946. Often regarded as the first randomized clinical trial. From: Medical Research Council, (1948)

There is no argument with the statement that the double-blind randomized prospective trial is the ideal way to test a causal relationship in the medical area. However the procedure is not necessarily a simple one to carry out, not so much for scientific reasons but for practical and ethical ones. For example, to compare the efficacy of two types of treatment whose aim is to reduce the long term mortality from a chronic disease such as cancer, a large number of patients who all have a similar type of disease will have to be randomized, receive treatment, and be followed up for many years. Such a trial is obviously an expensive undertaking and has major logistic problems. Its results apply to the therapies used during the trial, and may be made obsolete by new therapies. The absolute limitation of the prospective randomized trial is that it can be used only to assess interventions which are likely to be beneficial. Many important relationships concern harmful rather than beneficial exposures, and it is clearly unethical to randomize individuals to receive a harmful exposure, such as being exposed to smoking, industrial pollutants, or other toxins. Even when the comparisons are to be made between exposures which we would hope are beneficial, for example different treatments, there may well be sufficient disparity of professional opinion so that many individual physicians may not judge it ethical to enter patients under their care into randomized trials.

One response to this situation is to define causation as that which can be demonstrated in a randomized trial, and to discount all other situations. This is an unrealistic stance. On this definition, we could not assume a causal relationship between the multiple fractures and the bus accident. This viewpoint that a particular scientific method determines the definition of causation, is the root of the commonly made assertion that epidemiological or observational studies, can show 'only associations'. It is the purpose of much of this work to argue that this is not true.

The thesis which will be presented is that the decision as to whether a certain relationship is causal must in all cases be a balanced professional judgment. We will argue that even prospective randomized trials do not 'prove' causation, because there are many practical and methodological pitfalls of such trials which can lead them to produce inaccurate results. Moreover, it will be argued that causation can be adequately demonstrated by other scientific methods, and that the acceptance of causation on the basis of results of such methods is essential to medical practice. Only a small fraction of therapeutic decisions in medicine can be supported by the results of randomized trials. Almost no managerial or policy decisions can be so supported. Almost no conclusions as to the causes and natural history of disease can be supported by such evidence. For most of our knowledge of medicine in terms of therapy, aetiology and health care planning, we must use observational studies, because of the ethical and logistical impossibility of mounting randomized trials in more than a tiny proportion of circumstances. We must therefore be prepared to consider such observational evidence and to gain skill in judging such evidence in terms of the extent to which it supports a causal relationship.

2. Study designs which can demonstrate and test causation

All true and fruitful natural philosophy hath a double scale or ladder, ascendent and descendent, ascending from experiments to the inventions of causes, and descending from causes to the invention of new experiments.
—Francis Bacon: The advancement of learning, II; 1605

The definition of a causal factor given in Chapter 1 was, 'a factor whose operation increases the frequency of an event'. This implies that people who are affected by the causal agent will have a higher frequency of the defined outcome, and also individuals with the defined outcome will have a greater frequency of past exposure to the cause. Thus there are two general types of comparative study which can be done. One will compare individuals exposed to the putative causative factor with individuals not exposed, and the other will compare individuals with the outcome in question to those without the outcome. We will refer to these studies as *cohort* studies and *case–control* studies respectively. The randomized trial introduced in Chapter 1 is a special type of cohort study, where the two groups are defined after randomization.

These studies are set up to test causal hypotheses. If the hypothesis is that the causal agent is either necessary or sufficient, or both, the results are simple to interpret. A single demonstration from unequivocal data that the defined outcome has occurred without the operation of the putative causal factor shows that that causal factor is not necessary. A single demonstration from unequivocal data that the causal factor is not followed by the defined outcome is enough to show that that causal factor is not sufficient. These are of course theoretical propositions, and in real situations a single demonstration would not be enough, as questions of error or incompleteness in the reliability of the observations would always be raised. It is theoretically impossible to demonstrate necessary or sufficient causation. It is only possible to conclude on the basis of all reliably ascertained situations that the cause appears to be necessary or sufficient.

We need not pay much further attention to the unusual situations of necessary or sufficient causation. From now on we shall concentrate on the common situation: causation which is neither necessary nor sufficient. This causation gives a quantitative relationship between the causative factor and the outcome, and therefore the results of the study must be expressed in quantitative terms.

A classification of comparative studies

Classification by the main comparison

The definition of causation therefore leads us naturally to two basic groups of studies. The definition of these studies rests on the essential comparison being made. In *cohort* and *intervention* studies, groups of individuals are definied in terms of their exposure to the putative causative factor, and the outcome is then measured (Ex. 2.1). In *case-control* studies, groups of individuals are defined in terms of whether they have or have not already experienced the outcome under consideration, and the exposure is then measured (Ex. 2.2).

Classification by time relationships

The studies may also be defined in terms of their relationship to time (Ex. 2.3). A study in which subjects are entered and data are collected at a point in time, and then the subjects are followed and further events recorded as they happen is a *prospective* study. If we take a group of current users of oral contraceptives, and a group of non-users, and follow them over time to see which of them develop heart disease, we are doing a prospective cohort study. In intervention studies, we, as investigators, control the assignment of individuals to receive or not to receive the 'exposure' or intervention, and for this reason such studies are cohort studies and are prospective. Randomized trials are one type of intervention study.

A *retrospective* study includes observations relating to the time at which data are collected, and also previous time. Case-control studies are by definition retrospective, because the outcome has already happened. To explore the relationship between heart disease and oral contraceptive use by a retrospective case-control design, we would take a group of women with heart disease and a group of women without, and measure for each group the frequency of exposure to oral contraceptives in the time period prior to the diagnosis of heart disease. If the frequency is higher in the affected group than in the comparison group, an association exists which is consistent with causality.

The simplest, but weakest, type of study is one where all the information is related to one point in time and is collected at that time. Thus to assess whether hypertension is related to blood group O, we could survey a group of subjects, and determine which of them had hypertension, and which were of blood group O. We refer to such a study as a *cross-sectional* study, in that all data collected in the study can be considered as representing a cross-section in time. Where both the putative causal factor and the outcome state are stable, so that an adequate assessment can be made (e.g. blood group), this study design may be adequate. More commonly, the exposure or outcome changes

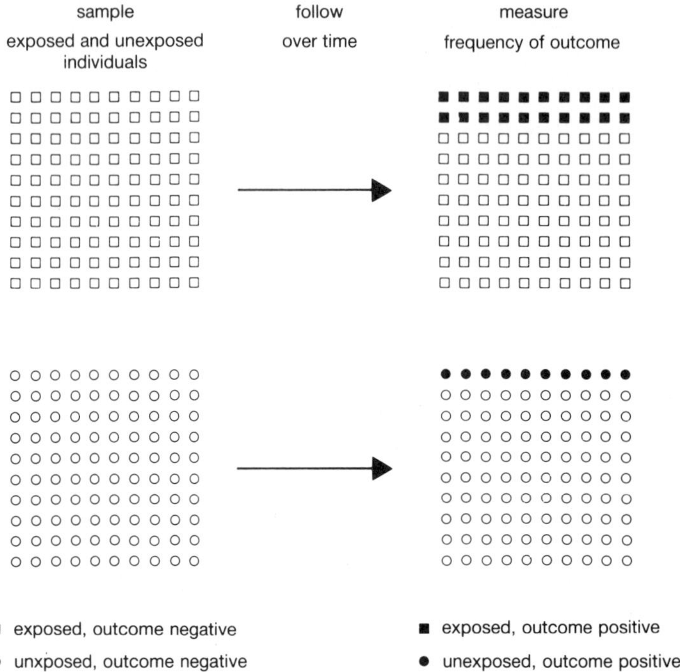

Ex. 2.1. The principle of a cohort study to test for causality. Groups of individuals are chosen, 'exposed' and 'unexposed' to the putative causal factor. The frequency of the outcome is measured in each group. The results would be expressed as:

	Outcome		Total subjects
	yes	no	
Exposed group	20	80	100
Unexposed group	10	90	100

over time, and so this design is weak. For example, to assess an association between oral contraceptive use and hypertension in women, a cross-sectional study which compares current oral contraceptive use with current hypertension is a very poor method. The relevant causal relationship is that the use of oral contraceptives may lead, after an unknown interval of time, to the development of hypertension.

More complex designs

The feature which defines the study is the comparison which is being made; where the groups compared are defined by differences in regard to the exposure factor in the postulated causal relationship, the study is a cohort study; where the groups are defined in terms of the outcome, it is a

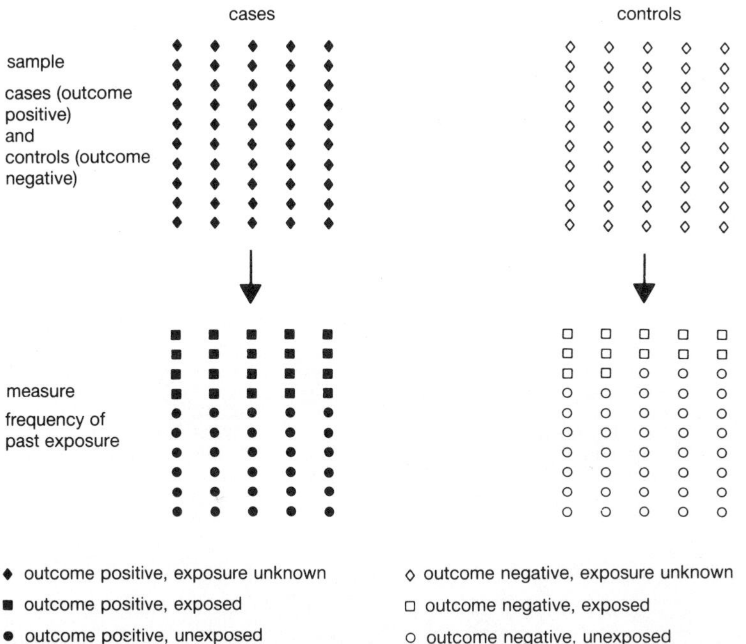

Ex. 2.2. The principle of a case–control design. A group of individuals who have experienced the outcome under assessment, and a group who have not, are assessed and the frequency of exposure measured in each group. The results would be expressed as:

	Cases Outcome positive	Controls Outcome negative
Exposed	20	12
Unexposed	30	38
Total subjects	50	50

case–control study. This principle is useful when rather more complex designs are considered.

Thus while cohort studies are usually prospective they can be retrospective, in that cohorts can be defined and information collected which applies to past time. Suppose we are able to identify from the medical records of a health care facility a group of women who ten years ago were using oral contraceptives, and a group of women who were not. We could then go to these women or use the medical records to determine their subsequent history from that point to the present in terms of hypertension. This design can be called a *retrospective cohort study*.

In a cohort study, a large number of subjects may be enrolled while only a

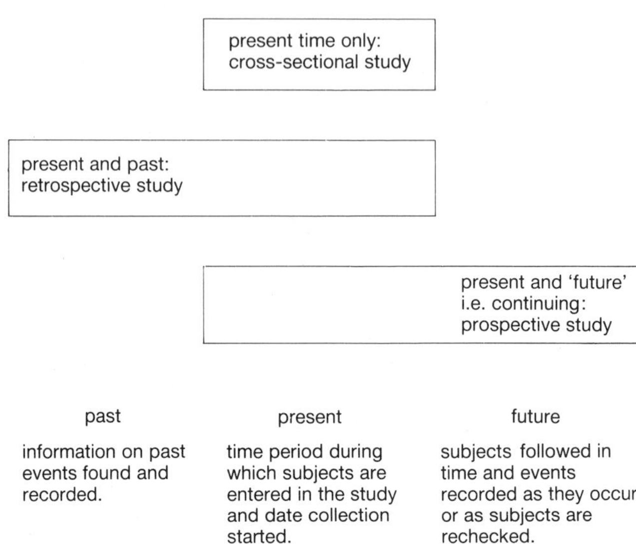

Ex. 2.3. The time relationships of studies

few suffer the outcome of interest. It may be useful to compare these subjects specifically with a sample of those without the outcome: this gives a *case–control study within the original cohort.*

Most analyses of a cross-sectional survey will examine the frequency of characteristics and associations between them in the sampled group without considerations of causality; but in addition to such 'survey' analysis, exposure or outcome based comparisons can be made between sub-groups of subjects. A survey may be used to identify sub-groups with different exposures, who are then followed giving a prospective cohort study: sub-groups can also be defined in terms of more detailed case–control comparisons.

Thus by defining both the sampling system and the time relationships, studies can be categorized in a way which is useful in their interpretation (Ex. 2.4). The method of analysis depends on the sampling system used rather than on the time relationships. This is why it is essential to understand the sampling system used in a study, as only by so doing will the correct method of analysis be chosen.

Characteristics of the different study designs

The major characteristics of the different study designs will now be described, because in assessing studies it is useful to bear in mind the areas where they are likely to have the greatest strengths and those where they may

STUDY DESIGN: SAMPLING, TIME RELATIONSHIP, AND ANALYSIS

Sampling system	Time relationship	Type of analysis
COHORT:		
Select on exposure	prospective, retrospective, or cross-sectional	cohort
INTERVENTION:		
Assign exposure	prospective	cohort
CASE–CONTROL:		
Select on outcome	retrospective, or cross-sectional	case–control
SURVEY:		
Total or sample of a defined population	cross-sectional, or retrospective	survey, plus cohort or case–control analyses comparing subgroups

Ex. 2.4. The different types of study design

have the greatest problems. These main study designs have different applications, and answer different questions; often the design of choice will be determined by the question to be answered, or will be dictated by practical and resource restraints.

Intervention trials

The purpose of an intervention trial is to estimate certain predetermined outcomes of a well defined intervention which is deliberately administered to certain individuals. These trials are limited to the evaluation of exposures which are likely to be beneficial. Their main role is in the assessment of treatment, where the randomized clinical trial is the optimal method.

The prime advantage of this method is that the investigator controls which subjects receive the intervention under test. Trials should be designed so that subjects receiving the intervention are similar to those in the comparison group both in regard to any other care they receive and in regard to other characteristics which might influence the outcome being asssessed. These features can be best achieved by using randomization; that is, by entering into the trial subjects who are eligible for, and have agreed to accept, either the intervention under test or any comparison procedure, and then selecting by a random process those who will receive the test intervention. A randomized design may also make it easier to use techniques such as single or double blind methods to minimize bias in the recording of the outcome, as will be discussed in Chapter 5. Intervention trials provide a direct test of the causal hypothesis that a change in the exposure factor produces a change in the outcome.

The main disadvantage of intervention trials is that their applicability is limited to exposures which are likely to be beneficial. They are therefore of little importance in questions of aetiology and the study of natural or artificial hazards. Beyond this, their limitations lie in the difficulties they pose in terms of organization, time, cost, and resources. Clinical trials of therapy have to involve relatively large numbers of subjects to be effective, as will be discussed in Chapter 7, and to identify and study such numbers of patients requires a high degree of commitment and co-operation from physicians and from their patients. It is the former rather than the latter which is usually the limiting step; and there are few incentives and many disincentives to physicians to be involved in such trials, particularly if they are engaged in individual private practice. Clinical trials are appropriate when a new therapy looks as if it may give better results than an established therapy, while trials are unethical either if the new therapy has very little chance of being better, or if the new therapy is so much better than it is clearly the treatment of choice. There is room for much professional disagreement over the necessity for a clinical trial in a particular instance. Time is a problem in regard to many outcome measures, such as survival in diseases like cancer, where long follow-up is required. This may mean that the therapy assessed is obsolescent by the time the results are available.

All those issues aside, it is useful to stress that a randomized intervention study has advantages which are shared by no other type of study; these are the particular advantages of randomization as a method of obtaining groups of subjects whose outcome rates, in the absence of any treatment effect, are likely to be the same; and the opportunities for standardized and double blind procedures, thereby avoiding observation bias. So whenever a major question arises, consideration must be given to whether a randomized intervention trial can be mounted. Often the possibility is too readily dismissed. The result may be that for many years treatments are used and studies of an unsatisfactory nature are carried out, and at the end there is still no adequate evidence indicating the best course of action. This applies not only to aspects of therapy, but also to questions of prevention, public education, and the provision of services; it applies also to many issues of life outside the medical area.

A few examples of intervention trials will illustrate the range of applicability of the technique. The randomized clinical trial is accepted as the primary method of investigation of a new therapy, and is a routine and virtually universal method in connection with medical therapies; an example of its use in cancer therapy will be given in Chapter 5 (p 72), and a detailed review of a trial of treatment after myocardial infarction will be given in

Chapter 11 (p 230). Much more difficult have been studies concerning major surgical therapies, or comparing surgery with medical treatment. Studies such as the large scale trials comparing different methods for the primary treatment of breast cancer represent triumphs of organization and of persistence in the face of prejudice and apathy (e.g. Veronesi *et al.*, 1981; Taylor *et al.*, 1984). Also difficult to accomplish are trials which compare radically different methods of providing care, such as the comparison between in-hospital and home-based care for acute myocardial infarction (e.g. Hill *et al.*, 1978). Intervention trials are relevant to active preventive measures, and have been heavily used in immunization; for example, the American trials of poliomyelitis vaccine involved 750 000 school children in a placebo controlled trial and over one million in a non-randomized study; for an interesting comment on this, see Susser (1977). Equally challenging was the randomized trial of breast cancer screening in which some 62 000 members of a health plan in New York were randomized to be offered regular mammography and physical examination, and compared with their peers who received routine care (Shapiro *et al.*, 1982).

Intervention trials do not have to involve comparisons at the individual level, and where the intervention is made on a community basis, trials in which communities are compared are appropriate. Thus to evaluate the impact of improved water supplies or village health workers' activities in a developing country, comparisons between villages are appropriate. To evaluate health promotion activities, comparisons between towns, workforces, or schools may be appropriate: an example is the European trial of prevention of coronary heart disease in which workforces receiving the complex intervention programme are compared to those not receiving it. Useful reviews of the issues of community trials are given by Buck and Donner (1982), and in a symposium in the *American Journal of Epidemiology*, volume 108, no. 2, 1978.

Intervention trials do not have to be randomized, and non-randomized intervention trials are often of great importance. Their results are more difficult to interpret, as the evidence must show that any differences in outcome are not likely to be due to factors other than the intervention under test. Such intervention trials include studies of fluoridation of water supplies in which communities using fluoridated water were compared to generally similar communities continuing with unflouridated supplies (Arnold *et al.*, 1956). In health education, the Stanford Heart Prevention project compared intensive methods of health education in a community, comparing it with rather similar communities which did not receive the intervention (Farquhar *et al.*, 1977; Farquhar, 1978).

Observational cohort studies

The remaining types of studies involve observation rather than intervention;

that is, the scientist does not control the intervention, but merely observes its effects. The function of a cohort study is to answer the question: 'What are the effects of this particular exposure?' The studies therefore start by defining a group of subjects with the exposure under consideration, and comparing that group to a group without the exposure, or with a different level of exposure. This study design allows the definition of exposure and the selection of subjects to be made before the outcome events have happened, and therefore ensures that the time relationship between exposure and outcome is appropriate; then the follow-up procedures allow direct measurement of the incidence rate† of the outcome(s) in each of the groups being studied.

The major disadvantages of cohort studies follow directly from their design. For many causal relationships, the outcome does not follow the exposure until after a long period, and therefore the study has to be designed to allow for many years of active follow-up. The study may be performed quickly if a retrospective cohort design is used, as defined previously, but this is possible only if adequate records are available which cover the appropriate subjects and the appropriate time period. The other major disadvantage of cohort studies is that many important questions relate to outcomes which do not happen frequently. Investigators must therefore enrol, study and follow-up very large numbers of subjects, to observe even a reasonable number of events. Issues of the necessary size of the study will be discussed in Chapter 7. At a very simple level, it is appropriate to note that the effective size of a study depends primarily on the number of events of interest which are observed. We will show some results from a prospective study of pregnancies in the next chapter; data from 50 282 pregnancies were obtained, but in assessing the association between maternal epilepsy and congenital malformations, the critical figure is the number of malformed births occurring to exposed mothers which was only 32.

Some examples of cohort studies will show the relevance of the general definition of their purpose, that of assessing the effect or effects of a certain exposure. One way to do this is to identify groups of subjects who have a particularly high level of exposure to the factor under consideration, and this accounts for the importance of cohort studies in the occupational health area. The effects of many occupational hazards have been established by studying cohorts of exposed workers, comparing their subsequent mortality or morbidity either to defined comparison groups or to the general population, which can be regarded as unexposed to the particular chemical or process. A cohort study is the best way to assess the outcomes of an unusual and severe exposure, and such studies have been set up to follow survivors of the atomic bomb explosions in Japan in 1945 (Wakabayashi *et al.*, 1983), and those affected by the Chernobyl nuclear plant accident in 1986.

† For definitions of incidence and prevalence, see p 26.

Subjects may also be chosen for cohort studies not because they are particularly unusual in terms of exposure, but because they can be kept under surveillance over a long period. An example of this type of study is the cohort study of the effects of smoking in British doctors started in the 1950s, selecting doctors not because their smoking habits were particularly unusual, but because they could be followed through annual registration procedures and their rate of co-operation was expected to be high (Doll and Hill, 1964; Doll and Peto, 1976; Doll *et al.*, 1980). Using similar logic, a cohort study of American nurses was started in the late 1970s as an opportunity to assess many major health issues in women (Hennekens *et al.*, 1979). We shall discuss in Chapters 5 and 9, studies in which women using oral contraceptives were recruited either through particular clinics or through their regular doctors, and followed up over time to assess many different types of morbidity and mortality.

A cohort can be set up by doing an initial survey of a sample of subjects or of a whole community, chosen not because of any unusual characteristic of exposure but because of availability and practical considerations. Such general population follow-up studies are analysed as cohort studies comparing subjects with different exposures from within the same initial group. An important example is the Framingham Heart Study, started in the 1950s by asking for volunteers from the small town of Framingham, a short distance from Boston, Massachusetts, enrolling those who volunteered, and following them up over a long period of time (Dawber, 1980; Gordon *et al.*, 1977).

Case–control studies

The question asked in a case–control study is: 'What are the factors which caused this event?' Case–control studies start after the outcome event, and therefore have the opportunity to assess multiple causes relating to one event. They are therefore the prime method to assess the causes of a new set of occurrences. Examples include the unprecedented occurrence of several cases of vaginal adenocarcinoma in young women in Boston in the 1970s. The causal agent, the use of diethylstilboestrol (DES) by their mothers, was demonstrated by a case–control study (Herbst *et al.*, 1971), although to estimate the absolute risk of disease in those exposed required a retrospective cohort study (Herbst *et al.*, 1977). The case–control study is a natural development from the case series, in that the clinician faced with an unusual situation will start by considering the characteristics of those subjects who have the new condition, and will then have to consider how common those characteristics would be in an unaffected population. Beyond this, the major advantage of case–control studies is that they are highly efficient in terms of the numbers of subjects required. Thus, for example, in a study of the causes of breast cancer, in principle the amount of information given by studying

100 women who have developed breast cancer and 100 controls, is similar to or greater than that produced by asking the same questions of a group of some 50 000 middle-aged women and following them for a year, during which 100 of them might develop breast cancer.

Whereas this advantage of numbers is because the outcome has already happened, it is that fact that gives the greatest disadvantages to case–control studies. All information on previous events has to be collected after the outcome. This causes difficulty not merely because of the long period of time which might have elapsed since the relevant event, but because the information often has to be obtained from the study subjects, whose recollection of previous events may well be biased if they have developed the condition of interest. The advantages in the numbers of subjects and the resources needed for a case–control study must be compared with the disadvantages of unreliability of exposure information and biased recall of events. Often these biases are severe enough to justify a more expensive and time consuming cohort study.

With regard to examples, some situations, where a new and unusual event occurred, have been noted where it was necessary to assess a range of possible

---

RISKS GIVEN BY DIFFERENT STUDIES

Relative risks of lung cancer by daily cigarette smoking from different studies

Non-smokers (referent)	1.0	1.0	1.0	1.0
1–14	11.0	7.0	8.1	7.8
15–24	13.9	9.5	19.9	12.7
25 +	27.0	16.3	32.4	25.1
Publication date:	1950	1952	1964	1976
	(1)	(2)	(3)	(4)

1. Doll and Hill (1950): 3 years' study: 1298 subjects: case-control, incidence, odds ratio.
2. Doll and Hill (1952): 5 years' study: 2714 subjects: case-control, incidence, odds ratio.
3. Doll and Hill (1964): 13 years' study: 34 445 subjects: cohort, mortality, relative risk.
4. Doll and Peto (1976): 25 years' study: 34 445 subjects: cohort, mortality, relative risk.

Ex. 2.5. Comparison of results. The relationship between smoking and lung cancer in men, as shown by different British reports.
Relative risk or its close approximation, odds ratio, is the basic measure of association given by these studies and shows the ratio of the frequency of lung cancer at each level of smoking compared to the frequency in non-smokers; see Chapter 3

causal factors. Case–control studies have been of immense importance in elucidating the causes of chronic diseases, such as cancer, and the first indications of causes have often come from such studies. A good example is the association between smoking and lung cancer, which was shown in the results of a 1950 case–control study by Doll and Hill; their prospective study of British doctors, published fourteen years later, gave substantially the same results, as shown in Ex. 2.5. While the details of the results vary considerably, even the first study is sufficient to show the strong relationship. When published, it was one of the first case–control studies, and acceptance of its results required several years of debate about, amongst other things, the value of the case–control approach. Case–control studies are applicable to many questions other than aetiology, although their value in other issues has been recognized only in recent years. For example, the effect of population based interventions can be assessed efficiently, and studies of cervical cytology and of breast cancer screening have been done by comparing subjects who develop or die from the diseases in question with samples of the unaffected population (MacGregor *et al.*, 1985; Collette *et al.*, 1984). The benefits of screening are shown by a less frequent history of screening in those who develop the condition or die of it. Case–control studies deserve to be more widely used in assessments of such population interventions, and also in assessments of different types of medical care. An interesting example of the case–control approach to a clinical topic is a study of prognostic factors in breast cancer which compared long-term survivors with patients who had died (Fentiman *et al.*, 1984).

Unfortunately there are also many examples of badly performed case–control studies, which have led to erroneous results. There are more examples of bad case–contol studies than there are of bad cohort studies. This is partly because the case–control design is more subtle and more difficult to apply than a cohort design, but also because case–control studies may appear deceptively easy. A factor in this may be the simplistic view that case–control studies are 'quick, simple, and cheap' compared to cohort studies, whereas in fact they may not be; to mount a well designed case–control study of an important question is often a complex and expensive endeavour. However, because of this impression, many case–control studies have been done with inadequate resources and poor design, and not surprisingly have given erratic results. The issues are those of appropriate study design and quality control of the information collected, which will be discussed in Chapters 4 and 5; and the issues of appropriate analysis, sample size, power and publication bias, which will be discussed in Chapters 6 and 7.

Cross-sectional surveys

The basic purpose of a survey is to measure the prevalence (frequency at one point in time) of a condition. It is therefore the appropriate method to answer questions such as: is anaemia common in my patients? what is the prevalence of hypertension in the community? how satisfied are our patients with the health services? Surveys also allow the assessment of associations, such as whether hypertension or a poor diet is more common in one social group than in another, and such comparisons can lend themselves to causal thinking. Cross-sectional surveys are limited to making observations which apply to one point in time, and therefore judgments about causation based on survey data have to be very cautious. This is because causation by its definition includes a time function, and therefore to assess it, studies must cover a time period, either prospectively or retrospectively. Our definition of a cross-sectional survey is quite narrow; if a population is surveyed to find out which subjects have a poor diet, and these subjects are then compared to those with a better diet in terms of subsequent health care utilization, we classify the first part as a survey, but the second as a prospective cohort study.

The advantages of a cross-sectional survey arise primarily because of its relative simplicity, as the complications of retrospective data collection and prospective follow-up are both avoided. Thus the methods to be used can be extensively pre-tested, applied on a large scale, and made reproducible and at least single-blind, in that the investigators need know nothing about the state of the individuals being assessed. Because of their simplicity, co-operation can be high as little is demanded of the subjects. Recently we completed a survey of smoking prevalence and a few associated factors in all school children aged 15 to 16 in a region with a population of five million; co-operation for this simple survey could be obtained, whereas a more ambitious study in which extensive interviews or tests were necessary, or individuals had to be identified for further follow-up, would have raised many more difficulties (Gillies *et al.*, 1987).

As the primary function of a survey is often to assess prevalence, the methods obtained to draw samples from a defined population are crucial, and various randomized or systematic methods are available which have been discussed in detail in standard texts (e.g. Moser and Kalton, 1979). The use of such methods can ensure that the subjects surveyed are a representative sample of the community, and allows the repetition of the survey at other times or in other communities using identical methods and yielding comparable results. Thus, surveys can monitor changes in a population in time and assess differences between population subgroups.

The main disadvantages of survey methods also arise from their simplicity. Because of their lack of a time dimension, the interpretation of their results in terms of cause and effect is very limited, and over-interpretation in this regard is a considerable danger. Their power in assessing prevalence, and therefore in assessing associations between different states, requires a reasonable prevalence of that condition in the population, otherwise they will be inefficient.

MAIN PROPERTIES OF DIFFERENT STUDY DESIGNS

Design	Intervention trials	Cohort studies	Case–control studies	Surveys
Question asked:	What is the effect of this intervention?	What are the effects of this exposure?	What were the causes of this event?	How common is this condition? Are conditions and exposures associated?
Applicability:	Controlled interventions of likely benefit Primary method of studying new therapies	Any exposure for which adequate numbers of exposed subjects can be found and studied, and outcome can be assessed Primary method of studying unusual or new exposures	Any event for which groups of cases and appropriate controls can be found, and exposure factors can be assessed retrospectively Primary method of studying unusual or new outcomes	Any exposure, condition or association which is reasonably common and for which assessment at one point in time is sufficient Primary method of assessing prevalence
Major strengths:	Allows randomization—best way to control confounding Allows double-blind assessment—best way to control bias	Allows multiple endpoints to be assessed Cause to effect time sequence clear All measures of risk can be assessed Exposure is assessed prior to outcome, avoiding bias	Usually can be done with moderate numbers of subjects; feasible even on small numbers Retrospective method is rapid Multiple exposure factors can be assessed	Representative samples of a population can be drawn Methods can be standardized, reliable and single blind Efficient in resources needed Co-operation may be high Can be repeated using similar methods
Major weaknesses:	Ethical limitations Organizational problems Time scale	Usually requires large numbers Long time scale for some effects	Retrospective method limits exposure information, and is open to bias Adequate control group may be difficult to define or obtain	Lack of time dimension limits causal interpretations Inefficient for rare exposures or conditions

Ex. 2.6. Some properties of the four major study designs

Summary of comparisons

The major properties of the different study designs are summarized in Ex. 2.6. In deciding which approach to adopt to deal with a specific question, these properties can be used as a general guide, but the final decision on the appropriate method will be based on a detailed consideration of the issues to be addressed in the study, including the likely effects of bias, confounding and chance on the interpretation of the results. These concepts will be explored in subsequent chapters.

3. The results obtained from studies of causation

When you can measure what you are speaking about, and express it in numbers, you know something about it; but when you cannot measure it, when you cannot express it in numbers, your knowledge is of a meagre and unsatisfactory kind: it may be the beginning of knowledge, but you have scarcely, in your thoughts, advanced to the stage of science.
—*William Thomson, Lord Kelvin: Popular lectures and addresses; 1891–94*

In the last section, we presented a classification of study design which separated the sampling procedure used to select the individuals for inclusion in the study from the time relationships of the study. The logic of this system will appear clear when we come to discuss the types of results obtained from these studies. The format of the results and therefore the appropriate methods of interpreting them depend on the sampling frame of the study. The extent to which particular problems and biases are likely to occur depends largely on the time relationships.

Cohort and intervention studies

We shall first consider the cohort design, which applies both to observational cohort studies and to intervention trials. In this design we are comparing groups of individuals who are classified by their exposure to the putative causal factor. We shall consider the simplest situation where we have two groups which we can regard as 'exposed' and 'non-exposed'. This will often be the real situation; for example, we might compare women using oral contraceptives with women who do not use oral contraceptives, or patients on one therapy with patients on another. In other situations, the cohorts may be more numerous and may be ordered; we may consider groups of individuals characterized by the amount they smoke, or groups of patients with different severities of disease. The format of the results in any cohort study is the same, so understanding the cohort study allows us to deal with aetiological studies looking at individuals exposed to external agents in the environment, clinical studies comparing the outcome of groups of patients given different therapies, and randomized trials, which are a special form of cohort study where the two groups are derived from a common pool of individuals by randomization. Similarly, whether the cohort study is

RESULTS OF A COHORT STUDY (1)

Exposure	Number of Infants: Malformed	Not malformed	Total	Prevalence of malformation (%)
Epilepsy	32	273	305	10.49
No epilepsy	3216	46 761	49 977	6.43

Ex. 3.1. Results of a cohort study, comparing mothers with epilepsy with unaffected mothers in regard to total congenital defects in their infants; part of a large multi-centre prospective study of pregnancies. From Shapiro *et al.* (1976)

prospective in that we identify individuals at the start of the study and follow them forward in time, or whether the study is retrospective, in that we identify individuals using past records and review their experience up to the current time, makes no difference to the analysis.

The simplest situation is illustrated by Ex. 3.1 which shows the results of a study which compared two groups of expectant mothers. One group of these mothers was classified as having epilepsy at the time of pregnancy, and the second group was not affected. This study is a prospective cohort study, in which women were entered into the study at the time of an ante-natal visit, and the classification of exposure was made from medical records and an interview. Being a study of pregnancy and its outcome, the follow-up was of fixed and relatively short duration, and the outcome of interest is the frequency of congenital abnormalities in the offspring of the mothers. The results therefore have a simple format, in that for each of the exposed and unexposed groups we have the number of infants delivered, and the number of these infants who were abnormal.†

The results show the two proportions, or prevalence rates at birth. If there were no difference in outcome between the two groups—that is, if the 'null hypothesis' were true—we should expect the prevalence rates in the two groups to be the same. It is logical to compare either the difference in these rates, or the ratio of these rates, and these considerations lead us to important

† A reminder about measures of frequency may be in order. The simplest measure is *prevalence*: the frequency of a characteristic, or the proportion of a group which has the characteristic, at one point in time; it is a simple proportion, has no units, and can be measured by one observation. *Incidence rate* is the frequency of incidents: events such as deaths or new diagnoses of disease, over a defined time period; it has units of time^{-1}; for example, an annual mortality rate is the number of deaths occurring in one year divided by the population at risk. To measure the incidence rate therefore requires counting events over a period of time. The term is frequently misused in place of prevalence. *Cumulative incidence* is the proportion of a group of subjects which experiences an event from the start to the end of a given time period, i.e., the cumulative frequency of the event; being a measure based on incidents it requires counting events over a period of time, although it is a simple proportion, with no units.

RESULTS OF A COHORT STUDY (2)

Exposure	Number of Infants: Malformed	Not malformed	Total	Prevalence of malformation (%)
Epilepsy	32	273	305	10.49
No epilepsy	3216	46 761	49 977	6.43

RR, *Relative risk*, or risk ratio = 10.49/6.43 = 1.63
OR, *Odds ratio* = (32/273)/(3216/46761) = 1.70
AR, *Attributable risk*, or risk difference = 10.49 − 6.43 = 4.06%
AP_{exp}, *Attributable proportion in exposed subjects* = 4.06/10.49 = 38.7%
This is also given by $(RR - 1)/RR$
AP_{pop}, *Attributable proportion in the population*:
For the whole population, risk = 3248/50282 = 6.46%,
Attributable proportion in the population = (6.46 − 6.43)/6.46 = 0.4%.
More generally, where p = the proportion of the population exposed, estimated from the study or from other sources, the attributable proportion in the population is given by $\frac{p(RR-1)}{p(RR-1)+1}$
here p = 305/50282 = 0.0061

$$AP_{pop} = \frac{0.0061\ (1.63-1)}{0.0061\ (1.63-1)+1} = 0.4\%$$

Ex. 3.2. Derivation of measures of association, from the results of the cohort study shown in Ex. 3.1

and widely used epidemiological measures. Exhibit 3.2 shows the measures which can be derived.

Relative risk and relative odds

The 'relative risk' or 'risk ratio' is the ratio of the rate of disease among those exposed to the rate in those not exposed, and being a ratio has no units. In this example the relative risk is 1.63.

We can also consider a further measure, which is the 'odds ratio'. The odds of a baby in the exposed group being malformed are 32:273 (approximately 1:8.5), compared to the odds in the unexposed group of 3216:46761, (about 1:14.5). The ratio of these is the odds ratio, which is 1.70, similar to the relative risk. The odds ratio and the relative risk are similar where the frequency of the outcome is low; they diverge as the outcome becomes more frequent. For both relative risk and odds ratio, the value of 1.0 corresponds to the situation of no association between exposure and outcome.

Attributable risk

We refer to the difference between the two rates as the 'attributable risk' or 'risk difference'. The former term is a somewhat dangerous one as it implies that there is a causal relationship, but if we accept that this assumption has to be justified, the attributable risk gives a measure in absolute terms of the frequency of the outcome which is associated with the exposure. In this example the attributable risk is 4.06 per cent. If there were no association present, we should expect an attributable risk of zero.

If we divide the attributable risk by the total risk in those exposed to the causative factor, the result is the proportion of disease in those exposed to the factor which is associated with the exposure; this may be called the 'attributable proportion in exposed subjects'. Here it is 4.06/10.49 = 38.7 per cent.

If for the population under study the proportion of subjects who are exposed is known, the proportion of total disease in the population which is associated with the causal factor can be calculated; this is the 'attributable proportion in the population'. In this example it is 0.4 per cent.

The uses of attributable and relative risk

Attributable risk, unlike relative risk, describes the absolute quantity of the outcome measure which is associated with the exposure. It is therefore useful in considering the practical implications of studies in which a decision has been reached that the association represents causation. Thus a comparison of the attributable risks in terms of total mortality conferred by a number of environmental exposures gives an indication of how much mortality will be prevented by successful action on each one of the exposures, and such an approach has been useful in setting priorities for public health and health promotion campaigns. A similar consideration in terms of the long term outcome of a complex disease such as diabetes, whose course may be influenced by a large number of factors, may be used to indicate what aspects of care, if dealt with successfully, will result in the greatest improvement in outcome. Attributable risk is therefore particularly useful in well researched situations where the implications of soundly supported results are being considered. It is of less value in the preliminary stages of assessment of a putative causal relationship.

The great advantage of the relative risk estimate is the empiric finding that in many human disease situations, the relative risk of disease incidence or mortality associated with a particular exposure is fairly constant over a wide range of populations and groups of patients, even where other factors differ. If the relative risk of a particular exposure is the same in two different populations, but because of differences in other factors the total risks of the outcome are different, then the attributable risks will be different. In comparing evidence from a number of sources concerning a particular causal relationship, it is therefore more reasonable to expect consistency in terms of relative risk than of attributable risk, and this property of consistency makes relative risk more valuable in evaluating whether a particular relationship is or is not likely to be causal. It is also rather easier to predict the effects of non-causal factors on the observed relative risk than on the observed attributable risk.

There is another important reason for concentrating on relative risk, and that is because this measure, unlike attributable risk, can be derived from any of the main study designs. As will be shown, case–control studies provide estimates of relative risk (by the odds ratio), but do not provide direct measures of attributable risk.

For these reasons the relative risk is the more useful index to summarize the results of a study in order to discuss the interpretation of the association. In the rest of this book we will therefore concentrate on the interpretation of relative risk.

Person-time as the denominator of rates

In the data for pregnancies in Ex. 3.2, the outcome measure is the proportion of malformed births. In cohort studies of other outcomes, the follow-up time is not fixed and may not be the same for each subject. Consider a cohort study in which men are classified by their level of exercise, and subsequently the occurrence of deaths from heart disease is recorded. Each subject contributes information from the time he enters the study until his death, until the end of the follow-up period, or until some specified time at which the data are collected for analysis, even though follow-up may continue. Some subjects may leave the study before any of these end points; they become 'lost to follow-up', and contribute to the study up to the time at which their outcome status was last known. To assess an incidence rate, the number of heart disease deaths is divided by the total follow-up period: that is, the sum of the follow-up times for all individuals, expressed as person-time (person-years, man-months, etc.). To evaluate the relationship between physical exercise and coronary heart disease mortality, Paffenbarger and Hale (1975) performed a prospective cohort study on longshoremen (dock workers) in San Francisco. Between 1951 and 1961, men who were assessed at a health screening clinic and were aged 35–74 were entered into the study; men first assessed at a younger age entered the study when they turned 35. The follow-up continued until death, attaining the age of 75, the end of the follow-up period in 1972, or the date of loss to follow-up. Less than 1 per cent were lost to follow-up. Thus the follow-up varied from very short, if an early death occurred, to 22 years. In total, 6351 men entered the study, contributing 92 645 man-years of experience; there were 598 deaths from coronary heart disease, giving a crude death rate of 598/92 645 = 64.5 deaths per 10 000 man-years. This value is an average for the whole follow-up period. If the rate of outcome varies greatly over the follow-up period this simple average will not be adequate. For example, in a clinical study of survival after a myocardial infarction, the death rate is high immediately after the infarct and then falls rapidly. In this situation, more complex methods of analysis are necessary. As the issues of interpretation can be adequately dealt with using simple data, such methods are not discussed here but are presented in Appendix 2, p 295.

Beneficial exposures

There are no mathematical difficulties in dealing with 'exposures' which are beneficial rather than harmful, but more appropriate terminology is useful. Relative risk and odds ratio can be used, and will give values of less than one. An alternative is to use their reciprocals and refer to them as the 'relative protection' and 'relative odds of protection'. Some results from the study of longshoremen referred to above are shown in Ex. 3.3, showing the use of the person-years denominator and the use of terminology appropriate to the beneficial factor of heavy physical activity. The results are shown for one age group only to avoid the problems introduced by the two exercise groups having different age distributions. The 'relative protection'—the inverse of relative risk—is 1.92. The attributable risk calculated as above will be negative, and it may be replaced by the positive quantity of 'attributable benefit'. The ratio of the attributable benefit to the absolute risk in subjects who have *not* had the beneficial exposure gives the proportion of disease

COHORT RESULTS SHOWING A BENEFICIAL FACTOR

Physical activity	Coronary heart disease deaths	Man-years thousands	Death rate per 10 000 man-years	Relative risk
Light or moderate	62	17.6	35.2	1.0 (R)
Heavy	20	11.0	18.2	0.52

Comparing 'heavy' with 'light or moderate' physical activity:
relative risk = 0.52
relative protection = 1/0.52 = 1.92
attributable benefit = 35.2 − 18.2 = 17.0 deaths per 10 000 man-years
preventable proportion in subjects
without the beneficial factor = (35.2 − 18.2)/35.2 = 48.3% = $(RP-1)/RP$

Ex. 3.3. Results of a cohort study showing a beneficial exposure, heavy physical activity at work, in San Francisco longshoremen, aged 45–54, and showing the use of a person-time denominator. From Paffenbarger and Hale (1975)

occurrence in those subjects which could be prevented (theoretically), which can be referred to as the 'preventable proportion'. The proportion of disease in the population which could be prevented by all subjects having the beneficial exposure will depend on the existing frequency of the beneficial exposure in the population, and can be assessed by methods analogous to the population attributable proportion. In Exhibit 3.3 it can be calculated from the risk in the whole population studied as (28.7 – 18.2)/28.7 = 36.5 per cent, but as the study is of a specially chosen workforce this value is applicable only to that population.

More than one causal agent

Exhibit 3.4 shows death rates from cardiovascular disease in cohorts of women defined by two exposures, smoking and contraceptive usage, from a large prospective cohort study.

Women exposed to neither oral contraceptives nor smoking had a cardiovascular death rate of 3 per 100 000 woman-years; those who smoked but did not use oral contraceptives had a rate of 8.9, while those who used oral contraceptives but did not smoke had a rate of 13.8. In this joint exposure situation, it is appropriate to regard the women who were exposed to neither factor as the baseline or 'referent' group, and to consider attributable risks and relative risks as compared to this group. What rate would we expect in women who both used oral contraceptives and smoked?

There would seem to be two simple methods by which we could derive such a rate. The first is to assume that women who are exposed to both agents have the baseline risk of the unexposed group, plus the attributable risk associated with smoking, plus the attributable risk due to oral contraceptive use, and so end up with a cardiovascular mortality rate of 3 + 5.9 + 10.8 = 19.7 deaths

COHORT STUDY WITH TWO CAUSAL FACTORS

Exposure	Mortality from circulatory system diseases, per 100 000 women-years	Relative risk	Attributable risk/10^5 w-yrs
Non-smoker, no O.C. use	3.0	1.0	0 (referent)
Smoker, no O.C. use	8.9	3.0	5.9
Non-smoker, O.C. user	13.8	4.6	10.8
Smoker, O.C. user	?	?	?

Ex. 3.4. Two causal factors. Results of a prospective cohort study, comparing women classified by smoking habit and by oral contraceptive (O.C.) use in terms of deaths from circulatory system diseases. For effects of joint exposure, see text. From Royal College of General Practitioners (1977)

per 100 000 woman-years. This gives a relative risk for the group exposed to both factors, compared to the unexposed, of 19.7/3.0 = 6.6. We are assuming that the two effects work in an additive fashion, in that the excess risks produced by each exposure add together, and add to the baseline risk which is due to the effects of other factors, to give the total risk. We can derive the same figure using relative risk estimates by combining what is called the *excess relative risk*, which is the relative risk minus one. The additive calculation therefore is the excess relative risk from smoking (3.0 − 1 = 2.0), added to the excess relative risk from oral contraceptive use (4.6 − 1 = 3.6) plus the baseline relative risk (1.0), sums to give us 6.6 as the relative risk for subjects with both exposures, compared to those with neither.

Another simple argument is that if smoking increases an individual's risk by 3 times, and oral contraceptive use increases it by 4.6 times, then the joint effect of smoking and oral contraceptive use may increase the risk by 3.0 × 4.6, that is 13.8 times. If we multiply this 13.8 relative risk with the baseline absolute risk of 3.0 deaths per 100 000 woman-years, we get an expected death rate of 41.4 deaths per 100 000 woman-years. We are assuming here a multiplicative model, that is the effect of two exposures is the multiple of the effects of each. In few studies of human disease have we enough information on biological mechanisms to predict confidently which of these models, or indeed which of a large range of other models, fit the real situation. We have to observe what happens in practice, and in this oral contraceptive study the cardiovascular death rate per 100 000 woman-years in women who both smoked and were exposed to oral contraceptives was in fact 39.5 per 100 000 woman-years. This is close to the expected result on a multiplicative model, and would lead us to suggest that for these data it is the more appropriate model. We should be cautious, however, as the numbers of deaths in each group shown in Ex. 3.4 are small (2, 3, 5, and 19 in the four groups) and more information would be needed to be confident that the multiplicative model was a better fit to the data than the additive model.

Case–control studies

The other major design is the case–control format, where we select a group of individuals who have experienced the outcome under study, and a group of comparison subjects. We then assess for each subject in the study their exposure to the factor under consideration. The results will appear as a fourfold table as shown in Ex. 3.5. In the case–control design, a sample of all available cases is taken ($a + c$), and independently a sample of unaffected subjects (controls) is drawn ($b + d$). As these two groups are sampled separately, rates of disease in the exposed or unexposed groups cannot be calculated, nor can relative risk be directly measured. However, the odds

CASE-CONTROL STUDY RESULTS

	Cases	Controls
Exposed	a	b
Unexposed	c	d
	$a + c$	$b + d$

Odds ratio $= (a/b)/(c/d)$
$= ad/bc$ the 'cross products' ratio

Ex. 3.5. Simplest form of results for a case–control study. The odds ratio, or relative odds, is the key measure of association. Because of the sampling used, the total number of exposed subjects is *not* $a + b$, and the risk in exposed subjects is *not* $a/(a + b)$; see text for explanation

ratio can be obtained, and so it is the primary measure of association in case–control studies.

To understand how the odds ratio in a case–control study is derived, it is useful to consider an unusual example in which we can compare the results with the situation in the population from which the study participants were selected. Exhibit 3.6 shows the results of a case–control study in which 1391 births with anencephalus, a severe and fatal abnormality, were compared to 5000 live births, the exposure being the mother's past history of a stillbirth. The odds ratio is 4.13, showing a strong association. Ignore the results under (b) at present.

To see how these results were derived, Ex. 3.7 shows the source population, that of all births in certain cities in Canada over a 20-year period. There were 1391 births with anencephalus, all of which were included in the case–control study; and there were 1 193 600 live births, of which only 5000 were selected to form the control series. From Ex. 3.7, all the measures of risk can be calculated, as shown. Note that the relative odds and the relative risk are virtually the same: this is because the frequency of the disease is low, so the numbers of unaffected and of total subjects are not very different.

Now, return to Ex. 3.6 and see what measures can be calculated. The odds ratio estimate is valid, differing from that in the whole population only by sampling variation; knowing that anencephalus is uncommon allows us to use the odds ratio as an estimate of relative risk. What cannot be calculated from Ex. 3.6 is the actual rate of disease in either the exposed or unexposed groups, or the attributable risk. If Exhibit 3.6 is misinterpreted, by a failure to consider that the data come from a case–control study, it might be thought that the risk of anencephalus in mothers who had had a previous stillbirth was $141/(141 + 133) = 51$ per cent—an order of magnitude different from the true value given in Ex. 3.7.

CASE–CONTROL STUDY RESULTS

	Cases numbers	Controls numbers
Exposed (one or more previous stillbirths)	141	133
Unexposed (no previous stillbirths)	1250	4867
	1391	5000

(a) Odds ratio = (141 × 4867)/(133 × 1250) = 4.13

(b) Relative risk undetermined but will be similar to relative odds as other information shows that anencephalus is uncommon (about 1–2 per 1000 births).
Attributable risk undetermined.

Attributable proportion in exposed subjects $= \left\{\frac{(4.13 - 1)}{(4.13)}\right\} = 75.8\%$

Attributable proportion in population; if controls are representative of all unaffected births, then prevalence of exposure, p = 133/5000 = 0.0266
and attributable proportion in the population =

$$\frac{p(RR-1)}{p(RR-1)+1} = \frac{0.0266 \times 3.13}{(0.0266 \times 3.13)+1} = 7.7\%$$

Ex. 3.6. Format of results from a case–control study, assessing the relationship between a history of a previous stillbirth and the occurrence of anencephalus. Mothers of all notified babies with anencephalus in a defined population form the case series (n = 1391); an arbitrary number of 5000 mothers of liveborn babies were chosen as controls. From Elwood *et al.* (1978)

A RELATIONSHIP IN A POPULATION

	Anencephalus births	Unaffected births	Total births	Prevalence of anencephalus per 1000 births
Previous stillbirth	141	31 750	31 891	4.42
No previous stillbirth	1250	1 161 850	1 163 100	1.07
	1391	1 193 600	1 194 991	1.16

relative odds = (141/31 750)/(1250/1 161 850) = 4.13
relative risk = (141/31 891)/(1250/1 163 100) = 4.11
attributable risk = 4.42 − 1.07 = 3.35 per 1000 births
attributable proportion in exposed subjects = 3.35/4.42 = 75.8%
attributable proportion in population = (1.16 − 1.07)/1.16 = 7.8%

Ex. 3.7. Relationships in a population. The relationships between anencephalus and previous stillbirths in all pregnancies in the population in which the case–control study shown in Ex. 3.6 was conducted. From Elwood *et al.* (1978)

Attributable proportion in case–control studies

In Exhibit 3.2 it was shown that there is a simple formula linking the attributable proportion in exposed subjects to the relative risk, the attributable proportion being equal to $(RR - 1)/RR$; thus, this can be estimated in a case–control study. The attributable proportion in the population can be calculated using an estimate of the proportion of the total population which is exposed to the causative factor (Ex. 3.6). In some circumstances the control group in a case–control study can be considered as a representative sample of the total population, and this proportion is given by the proportion of controls exposed. However, if the controls have to be chosen to be matched to the cases on certain characteristics, they will not be representative of the population and an independent source of evidence will be necessary to give the proportion of the population which is exposed.

Case–control studies: a more formal derivation

The difference between the results from a case–control study and those from the entire source population arise because the sampling fractions are different for the cases and for the controls. In the study shown in Ex. 3.6 and Ex. 3.7, the sampling fraction for the cases was 1.0, and that for the controls was 5000/1 193 600 = 0.00419.

ODDS RATIO IN A CASE–CONTROL STUDY

	Cases	Controls
Exposed	$a = f.A$	$b = g.B$
Unexposed	$c = f.C$	$d = g.D$
	$a + c = f(A + C)$	$b + d = g(B + D)$

odds ratio in population = (A/B)/(C/D) = AD/BC

$$\text{odds ratio in study} = (a/b)/(c/d) = (f.A/g.B)/(f.C/g.D) = AD/BC$$

Ex. 3.8. Algebraic justification for the calculation of odds ratio from a case–control study

Capital letters = numbers of individuals in the population, A, B, C, D.
Lower case letters = numbers of individuals in the study, a, b, c, d.
f = sampling fraction for cases = $(a + c)/(A + C)$
g = sampling fraction for controls = $(b + d)/(B + D)$

The essential design characteristic of case–control studies is that the fractions f and g are the same for exposed and for unexposed subjects

In the usual case–control situation, the sampling fractions are unknown but will be often of this nature, in that the sampling fraction of the cases will be 1.0 or very high, and the sampling fraction of controls will be very low.

Exhibit 3.8 summarizes the algebra of case–control studies, showing that in the odds ratio calculations the sampling fractions cancel out, and therefore the odds ratio is a direct estimate of the odds ratio in the source population, even if the sampling fractions are unknown. This simple algebra emphasizes a crucial point in the design of case–control studies: the sampling system used for cases must be without bias in respect to exposure, so that the ratio of the numbers of exposed to unexposed cases in the study will be the same as the ratio in the population, as the same sampling fraction f applies to both exposed and unexposed cases. The same applies to the controls, which must

RESULTS OF A CROSS-SECTIONAL SURVEY

Parents' smoking	Smoking in young children		Total	Prevalence, ever smoked (%)
	Ever smoked	Never smoked		
One or both smoke	3203	2418	5621	57.0
Neither smokes	1601	1508	3109	51.5
Total	4804	3926	8730	55.0

Prevalence ratio (relative risk) = 57.0/51.5 = 1.11
Odds ratio = (3203/2418)/(1601/1508) = 1.25

The odds ratio is not a very useful measure, as the prevalence ratio can be calculated as easily, and it is substantially different from the prevalence ratio as the outcome is common.

Attributable risk or prevalence difference = 57.0 − 51.5 = 5.5%

$$\text{Attributable proportion in exposed} = \frac{5.5}{57.0} = 9.6\% = \frac{(RR - 1)}{RR}$$

$$\text{Attributable proportion in population} = \frac{55.0 - 51.5}{55.0} = 6.4\%$$

$$= \frac{p(RR - 1)}{p(RR - 1) + 1}$$

where $p = 5621/8730 = 0.64$

Ex. 3.9. Results of a cross-sectional survey, in which questionnaires were given to 8–9 year old subjects in industrial areas of northern England; these results show the smoking history of the subjects, compared to their report on their parents' smoking Note: for the attributable proportion calculation, rounding errors are considerable and the raw data should be used in the calculations; Thus RR = (3203/5621)/(1601/3109) = 1.1066; $(RR - 1)/RR$ = 0.1066/1.1066 = 9.6% although (1.11 − 1)/1.11 = 9.9% (from Charlton, 1984)

also be sampled without bias in regard to exposure status, so that the sampling fraction g applies both to exposed and to unexposed controls.

As has been already shown, the odds ratio is a very good estimate of relative risk in most situations, the exception being where the outcome is very frequent. For conditions with a very frequent outcome, cohort designs will be efficient, as only a reasonable number of subjects will have to be followed to obtain an adequate number who experience the outcome under study. The great disadvantage of cohort studies is in attempting to study outcomes which are uncommon, so that many hundreds or thousands of individuals have to be followed before a reasonable number of them experience the outcome. It is in this situation that case–control studies are most useful, and therefore in most situations for which case–control studies are advantageous, the difference between relative odds and relative risk will be trivial, and certainly much less important than other potential sources of error in the study. So in much modern scientific literature the results of case–control studies are referred to in terms of relative risk, and the estimates thus produced can be considered as comparable to those produced by cohort designs.

Surveys

In principle, survey designs yield the same type of results as cohort studies, with the important limitation that all information on both exposures and outcomes exists as measures of prevalence (Ex. 3.9). Thus a survey measures the proportion of subjects surveyed who have a particular condition or health state which may be regarded as the outcome in a cause–effect equation, and measures the proportion of subjects who have a particular exposure. The terms relative risk, relative odds, and so on may be used, remembering that in this situation these apply to ratios of prevalence rates rather than ratios of incidence rates as will apply in a prospective cohort design. The use of relative odds is also more limited because frequently in a survey the prevalences of conditions being studied are quite substantial, and therefore the relative odds may be substantially different from the relative risk.

4. Selection of subjects for study

On the 20th of May, 1747, I took twelve patients in the scurvy, on board the Salisbury at sea. Their cases were as similar as I could have them. They all in general had putrid gums, the spots and lassitude, with weakness of their knees. They lay together in one place . . . and had one diet common to all . . . . Two of these were ordered each a quart of cyder a-day. Two others took twenty-five gutts of elixir vitriol three times a day . . . . Two others took two spoonfuls of vinegar three times a day . . . . Two of the worst patients . . . were put under a course of sea water . . . . Two others had each two oranges and one lemon given them every day . . . . The two remaining patients, took the bigness of a nutmeg three times a-day, of an electuary recommended by an hospital-surgeon . . . . The consequence was, that the most sudden and visible good effects were perceived from the use of the oranges and lemons . . . .

—James Lind: A treatise of the scurvy; 1753

This chapter deals with the topic of how subjects are selected for inclusion in analytical and intervention studies. The interpretation of many studies is dependent on an assessment of the problems which may have been overcome, or introduced, by the particular methods used to select subjects for study. Again we shall be dealing with the simplest possible situation, where two groups of subjects are being compared. In cohort and intervention studies, we compare subjects who are exposed to the putative causal factor with an unexposed group of subjects, the control group. In the case-control design, subjects in whom the outcome has occurred (cases) are compared to subjects in whom the outcome has not occurred (controls).

Target, source, eligible, and participant populations

As the derivation of subjects in a study is sometimes quite complex, we shall introduce four terms which will allow us to describe the selection process in most studies (Ex. 4.1).

The information in any study applies directly only to individuals who enter the study and contribute information to it, and we refer to these subjects as

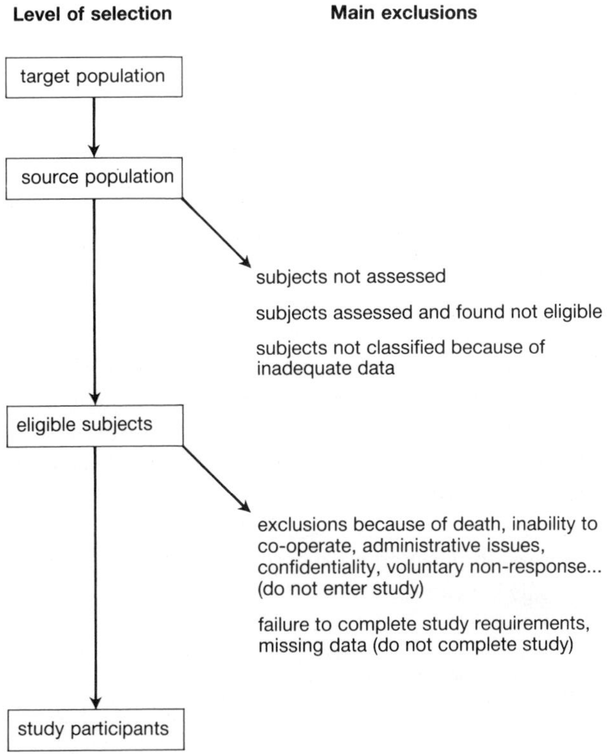

Ex. 4.1. Formation of different levels in subject selection

participants. They are derived from the *eligible* population, which consists of those individuals who have been defined as eligible for entry into the study. Members of the eligible population who do not become study participants may do so because they are unable to participate, because of death, severe illness, administrative or confidentiality issues, or because they do not wish to participate once they have been approached. Such subjects do not enter the study. Eligible subjects may also fail to become study participants because although they enter the study they do not complete its requirements and undergo procedures or provide information which is necessary. The correct handling of subjects who enter but who do not complete the study is an important issue, particularly in intervention trials, and will be discussed specifically in that context.

The eligible population is in turn a subset of the *source* population. The source population is usually determined by practical considerations, and might consist of patients in a hospital or in an individual physician's practice, members of a particular community, a workforce, or some other group which can be defined. For some studies the source population can be strictly defined and enumerated, and the proportion who are eligible can be calculated; in other studies the source population cannot be measured exactly, although it still needs definition. Within the source population there will be four groups of subjects; those who are eligible, those who are adequately assessed and found not to be eligible, those who cannot be classified because of inadequate information, and those who are not assessed because of lack of resources, unavailability, or other reasons.

To have practical value the study results must be applicable to subjects other than those in the original source population; for example a study of medical treatment has the purpose of providing information which will be relevant to future patients. The population to which we aim to apply the results we shall call the *target* population, or rather target populations; unlike the other entities in the scheme, the target population is not fixed, and its definition can be modified by information from outside the study results.

In terms of subject selection, these four levels give four successively smaller subsets of subjects, each derived from the one preceding (Ex. 4.2). In terms of the application of the study results, they are four successively larger populations, for each of which a generalization of the results applicable to the preceding stage is needed.

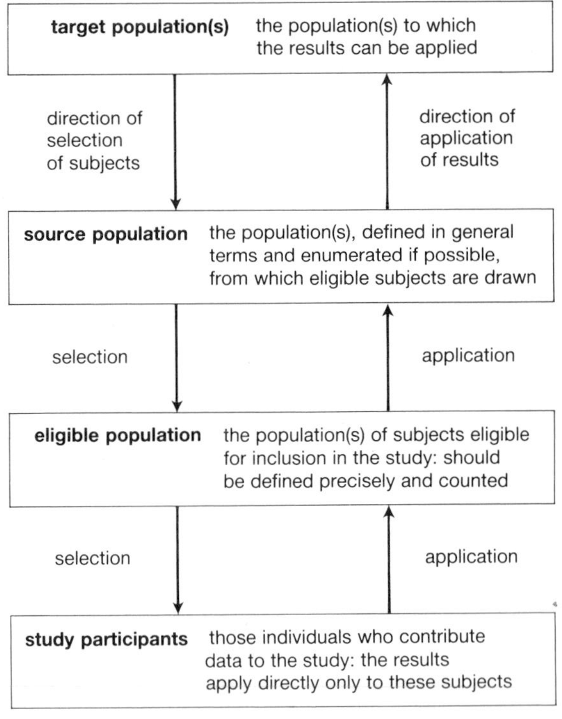

Ex. 4.2. The different groups of subjects to be considered in interpreting studies

As an example, consider a clinical trial assessing different treatments in the management of acute myocardial infarction, carried out, as most such trials are, in a major teaching hospital. The study participants will be those patients who are entered into the study and randomized; their outcome information is used in the results. The eligible population will consist of all patients with an appropriate diagnosis seen at the participating hospital, within preset limits of age and perhaps other factors, who do not have the various clinical contra-indications which will be defined in the trial protocol. The study will be of little value unless we can assume that the results based on the study participants apply to this eligible population. If they do, we can say that the results obtained are a measure of the effects of the different treatments, in patients defined by the eligibility criteria, who have been seen in the institution involved in the trial. Should there be substantial differences between the eligible and participant populations, which might occur if many patients did not give their consent to enter the trial, if many were excluded for reasons other than those stipulated in the trial protocol, or if many patients were lost to follow-up after entering the trial, we should question whether the results can be assumed to apply to the eligible population.

The source population in this situation consists of the patients admitted to the teaching hospital, or to the particular clinical unit, over a certain period of time. In principle all such patients should be assessed to see if they are eligible for the study. The target population is much wider, and will include patients seen in other geographical areas, perhaps even other countries, and certainly include patients seen at a future time. The definition of the target population will reflect the eligibility criteria, but also the characteristics of the source population in regard to how patients reach that institution and become part of the source population. The particular issues will be specific to the subject matter. For example, if the trial concerns therapy for myocardial infarction given immediately on admission to the clinical unit, results based on a unit which has a very rapid referral procedure from the community might not be applicable to another institution which admits only patients who have survived a considerable time since the infarct.

The procedure of selection of subjects who participate in the study can affect not only how widely the results of the study can be applied, but whether the results of the study are in fact valid. To go further, it is helpful to distinguish two important aspects of study validity.

The distinction between internal and external validity

In discussing how the selection of subjects for inclusion in a study is accomplished, it is useful to distinguish two important concepts. All the studies we are discussing involve a comparison between, at the simplest level, two groups of subjects. Thus, in the cohort or trial design we compare subjects who have been exposed to the putative causative factor with subjects who have not been exposed. The *internal validity* of such a study is a measure of how easily a difference in outcome between these two groups can be attributed to the effects of the exposure or intervention. The alternative explanations, which will each be discussed in detail in subsequent chapters, are that the observed difference in outcome between the groups being compared is due to *bias* in the way the observations are made, to differences between the groups in terms of other relevant factors (*confounding*), or to *chance* variation. As an example of a study with high internal validity, consider an experiment to test the carcinogenic potential of a chemical. This can be done by taking a large number of laboratory rats, bred from the same strains, kept under identical conditions of diet, environment and handling, and from these randomly selecting some animals to receive the chemical in their food, while the other animals receive a similar amount of an inert substance. The outcome would be determined by postmortem examination of all animals at the end of their natural lifespan to determine the prevalence of tumours, these examinations being done by a pathologist who is unaware of which animals have been given the chemical. In such a study the possibility of the observations of tumour occurrence being biased can be dismissed, the likelihood of there being some systematic difference between the animals who received the chemical and those who did not is small, and if adequate numbers are used the possibility of chance variation will be small. It is therefore relatively easy to interpret differences in tumour occurrence between the exposed and unexposed animals as reflecting a cause and effect relationship; this ease of interpretation is due to the high internal validity of the study.

In contrast, consider a study attempting to look at the relationship between regular exercise and heart disease, in which a group of men who report that they take regular exercise is compared to a group of men who do not take regular exercise, the outcome of the study being determined by the diagnoses of heart disease made by the subjects' physicians over the following few years. A difference in the recorded frequency of heart disease between these groups could be due to differences in ascertainment; for example, if there were differences in the frequency with which subjects visit their physicians, or differences in the physicians' categorization and recording of symptoms and diagnoses. A difference in outcome could also occur because of other differences between the two groups of men which could affect their frequency of heart disease, such as variations in cigarette smoking or diet. If the two groups of men being compared were small, the likelihood of the difference seen having arisen through chance variation might be considerable. We would say that such a study has low internal validity.

The *external validity* of a study refers to the way in which the results of the study can be generalized to a wider population. For example, despite the very high internal validity of the rat experiment described above, we would hesitate to use the results to conclude that the chemical causes cancer in humans, because the species, the dosages given, the route of administration, and various other factors differ between the experimental situation and the situation which interests us. An epidemiological study of the same topic, for example comparing workers who use the chemical concerned in their job to workers who do rather similar jobs but without such exposure could give us a result which would have much higher external validity.

It is obvious that the best studies are those which have high internal validity and also high external validity; but such studies may be difficult or impossible to design, and often the design considerations which help to increase the internal validity of a study may work against its external validity. Difficult choices in study design often have to be made. Going back to the example of the comparison between exercising and non-exercising men, one could argue that this study might have acceptable external validity, as it is after all looking at the topic in free living individuals. However, the internal validity of that study is so low that its external validity is obviously irrelevant. It is important to realize that external validity is only useful if the internal validity of a study is acceptable; studies with very low internal validity have very little value. Studies which have high internal validity always have some value, even if the external validity is low. We can conclude therefore that in designing and interpreting studies we need to pay attention both to internal validity and to external validity; but of these two, internal validity is the more important.

In considering a study, each step in the chain from target population to study participants should be examined. We should ask whether the losses seen at each point produce differences between the groups of individuals being compared which may compromise the internal validity of the study, or produce a limited or atypical group of study participants, thus compromising the external validity of the results.

The effects of selection on internal and external validity

Let us now put together the concepts of internal and external validity, the different levels of selection, and the object of the study, which is to compare two (or more) groups of subjects who are chosen because they differ either in regard to an exposure (cohort study), or in regard to an outcome (case–control study). The selection processes by which the two groups have been derived can have three types of influence on the study: they can affect the external validity, affect the internal validity, or modify the hypothesis.

First, they can affect the external validity of the study. If we perform a comparison of therapy for myocardial infarction, and only accept patients who are female, aged under 55, and have a particular pattern of infarction, clearly that defines the target population to which we can apply the results of the study. Thus the selection criteria control the nature of the target population. This influence on external validity is controlled by the eligibility criteria which apply to each of the groups being compared. It may also be influenced by the participation rate, that is the proportion of eligible subjects who participate in the study.

Second, and rather more subtly, the selection criteria can influence the internal validity of the study. Suppose a physician sends a postal questionnaire on smoking to all his patients. Let us say the response rate is high for women, but lower for men; and for the men, the response rate is lower for smokers than for non-smokers. The survey will then give a valid estimate of the prevalence of smoking in women, but will underestimate smoking in men. The internal validity of the study in assessing differences in smoking between men and women is thus compromised. Selection factors can act in this way only if they have different effects on the groups of subjects being compared within the study; this is the important distinction between this effect on internal validity and the effect on external validity noted above. As we have seen, internal validity is the more important concept, so the primary objective in designing appropriate selection procedures is to preserve internal validity.

The stronger study designs are therefore those in which the selection criteria apply equally and with the same effects in each of the groups being

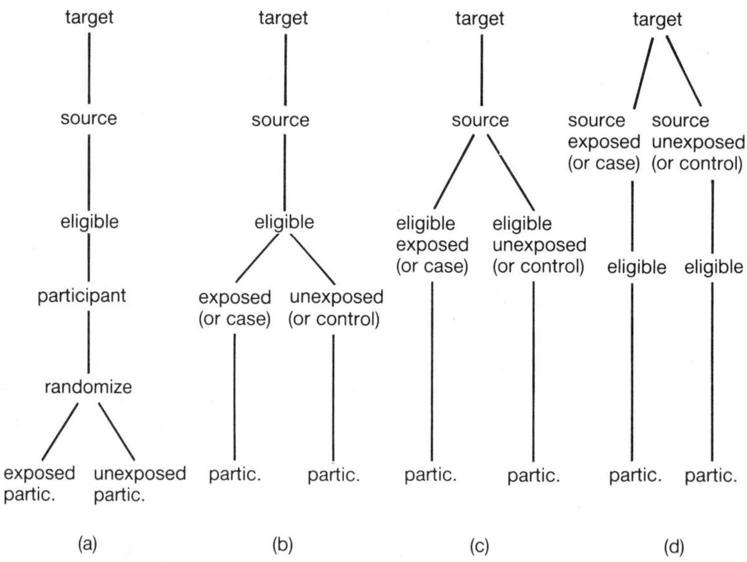

Ex. 4.3. Study designs showing different selection schemes. From (a) to (d), the pathways for selection of the groups to be compared become more different, and so the possible influence of selection on *internal* validity increases. (a) is a randomized trial design; (b), (c), and (d) varieties of non-randomized intervention, cohort or case–control designs. Partic. = participants

compared. The outline diagram of a randomized intervention trial (Ex. 4.3, type a) illustrates the value of this design. The selection criteria are identical to the point of randomization. A large element of the participation factor is included prior to randomization, by entering into the study only subjects who are eligible and have given their consent to the study, including consent to all the interventions being offered. From the point of randomization, all subjects will be included in the analysis, irrespective of whether they accept the prescribed intervention and complete the follow-up procedures or not. This issue will be described more fully when we consider the role of randomization in preventing confounding in Chapter 6. As the selection criteria apply to each of the groups in an identical fashion, selection issues will not affect internal validity. However, the external validity of this design may be quite limited, as the strict eligibility criteria and the requirement for consent prior to randomization may act to make the participant group a relatively small and perhaps unrepresentative sample of the eligible, source, and target populations. While the association seen in the study may hold even if the participants in the study are not in general a representative sample of the target population, the external validity of the design may be compromised.

The effects of selection on internal validity become more severe as the design departs from the ideal of the randomized trial. In Exhibit 4.3 diagrams b, c, and d, there are shown designs in which the differences in selection appear at the levels of the participant, eligible, and source populations respectively. As an illustration, consider the design of a prospective study evaluating the later effects of contraceptive methods by comparing women using oral contraceptives with those using other methods. The ideal scientific design would be a randomized trial, but this is clearly ethically impossible. The next strongest design is one in which a suitable source population is identified and eligibility criteria are set which are identical for exposed and unexposed women; this is design b, and an example of this design will be described subsequently (p 77). In this design, the eligible women using oral contraceptives and the eligible comparison women may differ in terms of other factors which may affect their outcome rates. Moreover, the participation rates for the oral contraceptive users and for the comparison subjects may differ, introducing further differences between the groups being compared. The analysis of the study needs to take account of these possible differences between the groups. If the eligibility criteria for oral contraceptive users and for the comparison subjects are not the same, further problems will be introduced, and this becomes design c. For example, oral contraceptive users might enter the study from the time of their first use of an oral contraceptive, but it may be convenient to enrol comparison subjects using other contraceptive methods whether they were just starting on these methods or had used them for some time. This difference in eligibility criteria could introduce further differences between the groups being compared, giving greater effects on internal validity. Another design would be of type d, where the source populations are different. For example, the oral contraceptive users might be identified as women who had received their contraceptive prescriptions from a certain clinic, while comparison subjects might be taken as women using other methods of contraception, identified in other ways. The source populations are therefore different, and factors affecting this difference in source populations, such as factors influencing whether women go to a particular clinic, can then contribute to the differences between the exposed and unexposed groups.

The same types of consideration apply to case–control studies. It is therefore helpful in assessing or designing studies to define the participant, eligible, source and target populations, as this may illustrate where problems of validity may arise.

Selection, the hypothesis under test, and misclassification

The third effect selection processes can have on a study is to modify the hypothesis which is being tested. This relates to the eligibility criteria for the subject groups being compared.

Consider first the criteria for the group of prime interest—the exposed group, or the cases. Whereas the original objective might be to study the causes of 'rheumatoid arthritis' the selection procedure used to identify cases for a case–control study may mean that the study actually assesses possible causative factors for 'rheumatoid arthritis which is sufficiently severe to lead to hospital treatment', which may be an hypothesis considerably different from that originally envisaged.

This issue is closely related to that of misclassification. External validity will be highest where the cases in the case–control study, or the exposed group in a cohort study, can be regarded as representative of all cases or of all exposed individuals in the source population. However, frequently the attempt to maintain high external validity introduces the risk of inaccuracies in the definition of these study groups, so that they include non-cases or non-exposed individuals. For example, in mounting a case–control study of rheumatoid arthritis there are choices between the two extremes of entering all individuals in a defined community (the source population) who have any type of diagnosis of rheumatoid arthritis, or of entering only those who have rheumatoid arthritis defined by specific criteria and supported by specific laboratory and radiological investigations. The latter procedure will lead to less misclassification, but if full investigation is performed only on patients with severe disease, the participants will be less likely to be representative of all individuals with rheumatoid arthritis. The balance between these two options will depend on the particular circumstances of the investigation.

In cohort studies, misclassification is often severe because an indirect indicator of exposure is used. To assess the health effects of exposure to asbestos, for example, an 'exposed' group of subjects who have worked in an environment where asbestos was used may be chosen, even though many of them may have had no exposure. The results will demonstrate the health effects of the average exposure of this group; a real effect may be missed if there are many individuals in the group who have no exposure.

A related issue in cohort studies is that the exposure may change over time. In the above example if cohorts of those exposed in asbestos and those not exposed are set up at a given point in time, as the study follow-up proceeds some exposed workers will cease exposure and some unexposed workers may begin exposure, introducing further misclassification. If such variations are large, special types of analysis will be necessary, such as defining each subject on the basis of total length of exposure. This method is used in the study of oral contraceptive users discussed in Chapter 9.

In an intervention study, some subjects offered or randomized to the intervention may never receive it because they do not accept it, or clinical contra-indications arise, or there are administrative difficulties; and some of those who start the new therapy may not continue it for very long. Despite the misclassification thus produced, the appropriate comparison in any randomized trial is between the groups who are selected by the random process. Only this comparison maintains the advantages of the randomized design, and therefore the standard appropriate analysis is on an 'intention to treat' or 'management' basis. The trial thus compares the ultimate outcome in those who are offered different therapies. If comparisons are based only on the subjects who accept the therapy, or complete the course of therapy, these groups may no longer represent the randomized groups, and the comparisons are open to all the difficulties of comparing non-randomized cohorts.

The hypothesis under test may also be modified by the eligibility criteria for the comparison group used. For example, a respiratory medicine specialist might be tempted to assess the relationship of smoking to lung cancer by performing a case–control study in which the cases are the patients with lung cancer whom he sees, and the controls are other patients he sees in his clinic. The association being assessed in that study is whether there is a difference in smoking between lung cancer patients, and other patients with respiratory disease. If the result showed no association, this could occur because smoking was related neither to lung cancer nor to the diseases affecting the controls, or because smoking was related to both sets of conditions in a similar way.

A misclassification issue may arise in terms of the comparison group in a case–control study. If the outcome under study is fairly common, like hypertension, it may be necessary to assess each potential member of the control group to make sure that he or she does not have the disease under study. If the disease under study is fairly rare the risk of this misclassification may be too small to be important, and the likely fall in participation rate produced by such an assessment may be the larger problem.

In intervention studies also the association actually assessed may be different from that which was originally envisaged. For example, in a trial of health education, an intervention group may be defined, perhaps by randomization, and offered a new education programme; but the comparison group which is not offered the intervention may obtain similar advice for themselves. In this situation, it has to be realized that the comparison being made is between the specific intervention and the other educational activities affecting the control group. This has been an important question in the interpretation of the results of some major trials of disease prevention, such as the North Karelia project in Finland which compared a county in which preventive programmes were mounted to a neighbouring county (Puska *et al.*, 1983), and the MRFIT (Multiple Risk Factor Intervention Trial) in the United States, in which 12 866 men judged to be at high risk of coronary heart disease were randomly allocated to a special intervention programme or to normal care (Multiple Risk Factor Intervention Trial Research Group, 1982).

Selection of the subjects of prime interest

We shall now consider some practical guidelines for the selection of subjects. Keeping to the simplest model, we are dealing with cohort or intervention studies which compare exposed with unexposed subjects, and with case–control designs where we compare subjects who have had the outcome of interest with those who have not. In each type of study therefore, there is a group of subjects of prime interest, the exposed or case group, and for each type of study there is a comparison or control group. Let us first consider the essential characteristics of the exposed or case groups (Ex. 4.4). There are four ideal criteria for these subjects.

(1) They must truly be exposed, or be a case. If we include amongst a cohort of subjects defined as exposed some subjects who are not exposed, we will

---

QUALITIES OF THE 'EXPOSED' GROUP IN A COHORT STUDY AND THE 'CASE' GROUP IN A CASE–CONTROL STUDY

1. Should be truly 'exposed' or a 'case'
2. Should be newly exposed, or be a newly incident case
3. Should be representative of a defined eligible population
4. Should be available for study so that necessary information can be collected in the same way as it is for the comparison subjects

---

Ex. 4.4. Criteria for the groups of prime interest in a comparative study. Total fulfilment of all criteria is rarely possible

under-estimate the true size of the association between exposure and outcome. Misclassification by exposure status in a cohort study, or case status in a case–control study, will bias the results of the study towards the null hypothesis. The direction of this effect is useful to note. In assessing published work, misclassification is not a serious issue in studies which show a strong association, as a reduction of the misclassification will actually increase the observed association. In interpreting studies which show no association, a possibility is that a true association exists and there has been sufficient misclassification to disguise it. In some circumstances quantitative estimates of the degree of misclassification can be made, and the results adjusted accordingly, but we shall not deal with this in detail.

(2) Subjects should either be newly exposed to the causative agent under study, or in case–control studies should have recently had the outcome under investigation. Consider the design of a study to look at the frequency of muscular pain in workers doing repetitive jobs in a factory. The simplest design is to go to the factory, examine workers who are doing the particular job, and find out how many of them have evidence of muscular problems. This will almost certainly underestimate the problem, as one is examining workers who have started the job and continued it for various periods until the time of the investigation. If instead, we study all workers who start on the job, we might find that many of them develop muscular problems and then change their job or leave the workforce entirely. In studies of the outcome of disease in groups of subjects seen in hospital, a frequent error is to study only those subjects who are still under follow-up by the hospital, rather than all patients diagnosed with the disease, irrespective of whether they are being followed up or not. The patients not under follow-up include those with particularly bad outcomes, who may have died or been admitted elsewhere, and sometimes those with particularly good outcomes, who need not return for further care.

This consideration of being newly exposed must be taken along with the definition of the exposure. In studying the frequency of cancer in workers exposed to a particular chemical through their occupation, we might assume that a substantial amount of exposure would be necessary before any detectable increase would occur, and therefore might define exposure as a minimum of five years' occupational exposure to the chemical. In this situation being newly exposed means that this five-year period has just been completed, and a study design which includes the total follow-up period subsequent to that time for each subject, but excludes subjects who leave the workforce or change jobs before they have five years' exposure, will give appropriate results.

In a case–control study a similar consideration applies, that the cases should be newly incident with the outcome or disease under investigation. A series of prevalent cases, such as all cases being currently seen in a clinic or existing in a community, will exclude those subjects who have developed the disease and then left the area, died, or recovered. Such subjects will be different in a number of ways from those who still have the disease and therefore are included in the sample.

(3) The exposed or case subjects should be representative of a defined eligible population. As we have seen, this defined eligible population is the essential link between the exposed or case group in the study, and the comparison group. Differences between the eligible population and the participant population are of great importance as they may influence both the internal and the external validity of the study, and therefore an examination of these differences is an important part of study evaluation. A useful summary is given by the *participation rate*, which is defined as the number of study participants divided by the number of eligible subjects. This rate gives a measure of the extent to which problems in the interpretation of the results may be present. It is particularly useful to compare the participation rates of the different groups being compared, as this may give a simple indication of major differences between the groups.

The participation rate is a stricter and more useful figure than the *response rate*, which is one component of it. The response rate is the number of study participants divided by the number of eligible subjects who were identified, contacted, and asked to participate: it is a measure of the completeness of voluntary response by the subjects. As such, it is useful and indicates one important part of the selection process. As it does not account for losses by mortality, failure to locate, exclusion by physicians, and so on, it should not be used as the only or main estimate of participation, although it often is in publications, perhaps because it is often impressively high. The participation rate is of course always lower than, or at the maximum equal to, the response rate.

(4) The subjects must be chosen so that the appropriate other investigations can be carried out; that is, the assessment of outcome in a cohort study, of exposure in a case–control design, and of related factors in either. These other investigations should be carried out in a similar manner in the control groups chosen, and with similar completeness. For example, one of the main cohort studies of the effects of smoking was the study of British doctors started in the 1950's. The decision to base the study on doctors was made largely because physicians would be expected to be interested in participating in the study, and as they must formally reregister each year to maintain their licence to practice, the difficulties of keeping them under follow-up were minimized.

Selection of the comparison subjects

The essential characteristics of the comparison group, whether it be the unexposed group in a cohort study, or the unaffected group in a case–control study, follow logically from, and are equivalent to, the criteria for the exposed or case groups (Ex. 4.5).

QUALITIES OF THE COMPARISON GROUP IN A COHORT OR CASE–CONTROL STUDY

1. Should be truly 'non-exposed' or 'non-diseased'
2. Should be available for study so that necessary information can be obtained in the same way as it is for the exposed or case subjects
3. Should be representative of a defined eligible population, analogous to that for the 'exposed' or 'case' series; this can be modified, in that comparison subjects may be chosen specifically to be similar to the exposed or case series in regard to particular factors

---

Ex. 4.5. Criteria for the comparison groups in a cohort or case–control study. Total fulfilment of all criteria is rarely possible

(1) The subjects who are regarded as unexposed or as controls must actually be unexposed, or in a case–control design be free of the outcome of interest. As pointed out above, misclassification in this regard will have the effect of biasing the measured association towards the null value, and cannot exaggerate the true association. A small degree of misclassification may therefore be acceptable, particularly if to avoid it would compromise other valuable parts of the research design.

(2) They should be chosen so that the relevant information can be collected in a manner analogous to that used for the exposed or case series.

(3) A useful general concept is that comparison subjects should be representative of the unaffected members of the same eligible population which provided the exposed or case subjects. While this general statement is usually applicable, the choice of appropriate comparison subjects is a complex issue and the ideal characteristics cannot be fully described in a simple inclusive statement. Therefore we shall explore this issue more fully, and to do so we shall discuss the two major study designs separately.

Choice of the control group in cohort or intervention studies

It is helpful to concentrate on the purpose of the control group in the different study designs. Considering the cohort design first, the exposed group gives a measurement of the incidence rate of the outcome under investigation in exposed subjects. The function of the control group is to estimate what that incidence rate would be in those exposed subjects had they not been exposed. The incidence rate which is observed in the exposed group will depend on the effects of the exposure factor, but also on the characteristics of that exposed group, other than the exposure factor, which influence the incidence rate. An appropriate comparison group would be a group of subjects who share all the other factors which influence the outcome, apart from the exposure. The randomized trial design achieves this objective by taking an eligible population, and randomly selecting from it a sub-group who become the exposed group and a sub-group who remain unexposed. The random selection procedure, if done on adequate numbers, will result in two groups who will not differ systematically from each other in terms of any particular factor. Further, the exposure is added independently to one group, and so will not be associated with other factors influencing the outcome. Thus it is reasonable to assume that the frequency of outcome which is observed in the comparison group would also be seen in the exposed group if the exposure had not occurred, or had no effect.

In a cohort study of a hazardous exposure such as smoking, random allocation and an intervention design are not possible. In the randomized trial design, the control group has two properties; it is a representative sample of the original eligible population, and it is likely to be similar to the exposed group in regard to other relevant factors. Procedures for selecting controls in non-randomized studies can be logically determined by starting from one or other of these properties.

The control series can be chosen as a representative sample of the unexposed members of the eligible population from which the exposed subjects are also drawn—design (b) in Ex. 4.3. A useful practical guiding point on this issue is that unexposed subjects, if they were exposed, should be eligible for inclusion in the exposed group. This approach has the advantage of ensuring comparability of the exposed and unexposed groups in regard to characteristics which define the eligible population, and separate it from the source population. However, the major difference between this and a randomized design is that the subjects themselves, or, in the case of therapy, their medical advisers, have chosen whether they are to be exposed or unexposed to the factor in question. This self-selection will usually mean that the exposed and unexposed groups differ in regard to other factors which themselves may influence the outcome. For example, smokers and non-smokers will differ in regard to other aspects of lifestyle such as alcohol use and diet; a non-randomized comparison of patients who have been given different treatments will often be made difficult because the patient's clinical findings and current prognosis will influence the treatment given.

Where we know a great deal about the factors which influence the outcome under study, it is appropriate to choose a comparison group which is deliberately made similar to the exposed group in terms of the other factors which determine outcome. This results in a matched design, in which for each exposed subject, one or more unexposed subjects are chosen because they share the other characteristics which affect the frequency of the outcome variable. This can be a powerful design, but its disadvantages are several. It is not often that we know all the factors which influence the outcome under study, and for this design we not only have to know them but we have to be able to measure them, and we have to be able to find matched comparison subjects who share those characteristics with the exposed subjects. Matched designs although elegant in theory, are therefore often difficult to employ in practice. Matching is discussed more fully in Chapter 6.

The designs we have described so far involve internal control groups: that is, they are derived from the same source population as the cases. A rather

SOME OPTIONS IN THE DESIGN OF COHORT STUDIES

Design	Exposed group	Comparison group	Applicability
Randomized			
randomized trial	random selection from eligible population: intervention applied	random selection from same eligible population: intervention not applied	only for ethical interventions of likely benefit
Unmatched, internal controls			
one or more outcomes, confounders not fully known	exposed subset of an eligible population	representative sample of unexposed members of same eligible population; no individual matching	preferable if multiple outcomes; confounders controlled in analysis
Matched, internal controls			
specific outcome, main confounders known	exposed subset of an eligible population	unexposed subjects matched for other factors which influence outcome	only if outcome specified and main confounders known in advance
External controls			
	exposed subjects, or all members of a population with high exposure.	all or sample of another population with no exposure or lower exposure.	if internal controls not possible.

Ex. 4.6. Design of cohort studies. Some methods of selection of exposed and comparison groups in cohort and intervention studies. The list is not meant to be exhaustive

weaker design uses an external control group, in that exposed subjects are compared with a separate control group which is unexposed or which has lower exposure. While the source populations for the exposed and unexposed groups are therefore not the same, they must both relate to a common target population. Thus, the health effects of asbestos may be examined by comparing a group of workers who use asbestos with workers who have generally similar jobs but do not use asbestos. The health effects of asbestos may also be assessed by comparing the death rates of the group of workers using asbestos with the death rates for the whole population in that area or country. If the effects are large this may be an adequate design, but is clearly a rather weak one. The main options in the design of cohort studies are summarized in Ex. 4.6.

Choice of the control group in case control studies

The logic of choosing control groups in case–control studies is basically similar to that for cohort studies (Ex. 4.3, 4.5). Firstly, subjects in the control group should be truly without the outcome of interest at the time the study is performed; they may of course develop the outcome at some point in the future but that is not relevant. Secondly, they should be chosen so that the measurement of past exposure can be made in the same way as it is for the case series.

As for the third criterion, controls can be chosen to be a representative sample of the members of the eligible population who have not had the outcome, or alternatively can be chosen to be matched to the case series in regard to other factors which are associated with both outcome and exposure. Again it is useful to emphasize the function of the control group in a case–control study: its purpose is to estimate the frequency of exposure to the putative causative factor which would be expected in the case series in the absence of any association between that exposure factor and the outcome which defines the case series. Exhibit 4.7 illustrates some of the study designs which are often used in regard to case–control studies, and is set out in a way which is similar to that for cohort studies shown in Ex. 4.6.

There are two main distinctions to be made, between matched and unmatched studies, and between studies with community based control groups and with institutionally based control groups.

The more generally applicable design is an unmatched design, which is appropriate if a number of possibly causative factors are to be assessed, or if the main confounding factors—those which are related to the condition under study and to the putative causal factors—are not fully known. One strong design uses a case series which is a total or representative sample of all affected subjects drawn from a specified source population, and a control group which is chosen as a representative sample of unaffected members of that same source population.

SOME OPTIONS IN CASE-CONTROL STUDIES

Design	Case group	Control group	Applicability
Unmatched community-based	all or representative sample of all affected subjects in source population	representative sample of unaffected members of same source population; no individual matching	preferable for multiple exposures or if confounders not known; confounders controlled in analysis
Unmatched institution-based	all or representative sample of all affected subjects in eligible population	sample of unaffected members of same eligible population; no individual matching	preferable for multiple exposures or if confounders not known; confounders controlled in analysis
Matched community- or institution-based	affected members of eligible population	unaffected subjects chosen to be similar to cases on certain specified matching factors; from same eligible population	only if exposure specified and main confounders known in advance

Ex. 4.7. Design of case-control studies. Some methods of selection of case and control groups in case-control studies. The list is not meant to be exhaustive

This source population may be defined in terms of a community or of an institution. A community-based design has the advantage that the source population will be closely related to a definable target population, the particular community defined in time and space, which will make the further generalization of the results more straightforward. In a study based on an institution, for example, comparing patients with a particular condition in a hospital to patients with other conditions in the same hospital, the applicability of the results to an appropriate target population may be more difficult. In a community-based study, the data from the control group may be much easier to interpret, as the controls will probably be healthy subjects. In a hospital-based study, the comparison group will of course have other conditions, and it may be difficult to be sure that these other conditions are not related to the exposure under consideration. A useful protection with hospital-based case–control designs is to ensure that the unaffected subjects cover a wide range of other diagnoses, as it is unlikely that the exposure under consideration will be related to many of them. Moreover, patients who have diagnoses which are known to be related to the exposure factor under assessment in the case–control study should not be eligible as controls. From the above, the advantages of community-based case–control studies would seem considerable, but against these must be balanced the greater difficulty of carrying out such studies, and particularly of ensuring a high response rate in the control series. It is more difficult to obtain a high degree of co-operation from subjects in the community as they have less incentive to be involved with the study than have patients who have been treated. Further, some studies may require clinical information on comparison subjects which may not be easy to obtain from subjects chosen from the community.

ISSUES IN THE SELECTION OF SUBJECTS

General questions	Comparison of the groups
What is the definition of the eligible population?	Are the definitions comparable?
How do the participants relate to the eligible population?	
What is the participation rate?	Compare the groups
What are the reasons for losses, and how frequent is each?	Compare the groups. Are differences likely to affect internal validity? Do the losses compromise external validity?
What is the source population?	Is it the same for each group?
How do the source and eligible populations relate?	Is the relationship similar for each group? Is the main result likely to apply to the source population?
What is the target population?	Is the main result applicable to this target population?

Ex. 4.8. Selection of subjects. An outline scheme to assist in the consideration of issues of subject selection in a particular study. The questions should be considered generally, and specifically in regard to the comparability of the relevant groups—exposed and unexposed in cohort and intervention studies, affected and unaffected in case–control studies

Where a specific exposure is under assessment, and the main factors which are likely to be related to that exposure and to the outcome which defines the case series are known, a matched design may be used in which the control group consists of subjects who are unaffected by the condition which defines the case group but are chosen to be deliberately similar to the cases in regard to these specific 'confounding' factors. The advantages and disadvantages of matched designs are discussed further in Chapter 6. The requirement for the matching of the comparison subjects takes precedence over the other characteristics of the control subjects but beyond this, institutional or community sources of controls may be used.

Assessment of selection issues in a completed study

We have seen how the selection of subjects for a study can influence both internal and external validity, and affect the hypothesis under test. In assessing a study, it is useful to examine the component populations, and a simple scheme is shown in Ex. 4.8. The general questions, applying to the whole study, are relevant to external validity and to the hypothesis; the questions concerning differences between the groups being compared are relevant also to internal validity. Examples of this type of assessment will be given in the second part of Chapter 5 (p 70).

5. Error and bias in observations

Mathematics may be compared to a mill of exquisite workmanship, which grinds you stuff of any degree of fineness; but, nevertheless, what you get out depends on what you put in; and as the grandest mill in the world will not extract wheat-flour from peascod, so pages of formulae will not get a definite result out of loose data

—T.H. Huxley: Geological reform; 1869

Sources of error and of bias

In the previous chapter we dealt with the choice of the subjects for inclusion in the study, which defines one of the two variables in the causal hypothesis. In cohort studies and intervention trials, the subject selection defines the exposure or intervention, and the remaining variable to be assessed is the outcome. In the case–control approach, the outcome is defined by the subject selection process, and the remaining variable to be assessed is the exposure. As we have seen in Chapter 4, the way in which the subjects are chosen defines the study and determines the external validity of the study. For example, a study apparently assessing the value of physiotherapy in rheumatoid arthritis may be seen on closer examination to be studying the effect of physiotherapy on patients of a certain age who have a particular form of rheumatoid arthritis in terms of its pattern of joint involvement and its severity. The eligibility criteria and the participation rate will affect the external validity, in other words the applicability and usefulness of the results in a wider context.

In assessing scientific work, either our own or that of others, to go further we must be willing to accept what has been done in terms of the subjects who have been included in the study and the design which has been used, and proceed in terms of those studies in which we judge the external validity to be at least reasonable. This chapter and the subsequent ones, 6,7 and 8, now deal with this central issue: given that the study has been performed on a certain group of subjects, do the results support a causal relationship between the exposure and the outcome within the confines of the particular study?

If any association is shown within the study, it must be due to one of four mechanisms: *causation*, *observation bias*, *confounding* or *chance*. In this chapter we shall deal with observation bias. Observation bias is relevant to the measurement of the dependent variable in the study, that is, the outcome in studies of a cohort design and the exposure in studies of a case–control design.

At issue is the relationship between the *true value* of the factor being assessed, outcome or exposure, and the value of the variable which is chosen to represent that factor in the study. In the intervention study of physiotherapy and rheumatoid arthritis, the outcome variable might be defined as an improvement in the function of the affected joints. How this improvement can be best assessed will be a major question in the study design, and possibilities will range from physiological measures such as hand grip, to questionnaire assessments of degree of functional impairment. Expert knowledge of this specific issue is obviously required for the design or interpretation of such studies, and attention must be paid to the acceptability, reproducibility, and relevance of the measures considered. For a general discussion, we shall accept that the variable measured in the study is considerably far removed from the biological event which is a feature of the causal hypothesis.

Consider a case–control study assessing whether high vitamin C consumption is protective against colonic cancer. The causal hypothesis would relate the occurrence of colonic cancer to the level of intake of vitamin C over a long time period many years before the clinical diagnosis of the tumour. The variable used to represent this factor in the retrospective design could be the responses to a questionnaire on the frequency of consumption of a number of food items at a defined period in the past, converted through a chosen formula into an estimate of vitamin C consumption. The variable appearing in the results as 'exposure' is considerably different from the biological 'exposure' in the hypothesis.

Error

There are several influences which may cause differences between the *true value* of the factor being assessed and the *recorded value* of the variable chosen; these are shown in Ex. 5.1. We need to distinguish two different problems. First, is the problem of 'error', which means inaccuracy which is similar in the different groups of subjects being compared. In many studies the amount of error will be considerable, but some precautions will help to ensure that the error is equal in the different groups of subjects being compared. Error includes several components. Within subject variation includes true random variation, and also biological variations, such as circadian or seasonal rhythms, which may lead to the value of the factor at the time of measurement differing from the usual value over a longer time. All methods of measurement will have a degree of error which is a function of the instrument used. For all studies data which is collected has to be recorded, whether manually or electronically, and in many studies raw data is converted or manipulated to give the final variable representing the factor

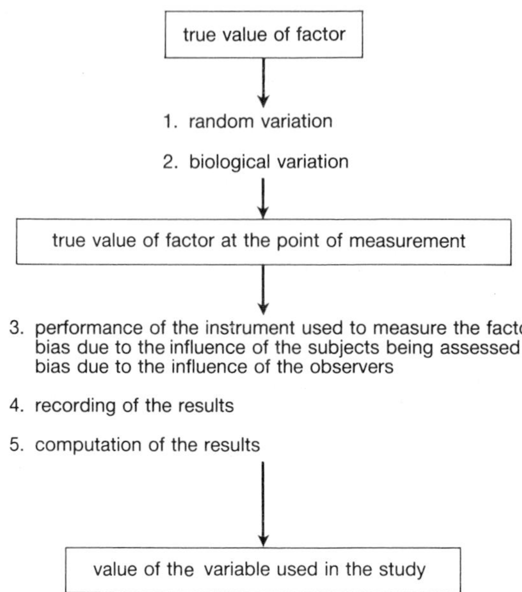

Ex. 5.1. Sources of error and of bias in the observed value of a variable compared to the true value of the factor it represents

under consideration. For all these issues, the general principle will be that the methods used will be applied in the same manner and with the same care to all the subjects in the study irrespective of the group to which they belong. If the methods used are the same for all subjects then we shall accept that a degree of error exists, but may be able to conclude that the possibility of systematic differences between the groups being compared is small.

Error is of course important. The greater the error, the more 'noise' there is in the system, and therefore the more difficult it will be to detect a true difference in the factor being assessed between the groups being compared. In the extreme situation, if the measurement used is so inaccurate that its value bears no relationship to the true value of the factor being assessed, we shall not be able to detect any differences between groups of subjects even if large differences exist. Thus, if physiotherapy is actually beneficial in improving joint function, a reasonably accurate method of assessing joint function will show this improvement, while a very inaccurate method will show no difference between treated and untreated groups of patients. The effect of error will always be to make the observed association, for example the relative risk estimate, closer to the null value than is the true situation. If a study shows a strong association, this association cannot be produced by error in the measurements used; on the other hand if a study shows no association or a weak association, error in the observations may be disguising a much stronger association.

Studies of disease causation often produce very weak associations, with relative risks of the order of two. The reason may be that the exposure variable measured is a very inaccurate estimate of the true biological factor concerned, because it is an extremely indirect measurement. Many studies show that the incidence of breast cancer is increased in association with obesity, with fairly low relative risks, and this may be because obesity is a very inaccurate estimator of the consumption of one particular nutrient which is related to breast cancer incidence. Where the factor assessed is a much closer estimate of the true biological agent, relative risks will be much higher. The inhalation of certain types of wood dust is a cause of cancers in the nose and nasal sinuses; if we compare employees in an industry which uses wood with the general working population, we may find a moderately increased relative risk, perhaps of two to three; if we compare workers employed on dusty processes which use wood with the general working population, we may find a much higher relative risk, perhaps a hundred or more, while if we compare workers who personally have had exposure over many years to particular types of wood with the general working population we may find a relative risk of a thousand or more. The closer we go to the biological causal factor, the higher the relative risk will become.

Bias

The other component of inaccuracy is *bias*, that is inaccuracy which is different in its size or direction in one of the groups under study than in the others. This is a much more serious problem, as bias can influence the results of a study in any direction and can produce measurements of association which are exaggerated, and may produce strong associations when there is no true difference between the groups being compared. The most common sources of bias (Ex. 5.1) are variation in the subject's response to the method of assessment, and variation in the observer's response. The best way in which these potential biases can be overcome is to ensure that when the measurement is made neither the subject nor the observer is aware of which group the subject is in. This is easiest to do in a prospective intervention trial, where the classical double-blind technique is used. Thus to evaluate the effect of a new drug on the relief of symptoms from rheumatoid arthritis, a placebo drug can be made up which looks and tastes the same as the new drug, and the study is designed so that neither the subject nor the physician making the observations of outcome is aware of whether the subject is taking the active drug or the placebo. Such a design in principle should avoid most sources of subject and observer bias. Care has to be taken that the double-blindness is in fact preserved, and not broken either inadvertently through administrative lapses or through the active drug having some side effect which makes its presence obvious. In many other prospective designs, double-blindness is not possible. If, for example, a comparison is being made between surgery and medical therapy for coronary artery disease, it is impossible to achieve double-blindness, but a single-blind assessment, where the observer is unaware of the treatment given to the subject may be possible. Obviously the normal medical carers of the patient cannot be unaware of the patient's treatment, but in this study the end points can be chosen to be those which can be verified by an independent group of assessors on the basis of electrocardiograms, X-rays and so on, or those in which observer bias is not an issue, e.g. total mortality.

In large scale observational cohort studies there is often no possibility of even single-blindness, as the outcome may not be assessed directly by the investigators, but may be dependent upon death certification, recorded morbidity, or functional outcomes such as self-reported symptoms, return to work, and so on; an example is the Royal College of General Practitioners' study of oral contraception, described later in this chapter. Where outcome measures are dependent upon observations by people other than the investigators, comparability of the exposed and comparison groups in terms of the frequency with which such observations are made, the individuals or types of persons who make them, and the degree of completeness and detail of the observations may attest to the comparability of the results. Another useful ploy is to look for specificity of the result, which can be tested by showing that outcomes which would be expected to be irrelevant to the causal hypothesis are similar in the groups being compared.

In a case–control design, where the outcome has already occurred, the opportunities for control of bias in the subjects' responses are very limited. A degree of blinding may be accomplished by doing the investigation on subjects with symptoms considered suggestive of the outcome under test, but who have not had or received a specific diagnosis. To deal with the issue of subject bias there may be value in enrolling as a control group subjects who have conditions of similar severity or nature to that of the cases. Thus in a retrospective study looking at events during pregnancy in mothers of infants with a specific congenital defect, it may be useful to use as controls mothers with babies with a range of other defects, who might be expected to be influenced by the same factors affecting recall. Observer variation is also difficult to control as it is not easy to keep the observer unaware of the status of the interviewee, but simple precautions such as ensuring that cases and controls are assessed by the same observer or group of observers, and by the same methods used under the same circumstances, are of help. Some simple observations may be helpful in judging whether subject or observer bias may be a problem, such as recording the length of time taken for examinations or interviews, recording the interviewer's assessment of the co-operation of the subject and the degree of difficulty experienced with some of the key questions, and even asking the subjects at the end of the interview whether they are aware of any relationship between their condition and some of the factors asked about. Similarly, the examiners or interviewers can be asked to record whether they became aware of the case or control status of the subject before or during the assessment. Such recordings give the possibility of analysing sub-sets of data for subjects who were aware or were not aware of the key hypothesis, and those in whom the observer did or did not know their status. Again the use of questions for which cases and controls would be expected to give similar answers is useful.

Many quite dramatic examples of severe recall bias can be found. Thus in a study to assess whether rheumatoid arthritis has a familial link, a group of affected patients were asked whether their parents had suffered from arthritis, and the responses compared to an unaffected control group. The results show that the frequency with which parents were affected was much higher for the rheumatoid arthritis patients than for controls, with a very high relative risk (Ex. 5.2). In a second comparison, another group of patients with rheumatoid arthritis were asked about arthritis in their parents, and independently the unaffected siblings of these rheumatoid arthritis patients were asked the same questions. The answers of course relate to the same parents, and therefore should be identical; however these results also

REPORTING BIAS IN A CASE-CONTROL STUDY

	Patients with RA	Controls	Odds ratio
(A) Arthritis in parents			
neither	3	111	1.0 (referent)
one	10	74	5.0
both	6	16	13.9
	19	201	
(B) Arthritis in parents			
neither	11	20	1.0 (referent)
one	23	17	2.5
both	6	3	3.6
	40	40	

Ex. 5.2. An example of subject recall bias. Results of case–control studies comparing patients with rheumatoid arthritis (RA) with unaffected controls, in terms of whether their parents had arthritis, as reported by these respondents. Study A shows a strong positive association between RA and arthritis in parents. Study B also shows a positive association which, as it compares responses of RA patients and their unaffected siblings in regard to the same parents, must be due to variation in reporting. Knowledge of the results of study B will influence the interpretation of study A. From Schull and Cobb (1969)

REPORTING BIAS IN A GENETIC STUDY OF CENTRAL NERVOUS SYSTEM MALFORMATIONS

	Total	With CNSM	% affected
(A) Cousins of index subjects			
mother's siblings' children	2327	26	1.12
father's siblings' children	2627	12	0.46
(B) Cousins of control subjects			
mother's siblings' children	1231	9	0.73
father's siblings' children	1333	4	0.30

Ex. 5.3. Recall bias in a genetic study. Table A compares the reported frequency of central nervous system malformations in cousins of an index series of 547 cases of these defects, and shows higher frequencies of CNS defects in maternal compared to paternal relatives (relative risk = 2.4). However, Table B shows the reported frequencies of CNS malformations in cousins of control births which did not have CNS defects, and shows a similar maternal-paternal difference (relative risk = 2.4). From Carter *et al.* (1968)

show that a higher frequency of parental arthritis was reported by the rheumatoid arthritis patients than by their unaffected siblings, and this result must be due to observation bias. Patients affected by a disease are more likely to know of family members with the same disease.

Studies of family history which depend upon asking mothers of babies with severe defects whether their relatives have had similarly affected babies have sometimes resulted in the conclusion that the disease occurred more commonly in the maternal than in the paternal relatives. Such observations have led to hypotheses of complex inheritance patterns, including even cytoplasmic inheritance. Such observations may be biased by the fact that mothers generally know more about the offspring of their own family than that of their husband's family, as can be seen if control families are investigated in the same way (Ex. 5.3). These data from a large family history study show that in the cousins of subjects with central nervous system malformations the reported frequency of similarly affected children was considerably higher in the mothers' relatives than in the fathers' relatives, suggesting a maternal inheritance pattern. However the same type of investigation carried out on families of normal control babies, showed a very similar degree of excess in the mothers' families as in the fathers', which must be due to biased reporting. These examples will emphasize that if the information is biased, the associations seen may be strong, and there is no point in applying statistical tests to biased data. The fact that the associations are statistically significant gives no protection against bias.

Assessment of bias and error

Clearly the principles of avoiding bias are to ensure that the same methods are used under the same circumstances by the same observers for all subjects involved in the study, and to employ double- or single-blind techniques as far as possible. In the consideration of study design the choice of outcome or exposure measures is important, and these must not only be relevant to the hypothesis, but be chosen to be objective, reproducible and robust; that is, likely to be little influenced by variations in the method of testing. One must guard against mistakes in both directions however; while an outcome which is extremely difficult to measure and open to highly subjective interpretation may be of little value, there is also the danger of choosing an outcome simply because it can be measured easily, even if it is not directly relevant to the hypothesis under test, or may even result in a distortion or change in that hypothesis. We may wish to evaluate if a health education programme results in subjects changing their diet, but may realize early on that this is a very difficult thing to measure; so we may choose to measure something much simpler, such as the subjects' responses to factual questions about diet. This is perfectly appropriate if we accept that the hypothesis under test has now changed, and we are assessing only if the educational programme results in increases in knowledge. The relationship between increases in knowledge and behaviour change must therefore be assessed in some other way.

ASSESSMENT OF OBSERVATION BIAS AND ERROR

What is the definition of the factor being assessed?	Is it the same for each group? Is it appropriate to the hypothesis?
What is the method of assessment? instrument used observer making the assessment circumstances of use subjects' circumstances subjects' knowledge and co-operation	Are the methods of assessment similar for each group? Are the subjects, or the observers, aware of the grouping of the subjects when the assessment is made? How accurate and reliable is the method of assessment?
When is the observation made? in calendar time in relation to the hypothesis	Is it the same for each group?
How are the data handled? recording and coding computation	Are the methods the same for each group?

Ex. 5.4. Bias and error. An outline scheme to assist in the consideration of issues of observation bias and error. The questions should be considered for the whole study, and specifically in regard to the comparability of the relevant groups—exposed and unexposed in cohort and intervention studies, affected and unaffected in case–control studies

To assess a completed study for the existence of bias, the methods used have to be examined in terms of the possible sources of error and bias shown in Ex. 5.1. As bias is the more serious problem, we concentrate on whether the methods used have been applied identically to all subjects in the study, and whether the subjects' responses to these methods are likely to have been similar. If we can be certain as to the precautions taken against severe bias, it is useful also to assess the likelihood of error, which will always be present, but may be a serious problem, causing the results of this study to be influenced towards a null result.

In Ex. 5.4, a check list is given which will be helpful in the assessment of bias and error. It consists of the questions relevant to judging whether the variable recorded is a valid measure of the biological factor which is a component of the hypothesis under test. For each aspect of this measurement, a general question relates to the accuracy of the measurement, that is primarily to error, and a more specific question deals with differences in the assessment between the groups under test, and therefore relates primarily to bias. Often the assessments can be made only in a qualitative and subjective manner, leading to a reasoned judgment as to whether the results can be accepted as valid. It is more satisfactory if evidence on the validity, reproducibility or consistency of the observations made can be obtained, and in designing a study opportunities for such assessment should be created.

Practical issues in reducing bias and error

The design of methods of investigation which minimize error and bias is a large subject in its own right, and will not be dealt with fully. It is however useful to summarize some of the main approaches. Whatever the method of assessment used, important issues will include those of *definition*, choice of *instrument*, *standardization*, and *quality control*. It is essential in any research study to define precisely the factor being assessed, even, one might say especially, when it appears simple; consider the definitional issues involved in items such as tumour stage, cardiac failure, pain relief, social class, diastolic blood pressure, high fat diet, or cellular atypia. The 'instrument' used to assess the factor must then be chosen: we use this general term to include any means of assessment, such as clinical examination, laboratory test, questionnaire, review of medical records, observation. Then the way in which the instrument is to be applied must be standardized: by whom, when, how, and under what circumstances. Finally, quality control procedures should be developed to monitor the information collected throughout the study, and, even more difficult, to produce useful data which will attest to its quality. These processes of definition, standardization, and quality control are relevant not only to the collection of information, but also to recording, coding and computer entry. Quality control should include systematic checks for gross errors—variables which are irreconcilable such as males with menstrual problems, contradictory such as non-matching age and date of birth, or outside an expected range; systematic checks for inconsistencies, such as addresses or diagnoses from different sources; and rechecking of all or a sample of examination, interview, coding and data entry procedures.

Assessment of the consistency of information

It is important not only to try to collect data of good quality, but to be able to demonstrate its quality. A first criterion is that of *consistency*: data collected on more than one occasion or by more than one method or observer should be consistent. Checks for consistency can be made within an observation procedure such as an interview or clinical examination by repeating key items at different points in the procedure, and by assessing factors in more than one way. In regard to variation within the subject, all or a sample of subjects can be reassessed; the likelihood of a true change over time must be considered in interpreting the results. Observer and instrument variation can be assessed on all or a sample of subjects, comparing data collected independently by a number of observers or by different methods. To capitalize on some of these techniques *quality control variables* can be deliberately included in the study, chosen not because they are of intrinsic interest but because they should be stable over time, between interviewers, between subjects, and so on, and therefore variation in their recorded values can be used to assess the consistency of the information used.

A quantitative measure of consistency: kappa

A quantitative method of assessing consistency will be described, which is applicable where two methods have been used on the same subjects (two observers, two occasions, or two procedures). Exhibit 5.5 shows some data from the world Fertility Survey, which was set up to collect reliable and comparable data on fertility and related factors in many developing countries; clearly not an easy task, and one where the consistency of the collected data is crucial. As a small part of this, two interviews were performed by similar methods but two to twelve weeks apart, on 371 women in Fiji; data for two factors are shown in Ex. 5.5. For use of contraception, the two surveys were virtually identical in terms of their gross results: the percentages of respondents reporting 'ever use' of contraception were 68.3 on the first survey and 68.0 on the second. This similarity hides a substantial variation in individual responses: a better measure of consistency is the proportion of women who gave the same response on each occasion, which is 57.7 + 21.3 = 79.0 per cent. Even this quantity may be misleading, as even if

CONSISTENCY OF INTERVIEW DATA

Ever use of contraception: percentages of respondents, $n = 371$

		Second interview		
		Yes	No	Total
	Yes	57.7	10.6	68.3
First interview	No	10.3	21.3	31.7
	Total	68.0	32.0	100.0

Observed agreement = 57.7 + 21.3 = 79.0%.
Expected agreement by chance = (68.3 × 68.0 + 31.7 × 32.0)/100 = 56.6%.
Kappa, κ = (observed – expected agreement)/(100 – expected agreement)
= 22.4/43.4
= 0.52

Status of first marriage: percentages of respondents, $n = 371$.

		Second interview			
		C	D, NR	D, R	Total
	C	86.2			86.9
First interview	D, NR		5.9		6.5
	D, R			5.8	6.6
	Total	87.4	6.1	6.5	100.0

C = continued D, NR = dissolved, not remarried D, R = dissolved, remarried.
Observed agreement = 97.9%
Expected agreement = (86.9 × 87.4 + 6.5 × 6.1 + 6.6 × 6.5)/100 = 76.8%.
Kappa = 0.91

Ex. 5.5. Use of a re-interview technique to assess consistency of data. For part of the World Fertility Survey, 371 women in Fiji were re-interviewed 2–12 weeks after the first interview; here the responses are compared for two factors: ever use of contraception, and status of the first marriage. From O'Muircheartaigh and Marckwardt (1980)

there were no relationship between an individual's responses to the two surveys, substantial agreement would be expected by chance alone: this amount can be calculated in the manner shown. The logic is that as 68.0 per cent of subjects gave a 'yes' response on the second survey, if their responses were totally unrelated to those they had previously given, the expected proportion giving 'yes' responses on both occasions would be 0.683 × 0.68, that is, the product of the proportions on each survey; the total expected agreement is therefore the sum of the expected agreement for each category: here it is 56.6 per cent. If we take the excess of agreement over expected agreement (79.0 – 56.6), and divide it by the potential excess which is (100 – 56.6), we obtain a statistic known as kappa, κ:

$$\kappa = \frac{(P_c - P_e)}{(1 - P_e)}$$

where P_c = the proportion of subjects giving consistent responses
and P_e = the proportion with consistent responses, expected by chance alone (Cohen, 1960).

Kappa has a range of + 1 (complete agreement), to 0 (agreement seen is equal to that expected by chance), to negative values (agreement less than that expected by chance). Here kappa is 0.52, which indicates substantial inconsistency. The results for the question on status of the first marriage are better, kappa being 0.91. The practical value of this information to the survey organizers is to suggest that the question on marriage status is acceptable, but that on contraceptive use needs improvement.

The variance of kappa can be calculated and used to test whether the observed agreement is statistically significantly better than that expected by chance alone. The index can also be generalized to apply to studies with many categories of result and many observers, and to take account of different degrees of disagreement; a fuller discussion is given by Fleiss (1973).

In a clinical application, physicians wished to develop a patient-completed questionnaire on gastrointestinal symptoms. They tested eighteen questions, comparing the patients' responses to the self-completed questionnaire with the results of a conventional medical history taken independently by a specialist. For fifteen questions, the kappa values were over 0.85; however the unsuitability of three other questions was shown by kappa values of 0.3 or less (Chisholm *et al.*, 1985). Other clinical applications are discussed by Sackett *et al.* (1985), who note studies of the consistency of clinical examinations yielding kappa values similar to that shown for the contraception survey in Fiji for the assessment of retinopathy, a dorsalis pedis pulse, and signs of chronic airflow obstruction; and considerably lower values for the interpretation of exercise electrocardiograms, and blood films for iron deficiency. Consistency is a particular issue in psychiatric diagnosis: its assessment has been reviewed by Shrout *et al.* (1987) who also discuss some further issues, such as the difficulties of consistency studies with conditions of low prevalence.

Assessment of the accuracy of information

Other measures are appropriate if one of the assessments can be regarded as giving the 'truth', and the issue is the accuracy of the other in giving the same results; for example, the second 'test' may be the final diagnosis achieved after full investigation, and the first a screening or diagnostic test. A measure of overall consistency is not so useful here, as the consequences of a positive and of a negative first test will be very different; hence the accuracy of each of these is assessed by the measures shown in Ex. 5.6. *Sensitivity* and *specificity*

ASSESSMENT OF ACCURACY OF DATA

		True result		
		Affected	Unaffected	Total
Screening result	abnormal	17	245	262
	normal	5	6176	6181
	Total	22	6421	6443

Sensitivity = proportion of affected subjects giving a positive test
= 17/22 = 77%.

Specificity = proportion of unaffected subjects giving a negative test
= 6176/6421 = 96.2%.

Predictive value positive = proportion of subjects with positive tests who are affected
= 17/262 = 6.5%.

Ex. 5.6. Assessment of accuracy of data, by comparison with a fully accurate method: the validity of antenatal screening for neural tube defects by a measurement of alphafetoprotein in maternal serum at 16–22 weeks' gestation, compared to the presence of a neural tube defect assessed after delivery. The test is only the first step in the screening process: the ultimate result was that terminations were carried out on 16 affected and on 2 unaffected pregnancies. For open neural tube defects, the sensitivity was 17/18 (94 per cent). From Wald *et al.* (1979)

together describe the performance of the test against the 'true' result, but can be calculated only where the true result is known for all subjects. In routine screening and diagnostic applications, only subjects giving a positive result to the first test will be investigated further; thus the *predictive value positive* will be the most easily measured parameter. It is a very relevant one, showing the proportion of all those testing positive, and suffering the consequences of worry and further testing, who do have the condition being sought. This predictive value increases with increases in the sensitivity and the specificity of the test, and in the prevalence of the condition in all those tested. Further discussion is given in works on diagnostic testing and on screening, including Sackett *et al.* (1985); a brief review of the arithmetic issues has been given by Vecchio (1966).

Examples of study design

To illustrate the concepts described so far in this book, we shall look at three examples, a randomized trial, a cohort study, and a case–control study. For each study, we will describe the study design, the selection of subjects, the observations made, and the main result. The studies are summarized in Ex. 5.7.

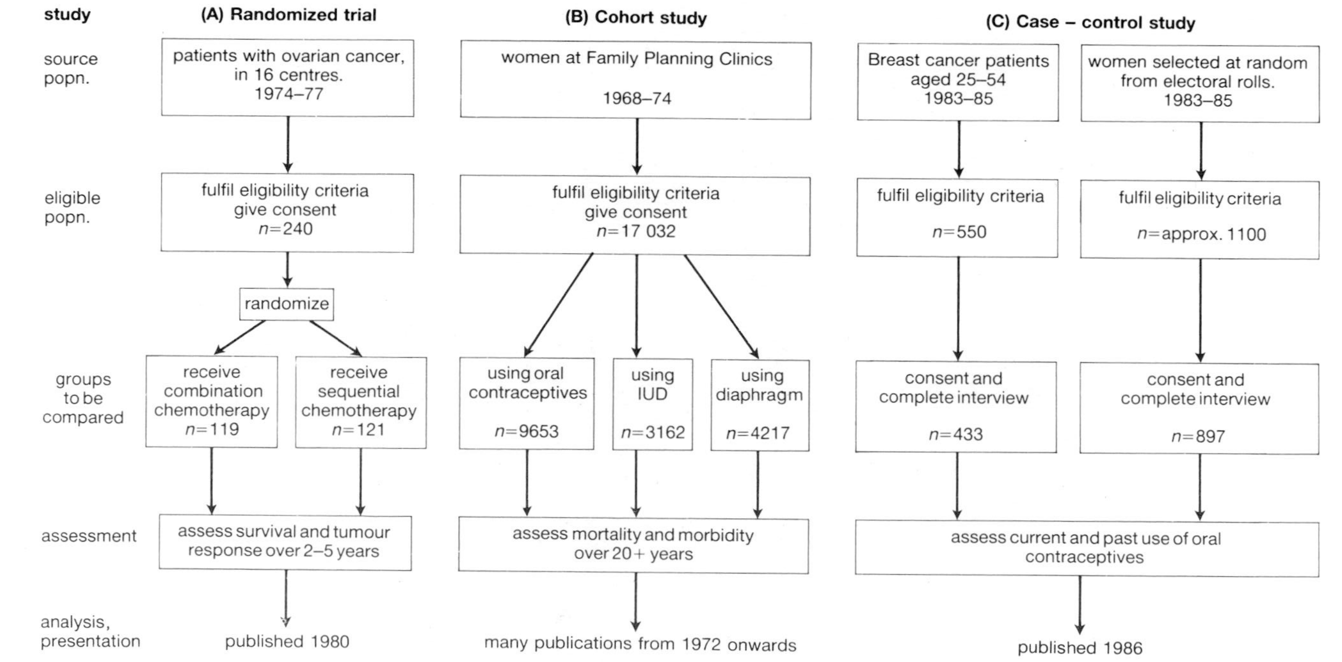

Ex. 5.7. Examples of study design

A: Randomized clinical trial (Miller *et al.*, 1980).

B: Prospective cohort study (Vessey *et al.*, 1976).

C: Case-control study (Paul *et al.*, 1986).

A randomized trial

'Combination v. sequential therapy with melphalan, 5-fluorouracil and methotrexate for advanced ovarian cancer.' Miller *et al.* (1980).

This study exemplifies the randomized trial design, and is shown in outline in Ex. 5.7A. This Canadian study was designed to compare the results of alternative treatments for advanced (stage 3 and 4) ovarian cancer: using three drugs simultaneously (combination therapy), or using them singly, in sequence (sequential therapy). Two outcome variables were used: survival, and tumour response. Calculations (such as will be shown in Chapter 7), showed that to detect a 15 per cent difference in survival rate, which was regarded as clinically important, required at least 100 patients in each treatment category. Such numbers could not be provided by one centre, so 16 cancer treatment centres were involved. Patient accrual started in 1974; follow-up continued for up to five years, and the results were published in 1980.

The emphasis in this design is on achieving high internal validity, so eligibility criteria were set to identify patients with the relevant condition who were suitable for treatment with either of the regimens, who were willing to enter the study and have either treatment, and who were likely to be available for follow-up (Ex. 5.8). Independent pathology review was used to standardize the diagnosis.

The 240 patients who entered the trial were randomly divided into two groups, 119 receiving combination chemotherapy and 121 receiving sequential chemotherapy. Because these two groups were derived by randomization, it is likely that they were similar in regard to the factors which affect their prognosis; thus we can assume that if the effects of the treatments were the same the subsequent course of these two groups would have been the same. The internal validity of this comparison is preserved by an analysis which compares the groups on the basis of this randomization, irrespective of what happened subsequently. In fact not all patients received their allocated treatment, and few received the full dosages, because of side effects. All patients were followed either until death or until the completion of the study; most of the patients had died by the time this analysis was done. The analysis of survival takes into account the fact of death and the time of death by life table methods which will be described in Appendix 2, but is based on total mortality, thereby avoiding any possible bias which might influence the certification of an individual death as being from ovarian cancer or from another cause. The comparison of survival is therefore very strong in terms of internal validity, as the two groups allocated by randomization are compared, complete data are available, and the outcome measure is simply death, giving no possibility of observation bias. The results showed that the survival experiences of the two groups were virtually identical, and the small differences seen were of an extent highly likely to occur through chance

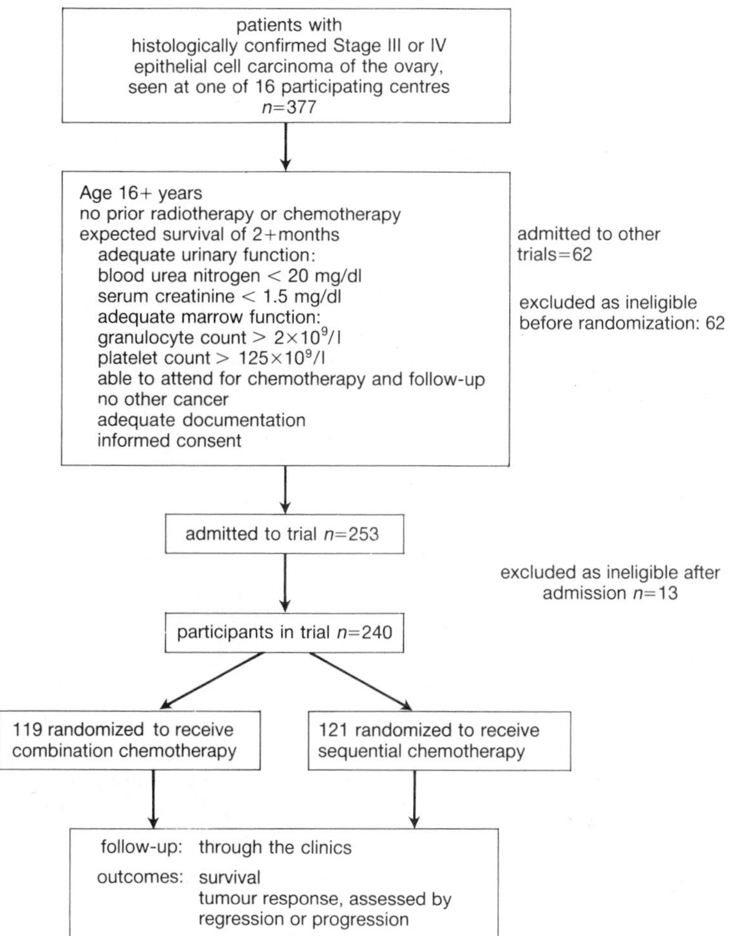

Ex. 5.8. Derivation of patient groups in a randomized trial, of two different regimens of drug therapy for ovarian cancer (Miller *et al.*, 1980)

variation; the conclusion therefore was that the two treatments had equal effects on survival.

The second outcome was tumour response. The internal validity of the assessment of the effect of treatment on tumour response is considerably weaker than that of survival, for two reasons. First, tumour response could be assessed only on patients who had measurable disease two months after entering the trial; there were 57 such patients in the combination therapy group and 52 in the sequential therapy group. These two sub-groups of patients with measurable disease have not been derived simply by randomization, and we can no longer assume that they are similar to each other in regard to all relevant factors. The randomization has been compromised, and this part of the study should be regarded as a non-randomized cohort comparison. Second, the assessment of response to treatment is conceivably open to observer variation. To minimize this, precise definitions of complete and partial response, no change, and progression of disease were set out in the protocol. Reports on each patient were sent regularly to the central unit, whether or not a change in state had been noted. This standardization of definition and procedure provides considerable protection against observer bias. Even better protection would be given by a single-blind technique; one could envisage a design in which patients were assessed regularly by a physician who was independent of the treatment teams and could be kept unaware of what treatment the patient had received; but the administrative difficulties of this would be considerable and its benefits marginal. Given the standardization procedures, it seems very unlikely that any major bias is present, but it cannot be dismissed as firmly as it can for the survival comparison. There is certainly considerable error in the response measurements, and so the results, which did not show any major difference between the two treatments in regard to tumour response, cannot be used to conclude firmly that there was not even a minor difference in response. This is not a severe limitation as such a difference would probably not be clinically relevant.

The internal validity of this design is therefore extremely high for the survival comparison, and reasonable for the comparison of tumour response. Let us now move to external validity. The source population comprises those patients with this particular disease seen in the participating centres during the trial period. Of the 377 such subjects, 240 (64 per cent) entered this trial (Ex. 5.8). Of the rest, 62 were admitted to other trials, and 75 excluded as ineligible. Thirteen patients were in fact entered into the trial and randomized to therapy, and it was subsequently realized that they were ineligible on the basis of clinical information recorded prior to randomization; these subjects were therefore appropriately excluded. It would not have been appropriate to exclude them if the question of their eligibility had depended on information recorded after the randomization. Basic information of this type, giving the numbers of patients in the source population and the total number of those eligible, should be recorded in clinical trials as a routine, but too often is not. In this trial we can be reasonably assured that the results of the trial can be applied to the eligible subjects. The target population is by implication subjects fulfilling the eligibility criteria seen in these and other treatment centres at future times. The eligibility criteria are in general objective and appear to be clinically appropriate, in that most relate to investigations which would be used in normal clinical care. The more subjective ones, such as the 'expected survival of at least two months' are open to more variation in interpretation.

Thus this trial design has succeeded in making a comparison between patients treated on alternative therapies which has very high internal validity in regard to the major end point of survival, reasonable internal validity in regard to tumour response, and acceptable external validity. The results, which showed no important difference between the two treatment groups in either outcome, can be applied to clinical practice relatively easily. Other results from this study showed that the toxicity appeared to be higher on the sequential regimen.

Cohort studies of oral contraceptive users

Two major studies will be discussed. Both have given many important papers, but the design of the studies is best described in the reports of Vessey *et al.* (1976), and the Royal College of General Practitioners (1974).

Consider the situation faced by investigators in the mid-1960s concerning the effects of the contraceptive pill. Here was a new pharmacological preparation being used by very large numbers of women and which could have major effects on their health. To show such effects, or to demonstrate their absence, required a long-term cohort study capable of assessing multiple end points and of giving results which would be widely applicable. Such a study would be a large, expensive and long-term commitment, not easily repeated; therefore the design needed to optimize both internal and external validity. Two such studies were set up in the United Kingdom.

The Royal College of General Practitioners based their study on oral contraceptive users and comparison subjects selected by general practitioners. The source population comprised the registered patients of the 1400 general practitioners who responded to the College's invitation to participate. They selected the first two women in each calendar month for whom they prescribed an oral contraceptive, either for the first time or as a repeat prescription. For each, a control was selected as the next woman identified in the practice records whose year of birth was within three years of that of the oral contraceptive user, but who had never used an oral contraceptive (Ex. 5.9). Both users and non-users had to be married or living as married, and thus were likely to be sexually active. Follow-up was done by the general practitioners recording diagnoses of all future episodes of illness newly presenting after the date of recruitment, and continuing to record information on oral contraceptive use, pregnancies, and related events. Patients who left their original general practitioner, or whose general practitioner withdrew from the study, ceased follow-up at that time, as did patients who began to be supplied with oral contraceptives by sources other than the general practice.

The other study was set up in collaboration with the Family Planning Association (FPA), a voluntary group which runs clinics giving family planning and contraceptive advice (Vessey *et al.*, 1976). Through seventeen of the largest FPA clinics (the source population), 17 032 women were

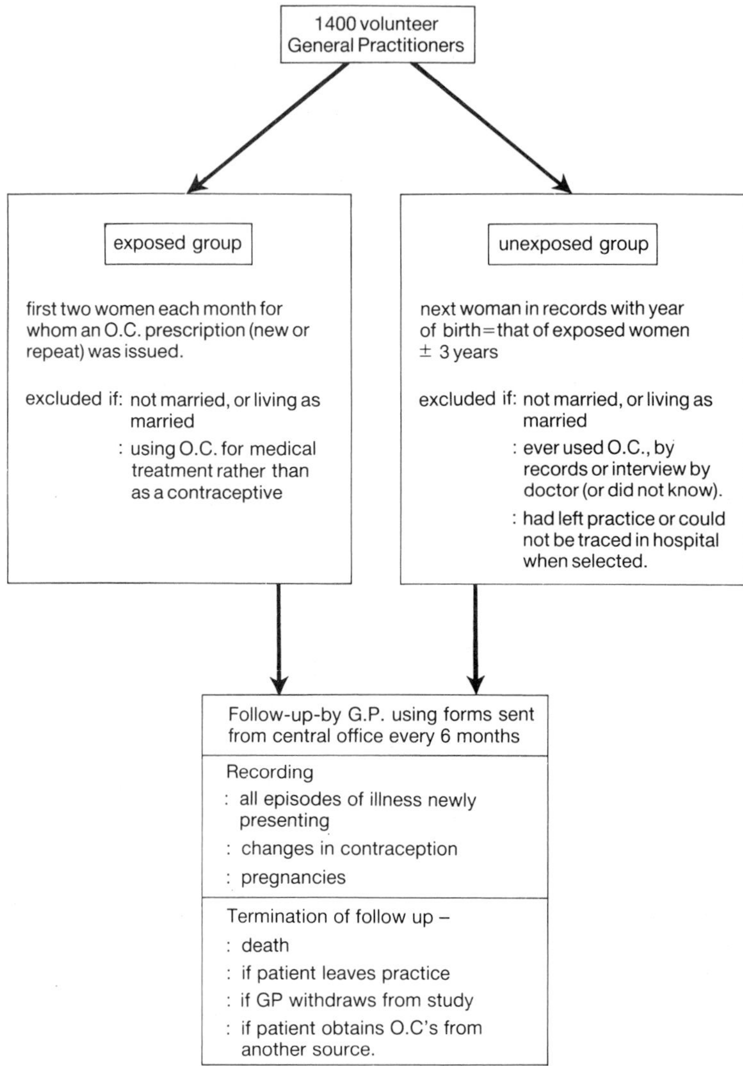

Ex. 5.9. Design of a prospective cohort study: derivation of groups of exposed and non-exposed women in a prospective cohort study of oral contraceptive use, from Royal College of General Practitioners (1974)

recruited (Ex. 5.10). To be eligible, a clinic patient had to be married, aged 25 to 39, a white British subject, and be willing to participate; these criteria were primarily to ensure adequate follow-up. Oral contraceptive users were defined as currently using oral contraceptives and having used them for at least five months, and the unexposed groups were currently using either a diaphragm or an intra-uterine device, having used it for at least five months,

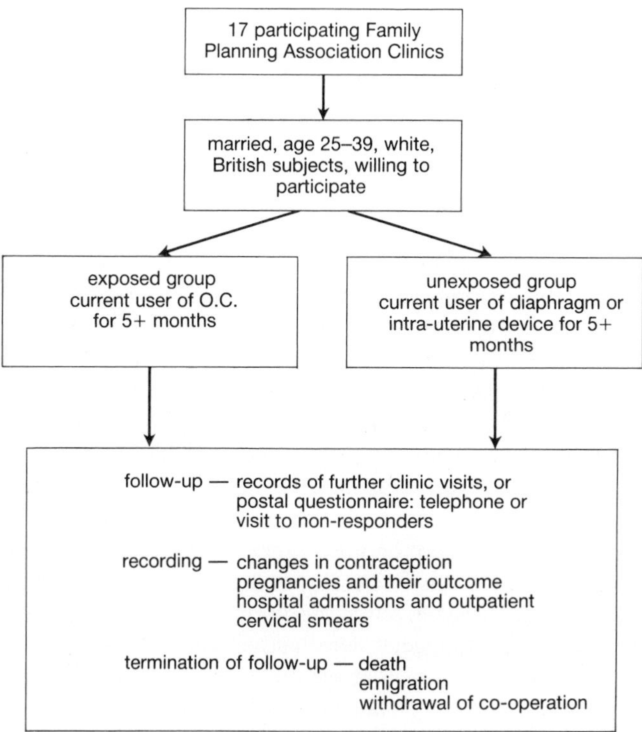

Ex. 5.10. Design of a prospective cohort study, of oral contraceptive use: based on Family Planning Clinics (Vessey *et al.*, 1976)

without prior exposure to oral contraceptives. The five months criterion was included to eliminate substantial numbers of women who would change their method of contraception only a few months after starting. Patients were followed primarily through the FPA clinics, with records being filled out at each subsequent visit, but if no appointment was made or the appointment was not kept, a follow-up form was sent directly to the patient, and if this failed telephone calls or home visits were made. On recruitment, as well as the usual identification information, patients were asked to give the name of their family doctor and of two contact persons who could be used to find out, for example, their further address if they moved. On the clinic follow-up and postal follow-up forms, information was requested about any hospital visit either as an inpatient or outpatient made since the last follow-up, and therefore the outcome measures were primarily mortality and morbidity recorded at inpatient or outpatient visits. Follow-up was terminated at death, at emigration outside the United Kingdom, or if the subject requested to withdraw from the study.

Both these cohort designs show that the prime considerations were to achieve adequate follow-up and high internal validity, after choosing source populations to give reasonable external validity. The FPA study has shown few losses to follow-up, about 0.7 per cent per year, and the loss rates have been similar in the different contraceptive groups. This good follow-up is due to the use of a source population and eligibility criteria which will tend to select women with a stable life style. Internal validity is preserved as these criteria apply to both the oral contraceptive users and the comparison groups. The price of these advantages is some limitation of external validity, which however is probably not of major importance. The women in the FPA study are certainly not 'representative' of all oral contraceptive users in the United Kingdom; but it seems unlikely that any major biological association seen will be markedly different outside this selected group. A greater problem is the nature of the comparison group: the non-oral contraceptive users were all using another method of contraception, and so differences in a particular outcome between the oral contraceptive users and the other groups might be due to an effect either of the oral contraceptive or of the other method. The fact that the non-oral contraceptive users comprised two major groups, users of the diaphragm and users of an intra-uterine device, has been useful in this respect. For example, it has been shown that rates of cervical cancer and cervical dysplasia have been lower in the diaphragm users than in either of the other two groups, which suggests a protective effect of the diaphragm rather than increased risks in both other groups. To assess whether oral contraceptives are related to cervical cancer, the relevant comparison is therefore between oral contraceptive users and users of an intra-uterine device; this study is discussed further in Chapter 9.

The Royal College of General Practitioners' study may have a somewhat higher degree of external validity. The sampling system suggests that the oral contraceptive users might be a reasonably representative sample of all users in that particular practice, although the number of eligible women who did not enter the study cannot be ascertained. The non-users included married women who were not using any method of contraception as well as those who were using some; it is doubtful if this is a benefit, as differences between oral contraceptive users and non-users in this study in regard to factors such as sexual activity may then be greater than those in the FPA study. The participating general practitioners were volunteers, and therefore the oral contraceptive users even in this study are not a representative sample of all users. Both these designs fail to fulfil one of the criteria set out in Ex. 4.4; the exposed group were not included from the time of first exposure, but were identified as a prevalent sample of oral contraceptive users. The reason is again practical: the recruitment process would have been much more difficult if women were recruited at first use only, and many women would stop oral contraceptive use after only a short time. As a result, neither of these studies is powerful in the assessment of short-term effects of oral contraceptive use, as women who started using oral contraceptives and had ill-effects immediately would be under-represented.

Thus in both studies a degree of external validity has been sacrificed to achieve good internal validity and to facilitate follow-up.

These cohort studies involved many outcome measures, with various problems of observation bias. Observation bias is likely to be at its maximum in the recording of minor morbidity and at its minimum in mortality; thus consistency between different measures of outcome is valuable in its assessment. It will be most likely to occur for conditions which have been shown by these or other studies to be associated with oral contraceptive use. An example is venous thrombosis and embolism. A useful result from the FPA study is that the relationship between oral contraceptive use and venous embolism was stronger where the evidence for the diagnosis was more objective; if observation bias was a major contributor to the association the difference would be greater where the evidence was more subjective (Vessey and Doll 1969; also see Vessey 1971 for some useful discussion).

Observation bias in recorded morbidity could arise because doctors are more likely to diagnose a certain condition in oral contraceptive users, because they might diagnose all illness more readily in oral contraceptive users, because patients taking oral contraceptives might report ailments more readily, or because patients taking oral contraceptives might see their general practitioners more frequently. Thus bias might occur particularly in regard to data based on general practitioner diagnoses, as recorded in the Royal College's study. That study showed that of all diagnoses, 18 per cent were recorded on the prescription date of the oral contraceptive. This suggests that some complaints came to the general practitioner's notice only because the patient had to visit for the prescription (Royal College of General Practitioners 1974, pp 18–19). In the Family Planning Association study the morbidity information was restricted to hospital referrals for inpatient or outpatient care, partly in order to avoid such problems. A sub-study in which for certain FPA clinics the information from the study could be directly compared to linked hospital and maternity records showed that the method of investigation used identified all births and pregnancy terminations, and 90 per cent of all other hospital admissions (Vessey *et al.*, 1976, p 389; Vessey *et al.*, 1974).

As both these cohort studies have given rise to many individual reports, it is not appropriate to discuss any particular main result. An example of these results has been shown in Ex. 3.4 (p 31) and one study from the FPA cohort will be discussed in detail in Chapter 9 (p 184).

A case-control study of breast cancer

'Oral contraceptives and breast cancer: a national study'. Paul *et al.* (1986).

This case-control study is chosen as a more complex design, showing how the scientific objectives are met within practical limitations. It is a recent study of the aetiology of breast cancer in New Zealand, examining oral contraceptive use primarily, and in principle sets out to compare a series of newly incident cases from a defined population to a representative sample of unaffected subjects.

The source population was defined as all New Zealand women within a stated age range, 25 to 54, who were diagnosed with breast cancer between July 1983 and June 1985 (Ex. 5.11). Thus an objective of the study is that the results should be directly applicable to patients with breast cancer diagnosed in New Zealand within that age range and at that time period. The value of the study goes beyond this; if the study has high internal validity and the results are applicable to New Zealand, they will be relevant to other populations. In theory, the eligible population might be identical to the source population. However practical issues arise in that the cases have to be identified and approached by the same method as is used for the control series. The investigators decided to choose controls from the electoral rolls, and to use telephone interviews to conduct the study; therefore all the controls, and so all the cases, had to be on the electoral roll and had to have an available telephone number. The breast cancer cases were identified through a cancer registry and a special study group in a major city, and women with a previous breast cancer were excluded. The eligible population defined on

THE CASE SERIES IN A CASE-CONTROL STUDY

Source population	all New Zealand women aged 25–54 diagnosed with breast cancer between 1st July 1983 and 30th June 1985
Eligible population n = 550	women aged 25–54, with histologically confirmed breast cancer notified to the N.Z. National Cancer Registry or to the Auckland Breast Cancer Study group between above dates (n = 739); no previous breast cancer; on current electoral roll; whose telephone number was found; exclusions = 189, eligible population = 550
Participant population n = 433	had to have permission from their physician (28 not given) be identified in time to allow interview 4–8 months from diagnosis (49 too late) still alive (8 had died) well enough (4 too ill) exclusions (14 other exclusions) agreed to participate (14 refused) participant population 433; exclusions 117 all participants gave usable information on oral contraceptive use

Participants/eligible = 78.7%
Participants/source = 58.6%

Ex. 5.11. A case–control study. The source, eligible and participant populations in the case series of a case–control study of breast cancer in New Zealand (Paul *et al.* 1986)

those criteria numbered 550. The best estimate of the source population is the number of women notified to the registries used, 739; in addition there may have been small numbers of women diagnosed without histological confirmation or not notified to the registries. Thus 189 women were excluded, and the eligible population is 74 per cent of the estimated source population. The stipulation of no previous breast cancer could have been made part of the definition of the source population, and those exclusions discounted. The defence of the large number of exclusions is that exactly the same exclusions were made for the comparison group, and therefore any non-representativeness introduced is the same in the control group as in the case group, and should not affect the internal validity of the study.

The investigators then had to deal with the practical issues of approaching these 550 eligible women and asking them to participate in the study. As shown in Ex. 5.11, some 117 women did not participate, and there were 433 participants, 79 per cent of the eligible population. This figure of 79 per cent is the participation rate; however the participant population is only 59 per cent of the source population. The major reasons for non-participation were failure to identify patients quickly enough to allow an interview to be done within the stipulated time period of 4 to 8 months from diagnosis, failure to receive permission from the patient's physician, patients who had died or were too ill for interview, and the inevitable miscellaneous list of exclusions. It is noteworthy, and fairly typical of modern epidemiology, that the least of the investigators' problems was failure of the subjects to agree to interview, with only 14 refusals. The response rate, that is the proportion who agreed to participate out of all who were approached who were suitable for interview was 433/447, 97 per cent.

It is more difficult to describe precisely the constitution of the control group in the New Zealand study (Ex. 5.12). The source population comprised all New Zealand women aged 25 to 54 in the time period in question who did not have breast cancer. The eligibility criteria limited the study to women who were on the current electoral roll and who had telephone numbers. Because no list existed which included age, the investigators had to take a random sample of women from the electoral rolls, exclude those for whom a telephone number could not be found, and then write to the women asking for their participation; they could determine the age of the woman only if she responded. Whether a woman had had breast cancer was determined only after she was interviewed. The size of the eligible population therefore cannot be precisely determined, but the best estimate appears to be 1110. Of these women 39 were excluded because of death, illness, absence overseas or language difficulties, 99 refused to take part, and 75 were not traced, giving a participation rate of 897/1110, or 81 per cent. As the number of women not traced is likely to include some women who would not be eligible because of age, this participation rate will be a minimum estimate. As expected, the proportion of controls excluded because of illness or death was considerably

THE CONTROL SERIES IN A CASE-CONTROL STUDY

Source population	all New Zealand women aged 25–54 and without diagnosed breast cancer
Eligible population	women on electoral register, aged 25–54, with a telephone number, with no history of breast cancer: selected by random sampling from register; estimate of number =
n = 1110	1110
Participant population	still alive (10 had died) well enough (4 too ill) in New Zealand (12 overseas) no language difficulty (13 excluded) agreed to participate (99 refused) traced (75 not traced, of whom some were likely to be outside the age range)
n = 897	participant population 897; exclusions 213

Participants/eligible = 80.8%
Participants/source = unknown

Ex. 5.12. A case-control study. The source, eligible and participant populations in the control group in a case-control study of breast cancer in New Zealand (Paul *et al.*, 1986)

less than the proportion of the cases excluded for those reasons, and there were no exclusions because of failure to obtain permission from the physician as that was not required for the controls. The voluntary response rate of eligible controls was 897/996, 90 per cent; this is lower than that of the cases. This would be expected as subjects who have had a serious disease have a greater motivation to take part in a health study.

This case-control study is a complex one, and it is not easy to assess the extent of selection problems. The main issue of internal validity is whether the participating cases and controls differ from their respective eligible populations in terms of the exposure of interest (oral contraceptive use) because of factors affecting their participation in the study. The main losses of source population members, from the electoral roll and telephone requirements, were applied equally to each group and are unlikely to influence internal validity. The other losses are different in the case and control groups, although their overall extent is similar, and while there seems to be no particular reason why they would affect the association being examined, they do raise some doubts.

Information on the exposure, oral contraceptive use, and on related factors was collected by an interview conducted by telephone. The initial approach to the women was by letter, which included a calendar on which they were asked to mark important dates such as marriage and births of children for reference during the interview. The interview was totally standardized, and almost all the interviews were carried out by one nurse interviewer, who at least at the start of the interview did not know whether the interviewee was a cancer patient or a comparison subject. The reliability of the information therefore depends primarily on the standardization of the interview technique, and also on the blindness of the interviewer. However the subjects themselves were certainly not blind, being well aware of whether they had been treated for breast cancer or not. This is the major likely source of systematic bias, and one which is often unavoidable in a retrospective study. The standardized, non-emotive and systematic interview technique is the best protection against such bias, particularly if the primary issue in the study (here, oral contraceptive use) is not made clear to the subject and other issues are also assessed. If it were possible to obtain a full and complete history of oral contraceptive use from records made at the time the drugs were given, this of course would be free of such observer bias, but this is virtually impossible. In this study the investigators wrote to the general practitioners of women who had reported recent use of prescribed contraceptives, and concluded that there was 'close agreement' between the histories received from the general practitioners and from the women themselves. This is reassuring, but clearly incomplete.

The main result of the study can be given in a simple table, which shows that 310 of the 433 breast cancer patients (72 per cent) had ever used oral contraceptives, compared to 708 of the 897 controls (79 per cent). This gives a crude odds ratio of $(310 \times 189)/(708 \times 123) = 0.67$, but adjustment for six other factors including age, parity and age at first birth, by methods which will be described later, changed this to 0.94. Several other variables such as social class, obesity and alcohol consumption were also brought into the analysis, but did not affect the main result. More informative is a table showing the odds ratios by duration of use, which does not show any simple trend. The results therefore show no overall association, and statistical tests showed that the variations seen would be expected to occur frequently by chance variation alone. The study, while showing no overall effect, does not demonstrate the absence of any risk; in fact an increased risk was seen in women aged 25–34 years at diagnosis which could have occurred by chance but warrants further investigation. As information has been collected on many factors, such as other contraceptive methods and reproductive history, and as the study is continuing, we expect further analyses to be published in due course.

6. Confounding

Thus it is easy to prove that the wearing of tall hats and the carrying of umbrellas enlarges the chest, prolongs life, and confers comparative immunity from disease; for the statistics shew that the classes which use these articles are bigger, healthier, and live longer than the class which never dreams of possessing such things.

—George Bernard Shaw: Preface to 'The Doctor's Dilemma'; 1906

Confounding—definition and non-mathematical examples

One of the central concepts of science in general, and particularly biology, is that of the tightly controlled experiment. Consider the classical experimental situation in which animals are used. The investigator selects groups of animals as similar to each other as possible; for example, species of laboratory rats which have been bred under controlled conditions for many generations, are housed under identical circumstances of physical environment, fed and handled in the same way, and are then randomly allocated into the required groups. Observations are then made in a standardized manner, with the observer being 'blind' as to the allocation of the animal. The objective of this method is to achieve a situation where the groups of animals differ in terms of only one factor, the exposure factor under consideration, and therefore there is no alternative but to assume that a difference in the measured outcome between the groups of animals is due either to that exposure factor, or to chance. The randomization of animals from a common pool protects against there being factors other than the exposure under test which differ between the groups, and the standardized and blind assessment procedure protects against bias in the observations of outcome.

In observational studies on humans such tight control is not possible, for scientific or more commonly for ethical or logistic reasons. Even where a randomized design can be applied to a group of volunteers or a naturally selected population, one must be cautious as such individuals will differ from the population in general, weakening the external validity of the study. So we have to assess how to conduct studies of free living human subjects, which will still have a high degree of validity.

We have seen already that the results of a study, in terms of the differences in outcome between the groups being compared, may be due to any of four mechanisms: bias, confounding, chance or causation.

Confounding may be defined as (Ex. 6.1)

> a distortion of an exposure—outcome association brought about by the association of another factor with both outcome and exposure.

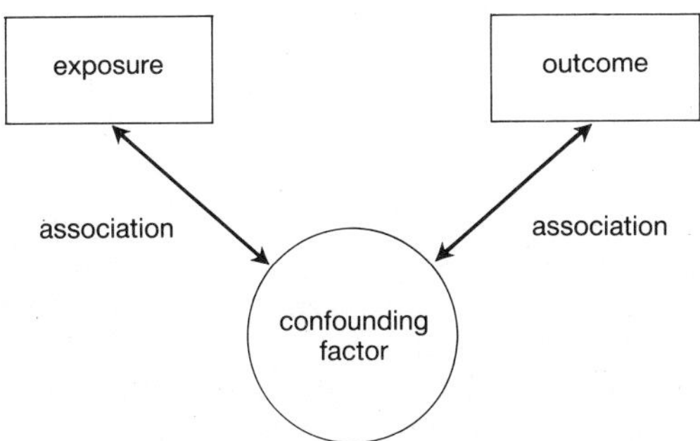

Ex. 6.1. A definition of confounding, and a diagram showing the two associations which are necessary for it to occur

Rather than deal with the formal definition it is perhaps easier to consider intuitively some situations. Consider a situation in which we are interested in the causal association between the use of oral contraceptives by women and the occurrence of myocardial infarction. We can imagine the two standard designs; a cohort study in which we compare oral contraceptive users with non-users, and a case–control study in which we compare women with myocardial infarction with an unaffected comparison group.

The issue we are to deal with now is: can the observed association between oral contraceptive use and myocardial infarction be influenced by differences between the two groups of women in terms of other factors? Consider first the issue of smoking. There is ample evidence that people who smoke have an increased risk of myocardial infarction. There is also considerable evidence that women who use oral contraceptives smoke more than women who do not. Now consider the effect of these two associations on the studies we are performing. Consider the situation where the null hypothesis is in fact the truth, that is, there is no causal association between oral contraceptive use and myocardial infarction. In the cohort study, because the oral contraceptive users smoke more than the non-users, they will have a higher risk of myocardial infarction. Therefore we shall see a higher incidence rate of myocardial infarction in the oral contraceptive users than in the non-users. In the case–control study, because smoking is a causal factor for myocardial infarction, the prevalence of smoking will be greater in the myocardial infarction patients than in the comparison patients. Because smoking is associated with oral contraceptive use, oral contraceptive use will also be more common in the myocardial infarction patients. Thus both studies will give a result suggesting a positive relationship between oral contraceptive use

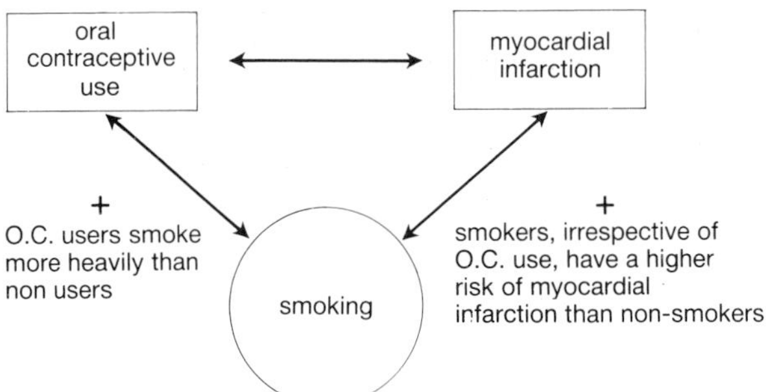

Ex. 6.2. An example of confounding: any comparison of the risks of myocardial infarction in oral contraceptive users and in non-users (cohort design), and any comparison of the prevalence of past O.C. use in myocardial infarction patients and in unaffected subjects (case–control design), will be influenced by the associations of both O.C. use and myocardial infarction with smoking, which is a confounding factor; the measured association between O.C. use and myocardial infarction will over-estimate the true association

and myocardial infarction, even if the null hypothesis of no association is in fact true (Ex. 6.2).

In this situation smoking is acting as a confounding factor. Confounding is produced by the two simultaneous and independent properties, that smoking is associated with the outcome in this study, and independently smoking is associated with the exposure.

The definition of confounding involves a definition of the study hypothesis, because it is true to say that both smoking and oral contraceptives are causal factors for myocardial infarction. If we were studying the relationship between smoking and myocardial infarction in women, we should have to consider oral contraceptive use as a confounding factor.

The effects of a confounding factor can be in either direction depending on the direction of the associations. In the situation given, the exposed group (oral contraceptive users) have a *higher* prevalence of smoking, and smoking is associated with an *increase* in risk of myocardial infarction. The net result of this confounding will be to give an apparent *excess* risk of myocardial infarction in the exposed group. In another situation, consider the relationship of oral contraceptive use to myocardial infarction in women, and the effect of obesity as a confounding factor (Ex. 6.3). Suppose that oral contraceptive users are *less* obese than non-users, but that obesity gives an *increased* risk of myocardial infarction. In this situation the 'exposed' group of oral contraceptive users will be less obese than the group of non-users, and because of this their risk of myocardial infarction will be *reduced*. If the null hypothesis of no association between oral contraception and myocardial infarction is true, the study will give a spurious indication of a protective effect. If there is a real increase in risk of myocardial infarction in oral

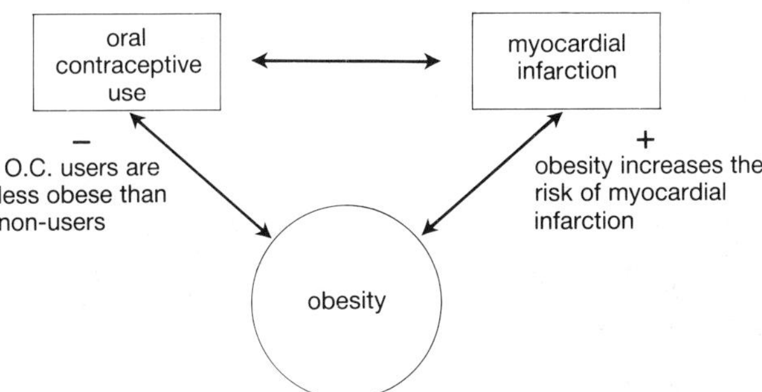

Ex. 6.3. Negative confounding: if obesity increases the risk of myocardial infarction, and O.C. users are less obese than non-users, the measured association between O.C. use and myocardial infarction will under-estimate the true association

contraceptive users, the study will under-estimate this risk if it fails to take into account the counteracting effect of the differences in obesity between contraceptive users and non-users.

How do we know if these associations exist? The issue is not whether the associations exist in general, for example whether it is true in general that oral contraceptive users tend to be less obese than non-users. That would be a difficult claim to substantiate, as the relationship is likely to vary between women of different ages, in different countries, and so on. That is not important. The crucial issue is, does the association exist within the study population; within the data used in the analysis? Thus, if within the data set given by a particular study, it is true that oral contraceptive users are less obese than non-users, and that obese subjects have a higher incidence of myocardial infarction, then obesity will be a confounding factor in the relationship between oral contraceptive use and myocardial infarction. The only other proviso is that the obesity–oral contraceptive and obesity–infarction associations must apply independently from the oral contraceptive–infarction relationship; that is, obesity must be associated with oral contraceptive use even in women without infarction, and obesity must be related to infarction even in women who do not use oral contraceptives. This may seem difficult logic, but should be clearer after some examples are presented.

A factor is therefore a confounding factor only when the two associations exist; when it is associated with both the exposure and the outcome under assessment. Oral contraceptive users and non-users may differ in terms of many other factors; for example, they may differ in their exposure to hair dyes, with oral contraceptive users more frequently using hair dyes. Do we have to consider hair dye use as a confounder in assessing the study? The answer is, only if hair dye use is itself related to myocardial infarction. If we have asked questions about hair dye use in our study, we can assess this by looking at the women who are not exposed to oral contraceptives, and within that sub-population see if there is an association between hair dye use and myocardial infarction. If there is not, there is no need to consider hair dye use as a confounder. Similarly, there may be factors related to the outcome which may not be related to the exposure. For example, the risk of myocardial infarction is increased in women who have certain types of familial hypercholesterolaemia. This will be a confounding factor only if in the study in question the prevalence of hypercholesterolaemia differs between oral contraceptive users and non-users.

Confounding in cohort and intervention studies

Because an understanding of confounding is so important, we shall look at a number of simple examples, using both hypothetical and real data. Consider a hypothetical example, Ex. 6.4. Here are the results of a cohort study in which subjects with low exercise levels are compared to subjects with high

CONFOUNDING IN A COHORT STUDY

	Myocardial infarctions	Person-years	Incidence/1000
Table A: all subjects ($n = 8000$ person-years)			
Low exercise	105	4000	26.25
High exercise	25	4000	6.25
Relative risk = 26.25/6.25 = 4.2			
Subtable B_1: obese subjects ($n = 4000$)			
Low exercise	90	3000	30.0
High exercise	10	1000	10.0
Relative risk = 3.0			
Subtable B_2: non-obese subjects ($n = 4000$)			
Low exercise	15	1000	15.0
High exercise	15	3000	5.0
Relative risk = 3.0			

Ex. 6.4. Confounding. A cohort study assessing the association between the incidence of myocardial infarction and exercise, where obesity is a confounding factor. Hypothetical data

exercise levels, the outcome under investigation being the incidence of myocardial infarction in a given follow-up period.

Table A shows the simplest form of the results, showing a strong association with a relative risk of 4.2. However, let us assume that the subjects vary in obesity, and that obesity and exercise are related; obesity is less common in the high exercise subjects than in the low exercise subjects. Sub-tables B_1 and B_2 show the results in an identical format to the first table, separately for obese subjects and non-obese subjects. The relative risk for low compared to high exercise in subjects who are obese is 3.0; the relative risk for low compared to high exercise in subjects who are not obese is also 3.0. So irrespective of obesity, the best estimate of the effect of exercise is clearly 3.0. Why then did we get the result of 4.2 in the first table for all subjects? The reason is that obesity is a confounding factor. Obesity is itself a risk factor for myocardial infarction, and this can be seen by comparing the risks for obese subjects for a given level of exercise (Subtable B_1) with those for non-obese subjects with the same level of exercise (Subtable B_2). For low exercise subjects, incidence rates per 1000 are 30.0 in obese and 15.0 in non-obese subjects; for high exercise subjects, the corresponding rates are 10.0 and 5.0. Moreover, obesity is related to exercise level, as comparison of the subtables shows that low exercise subjects are much more obese in terms of their distribution by person-years of experience; for the low exercise group, 75 per cent of the person-years apply to obese subjects, while for high exercise the proportion is 25 per cent.

The relationships between these factors, low exercise, obesity, and the outcome of myocardial infarction are shown diagrammatically in Ex. 6.5. Low exercise is a risk factor for myocardial infarction, with a true relative risk of 3.0. Obesity is also a risk factor for myocardial infarction, with a relative risk of 2.0, this result being derived from a comparison of Subtables B_1 and B_2. However, because low exercise and obesity are positively related to each other, the apparent relative risk of low exercise, that is the risk ratio

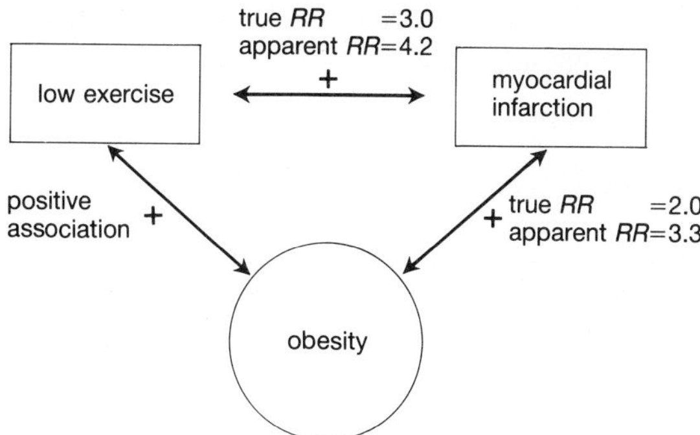

Ex. 6.5. Confounding. The associations which exist in Ex. 6.4.
RR = relative risk

obtained by comparing all low exercise subjects, many of whom are also obese, with all high exercise subjects, most of whom are not obese, is 4.2. If we add up the data in Subtables B_1 and B_2, to compare all obese subjects with all non-obese subjects we obtain the apparent risk ratio of 3.3 for the crude relationship between obesity and myocardial infarction. Thus in this situation there are two independent risk factors for myocardial infarction, low exercise and obesity, which are positively correlated with each other, and therefore each acts as a confounding factor when the relationship of the other to myocardial infarction is assessed.

If you have been able to work through and understand that hypothetical example, you can consider now a real example of rather simple confounding, shown in Ex. 6.6.

This is derived from a 1986 paper in a major journal which amongst other things compared the success rate for two different surgical procedures in the treatment of renal calculi. The upper table shows the results as they would be picked up by a casual reader, and as they were explained in the summary to the paper. For each surgical technique, open surgery and percutaneous nephrolithotomy, 350 patients were assessed, and the success rates were 78 per cent with open surgery and 83 per cent with percutaneous nephrolithotomy. In this paper patients were divided into those who had stones of less

CONFOUNDING: TREATMENT OF RENAL CALCULI

	Successes	Failures	Total patients	Successes (%)
All stones ($n = 700$)				
open surgery	273	77	350	78
percutaneous nephrolithotomy	289	61	350	83
Stones < 2 cm ($n = 357$)				
open surgery	81	6	87	93
percutaneous nephrolithotomy	234	36	270	87
Stones ⩾ 2 cm ($n = 343$)				
open surgery	192	71	263	73
percutaneous nephrolithotomy	55	25	80	69

Ex. 6.6. Confounding. A comparison of two surgical methods of treating renal calculi, showing success rates (per cent of patients with no stones at 3 months after treatment). The summary of this paper states 'success was achieved in 273 (78 per cent) of patients after open surgery, 289 (83 per cent) after percutaneous nephrolithotomy, . . .'. However, in fact the success rates for open surgery are higher, not lower, than those for the percutaneous technique. The main result of this paper concerns a third method, extracorporeal shockwave lithotripsy, which was followed by higher success rates than those shown (Charig *et al.*, 1986)

CONFOUNDING IN A COHORT STUDY

Activity level	Deaths	Man-years	Rate/10 000	Relative risk
Table A. All ages				
Light or moderate	532	65 000	81.8	3.4
Heavy	66	27 700	23.8	1.0 (reference)
Table B. Age 35–44				
Light or moderate	3	5 900	5.1	1.1
Heavy	4	8 300	4.8	
Age 45–54				
Light or moderate	62	17 600	35.2	1.9
Heavy	20	11 000	18.2	
Age 55–64				
Light or moderate	183	23 700	77.2	1.7
Heavy	34	7 400	45.9	
Age 65–74				
Light or moderate	284	17 800	159.6	2.0
Heavy	8	1 000	80.0	

Ex. 6.7. Confounding. Data from a cohort study of mortality from coronary heart disease and exercise. Confounding by age distorts the association between physical activity and mortality from heart disease. In Table A, a comparison of men with light or moderate physical activity with those with heavy activity gives a relative risk of 3.4. Table B shows that (1) mortality rises with age and (2) the proportion of men doing light or moderate work rises with age. Age is a confounding factor, and its effect gives an increase in the observed relative risk between light activity and CHD mortality. This excess is shown as the relative risks within each of 4 age bands are all much lower than the crude estimate of 3.4. From Paffenbarger and Hale (1975). See also Ex. 3.3. The situation can be represented as:

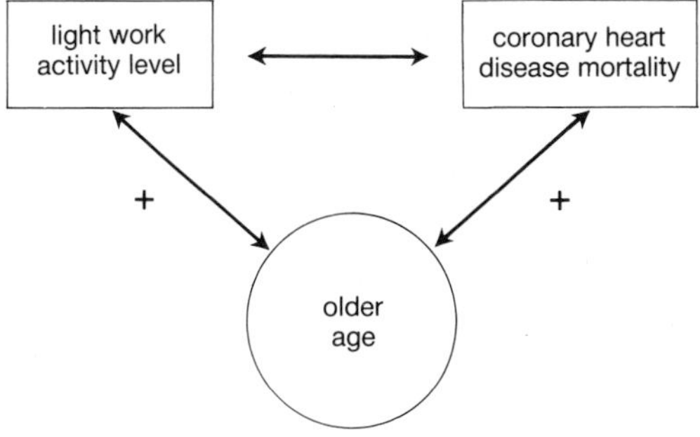

than 2 cm in diameter, and those with larger stones. For patients with small stones, the success rate of open surgery was better than that of the other technique, 93 per cent compared to 87 per cent, and for patients with larger stones open surgery also had the higher success rate, 73 per cent compared to 69 per cent. Thus, for either of the two groups of patients, open surgery gave better success rates, but an erroneous impression of a lower success rate is created from the pooled data, because open surgery was used much more often on patients with large stones, and those patients had a lower success rate irrespective of the technique used.

In most situations, of course, confounding cannot be dealt with quite so simply, and as a further example of real data, Ex. 6.7 looks at the relationship between physical activity and mortality from coronary heart disease in a major prospective study of longshoremen (dock workers) in California.

Table A shows the total data reconstructed from the original paper, comparing light or moderate exercise level workers with heavy exercise level workers, and shows a relative risk of 3.4 in the light exercise group. However, as one might predict, there was considerable confounding by age in this study, in that workers doing the lighter physical work tended to be older than those doing the heavier work, and therefore their high relative risk could have been because they were older, rather than a direct effect of their lower exercise levels. Thus, in Table B the results are sub-divided into four age groups, and the relative risks within each age group range from 1.1 to 2.0. We can see that the true effect of exercise averaged over all workers must be some figure between these numbers, and cannot be as high as the crude observed relative risk of 3.4, which is produced partly by the difference in age distribution. It is not intuitively obvious what the best single estimate of the effect of exercise would be; that will be discussed later (page 104).

Confounding in case–control studies

The logic of confounding in case–control studies is identical to that in cohort studies, but the arithmetic is slightly different. Exhibit 6.8 shows a simple hypothetical example, in which a case–control study is postulated comparing patients with Crohn's disease with controls, the exposure under interest being that of high sugar intake.

In Table A, the results for 500 cases and 500 controls are shown, which give an odds ratio of 1.59. However, smoking has been shown to be a risk factor for Crohn's disease, so Subtables B_1 and B_2 show the association between case–control status and sugar intake for non-smokers and for smokers separately. For non-smokers the odds ratio is 1.0, showing no association, and for smokers it is also 1.0. Clearly the best estimate of the association of high sugar intake with Crohn's disease is an odds ratio of 1.0, showing no association. We have an apparent association between high sugar intake and

CONFOUNDING IN A CASE-CONTROL STUDY

	Cases	Controls
Table A. All subjects ($n = 1000$)		
High sugar intake	257	200
Low sugar intake	243	300
Total	500	500
Odds ratio = $(257 \times 300)/(243 \times 200)$ = 1.59		
Subtable B_1. Non-smokers only ($n = 550$)		
High sugar intake	57	100
Low sugar intake	143	250
Total	200	350
Odds ratio = $(57 \times 250)/(143 \times 100)$ = 1.00		
Subtable B_2. Smokers only ($n = 450$)		
High sugar intake	200	100
Low sugar intake	100	50
Total	300	150
Odds ratio = $(200 \times 50)/(100 \times 100)$ = 1.00		

Ex. 6.8. Confounding in a case-control study: a hypothetical example, examining the relationship of sugar intake to Crohn's disease

Crohn's disease, with the odds ratio of 1.59, although there is no true association. The apparent excess risk in individuals with high sugar intake is because of a positive association between high sugar intake and smoking; this association can be seen by comparing Subtables B_1 and B_2 in terms of the control subjects: the proportion of high sugar consumers in smokers is 67 per cent (100/150); while the proportion of high sugar consumers in the non-smokers is 29 per cent (100/350). Subtables B_1 and B_2 can be used to look at the relationship between smoking and Crohn's disease. The apparent odds ratio, by comparing all smokers with all non-smokers, is 3.5 [$(300 \times 350)/(200 \times 150)$]. The true odds ratio is obtained by examining smoking within the categories of sugar consumption. For subjects with high sugar intake, the odds ratio for the relationship between smoking and Crohn's disease is $(200 \times 100)/(100 \times 57) = 3.5$; for subjects with low sugar intake it is $(100 \times 250)/(50 \times 143) = 3.5$. Whereas smoking is a confounder in regard to the relationship between sugar intake and Crohn's disease, sugar intake is not a confounder in the relationship between smoking and Crohn's disease. The reason sugar intake is not a confounder is that although it is associated with smoking, it is not itself a risk factor for Crohn's disease, as shown by its true odds ratio with Crohn's disease being 1.0. The associations are shown diagrammatically in Ex. 6.9. In fact, the calculation of odds ratio for smoking within the categories of sugar intake was unnecessary. Given that there is no association between sugar intake and Crohn's disease once smoking is controlled, we can deduce that sugar intake cannot be a confounder because it does not fit the definition of a confounder: it is not associated with the outcome under study. Therefore the crude odds ratio relating smoking to Crohn's disease will not be affected by controlling for sugar intake.

A further example of confounding in a case–control study, based on real data, will be shown in Ex. 6.17.

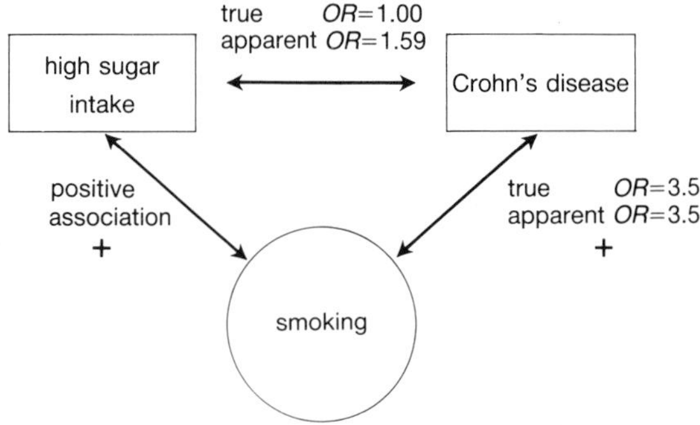

Ex. 6.9. Confounding. A diagram showing the relationships present in the data given in Ex. 6.8

Methods for the control of confounding

Having understood what confounding is, we can move to consider the methods available to deal with it. These are shown in Ex. 6.10, and there are only five methods available. In the design of a study we can *restrict* the

METHODS OF CONTROLLING CONFOUNDING

In the design of the study	restriction matching randomization
In the analysis of the study	restriction stratification multivariate methods

Ex. 6.10. The methods of controlling confounding. One or more may be used

participation in the study to certain individuals, we can decide to *match* individuals with others in the comparison group, and we may have the option of doing a *randomized* intervention study. Irrespective of what has been done at the design stage, when we come to the analysis we may again employ *restriction* to certain individuals in the data set, we may divide the data into subgroups by categories of the confounding factor, that is the process known as *stratification*, or we may use *multivariate* mathematical methods to take into account the effect of more than one factor simultaneously. In practice a combination of these methods is usually used. Each will now be dealt with in turn.

Control of confounding: restriction

Let us go back to our example of a study of oral contraception and myocardial infarction, and consider how we can avoid being misled by the effect of smoking.

One way would be to include only women who had never smoked in the study population. We can do this with either a cohort or a case–control design, and we refer to this method as 'restriction'. It is clearly an effective method, as it leaves no possibility of confounding, but obviously the disadvantage is that the study then becomes specific to the relationship between oral contraceptive use and myocardial infarction in non-smokers, and we cannot generalize the study beyond that target population.

Suppose then we do the entire study on women who smoke. Is there still the possibility of confounding by smoking in comparing, for example, a cohort of oral contraceptive users who smoke with non-oral contraceptive users who smoke? The answer is that there is still potential for confounding. The fact that all the women in the study smoke does not mean they all smoke the same amount, and if smoking has a dose–response relationship with myocardial infarction, and if the amount or duration of smoking is different in users and non-users, there is still potential for confounding. If, however, we restrict the entire study to women who had all smoked, for example, between 10 and 20 cigarettes per day for between 5 to 10 years, the extra specification in the design would reduce the possibility of confounding.

All studies involve some amount of restriction, if only for administrative reasons. The source and eligible populations will be restricted in terms of calendar time, geographical location, and frequently other factors such as age. Restriction should be considered if it is clear that within the study there may be relatively small groups of individuals whose results may be appreciably different from those of the main study population, and for whom the study is unlikely to provide much useful information because of the small numbers. A frequent situation is that of a racial or ethnic group which contributes only a small proportion of subjects. It may have substantially different outcome rates and exposure histories, but there is little value in including such subjects if their total number is likely to be too small for independent consideration.

Randomization

We have dealt with restriction first because some degree of restriction applies to all studies. We deal with randomization next because it has many advantages over the other methods, and therefore there is a major distinction between randomized and non-randomized studies, both in their design and their evaluation. If a randomized intervention study is feasible for the question under assessment, it has many advantages and should be considered first. But it is relevant only for certain situations: prospective intervention studies assessing the effects of an ethical, practical and acceptable intervention which is thought to be potentially beneficial and not likely to be harmful. Thus while of prime importance in issues of the effectiveness of clinical interventions, randomization is not relevant to most issues regarding the causes of disease, and cannot be applied to retrospective studies.

The principle of randomization is that from a pool of study participants, subjects are randomly assigned to the exposure and non-exposure groups. The definition of random is that each subject in the study has the same chance of being allocated to any particular group, and that the chance of one individual being allocated to one group is not influenced by the allocation of any other member to the group. The word is frequently misused even in the professional literature, and is not the same as simply unsystematic or haphazard assignment. It is normally done by reference to a series of numbers which are generated in such a way as to be completely random, obtained either from a computer programme or from a table of such numbers available in a standard statistical text. In principle, methods based on a random process, like tossing a coin, are acceptable but in practice these are too open to the possibility of conscious or unconscious manipulation. The essential logic is that if we use an appropriate random system, the likelihood is that the two groups created will be similar in respect of any particular variable. The essential limitation of randomization is that it is a method based on probability, and therefore it will succeed only if large numbers of subjects are used. If we are dealing with a large randomized study, it is highly likely that the two groups created by randomization will be comparable with respect to specific factors. If however the numbers in each group are relatively small, and a reasonable guideline might be numbers less than 100, then it is quite likely that purely by chance the groups will still vary. If they vary in terms of an important confounding factor, we must deal with that in the analysis. The practical message in this is that although randomization is a valuable technique which with reasonable numbers of subjects should work in most situations, we should not assume that simply because randomization has been used, the groups being compared cannot differ in terms of any confounding factor. Just as in any other study, data on the factors likely to be the main confounders should be used to compare the groups to make sure they are in fact similar. If they are not, even in a randomized design other methods of analysis such as stratification or multivariate methods may be used to take account of any differences in confounding factors.

The value of randomization

Exhibit 6.11 shows the value of randomization. In this study, patients with a suspected acute myocardial infarction were visited by a medical team at home, and if they fulfilled preset eligibility criteria they were randomly

RANDOMIZATION TO PRODUCE EQUIVALENT GROUPS

	Randomized to home care $n = 132$ % of subjects	Randomized to hospital care $n = 132$ % of subjects
Male	79	75
Previous infarction	28	25
Previous angina	33	33
ECG pattern:		
recent anterior change	17	17
recent inferior change	14	13
unhelpful	55	61
normal	14	9
ECG rhythm:		
sinus rhythm with ectopics	11	6
other dysrhythmias	4	7
Treatment given before randomization		
analgesia	77	77
anti-cardiac failure	11	8
anti-dysrhythmia	11	5
digoxin	2	1
Mean age (years)	58.6	59.9

Ex. 6.11. The benefits of randomization. In a study comparing home and hospital care for myocardial infarction, subjects with suspected infarction were visited and assessed at home; those fulfilling preset eligibility criteria were randomized into two groups. These data show the similarity of these two groups in regard to assessments before the point of randomization. From Hill *et al.* (1978)

assigned to receive further treatment at home or in a hospital. The table shows the characteristics of the two groups obtained by randomization, in terms of information known before randomization. Scanning this list shows that the two groups were similar in regard to a wide range of factors which would be expected to influence their subsequent prognosis, such as sex, age, previous infarction or angina, electrocardiogram pattern and rhythm, and treatment given on the spot. We can look at these two groups of subjects and consider whether, if they were subsequently treated in an identical manner, we should expect their outcome to be the same; there is little in the Table which would suggest otherwise. Randomization is much the simplest way to achieve such equivalent groups. In principle, we could have a design where the first person seen was treated in hospital, and was matched to a subsequent subject of the same age, sex, previous history, ECG characteristics, and so on, who would be treated at home, but the logistics of that type of design are difficult. The results of this study were that the mortality at six weeks was 13 per cent in those treated at home, and 11 per cent in those treated in hospital, a small and non-significant difference.

There is one advantage of randomization shared by no other technique. This is that randomization, given large samples, is likely to produce groups which are similar even in respect of variables which we have not anticipated, defined, or measured. Consider the randomization trial of home versus hospital management of myocardial infarction, and assume that after the study is completed new evidence appears that a biochemical measurement of blood clotting ability is a strong predictor of outcome after myocardial infarction. The study would have been better if that measurement had been made, and if it were shown that the two groups were similar in terms of it. But even without that data, if the original study was randomized and had adequate numbers, we can be reasonably sure that the distribution of the two groups in terms of this unmeasured factor would have been similar.

The limits of randomization

It is useful at this point to emphasize that the amount of confounding produced by a factor depends on the strength of its association with the outcome, and the strength of its association with the exposure. Consider a comparison of two treatments for a condition such as primary lung cancer. The outcome, mortality, is likely to vary greatly with the extent or stage of the disease; because this association (stage-outcome) is very strong, stage may have a major confounding effect even if the difference in stage distribution between the treatment groups is small. The difference between the treatment groups in terms of stage may not be statistically significant, but this is irrelevant; thus there is little value in applying statistical tests when comparing groups in terms of potential confounders.

It follows from this that in a randomized study where some major confounding factors can be predicted in advance, it may be wise not to rely only on the randomization procedure to produce similar groups. A more reliable procedure is to group the eligible subjects within categories of the strong confounder, and randomize within these categories. Thus in the above example we could classify all study entrants by stage of disease, and randomize within each stage, thus ensuring that the stage distribution of the treatment groups will be virtually identical. This is a combination of randomization and stratification, and is sometimes referred to as randomization within blocks, or pre-stratification. However, randomized trials are often difficult and time consuming in practice, and in clinical studies simple designs have great advantages, and pre-stratification should be used cautiously. It is often used to randomize within centres in multicentre studies, ensuring that each centre treats similar numbers of subjects on each of the alternative therapies. Several monographs on randomized clinical trials are available, for example the excellent text for the general reader by Pocock (1983), and the comprehensive work by Meinert (1986).

True randomization techniques are often difficult to use for practical reasons. For example, in a study evaluating the use of a new method of encouraging non-smoking in antenatal subjects, it is administratively much more convenient to offer the new programme to all women in a particular clinic, and compare them to women in a different clinic, than to allocate women randomly in each clinic. Such a systematic allocation method is weaker than randomization, as there is a greater chance of the groups chosen differing in terms of relevant factors. A preliminary assessment of possible confounding factors, and a pilot study to test whether there are any differences in these confounding factors between the groups who would be selected by systematic sampling, would be useful.

Randomization achieves its objectives by a random process. The principle is that it is *likely* that the groups produced by randomization will be equivalent, but it is to be expected that some differences between the groups may remain, and on some occasions these differences may be substantial. Exhibit 6.12 shows a table of baseline characteristics for subjects in an important randomized study of the treatment of diabetes, comparing those randomized to receive diet and tolbutamide, an oral glucose lowering agent, with those randomized to receive diet plus a placebo; the outcome of interest was subsequent deaths, of which the largest proportion was from cardiovascular disease.

Comparing these two groups shows that the patients randomized to receive tolbutamide were older, more frequently had a history of digitalis use or angina, and higher proportions had an ECG abnormality, high cholesterol levels, high glucose levels, increased relative body weight, and arterial calcification assessed by an X-ray of the lower limb. On the other hand they had a lower proportion with a history of hypertension. It is difficult to be confident that if the two treatments used had identical effects, the two groups

RANDOMIZED GROUPS MAY DIFFER

	Randomized to diet + tolbutamide $n = 204$ % of subjects	Randomized to diet + placebo $n = 205$ % of subjects
Age > 55	48.0	41.5
Digitalis use	7.6	4.5
Angina	7.0	5.0
ECG abnormality	4.0	3.0
Cholesterol > 300 mg/100 ml	15.1	8.6
Fasting glucose > 110 mg/100 ml	72.1	63.5
Relative body weight > 1.25	58.8	52.7
Arterial calcification	19.7	14.3
Hypertension	30.2	36.8

Ex. 6.12. The limits of randomization. This study compared four regimes for the management of diabetes; here the subjects randomized to diet + tolbutamide (an oral glucose lowering agent) are compared to those randomized to diet + placebo. From University Group Diabetes Program (1970)

would show the same results in terms of subsequent mortality. We should expect most of these factors to have considerable effects on subsequent mortality, and the differences between the groups appear substantial. Sometimes this issue is loosely referred to as a 'failure of randomization', but that is an inappropriate term; the randomization process has been carried out perfectly correctly, but being a probabilistic technique it does not ensure that the groups will always be similar in terms of all factors. Statistical tests of these differences between the two groups show that most of them are not statistically significant at the five per cent level, in other words differences of this or greater magnitude would be expected to occur on more than five per cent of occasions. However, that is not the relevant issue; the relevant issue is whether the actual differences between the groups being compared are sufficiently large to influence the subsequent outcome rates in the two groups, and a small difference in a factor which is strongly related to outcome may therefore be important, even if the difference in the distribution between the two groups being compared is not statistically significant. Thus in Ex. 6.12 we have a randomized study in which there appear to be differences between the groups being compared which may be important. The results of this study show that total mortality, particularly from cardiovascular disease, in the group treated with tolbutamide was substantially higher than in the group treated with the placebo, and therefore the crucial question is whether this difference in mortality can be attributed to the tolbutamide, or whether it is due to the other factors which appear to be somewhat different between the two groups. As will be shown later, other analytical techniques can be used to address this question.

Analysis of randomized trials

In many randomized trials not all individuals complete the treatment to which they have been randomized. Some patients may start the treatment but not complete the course either because they decide to discontinue, which may be for reasons related to the treatment (e.g. side effects) or for totally independent reasons (e.g. change of residence), or their clinical situation may change so that a change in treatment is indicated. Some patients may be randomized but not even commence treatment. Consider Ex. 6.13. This represents a clinical trial in which patients are randomized into two treatment groups, but only some of the patients complete the course of treatment offered. The question is: to assess the effect of the new therapy, which groups of patients should be compared?

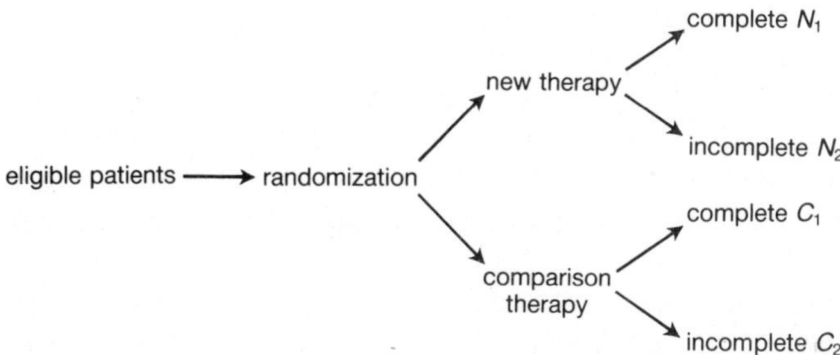

Ex. 6.13. Compliance. A randomized trial in which not all subjects complete the treatment course offered. Which groups should be compared?

The reply often given is to compare group N_1 with either all subjects allocated to placebo ($C_1 + C_2$), or to group C_1, or even to all other subjects ($C_1 + C_2 + N_2$). The logic is that only group N_1 patients have actually been given the test therapy, and therefore the comparison should be between them and the patients who have not had the new therapy.

If this is done, the value of randomization in controlling confounding is lost, because the comparisons are no longer being made between randomized groups. There may be very considerable differences between the subjects who remain on treatment (N_1), and those who withdraw or do not receive it (N_2) and these differences may influence the outcome. A classic example of this is shown in the coronary drug trial, a randomized double blind trial comparing lipid reducing drugs with placebo, carried out in the United States between March 1966 and October 1969. The outcome was mortality over the following five years. The mortality rate in those patients who were allocated to the lipid lowering agent clofibrate, and showed a reasonable adherence to this programme as estimated by whether they actually consumed over 80 per cent of the allocated dosages, was 15.0 per cent. This compares to the mortality rate of 19.4 per cent in patients allocated to the placebo, showing a statistically significant difference in favour of clofibrate. However this is a non-randomized comparison, and the difference could be due to factors which influence whether someone randomized to clofibrate actually takes the drug. As shown in Ex. 6.14, subjects who were randomized to clofibrate but did not take it efficiently had a much higher mortality, 24.6 per cent. This again of course is consistent with a drug effect; one would expect patients who did not take the drug adequately to have a higher mortality than those who took it well, but again it would be dangerous to ascribe this result to the pharmacological effect of the drug. This point is dramatically illustrated by the mortality experience in relation to compliance for the placebo; those who took more than 80 per cent of the allocated doses of the placebo had a mortality of 15.1 per cent, and those who took less a mortality rate of 28.2 per cent. Looking at all the data, it is obvious that the mortality rates in those randomized to clofibrate and those randomized to placebo are very similar; moreover irrespective of what drug is prescribed, subjects who follow the instructions carefully have a lower mortality rate than those who do not. This difference cannot be ascribed to any pharmacological drug action, but reflects the influence of factors which are related to compliance, which are confounding factors in the association between drug taking and outcome.

This demonstration shows the dangers of making any other comparison in a randomized trial except between the groups chosen by randomization. This is in spite of the fact that in many real trials, the proportions of patients who are originally randomized and who fulfil all the protocol criteria, particularly that of maintaining the allocated therapy for its full course, may be relatively small. An example of this will be shown in Chapter 11, in terms of a randomized trial for beta blockers, where it is shown that under 60 per cent of subjects randomized to either active drug or placebo actually met the protocol requirements. One could argue that analysis by comparison of randomized groups, while effective in controlling confounding, is therefore likely to be very inefficient, as there is a considerable dilution effect owing to the fact that many subjects in the active group are not actually receiving the active treatment. However, in considering this we have to go back to the question of what the trial is actually for, and how the results will be applied. It is a naive supposition that all the patients will follow a physician's advice or accept all treatment prescribed. It is logical to argue that unless a treatment results in an improved outcome, given that a substantial proportion of patients will not accept the treatment prescribed, it is not a useful course of action. It is useful to distinguish between trials which address the *management* question: what is the effect of prescribing a certain therapy in a

STRATIFICATION IN A COHORT STUDY

Table A: Data stratified by the confounder (age)

Age group	Heavy exercise			Light exercise			Light: heavy exercise Relative risk
	Deaths	Man-yrs	Rate/ 10 000	Deaths	Man-yrs	Rate/ 10 000	
35–44	4	8 300	4.8	3	5 900	5.1	1.1
45–54	20	11 000	18.2	62	17 600	35.2	1.9
55–64	34	7 400	45.9	183	23 700	77.2	1.7
65–74	8	1 000	80.0	284	17 800	159.6	2.0

The information relevant to the comparison of the two exercise groups is contained in the rates for each group in each age stratum. A relative risk based on all ages will be misleading as the two groups have different distributions by age. This can be 'controlled' if an artificial age distribution is applied to both groups: one possibility is to use the age distribution of all subjects in the study

Table B: Calculation of death rates, standardized for age

Age group	Standard distribution man-years	Heavy exercise		Light exercise	
		Rate/10 000 observed	'Expected' deaths	Rate/10 000 observed	'Expected' deaths
35–44	14 200	4.8	6.8	5.1	7.2
45–54	28 600	18.2	52.1	35.2	100.7
55–64	31 100	45.9	142.7	77.2	240.1
65–74	18 800	80.0	150.4	159.6	300.0
All ages	92 700		352.0		648.0

Standardized death rate/10 000 352.0/9.27 = 38.0 648/9.27 = 69.9

Standardized relative risk 69.9/38.0 = 648/352.4 = 1.84

Ex. 6.15. Stratification in a cohort study. The study shown in Ex. 6.7 gives, on simple analysis, a misleading result because of confounding by age. Stratification in age groups avoids this; standardization techniques such as the one above can be used to give a single measure of relative risk which is adjusted for the age differences. Data from Paffenbarger and Hale (1975)

specific risks. However, the numerical value of the standardized rates obtained will depend on what weighting is used, as will the standardized relative risk: in Ex. 6.15, if a weighting system were used which gave relatively more weight to the youngest age group, the standardized relative risk would be lower as that age group has the lowest stratum specific relative risk. Thus it is sensible to use a weighting which has some logical basis: for example the distribution of all subjects (as used in Ex. 6.15), or of the controls, or of some relevant external population. In using direct age standardization to compare death rates in different regions of one country, it is common to use the age distribution of the whole country population as the weighting system, or, as it is usually known, the 'standard population'. Using this system, if a region has the same age distribution as the whole country, its standardized mortality rate will be the same as its unadjusted or crude rate.

A very useful general method of calculating adjusted relative risks in cohort studies is however derived from the method used for case–control studies, which will now be described, and its application to cohort studies will be shown subsequently (p 110).

Stratification in case–control studies

The application of stratified analysis in a case–control study follows the same principle: the data are divided into strata defined by levels of the confounding factor, and the measure of association, the odds ratio, is assessed in each stratum. The same issues of small numbers and consequent instability of estimates will arise in case–control studies as in cohort studies, and therefore there is need for a method of producing a summary measure of association which is in the form of a weighted average of the stratum specific estimates. The most widely accepted method of doing this was developed by Mantel and Haenszel (1959) and is referred to as the Mantel–Haenszel estimate of odds ratio. The method gives a weighted average of the stratum specific odds ratios, the weights being dependent on the numbers of observations in each stratum, as shown in Ex. 6.16.

Exhibit 6.17 shows some simplified data from a case–control study comparing malignant melanoma patients with community based controls. Table

---

MANTEL–HAENSZEL ESTIMATION OF ODDS RATIO

In each subtable i, stratified by the potential confounder:

	Cases	Controls
exposed	a_i	b_i
unexposed	c_i	d_i

T_i = total in the subtable

Odds ratio for this subtable = $a_i d_i / b_i c_i$

The Mantel–Haenszel estimate of odds ratio uses the data from all subtables, but gives an estimate of the unconfounded odds ratio:

given by $\sum_i (a_i d_i / T_i) \Big/ \sum_i (b_i c_i / T_i)$

where $\sum_i$ indicates summation over all the subtables

Ex. 6.16. Stratification. Calculation of Mantel–Haenszel estimate of the summary odds ratio in a stratified analysis

A shows a positive association with a history of severe sunburn, giving an odds ratio of 1.40. However, such an association could be due to the trauma of the sunburn, to the sun exposure involved, or to the individual's susceptibility to sunburn. In the Subtables, control is made for susceptibility to sunburn. Both in subjects who burn easily and in those who do not, the odds ratio for the association between sunburn history and melanoma is lower than that in the crude analysis; the Mantel–Haenszel estimate gives 1.19 as the unconfounded odds ratio. Statistical tests on these data are shown in Ex. 7.5, p 136.

STRATIFICATION IN A CASE–CONTROL STUDY

	Cases	Controls
Table A: all subjects ($n = 924$)		
Exposed: severe sunburn	136	98
Unexposed: mild sunburn	343	347
Total	479	445
Odds ratio = (136 × 347)/(98 × 343) = 1.40		
Subtable B_1*: subjects who sunburn easily* ($n = 595$)		
Severe sunburn	119	76
Mild sunburn	227	173
Total	346	249
Odds ratio = (119 × 173)/(76 × 227) = 1.19		
Subtable B_2*: subjects who do not sunburn easily* ($n = 329$)		
Severe sunburn	17	22
Mild sunburn	116	174
Total	133	196
Odds ratio = (17 × 174)/(22 × 116) = 1.16		

Mantel–Haenszel estimate of odds ratio

$$= \frac{119 \times 173/595 + 17 \times 174/329}{76 \times 227/595 + 22 \times 116/329}$$

$= 1.19$

Ex. 6.17. Stratified analysis of a case-control study, comparing patients with malignant melanoma to community controls in regard to history of sunburn, and adjusting for tendency to sunburn. Simplified from Elwood *et al.* (1985)

In this example the odds ratios in individual strata are so similar that there is no obvious utility in the summary estimate. However with many subtables with small numbers of observations in each, the stratum specific odds ratios are unstable, but the summary estimate provides a stable measure of the overall odds ratio which is not affected by confounding by the factor which has been stratified. Of course, if the odds ratios in the different strata are very different from each other, it may be misleading to use a summary estimate: this issue will be discussed subsequently as that of 'interaction', p 150. An example of the use of the summary estimate in a more complex set of data is shown in Ex. 6.18.

These data are from a study comparing mothers of twins (cases) with mothers of singletons (controls). An examination of the relationship between twinning and parity gives the main Table A, which shows that the odds ratio for twinning rises steadily with increasing parity, reaching 1.84 in mothers with three or more previous births. However the frequency of twinning also increases with maternal age, and we should expect that mothers of high parity will tend to be older than mothers of low parity. Therefore without further analysis we cannot say whether the increased risk of twinning seen with increased parity shows a direct relationship with parity, or is due to the anticipated older age distribution of high parity mothers. To answer that question, tabulation of the distribution of twins and singletons by both parity and by maternal age is shown. Because the association of twinning with maternal age is strong, it is necessary to use a large number of sub-categories so that each has only a narrow range of maternal age; here six maternal age groups are used. One way to assess the data is to calculate within each maternal age category, the odds ratios of the different parity groups compared with a common reference group such as nulliparous mothers. This produces a matrix of odds ratios, shown in Table C, and suggests that even within maternal age groups the risk of twinning appears to rise with parity. This is most obvious for the youngest age group where those of para 3+ have an odds ratio of 3.87, but this is based on only one case and one control. The situation appears somewhat different in the oldest group of mothers, but here again the numbers are small, with the reference category having only six cases and six controls. Obviously to base the interpretation on these specific small tables is difficult. The Mantel–Haenszel procedure provides a method of estimating the odds ratio for each parity group, controlled for the six categories of maternal age shown. The calculation of the odds ratio follows that shown in Ex. 6.16, considering each parity category such as 3+ compared to the referent category of parity zero, and doing the summation over the six Subtables of maternal age. These calculations yield the odds ratios for different maternal parity groups, controlled for the differences in maternal age distribution, and these are shown in the Table. The results show that even after control for maternal age, there is an association of twinning with parity, although this is considerably weaker than that seen in the crude unadjusted

STRATIFIED ANALYSIS

Table A. All maternal ages

	Maternal parity				
	0	1	2	3 +	Total
Cases (twins)	716	582	454	720	2472
Controls (singletons)	1833	1269	853	1003	4958
Odds ratio	1.0 (R)	1.17	1.36	1.84	

Table B. Data stratified by maternal age

Maternal age (years)		Maternal parity 0	1	2	3 +	Total
15–19 Twins:	cases	105	22	4	1	132
Singletons:	controls	406	91	13	1	511
20–24	cases	312	205	90	53	660
	controls	833	467	184	86	1570
25–29	cases	171	196	147	166	680
	controls	389	401	303	264	1357
30–34	cases	85	111	136	251	583
	controls	148	226	225	337	936
35–39	cases	37	42	67	202	348
	controls	51	63	111	228	453
40–44	cases	6	6	10	47	69
	controls	6	21	17	87	131
Total all ages:	cases	716	582	454	720	2472
	controls	1833	1269	853	1003	4958
Crude odds ratio by parity		1.0 (R)	1.17	1.36	1.84	

Table C. Odds ratios by parity, within maternal age categories, and Mantel–Haenszel adjusted odds ratio

Maternal age (years)	Maternal parity 0	1	2	3 +
15–19	1.0 (R)	0.93	1.19	3.87
20–24	1.0	1.17	1.31	1.65
25–29	1.0	1.11	1.10	1.43
30–34	1.0	0.86	1.05	1.30
35–39	1.0	0.92	0.83	1.22
40–44	1.0	0.29	0.59	0.54
Mantel-Haenszel *OR*	1.0 (R)	1.06	1.11	1.38

Calculation of M–H odds ratio: for parity 3 + compared to parity 0

$$OR = \sum_i (a_i d_i / T_i) \Big/ \sum_i (b_i c_i / T_i)$$

$= \{(1 \times 406/513) + (53 \times 833/1284) + (166 \times 389/990)$ etc. for all 6 age groups$\}/\{(1 \times 105/513) + (86 \times 312/1284) + (264 \times 171/990)$ etc. for all 6 age groups$\}$

Ex. 6.18. A stratified analysis, examining the association of twinning with parity, stratified for maternal age, from a study comparing 2472 twin pregnancies with 4958 singleton pregnancies. From Elwood (1978) data. Appropriate statistical tests relevant to this example are shown in Ex. 7.11 and on p 149. With a strong confounding factor such as maternal age in this example, finer subdivision by maternal age would probably result in a further reduction in the odds ratio, because even within a five-year maternal age grouping there may be some residual confounding by differences in maternal age.

The same data can be used to assess the relationship of maternal age to twinning, and the extent to which the association with maternal age is modified by controlling for parity distribution. From the analysis which has been done, one can predict the effect; there is a positive association between twinning and parity, a positive association between parity and maternal age, and we anticipate a positive association between twinning and maternal age. On that basis one would anticipate that control of maternal parity will result in some reduction in the crude association between twinning and maternal age. The reader might like to test his understanding of the Mantel–Haenszel method by confirming that prediction.

Use of the Mantel–Haenszel method in cohort and intervention studies

The Mantel–Haenszel estimate of the summary odds ratio is a simple calculation, and has been shown to be a very good summary estimate: in most circumstances, it gives the 'maximum likelihood' estimator of the summary odds ratio. For such reasons, and because appropriate statistical tests can easily be applied to it, as discussed later (p 131), it is very widely used, in cohort and intervention studies as well as in case–control studies.

In Exhibit 6.12, some information from a randomized trial of tolbutamide and placebo in the management of diabetes was given, which suggested some substantial differences in the groups being compared. Exhibit 6.19, Table A, gives the main results of that study, showing death rates from all causes of 14.7 per cent in the tolbutamide treated patients and 10.2 per cent in the placebo treated patients, giving a relative risk of 1.44. We can assess whether these differences are influenced by the differences in the baseline characteristics shown in Ex. 6.12, by a stratified analysis in which we compare tolbutamide and placebo treated subjects who are similar in terms of each of these characteristics. In Ex. 6.19 the stratification by arterial calcification is shown. Arterial calcification is a true confounder; it is more common in the tolbutamide treated group than in the placebo treated group, and within each treatment group the death rate is higher in the subjects with arterial calcification. However both within subjects with arterial calcification and in those without arterial calcification, the death rate is higher in the tolbutamide treated subjects. Our best estimate of the relationship between tolbutamide treatment and mortality, adjusted for the differences in prevalence of arterial calcification, is given by a Mantel–Haenszel *relative risk* calculation, which

STRATIFIED ANALYSIS OF A RANDOMIZED TRIAL

Table A. Main results ($n = 409$)

Treatment	Deaths	Survivors	Total	% dead	Relative risk
Tolbutamide	30	174	204	14.7	1.44
Placebo	21	184	205	10.2	1.0 (R)

Table B. Stratified for arterial calcification

Treatment	Deaths	Survivors	Total	% dead	Relative risk
B_1: *arterial calcification present* ($n = 68$)					
Tolbutamide	13	26	39	33.3	1.93
Placebo	5	24	29	17.2	
B_2: *arterial calcification absent* ($n = 333$)					
Tolbutamide	16	143	159	10.1	1.09
Placebo	16	158	174	9.2	

Relative risk adjusted for arterial calcification:

$= (13 \times 29/68 + 16 \times 174/333)/(5 \times 39/68 + 16 \times 159/333)$

$= 1.32$

Ex. 6.19. Stratified analysis of a randomized trial. Main results of the trial shown in Ex. 6.12 (Table A), and results stratified for arterial calcification (Tables B_1 and B_2), and adjusted relative risk calculated by the modified Mantel–Haenszel method. (p 272)
Information on arterial calcification missing on 8 subjects. From University Group Diabetes Program (1970)

gives a relative risk of 1.32. We compare this with the original relative risk in Table A of 1.44. The conclusion is that the increased risk in the tolbutamide group is reduced by stratifying for arterial calcification, but is not abolished and most of the excess risk is still maintained. Analyses of this form can be carried out for each of the variables listed in Ex. 6.12. However it is clear that this method of analysis is still unsatisfactory, as although it is easy to adjust for each of the variables singly, we are still not answering the more general question which is: does the difference in mortality between tolbutamide and placebo treated patients persist when we take into account the effect of all the factors on which we have baseline information? That issue requires more complex analysis which will be shown later (p 119).

Matching

Another method of avoiding confounding is to choose the comparison subjects for a study so that they are deliberately made similar to the case or exposed subjects in regard to specified confounding factors. Consider a cohort study assessing the risks of myocardial infarction in women who use oral contraceptives. We would predict that factors such as age and cigarette smoking might be important confounders. If therefore for each woman using oral contraceptives entered into the study, we select a comparison woman who is not using oral contraceptives but is the same age and has the same smoking history, we shall create two groups of subjects who are similar in terms of these two factors. Within our study therefore there will be no association between age or smoking status and oral contraceptive exposure, and therefore these two factors will not be confounding. This process is referred to as matching.

Matching is a much more complex technique than it appears, and the applications and value of the method are very commonly misunderstood. This misunderstanding often arises from a lack of appreciation of the other methods of controlling confounding, particularly stratification, so that the specific advantages and disadvantages of matching are not recognized. More subtly, difficulties arise because matching has three different purposes; it can be used to increase the efficiency of the study, to control confounding, or to improve the comparability of the information collected.

Frequency matching

In regard to efficiency, that is the amount of information which is gained in relation to the size of the study, the value of matching is quite simple. In our above example, it is likely that the women using oral contraceptives will all be between 20 and 40 years old. There is no value is enrolling as comparison subjects women who are 50 years old, or even more obviously, no value in enrolling men in the study. Ideally the ratio of comparison subjects to exposed subjects in each age range should be reasonably constant. An age group in which there are many oral contraceptive users and very few non-users, or vice versa, will not give reliable information because of the small numbers in one category, and the same argument can be extended to other sub-groupings, for example by smoking status. Thus to increase the efficiency, matching can ensure that the groups of subjects being compared are similar in terms of the most important potential confounding factors in the study. This can be achieved by a process which we will call 'frequency matching': the study is designed so that the distribution of the groups of subjects being compared is similar in terms of major confounding factors. This is an easily applied, useful, and widely used technique; particularly for such characteristics as age and sex. Frequency matching should be considered only as a method of ensuring reasonable efficiency, and should not be regarded as a method of controlling confounding, because it involves only approximate matching and does not ensure total comparability. Major confounding factors should still be controlled by methods such as stratification, and the analysis of the study is best handled without specific regard to the frequency matching which has been done.

Individual matching

The second form of matching, which we will refer to as 'individual matching', is a precise technique. Rather than simply ensuring broad comparability between the groups being compared, comparison subjects are chosen to match index subjects in regard to one or more specified confounding factors. The purpose is not only to improve efficiency, but also to control for the confounding effects of these factors. There is an important distinction between the use of this technique in cohort design studies and in case–control studies.

In cohort studies, precise matching by important confounding factors will control for the effects of those factors. An analysis done in the same way as in an unmatched cohort study will give estimates of relative and attributable risks which can be regarded as free of the confounding effects of the variables on which matching has been done.

In a case–control study, controls are matched to the cases on specified factors. This will give an efficient study, but to control confounding it is necessary to analyse the study by special techniques which consider that data in matched form, in other words, consider each matched group of cases and controls as a unit. The simplest form of analysis is given by a fixed one to one matching ratio, where one matched control is chosen for each case (Ex. 6.20).

Note the format of the Table in Ex. 6.20: the table shows the numbers of pairs classified by exposure and by outcome, and the odds ratio is simply the ratio of the number of discordant pairs where only the case is exposed, to the number of discordant pairs where only the control is exposed. On the null hypothesis, these numbers will be equal. The (incorrect) unmatched table in the familiar two by two format uses exactly the same data, but the value of the matching is lost, and as the matching factors in this example had a strong confounding effect, the unmatched odds ratio is confounded and is substantially different from the matched, unconfounded, odds ratio. Where a fixed ratio of controls to cases (such as 3:1) is used the analysis is also relatively simple, but where the matching ratio is variable it becomes complex. Analysis of a fixed ratio matched study is shown in Appendix 1 (p 286); more complex situations are discussed by Breslow and Day, 1980, pp 176–187. Matched analyses also become complex if it is necessary to adjust for further confounding factors after the matched design is set up. Normal stratification procedures are difficult as the matched groups must be kept intact. Until some years ago, this situation could only be remedied by comparing matched sets which happened to be all the same in terms of the further confounding variable, resulting in a great loss of information and efficiency. Since then, complex multivariate statistical techniques and computer programmes have been developed which allow a matched design to be handled in an analysis

1:1 MATCHING IN A CASE–CONTROL STUDY

A. Distribution of 120 case control pairs by smoking history

		Controls	
		Smokers	Non-smokers
Cases	smokers	31	30
	non-smokers	7	52

Matched odds ratio = 30/7 = 4.3

B. An incorrect, unmatched analysis of the same 240 individuals

	Cases	Controls
smokers	61	38
non-smokers	59	82
	120	120

Unmatched odds ratio = (61 × 82)/(59 × 38) = 2.2

Ex. 6.20. 1:1 matching in a case control study. This yields a simple analysis. Here 120 male patients with nasal or nasal sinus cancer (a very rare cancer), seen in one clinic over a 38-year period, were matched to male controls with a range of other non-smoking related cancers by age and year of diagnosis.
Table A shows a matched analysis; the odds ratio is based only on the pairs with different exposures.
Table B shows the unmatched analysis of the same data—this analysis is incorrect as it loses the value of the matched pair comparison, and produces a substantially different odds ratio (Elwood, 1981)

which controls other confounding factors. Such procedures require expert statistical and computer programming assistance; see Breslow and Day (1980).

Uses of matching

What then are the *values* of matching? It has particular value where there is an important confounding variable which cannot be easily measured or easily defined. Examples include complex social factors, multiple environmental exposures, or circumstances in childhood, which might be controlled by matching with neighbours, co-workers, or siblings respectively. For example, to assess a possible relationship between tonsillectomy and Hodgkin's disease a suitable although logistically difficult design is to compare Hodgkin's disease patients with their unaffected siblings, to achieve control for childhood social and medical care factors (Johnson and Johnson, 1972; Cole *et al.*, 1973). Even closer matching for both genetic and environmental factors is given by matching subjects with twin siblings. Thus, a study comparing women with benign breast disease to unaffected twin sisters was used to assess the effects of coffee consumption and oral contraceptive use

(Odenheimer *et al.*, 1984). Comparisons between monozygotic (identical) and dizygotic (non-identical) twins are of course a fundamental method of distinguishing genetic from environment factors.

Using a twin registry in Sweden, Cederlof *et al.* (1966) compared respiratory symptoms in smokers with those in non-smoking co-twins; from 9319 pairs of twins, 1924 pairs who differed in their smoking were found; the prevalence of cough and of bronchitis was higher in the smoking twins, and the prevalence ratio was similar for non-identical and for identical twin pairs, showing that the association with smoking could not be explained by a genetic confounding factor.

Matching is also useful where the study has a limited number of cases. This may arise either from a particularly rare exposure, or a particularly rare outcome. For example, in the 1960s some eight cases of vaginal adenocarcinoma were diagnosed in young women in the Boston, Massachusetts, area. Vaginal cancer was previously virtually unknown in young women, and this particular disease was of an unusual histological type. To study the possible causes, the most efficient design is one in which causal factors are assessed using comparison subjects who are closely matched for the main confounders. To study the aetiology of this condition, for each patient with vaginal adenocarcinoma four comparison subjects were chosen who were matched on sex, date of birth (within five days), hospital of birth, and ward or private type of service (Herbst *et al.*, 1971).

A further use of matching is not to control confounding but to ensure comparability in terms of the information collected. In a study where some subjects of interest are interviewed by a doctor in a hospital and others by a lay-interviewer in their own homes, it is logical to ensure that the comparison subjects are similarly selected, and ideally the interviews can be conducted on at least a single blind basis. Similar considerations arise if several investigators or centres are involved.

Disadvantages of matching

Matching is a fairly complex technique, and involves both practical and conceptual difficulties. It has several disadvantages, compared to other methods of controlling confounding. To obtain an appropriate matched comparison subject, several potential comparison subjects may have to be approached and initial information gathered, making the study more expensive and difficult to set up. The design is prone to loss of data; if one member of a matched pair does not respond adequately to the study, the pair has to be excluded. A further disadvantage has been referred to above, that the analysis becomes complex if any difficulties arise in terms of other factors to be considered or in terms of variable matching ratios.

The most important disadvantage of matching is that the factor which is matched cannot itself be assessed in the analysis in terms of its relationship to the outcome. Therefore matching should be used only for factors which are known to be important risk factors and therefore important confounders, and should not be used if it is necessary to assess the relationship between the matched factor and the outcome in the study. Matching is thus inappropriate for an exploratory study in which it is wished to answer a general question as to what are the causes of the outcome in question.

Unnecessary matching: 'overmatching'

Thus the benefits of matching have to be compared to its disadvantages in operational terms. If the study is matched on a factor which is not a true confounder, the added complexity of the study is of no benefit: this is often referred to as 'overmatching', although 'unnecessary matching' is a clearer description. It may occur in two situations. Suppose in a case–control study the subjects are matched on a factor which is associated with the exposure, but which is not itself associated with the outcome; it is therefore not a confounding factor, and it is unnecessary to control its effects. The controls are selected to be matched to the cases in terms of this factor: because it is associated with exposure, the controls are being chosen in a way which will make them similar to the cases. Any difference in exposure between the case and control series which exists in the source population, will therefore be reduced in the study subjects, and an unmatched analysis will lead to an under-estimate of the true outcome–exposure association. If individual control to case matching is used and a correct matched analysis is done, the result of the unnecessary matching will be to increase the proportion of all case–control sets which are concordant for exposure; as these sets do not contribute to the estimate of odds ratio, the study results will not be biased; but the study will be less efficient as fewer sets of observations are contributing to the results. In a cohort study, unnecessary matching also leads to inefficiency, making it more difficult to enrol subject groups varying in their exposure, but the study results will still be valid.

As an example, consider a case–control study assessing the relationship between passive exposure to smoking and lung cancer. Should lung cancer subjects and controls be matched on their own smoking experience? As this is a major risk factor and is associated with passive smoking, it needs to be controlled, and matching or stratification is advisable. Should subjects be matched for the size of their family, or for the number of fellow workers they have? These factors are not themselves risk factors for lung cancer, but are associated with passive exposure to smoking: matching would be detrimental. If we wish to guard against the possibility of family size being a risk factor, perhaps by being an indicator of other exposures, we should be better to deal with it by stratification or multivariate analysis. Then we have freedom to assess if it is a risk factor, or a confounding factor; if we match on family size we do not have flexibility.

Unnecessary matching can also occur if the factor matched is not a confounding factor because it is part of a causal pathway linking exposure and outcome. Consider a case–control study to assess the causes of bladder cancer in a workforce where records of both a chemical exposure and previous bladder cytology are available for the employees; if the association between the chemical exposure and bladder cancer is to be assessed, should subjects be matched on prior cytology findings? If they are, and the true causal chain is

chemical exposure → abnormal cytology → bladder cancer,

then a matched study will likely show no difference in chemical exposure. To conclude from such results that chemical exposure was not linked to bladder cancer would be wrong.

Similarly, if in a prospective study assessing the association between the estimated size of a myocardial infarct and subsequent mortality, subjects are matched for the presence of hypotension or arrythmias, a null result should not be interpreted as meaning that the estimated infarct size is not a prognostic factor. In such situations, the study design is not so much wrong, as misapplied: the design used tests an hypothesis different from that contemplated: is chemical exposure related to bladder cancer irrespective of prior cytology findings, and does infarct size give prognostic information beyond that given by knowledge of hypotension and arrythmias? In these situations the interpretation cannot be made solely on the data: it requires assumptions regarding the causal model and is dependent on whether the third factor is a confounding factor or not. If subjects are chosen without matching, and information on the third factor collected, analyses can be done with and without control for that factor, and its associations with exposure and outcome can be assessed. If matching has been used, this flexibility is lost. The risks of unnecessary matching show again that matching should be used only after careful consideration based on a high level of knowledge about the confounding factors relevant in a given situation.

Multivariate methods

The final method of controlling confounding is to analyse the data by means of a mathematical model which takes the outcome under consideration as the dependent variable and includes both the postulated causal factor and confounding factors in the equation. For continuous variables, the techniques of multiple regression will be appropriate and may be familiar. For example, consider an assessment of whether maternal pre-pregnancy weight is related to the birth weight of the baby, taking account of any relationship with the mother's height. A multiple regression model could be used, where the dependent variable is birth weight, and the model includes the maternal pre-pregnancy weight as one independent variable, and height as another. Standard multiple regression methods would produce a coefficient for the maternal weight variable which would indicate the relationship between weight and birth weight, independent of height.

The mathematical expression is:

$$y = a + b_1x_1 + b_2x_2$$

where

y is the outcome, birth weight, and is the dependent variable in the equation;
x_1 is the mother's pre-pregnancy weight,
x_2 is the mother's height,
a is a constant with no intuitive meaning (it is the birth weight if x_1 and x_2 are both zero), and
b_1 and b_2 are the regression coefficients.

These are calculated to be the values which give the best fit of the equation set out above to the observed data.

This simple mathematical equation makes several assumptions. It assumes for example that the change in birth weight with the change in the mothers' pre-pregnancy weight is linear, and therefore the numerical value b_1 represents the amount of change in birth weight associated with a change in the mother's pre-pregnancy weight of one unit. A similar linear assumption holds for b_2. The equation also assumes that the change in birth weight with pre-pregnancy weight is the same irrespective of the value of the mothers' height, in other words there is no *interaction* between these two variables. These are assumptions inherent in the mathematical form of the equation. There are usually other assumptions involved in the ways in which the coefficients are calculated, for example the usual method of calculation will make the assumption that the variable y has a Normal distribution.

In many medical situations the main variables are not continuous. Outcomes are often dichotomous: diseased or not diseased, cured or not cured, and exposures may be continuous, dichotomous, or have several categories, e.g. age, sex, stage of disease. Thus, standard models designed for use with continuous variables are not always appropriate. Many other models have been developed and applied to these situations. A very useful one is the logistic model where the dependent variable is the logit of disease risk, which is regarded as having a linear relationship to the independent variables.

Consider P as the proportion of subjects in the study who have the outcome, or equivalently the probability that a randomly selected subject has the outcome; the *logit* of P is defined as

$$\ln\left(\frac{P}{1-P}\right).$$

The logistic regression equation takes the form

$$\ln\left(\frac{P}{1-P}\right) = a + b_1x_1 + b_2x_2 + b_3x_3. \ldots.$$

where the x variables represent exposure factors and confounders, and the b terms are their coefficients. If an x variable is a numerical value (e.g. height), the b coefficient gives the change in logit of P associated with a change of one unit of x, with the assumption of a linear relationship between the two.

A particularly useful result holds if x is binary, having the values of 0 or 1. For example, for sex we might use a variable such that $x_1 = 1$ for males and $x_1 = 0$ for females. For females, $x_1 = 0$, so b_1x_1 is zero. For males, $x_1 = 1$ so the equation for males differs from that for females by having the extra term b_1x_1, which is equal to b_1. The rest of the equation is the same. The difference in logit of P between males and females will be

$$\ln\left(\frac{P_m}{1-P_m}\right) - \ln\left(\frac{P_f}{1-P_f}\right) = b_1$$

where P_m = the risk for males, and P_f = the risk for females.

With two numbers r and s, $\ln(r) - \ln(s) = \ln(r/s)$,

so

$$\ln\left[\frac{P_m}{1-P_m} \Big/ \frac{P_f}{1-P_f}\right] = b_1$$

$P_m/(1 - P_m)$ is the odds of the outcome in males; $P_f/(1 - P_f)$ is the odds in females, so the quantity in the brackets is the odds ratio comparing male to female subjects:

$$\ln(OR) = b_1$$
$$\text{and } OR = \text{exponential}(b_1)$$

Thus with the logistic regression model the exponential of a coefficient b equals the odds ratio associated with the variable x, if this is a binary variable coded as 0 or 1. If x is continuous, b gives the odds ratio associated with a change in x of one unit.

A simple example of this is given by the comparison between tolbutamide and placebo in Ex. 6.19 (p 111).

Let us assume a model such as $\ln[P/(1\text{-}P)] = a + b_1x_1$

Where	$P =$	probability of death
and	$x_1 =$	1 for tolbutamide
	$x_1 =$	0 for placebo
For the placebo group	$P_p =$	0.1024 (from Ex. 6.19, Table A)
so	logit $P_p =$	$\ln(0.1024/0.8976) = -2.171 = a$
For the tolbutamide group	$P_t =$	0.1471
so	logit $P_t =$	$\ln(0.1471/0.8529) = -1.758 = a + b_1$
thus	$b_1 =$	0.413
and	$\exp(b_1) =$	$\exp(0.413) = 1.511$

From Ex. 6.19, Table A, relative odds $= (30 \times 184)/(21 \times 174) = 1.511$

To account for other factors, the model becomes

$$\ln[P/(1 - P)] = a + b_1x_1 + b_2x_2 + b_3x_3\ldots\text{etc.}$$

where the other x variables represent other factors.

Where fifteen other such factors were used (all of those shown in Ex. 6.12, plus sex, race, systolic blood pressure, diastolic blood pressure, visual acuity, and creatinine level), the value of b_1 in the presence of these other factors was 0.40, giving an odds ratio of 1.49. Thus although there were some considerable differences between the tolbutamide and placebo groups, these did not in aggregate produce any great difference in the main result, the relative odds for tolbutamide versus placebo changing only from 1.51 to 1.49. The results can also be expressed as the difference in mortality rate, as was done in the original paper (University Group Diabetes Program, 1970).

Frequently factors with several categories are relevant, and these are often best handled by using a number of 'dummy' binary variables to represent all the categories. Exhibit 6.21 gives some results from a simple application of this method. The data are from a case–control study comparing 83 patients with malignant melanoma with 83 controls chosen from the general population, and show the results for just two factors, the number of palpable moles on the upper arm assessed by an interviewer (three categories) and the response to a question on whether the subject had had a severe sunburn (two categories). The results from cross-tabulations showed strong associations with the number of moles, and with a history of sunburn. However in this study there were several other factors which would be expected to be related to these two factors, and which were also related to melanoma, and therefore could be confounding variables. These included the severity of skin freckling (three categories), the usual reaction to sun exposure (four categories), and hair colour (three categories). To control for each of these confounders singly can be done fairly easily by cross-tabulations. However to assess the relationship between moles and melanoma, with control for freckles, sun reaction,

MULTIVARIATE ANALYSIS

A: Cross tabulations	No. moles on upper arm			History of sunburn	
	0	1–2	3 +	No	Yes
Cases, number	32	16	35	34	49
Controls, number	62	17	4	57	26
Odds ratio	1.0 (R)	1.82	16.95	1.0 (R)	3.16
B: Logistic regression with one factor only					
Coefficient *b*		0.6008	2.830		1.150
Exp(*b*) = odds ratio		1.82	16.95		3.16
C: Logistic regression with both factors, plus quantity of freckles (3 categories), reaction to sun exposure (4 categories), and hair colour (3 categories)					
Coefficient *b*		0.3011	2.587		0.4276
Exp(*b*) = odds ratio		1.35	13.29		1.53

Ex. 6.21. Multivariate analysis. Results from a case–control study comparing 83 patients with malignant melanoma to 83 controls from the general population. Results are shown for two factors, number of moles on the upper arm, and history of severe sunburn, derived by (A) cross-tabulation, (B) a logistic regression fitting only the one factor, and (C) a logistic regression fitting five factors, represented by 10 binary variables. From: Elwood *et al.*, 1986: fuller results are given in that paper.

hair colour, and sunburn simultaneously by cross-tabulations would mean that 3 × 4 × 3 × 2 = 72 separate tables showing the case–control distribution by numbers of moles would have to be generated, and in this fairly small study many of these tables would have few or no observations.

It is therefore more useful to combine these five factors into a logistic regression equation, expressing each factor as a number of dummy variables, the number being one less than the number of categories. Thus for the number of moles, a binary variable is used which has the value 1 for subjects who had one to two moles on the upper arm, and 0 otherwise; and another which has the value of 1 for subjects with three or more moles, and 0 otherwise. Where both these factors are 0 the equation gives the risk in the referent category who have no moles. If a logistic regression is fitted with just one factor, the results will be identical to a simple cross-tabulation, and the exponential of the coefficient *b* will be equal to the odds ratio obtained by the usual calculation on the simple table. These results are shown in part B of Ex. 6.21. Then if a model is fitted which includes the variables representing all the factors listed above, the coefficient *b* for each variable will give the odds ratio associated with that variable controlled for the effects of all the other variables in the equation. Part (C) of Ex. 6.21 shows that with these coefficients, obtained from a model with ten variables, the odds ratios for number of moles are still high, whereas the odds ratio for history of sunburn is 1.53, considerably lower than the crude odds ratio of 3.16. The programme used to calculate the coefficients will also allow the estimation of the statistical significance of these adjusted coefficients, and that aspect of multivariate analysis is considered further with the same example in Chapter 7 (Ex. 7.14, p 156).

The logistic model has been found empirically to give a good fit to many sets of data, such as assessing combinations of risk factors for ischaemic heart disease in the context of the Framingham cohort study (Truett *et al.*, 1967). Discussion of the statistical issues of multivariate models is outside the scope of this text. To use such models the confounding factors must be recognized in advance, and quantitative information on them must be collected. Clearly, considerable statistical and programming expertise is necessary to use such models properly.

Multivariate analysis can deal with only a limited number of factors. All computer programs for such analyses have a limit to the number of factors they can satisfactorily deal with, and the number of study factors which can be used will depend on this and on how the factors are used; for example, whether a factor like age is entered as one continuous variable or represented by a number of categories, each with a corresponding variable. If interactions are to be examined, the number of factors which can be assessed is further reduced. Thus for studies which include data on many factors, the most relevant must be selected before a multivariate model is applied. The following section on the use of the principles of confounding in analysis will be helpful in this regard. Apart from computational limitations, factors to be included in a multivariate model must be studied in detail, and issues such as the distribution of observations, the need for transformations, the appropriateness of assumptions such as a linear relationship to risk, and so on, need to be addressed. Multivariate analysis is best regarded as a powerful but complex and demanding type of analysis, appropriate to the final stages of analysis of a study, rather than as a magical black box to provide short cuts to a final result.

Application of the definition of confounding to study design

Now that we have discussed confounding and the methods available to control it, it is useful to go back to the definition of confounding and see how this can assist us in the design of studies, and in their analysis. The definition of confounding provides a way in which we can protect ourselves against the danger of feeling that because there are so many possible confounding factors, no satisfactory study can be designed. In designing any study an important step is to make a list of factors which are likely to be associated with the exposure under study, and a list of factors which are likely to be associated with the outcome. These lists are made by considering our general knowledge of the topic, reviewing the literature, and consulting reference works and people with specialized knowledge. Any factor which appears on both of these lists should be treated as a potential confounding factor, and the method of dealing with it decided. Factors which may appear on only one list but which are likely to have a very strong association with either outcome or exposure, may be prudently included as potential confounding factors, as even a small difference in their distribution between the groups being compared may be sufficient to introduce confounding. The use of this approach will often reduce an apparently infinite number of potential confounders to a finite, and often fairly small, list of specific factors. The options available for confounder control (Ex. 6.10) can then be considered. In practice, many potential confounders will not in fact be confounding, in that their associations with outcome and exposure in the study data are often weak and unimportant: but this will be known only if data on the confounders are collected. The most commonly used approach in non-randomized studies is to apply some restriction, and to collect data on the potential confounders to allow stratification or multivariate methods to be used in the analysis. Individual matching should be used only when there are specific advantages to it.

In randomized studies, only one list, of factors likely to be related to the outcome, is needed, and data on these should be collected where possible to be able to assess if the groups are in fact comparable on those factors. In large scale randomized studies, for example of population interventions, samples of the groups may be selected for this purpose.

Application of the definition of confounding to analysis

Similarly in the analysis there are often a large number of other factors besides the outcome and the exposure under consideration. Initial data analysis can be used to decide which of these factors are related to the outcome and which are related to the exposure, most conveniently by generating cross-tabulations between each of the factors and outcome, and each of the factors and exposure. More strictly, the associations between the potential confounding factor and outcome should be examined within the non-exposed group, and the associations between the potential confounding factor and exposure should be examined within the group without the outcome under consideration. Only those factors which show associations with both exposure and outcome need to be considered further as confounding factors. It is important to emphasize again that it is the strength of the association which matters, not its statistical significance, although the latter may be used as a help in screening large numbers of variables. This type of initial analysis will often reduce a formidably large data set to a much simpler situation where only a few major confounding factors have to be dealt with, and these can be analysed further by stratification or multivariate methods.

An alternative method of deciding which factors are confounding is often easier, and relies on the fact that confounding is demonstrated if a stratified analysis is performed and the unconfounded relative risk or odds ratio estimate is different from the crude estimate. The ease of calculation of the Mantel–Haenszel summary odds ratio makes it ideal for this purpose both in cohort and in case–control designs, as illustrated in Ex. 6.17, 18 and 19. A practical approach to the analysis of a large data set is therefore to first produce the basic table comparing exposure with outcome, and calculate the crude odds ratio. Then each potential confounder is considered in a reasonable number of categories (five are usually sufficient), and stratified analyses performed using each potential confounder singly, calculating the adjusted Mantel–Haenszel odds ratio. If this adjusted odds ratio is similar to the crude odds ratio, there is no substantial confounding by that variable. Thus a large number of potential confounders can be reduced to a small number of actual confounders. It is possible of course that two or more potential confounders considered together may have a confounding effect, even if singly they do not, but it is not common. A reasonable approach is therefore to proceed further with a reduced data set, keeping factors which have shown a confounding effect on simpler analysis, plus those of major a priori importance. This data set should then present a less forbidding challenge.

7. Chance variation

Although men flatter themselves with their great actions, they are not so often the result of a great design as of chance.
—La Rochefoucauld: Maxims; 1665

The third non-causal explanation for an association is that it is due to chance variation, or random number variation, the fall of the dice, bad luck, or whatever synonym you prefer. The science of statistics is concerned with measuring the likelihood that a given set of results has been produced by this mechanism. In this chapter, therefore, we shall look at the probability of chance variation being responsible for an observed association, and show how the statistical methods are fitted into the overall concept of dealing with causality. This chapter is designed to act as a bridge between the rest of the text and a conventional basic course or text in biostatistics. The reason for including it is that I have found that many colleagues have some familiarity with basic statistics but find it difficult to integrate that knowledge into a general approach to causality.

A range of statistical techniques will be presented and discussed. For reference purposes, the tests most widely used for each type of study are summarized in Appendix 1 (p 265), and tables of probability distributions for the interpretation of the results of the tests are given in Appendix 3 (p 308); these are referred to as Statistical Tables 1 to 6.

In choosing which particular statistical methods to emphasize, we have taken a pragmatic approach. The first objective of this section is to see how the results of statistical tests can be interpreted and fitted in with other considerations relevant to causality. These principles can be appreciated using simple examples, but also apply to results which may use much more complex statistics. The non-statistical reader of medical literature will often find that important papers use complex methods with which the reader cannot be totally familiar, but an understanding of these can still be greatly helped by understanding some general principles of interpretation of statistical tests.

We shall, however, present in more detail a group of related and relatively simple statistical methods which have been shown to be powerful and reliable methods in most contexts, and can be applied to all the major study designs. These methods comprise the basic test for variation in a two-by-two table, often referred to as the Mantel–Haenszel statistic, and variations of it which can deal with cohort data using person-time denominators, life table methods, and matched studies. Because of the wide application and the excellent performance of these statistics, even in comparison with much more complex ones, we will present these in enough detail that the reader will be able to apply such statistics either to his own work or to the key results from published papers.

So far in this text we have discussed only the measurement of the association between the exposure variable and the outcome, measured in terms of the relative risk, relative odds, or attributable risk. We have already discussed methods to judge whether the relative risk estimate is acceptable on the basis of a lack of bias and a lack of confounding. The order of consideration of non-causal explanations, bias, confounding, and chance, is an appropriate one. If there is severe bias in the study we cannot be confident that the relevant factors have been measured in a similar fashion in the groups being compared, and there is no point in adding a statistical analysis to a biased result. The assessment of bias depends on consideration of the design characteristics of the study and the particular aspects of the question being assessed, and decisions will have to be made as to whether steps in the analysis can help to deal with the bias, for example by restricting the study to certain sub-groups, using a particular comparison group and so on. Once major biases have been dealt with, it is appropriate to consider confounding and, as we have seen, we may have situations in which there could be severe confounding by a factor not included in the study design, in which case further data manipulation is not helpful. More frequently, there may be confounding which can be dealt with by stratification or multivariate analysis or has been dealt with by randomization, matching or restriction in the study design. These methods have allowed us to reach the point of having available an estimate of the association which is, in our best judgment, not compromised by bias, and is adjusted as far as possible for any confounding. It is this estimate of the association on which we now concentrate and to which we can now apply statistical tests.

Discrete versus continuous measures

The statistical methods described here are limited to those applicable to discrete measures of exposure and of outcome. This is for two main reasons. We are concerned mainly with disease causation and with the evaluation of clinical therapy. In almost all of the former questions, and in most of the latter, the outcome measures are qualitative: the onset of disease, death, recurrence, recovery, return to work, and so on. Even where the biological issues are quantitative the practical issues are often qualitative, and it may be appropriate to convert continuous data to a discrete form. For example, in a comparison of agents used to control high blood sugar, the analysis may be based on a comparison of the change in blood glucose levels in each group of subjects, using methods appropriate for this quantitative outcome. However, it may be more relevant clinically to assess the value of the agents by the proportion of treated subjects who move from having clinically unacceptable blood sugar levels to being 'well-controlled', as defined by preset clinically relevant criteria.

The second reason is that introductory statistics courses and texts emphasize methods of dealing with continuous data: the normal distribution, t-tests, regression, analysis of variance, and so on. We have found that many of our colleagues who have had a little statistical teaching find that most of the methods they have come across are not applicable to the common clinical issues involving qualitative outcomes with which they have to deal. Generally trained statisticians also tend to be more experienced in methods for continuous variables and unless they have worked in epidemiological areas or in clinical trials, they are unlikely to be as familiar with the methods we emphasize here. Thus we have elected to concentrate almost exclusively on methods for discrete variables. Standard statistical texts should be consulted in regard to the analysis of data which uses continuous variables.

The concept of significance

The statistical method the reader is most likely to be familiar with is that of significance testing. The question is: is the difference in outcome between the two groups of subjects larger than we would expect to occur purely by chance? Consider a simple intervention study (Ex. 7.1).

A SIMPLE COMPARATIVE STUDY

Treatment group	Outcome			
	Success	No success	Total patients	Incidence of success (%)
New therapy	40	160	200	20
Conventional therapy	20	180	200	10
Total	60	340	400	15

Ex. 7.1. A simple comparative study, hypothetical data

For the new treatment, this study gives the success rate as 20 per cent. Even accepting the study design as being perfect with no bias, we would not interpret this as meaning that for all similar groups of subjects exposed to this intervention, the success rate would be 20.00 per cent. The 200 subjects chosen are a sample from the uncounted total of all possible subjects who could be given that intervention, and 20 per cent is the estimate of the success rate in that total group of potential subjects. On the basis of pure chance, we should understand that the next sample of 200 subjects would be likely to give a slightly different result. However, 20 per cent is our best estimate of the true success rate. Similarly in the comparison group, our best estimate is 10 per cent. The significance testing technique tests how likely it is that a difference as large as the one we have seen (or larger) could occur purely by chance, if the true situation is that both the intervention and the comparison groups have the same true success rate. This would occur on the *null hypothesis* that the effect of the intervention is no different from that of the comparison therapy. This is sometimes referred to as the concept that the two groups of subjects are independent samples drawn from the same population. Statistical tests therefore test the hypothesis that the true success rate in the two groups is the same, and that the observed differences are produced purely by chance variation around that common value. Our best estimate of the common value of the success rate will be based on all the subjects in the study, and will therefore be 15 per cent.

Simple statistical tests for a two-by-two table

One commonly used test in this situation is the chi-squared statistic, written χ^2, applied to the 2×2 table formed from the study results, which gives a value of 7.84 (Ex. 7.2). To interpret this we need to know the number of degrees of freedom of the statistic, which in an $n \times n$ table is $(n - 1) \times (n - 1)$, which in this case is 1, and looking up 7.84 in a table of the chi-squared distribution on one degree of freedom (Statistical Table 1, p 310) will show us that the probability or *P*-value is between 0.01 and 0.001. Thus the test shows that, if the true success rate is the same in the two groups, the probability of a difference as large or larger than the one we have observed occurring purely by chance variation, is considerably less than five per cent (0.05), which is conventionally accepted as 'statistically significant'.

Another familiar test is a test of difference in proportions, testing whether the 20 per cent success rate in the intervention group is different from the 10 per cent success rate in the control group. This formulation yields a standardized normal deviate of 2.80. This also corresponds to a two-sided *P*-value of between 0.01 and 0.001 (Statistical Table 1, p 310).

We have applied two very familiar statistical tests to the same data. They should give the same results. In fact, the chi-squared statistic on one degree of freedom is the square of the normal deviate; $2.8^2 = 7.84$. The cut-off point at 5 per cent significance for χ^2 on one degree of freedom is 3.84, which is the square of 1.96, the cut-off for the normal deviate. In fact, as an alternative to calculating the chi-squared statistic from the formula shown in Ex. 7.1 its square root, the chi statistic can be calculated and looked up in tables of the normal deviate, which are often more detailed than tables of the chi-squared statistic. This relationship between χ^2 and a standardized normal deviate holds only for the situation where χ^2 has one degree of freedom, and the sign of the χ value, like the relative risk value, depends on how the table is drawn up.

Studies which produce results which can be simplified to the two-by-two format exemplified here can be dealt with by the chi-squared statistic or

STATISTICAL TESTS OF A NULL HYPOTHESIS

Exposure	Outcome		Total no. patients	Success rate (%)
	Positive (success)	Negative		
New treatment	a (40)	b (160)	N_1 (200)	S_1 (20%)
Comparison	c (20)	d (180)	N_0 (200)	S_0 (10%)
Total	M_1 (60)	M_0 (340)	T (400)	S (15%)

Appropriate statistical tests for departures from the null hypothesis:

(a) Chi-square statistic $\chi^2 = \dfrac{(ad - bc)^2\,T}{N_1 N_0 M_1 M_0} = 7.84$

Equivalently $\chi^2 = \sum \dfrac{(\text{obs} - \text{exp})^2}{\text{exp}}$ for each of the four cells.

$$= \frac{(a - N_1M_1/T)^2}{N_1M_1/T} + \frac{(b - N_1M_0/T)^2}{N_1M_0/T} + \frac{(c - N_0M_1/T)^2}{N_0M_1/T} + \frac{(d - N_0M_0/T)^2}{N_0M_0/T}$$

$= 7.84$

From table of the χ^2 distribution on 1 d.f., the probability of this or a larger value occurring on the null hypothesis, P, lies between 0.01 and 0.001 (from Statistical Table 1, p 310).

(b) Comparison of two proportions:

Standardized normal deviate $= \dfrac{S_1 - S_0}{\sqrt{\left\{S(1 - S)\left(\dfrac{1}{N_1} + \dfrac{1}{N_0}\right)\right\}}}$

$= 2.80$

From a table of the normal distribution (Statistical Table 1), the two-sided probability corresponding to 2.80 lies between 0.01 and 0.001.

(c) For a continuity corrected version of the χ^2 statistic, the formulae are:

$$\chi^2_c = \frac{(|ad - bc| - \frac{1}{2}T)^2 T}{N_1N_0M_1M_0}$$

and $\chi^2_c = \dfrac{(|a - N_1M_1/T| - \frac{1}{2})^2}{N_1M_1/T} + \text{etc.}$

hence $\chi^2_c = 7.08$

From Statistical Table 1, P is between 0.01 and 0.001.

Ex. 7.2. Two appropriate statistical tests applied to a two-by-two table. Arithmetic examples use the data shown in Ex. 7.1

normal deviate techniques, and the format of the tables will make it clear that the statistics apply equally easily to cohort and to case–control designs. The statistic tests the departure of the data from the null hypothesis of no association: it may therefore be regarded both as a test of the significance of a risk difference (attributable risk) from the null value of 0, or of the risk ratio (relative risk or odds ratio) from the null value of 1.

One-sided and two-sided tests

The tests used above are 'two-sided' tests; that is, they estimate the probability that if the null hypothesis were true, a difference would occur which would be as large or larger than we observed, in either direction—that is, the intervention group having either the higher or the lower success rate. A 'one-sided' test estimates only the probability of occurrence, on the null hypothesis, of the observed result or results which are more different from the null hypothesis in the same direction. It is appropriate only in situations where the direction of the effect is established before the data are collected. Thus if example 7.1 were drawn from a study designed specifically to assess if the new therapy were better than the conventional, discounting any possibility that it could be worse, a one-sided test could be used. This will estimate the probability of occurrence, on the null hypothesis, of the difference observed (the success rate being 10 per cent higher in the new therapy group), or a larger difference in the pre-determined direction. Except with very small numbers, the two-sided probability is simply twice the one-sided probability, and therefore a one-sided test with a probability given as 0.05 would be equivalent to a two-sided test with a probability value of 0.1 (see Statistical Table 1, p 310). Note that chi-squared statistics, because they square the deviations between observed and expected values, directly give two-sided tests, while many tables of the distribution of the standardized normal deviate directly give a one-sided probability value, which is then doubled if a two-sided test is required. Statistical Tables 5 and 6 (p 322) show the relationship between one-sided and two-sided tests.

Continuity corrections

In some formulations for the chi-squared statistic, a 'continuity correction' is used (see Ex. 7.2). This is related to the fact that although the expected value of each cell in a two-by-two table has a continuous distribution, the observed values must of course be whole numbers, and therefore in calculating the probability of a particular whole number allowance has to be made for this. There is controversy about this point in the statistical literature†, and although

† For example, of current major texts, Rothman (1986) and Kleinbaum *et al.*, (1982) advocate not using a continuity correction, while Breslow and Day (1980) and Schlesselman (1982) favour its use; but even then not for some purposes, such as in calculating test based confidence limits.

some authorities feel that the use of a continuity correction gives a more accurate estimation of the P-value, others disagree. The effect of the continuity correction is to reduce by a small amount the calculated χ^2 statistic or normal deviate, and the extent of this reduction is greater when the number of observations in the table is small. With reasonably large numbers, the continuity correction will make very little difference. Thus the issue of whether to use a continuity correction is related to how P-values are interpreted, and if we reduce the stress on particular cut off values of the P-value, like 0.05, the problem is put into perspective. If the use of a continuity correction changes a result from being less than, to be greater than, 0.05, this merely shows that the true probability value is very close to 0.05 and should be interpreted accordingly. Also, if the difference is substantial, it means the numbers of observations are small, and a better solution is to use an exact probability test. One of these, the Fisher test for two-by-two tables, will be described in Appendix 1 (Ex. A1.4, p 280), but others are available for other situations and statistical advice should be sought. An approximate and traditional rule of thumb is that χ^2 statistics become unreliable where any expected numbers in the tables are less than 5. This often occurs if tables with many cells are generated, and the solution is often to reduce the size of the table by combining appropriate categories. The same general consideration applies where one statistical test gives a result which is somewhat different to another applicable statistical test, or even to the same test performed on a different calculator or computer programme, and all these serve to emphasize that we should guard against over-interpreting the precise value of the P-value, rather than using it as a general consideration of probability.

The continuity corrected χ^2 statistic calculated on the data in Ex. 7.2 has the value of 7.08, compared to the uncorrected value of 7.84, corresponding to P-values of 0.0078 and 0.0051 respectively (Statistical Table 4, p 318). The test of comparison of proportions makes an assumption of having reasonable numbers of subjects and gives the square root of the uncorrected χ^2 value.

The Mantel–Haenszel test

Although the usual χ^2 tests are appropriate for simple tables, more generally applicable methods, which can deal with stratified data, are very useful in epidemiological and clinical studies.

Many statistical tests are derived from the principle that if we calculate the difference between an observed value a and its expected value on the null hypothesis E, square that, and divide it by the variance of the observed value V, the quantity—the statistic—resulting will follow a χ^2 distribution, on one degree of freedom: that is

$$\chi^2 = \frac{(a - E)^2}{V}$$

As we shall see, this general formula can be applied to several different situations, using appropriate calculations to obtain E and V.

The χ^2 distribution on 1 d.f. is simply related to the normal distribution. If a variable χ follows a normal distribution, its square χ^2 will follow a χ^2 distribution on 1 d.f. Thus an equivalent formula to that given above is,

$$\chi = \sqrt{\chi^2} = \frac{a - E}{\sqrt{V}}$$

That is, the difference between the observed value, a, and its expected value E, divided by the standard deviation of a (that is, the square root of the variance) gives a normal deviate, often referred to as chi, χ or as Z.

A most useful test, the Mantel–Haenszel test, for a two-by-two table is shown in Ex. 7.3 (Mantel and Haenszel, 1959). It is of the above form, the χ^2 statistic being given by the squared difference between one value in the table and its expected value, and the variance calculated from a formula based on

---

GENERAL TEST FOR A TWO-BY-TWO TABLE

Table showing fixed marginal totals

	Success	No success	Total
New treatment	a	b	N_1
Old treatment	c	d	N_0
Total	M_1	M_0	T

General formulae

Observed number of 'exposed cases' $= a$

Expected value of a on null hypothesis $= E = N_1M_1/T$

Variance of a under hypergeometric distribution $= V = \left(\frac{N_1N_0M_0M_1}{T^2(T-1)}\right)$

Chi-squared statistic, 1 degree of freedom $= \frac{(a-E)^2}{V} = \frac{(a - N_1M_1/T)^2}{N_1N_0M_0M_1/T^2(T-1)}$

Normal deviate, χ $= \sqrt{\chi^2} = \frac{(a-E)}{\sqrt{V}}$

Continuity corrected versions: $\chi^2_c = \frac{(|a-E| - 0.5)^2}{V}$

$$\chi_c = \frac{|a-E| - 0.5}{\sqrt{V}}$$

Ex. 7.3. The Mantel–Haenszel test, for a two-by-two table with reasonable numbers. This is applicable to both cohort and case–control data.

the 'hypergeometric' distribution. A brief note on its derivation is now given, but readers to whom this is not of interest should skip to the next section.

In the data shown in Ex. 7.1, there are two independent groups of subjects and within each group, each independent subject may become a 'success' or not. The distribution of the number of 'successes' in each group under these conditions follows a binomial distribution, and the probability of observing the number of events seen (or a more extreme number) on the null hypothesis of the underlying rate being that given by all the data, can be calculated from first principles by considering the two-by-two table as giving the results from two independent binomial distributions. Such methods are practical and appropriate, with small numbers of observations. An example is Fisher's test, described in Ex. A1.4, (p 280), but with larger numbers the calculations involved become very tedious even with a computer.

The analysis can be greatly simplified by a slightly different derivation. In the trial in Ex. 7.1, the numbers of subjects in each treatment group are fixed: they were chosen by the investigator. Let us further assume that the number of 'successes' in the total study group can be regarded as fixed: this is not illogical as this number will depend on the choice of subjects, the natural history of the disease, the follow-up period, and so on. We thus have a table where the 'marginal totals' are fixed (Ex. 7.3). (This assumption is also made in the Fisher and the usual χ^2 tests). The way in which the numbers fall inside the table will depend only on the degree of association between success and the treatment group, which can be expressed as the odds ratio. We can note two further points. If we know one of the numbers of the body of the table, we can calculate the rest by subtraction: hence the table has one 'degree of freedom'. We can base a test on any one table entry, for example the number of 'exposed cases', here successes on the new treatment, which we shall call a. The deviation of the data from the null hypothesis can be expressed as the difference between this observed number a and its expected value on the null hypothesis. Given the marginal totals, this expected number is N_1M_1/T.

Thus we know a and its expected value, E. The variance of a is derived according to the distribution appropriate to a two-by-two table with fixed marginal totals: this is the hypergeometric distribution, and the variance of a is given by $N_1N_0M_1M_0/T^2(T-1)$. From this, we can calculate χ^2 or χ by the formulae given above. For a continuity correction, we reduce the absolute value $|a - E|$ by 0.5, before squaring.

For the table in Ex. 7.1

observed value of a = 40

expected value of a = $N_1M_1/T = 200 \times 60/400 = 30$

Variance of a = $N_1N_0M_1M_0/T^2(T-1)$

$= 200 \times 200 \times 60 \times 340/(400 \times 400 \times 399)$

$= 12.78$

$$\chi^2 = (a - E)^2/V$$
$$= (40 - 30)^2/12.78$$
$$= 7.82$$ From Statistical Table 1, P lies between 0.01 and 0.001.

Equivalently,

$$\chi = 2.80$$ From Statistical Table 4, $P = 0.005$ (two-sided).

The values are almost identical to those given by the tests used in Ex. 7.2. If a continuity correction is used, $\chi^2 = 7.06$ and $P = 0.008$.

Applications of the Mantel–Haenszel test

Although the formula above, based on the hypergeometric distribution was developed earlier, its widespread use dates from a major paper by Mantel and Haenszel (1959) who showed its applicability to case–control studies, and its ready adaptation to stratified data. Thus it is very frequently known as the Mantel–Haenszel statistic.

For cohort data with a person-time denominator, a very similar formula is used, shown in Ex. 7.4. As noted in Chapter 3, this analysis assumes that the risk to each individual subject is constant in time, as it treats each unit of person-time similarly. To avoid this assumption, lifetable methods may be applied, and a powerful and relatively simple test known as the log-rank test provides a useful method of comparing two survival distributions; this test is in fact the Mantel–Haenszel test applied to many subtables representing different time intervals during the follow-up period. These methods are described in Appendix 2 (p 295). Even the statistical test for 1:1 matched

TEST FOR COHORT STUDY WITH PERSON-TIME DATA

	Outcome positive	Person-time
Exposed	a	N_1
Unexposed	b	N_0
Total	M_1	T

Statistical test

Observed no. of 'exposed cases' $= a$

expected value of a $E = N_1M_1/T$

variance of a $V = N_1N_0M_1/T^2$

Chi-squared statistic χ^2, 1 degree of freedom $= \dfrac{(a - E)^2}{V} = \dfrac{(a - N_1M_1/T)^2}{N_1N_0M_1/T^2}$

Ex. 7.4. Person-time data. For cohort data using person-time denominators, formulae very similar to those shown in Ex. 7.3 are applicable. For a continuity correction, subtract 0.5 from the absolute value of $|a - E|$ (Rothman and Boice, 1982)

case–control studies, also discussed below, is a special case of the Mantel–Haenszel test for subtables each representing one matched pair. It is because of the interrelationship between all these tests, and their common dependence on the characteristics of the distribution noted above, that we emphasize it as the most useful statistical approach for the general reader.

These formulae are 'asymptotic', that is they are derived by making assumptions which are valid only where there are reasonable numbers of observations available; a guide to 'reasonable' would be that the smallest expected number in the two-by-two table on which the result is based should be greater than five. This limitation does not apply to stratified subtables which can be smaller if only the summary estimates are to be used. Where numbers of observations are smaller, 'exact' tests should be used instead, such as Fisher's test for a simple two-by-two table; for other examples and a full discussion see for example Rothman (1986).

Statistical tests in stratified analysis

The use of stratification to control for a confounding variable was discussed in Chapter 6. The Mantel–Haenszel test is easily applied to stratified data, from any type of study. The test can be regarded as a test of the summary relative risk or odds ratio estimate.

We recall that the Mantel–Haenszel χ^2 test for a two-by-two table is calculated as (Ex. 7.3)

$$\chi^2 = \frac{(a - E)^2}{V}$$

where a is one of the values in the table, such as the number of exposed cases, E is its expected value, and V its variance. If the data are stratified into several two by two tables, a χ^2 test for the association after stratification is given by

$$\chi^2 = \frac{\left(\sum_i a_i - \sum_i E_i\right)^2}{\sum_i V_i}$$

where $\Sigma_i\, a_i$ means 'the sum of the values a in each table, represented by $a_1, a_2, a_3 ....$ etc. over I tables, where I is the number of tables'. That is, the values of a, E, and V are calculated in each table, summed, and the χ^2 calculated; it still has 1 degree of freedom irrespective of the number of subtables.

An application to a simple case–control study is shown in Ex. 7.5; these data were shown previously in Ex. 6.17, and relate to the association between melanoma and sunburn history. The single factor table shows an odds ratio of 1.40, which is statistically significant: $\chi^2 = 4.94$, $P = 0.03$ (Statistical

MANTEL–HAENSZEL ANALYSIS OF STRATIFIED DATA

Table A. All subjects

	Cases	Controls	Total	
Severe sunburn	136	98	234	$OR = 1.40$
Mild sunburn	343	347	690	$a = 136 \quad E = 121.31 \quad V = 43.67$
	479	445	924	$\chi^2 = 4.94 \quad P = 0.03$

Subtable B_1. Subjects who sunburn easily

	Cases	Controls	Total	
Severe sunburn	119	76	195	$OR = 1.19$
Mild sunburn	227	173	400	$a = 119 \quad E = 113.39 \quad V = 31.96$
	346	249	595	

Subtable B_2. Subjects who do not sunburn easily

	Cases	Controls	Total	
Severe sunburn	17	22	39	$OR = 1.16$
Mild sunburn	116	174	290	$a = 17 \quad E = 15.77 \quad V = 8.30$
	133	196	329	

Stratified analysis, adjusting for tendency to sunburn

Summary OR = 1.19 (see Ex. 6.17 for calculation).

$$\text{Summary } \chi^2 = \frac{\left(\sum_i a_i - \sum_i E_i\right)^2}{\sum_i V_i} = \frac{\{(119 + 17) - (113.39 + 15.77)\}^2}{(31.96 + 8.30)}$$

$= 1.16 \quad P = 0.3$ (Statistical Table 1, p 310).

Ex. 7.5. Calculation of the Mantel–Haenszel χ^2 statistic from the case–control data shown in Ex. 6.17 (p 107)

Table 1, p 310). However, part of the association is produced by confounding by tendency to sunburn; adjustment for this by stratification gives an odds ratio of 1.19, which is not statistically significant; the summary χ^2 = 1.16, $P = 0.3$, that is these or more extreme results would occur in nearly one of three studies if the null hypothesis were true.

The same formula is applicable to cohort or intervention studies with observations on individuals. For person-time data from a cohort study, the formulation of the χ^2 is the same as that above, using the slightly different formula for the variance which is given in Ex. 7.4.

The concept of precision and confidence limits

These tests of significance yield a single value, which is the probability of a difference the same as or larger than that observed in the study occurring purely by chance, on the null hypothesis that the outcome is the same in each of the groups being compared. Two sets of data representing trials of therapy are shown in Ex. 7.6. In study A, the test shows that the difference is 'significant', in other words it could have occurred purely by chance on less than five per cent of occasions. In study B, the difference is not statistically significant, as it would occur purely by chance on more than five per cent of occasions. The thoughtful reader however will realise that this dependence on an arbitrary cut-off which is usually five per cent is rather limiting. It makes no distinction between studies where the probability of the difference being due to chance is 4.5 per cent or is 0.01 per cent, and at the other extreme, makes no difference between studies where that probability is six per cent, or is fifty per cent.

TWO COMPARATIVE STUDIES

	Numbers of subjects			
	Success	No success	Total	Success rate (%)
Study A				
New therapy	40	160	200	20
Old therapy	20	180	200	10
Study B				
New therapy	10	26	36	28
Old therapy	5	31	36	14

Study A: relative risk = 2.0 χ^2 = 7.84 P = 0.005

Study B: relative risk = 2.0 χ^2 = 2.11 P = 0.14

Ex. 7.6. Two simple comparative studies: hypothetical data. Statistics calculated without continuity corrections; with a continuity correction they are 7.08 and 1.35 respectively

A way to avoid this dependency on an arbitrary cut-off, and to use the information in the study more fully, is to calculate confidence limits for the result rather than the P-value. The concept is as follows. Any one study provides one observation of the quantity which it estimates, for example the relative risk. We accept that this has variability, in that another study on another group of participants would give a somewhat different estimate of this relative risk. Yet what we are interested in is the true relative risk in the

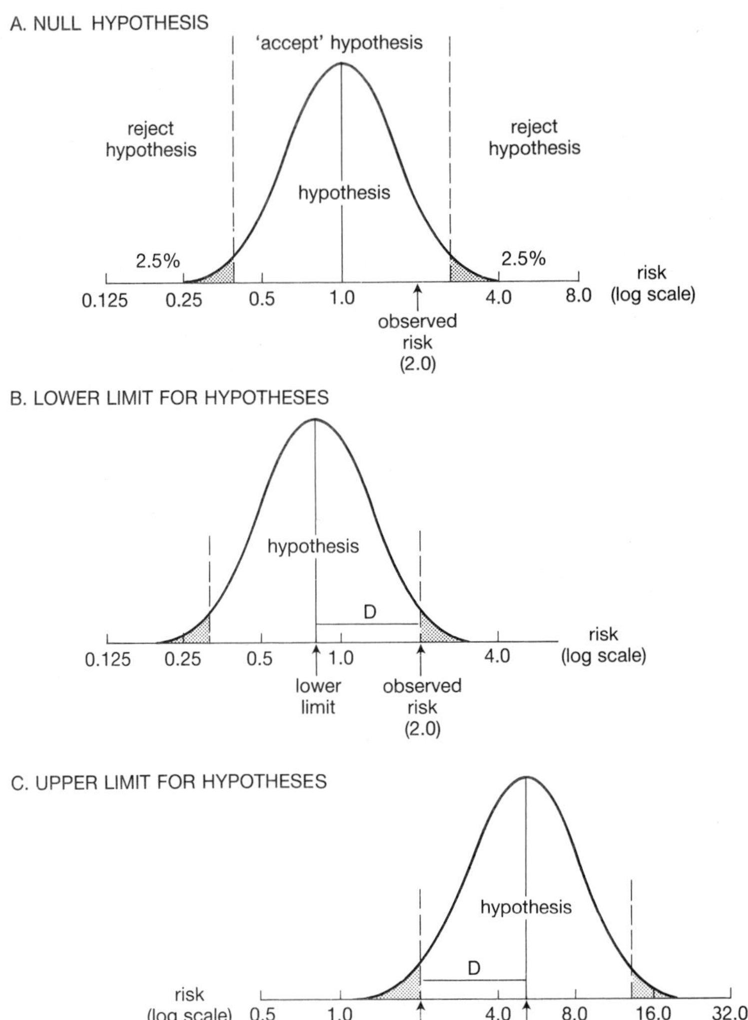

Ex. 7.7. Illustration of confidence limits, based on the data in Ex. 7.6, study B. The limits shown are 95 per cent, two-sided limits: that is, the unacceptable values of relative risk are those corresponding to the highest 2.5 per cent and the lowest 2.5 per cent of the distribution

population from which these samples of participants have been drawn. Exhibit 7.7 shows a diagrammatic representation of the statistical test applied to the data from study B in Exhibit 7.6. In hypothesis testing, a specific value is stated as the prior hypothesis, usually as here a relative risk of one, representing the null hypothesis of no association. The statistical test then assesses if the observed value of the relative risk is consistent or inconsistent with this prior value, using a preset level of probability. To be able to do this we must hypothesize what the true relative risk in the underlying population is, and how the risks observed in a multitude of small samples will be distributed. Exhibit 7.7, part A, shows the expected distribution of the observed relative risk in a multitude of samples of the same size as the one we have used. The distribution is centred on the null hypothesis value of 1.0. It has a normal distribution, but the scale of relative risk is logarithmic. This is because relative risk is a ratio measurement; relative risk values of 2.0 and 0.5 are different from the null value of 1.0 by different amounts on an arithmetic scale, but by the same amount on a logarithmic scale. The width of the normal curve is determined by the standard deviation of these estimates, which is given by the standard deviation of the observed relative risk value. We shall come to the issue of how we can calculate that in due course. Note that in the diagram the observed value of relative risk, 2.0, lies within the central part of the distribution and is therefore a value quite 'likely' to occur in taking a sample from such a distribution centred on 1.0. As a definition of 'likely' an arbitrary value of 5 per cent probability has been used. We conclude that although a relative risk of 2.0 has been observed, the relative risk in the population from which the sample was drawn is quite likely to be one; this is what we mean when we say that the result is not statistically significant.

However, it is clear that the distribution could be moved and centred on many other values, while still keeping our observed value in the central 'acceptable' region. If we take successively lower values for the population relative risk as the hypothesis, this is equivalent to moving the distribution to the left. The standard deviation does not change, since it does not depend on the central value. We can move the distribution to the left until it reaches the point shown in part B of Ex. 7.7. If we moved it any further, then the observed value would be moved into the region defining values with a probability less than 0.05, such that we should reject the hypothesis that the observed relative risk is consistent with the hypothesized value of the relative risk in the population. The value of the centre of the distribution, when the observed relative risk is at this cut-off point, is then the lowest 'acceptable' value for the population relative risk; it is referred to as the lower 95 per cent confidence limit. Similarly, moving the distribution to the right gives successively higher values of the population relative risk, until we reach a value so that the observed relative risk reaches the critical point in the lower tail of the distribution (part C of Ex. 7.7). This gives the upper limit of the 'acceptable' population relative risk; the upper 95 per cent confidence limit.

Any value between the two limits defined in this way is 'acceptable' as a value for the relative risk in the population from which our sample is drawn. In this way we can define limits for the relative risk, and we can be 95 per cent confident that these limits will include the true value.

While the use of the diagrams can aid in the understanding of confidence limits, it does not provide a practical method for calculating them. However, the basic formulae can be derived from the diagram. Given reasonable numbers in the samples studied, these distributions are normal in shape, and therefore the points which define the 5 per cent rejection region are located 1.96 standard deviations from the mean, and this standard deviation is equal to the standard deviation of the logarithm of the estimated relative risk. Thus, if we know the logarithm of the observed relative risk (ln *RR*) and its standard deviation (dev ln *RR*), we can calculate the 95 per cent confidence limits as follows:

$$\text{95 per cent confidence limits of } \ln RR = (\ln RR - 1.96 \text{ dev } \ln RR) \text{ and } (\ln RR + 1.96 \text{ dev } \ln RR)$$

$$\text{95 per cent confidence limits of } RR = \text{exponential} (\ln RR - 1.96 \text{ dev } \ln RR) \text{ and exponential } (\ln RR + 1.96 \text{ dev } \ln RR).$$

Of course limits other than 95 per cent can be calculated using different values of the normal deviate corresponding to that proportion, which can be obtained from a table of the normal distribution, such as that given in Ex. 7.10 or statistical Table 1. Thus, for 99 per cent two-sided confidence limits, we should use a value of 2.58 instead of 1.96. Just as we have discussed one-sided and two-sided statistical tests, we can use one-sided or two-sided confidence limits, the same issues being involved. The above example is based on two-sided limits.

The calculation of the standard deviation of the logarithm of the relative risk is not always simple. Formulae for the calculation of standard deviations for various study designs are given in Appendix 1. In addition to these, it is valuable to mention an approximate simple method which allows the standard deviation, and therefore confidence limits, to be calculated from a test statistic.

One simple method of calculating confidence limits is the 'test based' method, a short cut approximation, derived from the chi statistic given above (Miettinen, 1976), and should be based on the χ statistic without a continuity correction. It is derived from the logic that for a normally distributed variable the difference between its observed value and its expected value, divided by its standard deviation (the square root of the variance *V*) gives a normal deviate. This normal deviate can also be calculated as the test statistic, χ or $\sqrt{\chi^2}$ from any of the tests we have described; knowing χ and ln *RR* allows the calculation of the standard deviation of ln *RR* (Ex. 7.8).

TEST-BASED CONFIDENCE LIMITS

Given that the logarithm of the relative risk, ln *RR*, is normally distributed, and on the null hypothesis the expected value of ln *RR* is 0, a standardized normal deviate will be given by

$$\chi = \frac{\text{observed (ln } RR) - \text{expected (ln } RR)}{\text{standard deviation of (ln } RR)} = \frac{\ln RR}{\text{dev ln } RR}$$

This is equal to χ, calculated by the formulae in Ex. 7.3 and Ex. 7.4, or by other appropriate methods,

hence, standard deviation of ln *RR* = dev ln *RR* = ln RR/χ

The $y\%$ confidence limits of ln *RR* are

$\ln RR - Z_y(\text{dev ln } RR)$ and $\ln RR + Z_y(\text{dev ln } RR)$

where Z_y is the normal deviate corresponding to $y\%$; e.g. 1.96 for 95% two-sided limits;

hence $y\%$ confidence limits for ln *RR* $= \ln RR \pm Z_y(\text{dev ln } RR)$
$= \ln RR \pm Z_y(\ln RR/\chi)$
$= \ln RR\,(1 \pm Z_y/\chi)$

and the 95% confidence limits for *RR* $= \exp\{\ln RR(1 \pm Z_y/\chi)\}$

Ex. 7.8. Calculation of 'test-based' confidence limits

Thus for the data shown in Ex. 7.6, for study A the dev ln *RR* is ln 2.0/ $\surd(7.84) = 0.248$; the 95 per cent two-sided confidence limits for ln *RR* are

$$\ln RR \pm (1.96 \times \text{dev ln } RR))$$

and the limits for the relative risk itself are

$$\text{exponential } [\ln RR \pm (1.96 \times \text{dev ln } RR)]$$

which gives limits of 1.23 and 3.25. As we already know from the *P*-value, these limits do not include the value 1.0.

For study B the limits are 0.79 and 5.10, and these are shown in the diagram in Ex. 7.7. They do include the null hypothesis value.

The confidence limits are derived from exactly the same information as went into the *P*-values, but are a preferable method of presenting study results. They are particularly useful where the result of the study is non-significant. The presentation of confidence limits may guard against the common fallacy of interpreting studies like study B as showing 'no difference' between the intervention and control group. While the overall result is consistent with the null hypothesis, the confidence limits show that the study is also consistent with a relative risk of 5.0, a considerable effect. A better interpretation of study B is that while it has demonstrated a relative risk of 2.0, the 95 per cent confidence limits show that the study result is consistent with anything from a small detrimental effect of the intervention to a large beneficial effect, and therefore the study is inconclusive, rather than demonstrating that the intervention has no effect.

The test based method is quick and simple, and reasonably accurate for relative risks and odds ratios reasonably close to 1 (but not exactly 1, where it gives no result), which are based on fairly large numbers of observations. Some other relatively simple standard deviation formulae are given in Appendix 1 (p 265), which also shows how the test based estimate can be applied to risk difference (attributable risk) calculations.

The concept of statistical power

Look again at study B in Ex. 7.6. From an investigator's point of view this result is rather unsatisfactory. He has studied 72 subjects, he has observed a higher success rate in the intervention compared to the comparison group, and yet this effect is not statistically significant, and the confidence limits show that he cannot confidently decide whether the intervention is beneficial or not. The basic problem is that the study is too small. It does not provide a definite answer. In technical terms, the study lacks power. To avoid committing ourselves to performing studies like study B, it would be helpful to be able to predict the power of a study. We shall now present some fairly simple mathematical aspects of this; but readers who wish to avoid these may go on to the section on 'dealing with a statistician' on p 147.

Factors affecting the power of a study

Several factors affect the power of a study. First is the *strength of the true association*, for example, the difference in outcome rates between the two groups. The larger the true difference, the easier it will be to detect.

Second, is the *frequency of the outcome*. The 'size' of a cohort or intervention study can be thought of as the number of outcome events which are observed in the groups being compared, and in a case–control study, the number of cases and controls who have the exposure under consideration. In study B in Ex. 7.6, the number of outcome events is considerably less than the total number of subjects, 15 instead of 72. If this number were increased, for example by doing the study on patients with a higher frequency of success, or by extending the follow-up time, the study would have more power even though the same number of patients were entered initially. The maximum power for a fixed total number of subjects and a particular odds ratio will be when about half of them have the outcome, or in a case–control design where half have the exposure under consideration.

The next factors to be considered are the significance level and the power. The *significance level* is the cut-off point which will be used to determine whether the association found is regarded as statistically significant. It is most frequently at the $P = 0.05$ level, using a two-sided test. In some circumstances the direction of the effect may be regarded as fixed, and tests used which assess only effects in one direction, and a one-sided test may be used. If we are to apply a 5 per cent one-sided rather than a 5 per cent two-sided test, fewer subjects will be required.

The *power* of a study is its ability to demonstrate an association, given that the association exists. If in reality a true association is present, our ability to recognize it will be greater with a larger sample. For the specified size of the association, frequency of outcome, and significance level chosen, the power is the probability of the study showing this difference as statistically significant. A typical value is 80 per cent: the study is designed so that the chance of detecting a true difference is 80 per cent, and we accept that we will miss the true difference in 20 per cent of instances. For an exploratory study we may decide that missing a true difference (that is, getting a false negative result) is unimportant, and we may be content with a lower power, requiring fewer subjects. If we need to be confident that we will not miss a true effect, we may need a power of 90 per cent or more, which will require many more subjects.

Estimating the size of study which is needed

From the four parameters of the expected frequency of the outcome in the control group, the difference in outcome rates, the significance level, and the power, calculations of the sample size to satisfy those criteria can be made, and some appropriate formulae are illustrated in Ex. 7.9. The formulae can obviously be used in other ways, and another useful application is to calculate the power of the study from the sample size available, the significance level, frequency of outcome and difference in outcome rates. This often will show if a proposed investigation is worthwhile or if more ambitious methods need to be used.

Examples

(1) For a clinical trial. Suppose the mortality rate in two years from conventional therapy is 40 per cent, and a new therapy would be useful if the rate fell to 30 per cent. How many patients do we need? Setting a significance level of 0.05 one-sided, power of 80 per cent yields $K = 6.2$, $n = 279$; that is, 279 subjects in each group. If we were content to detect a larger difference, such as 20 per cent mortality with the new therapy, then $n = 62$; note the large change in n for a substantial change in $(p_1 - p_2)$.

(2) For an epidemiological cohort study. We wish to test whether the breast cancer rate is increased in oral contraceptive users, and estimate a 10-year cumulative incidence in unaffected women of 0.01 (1 per cent); we set significance at 0.05, two-sided, power at 90 per cent and wish to be able to detect a doubling of risk to 0.02; hence $K = 10.5$ and $n = 3098$.

FORMULAE FOR SAMPLE SIZE ESTIMATION

For cohort or trial design, with equal groups

$$n = \frac{(p_1q_1 + p_2q_2) \cdot K}{(p_1 - p_2)^2}$$ n = number of subjects in each group

where p_1 = frequency of outcome in group 1 $q_1 = 1 - p_1$
p_2 = frequency of outcome in group 2 $q_2 = 1 - p_2$

$K = (Z_\alpha + Z_\beta)^2$ where Z_α and Z_β are normal deviates corresponding to significance level α and power $(1 - \beta)$.

To calculate power

$$Z_\beta = \frac{(p_1 - p_2) \cdot \sqrt{n}}{\sqrt{(p_1q_1 + p_2q_2)}} - Z_\alpha$$

For case–control study

Same formulae, where
p_1 = frequency of exposure in cases
p_2 = frequency of exposure in controls

Use of odds ratio

Given the proportion of controls exposed, p_2, and the odds ratio predicted, *OR*, the proportion of cases exposed p_1 is given by:

$$p_1 = \frac{p_2 \cdot OR}{1 + p_2(OR - 1)}$$

Unequal groups

If there are c comparison subjects for each exposed subject or case,

$$n = \frac{(1 + 1/c) \cdot \bar{p}\bar{q} \cdot K}{(p_1 - p_2)^2} \quad \text{where } \bar{p} = \left(\frac{p_1 + p_2}{2}\right) \text{ and } \bar{q} = 1 - \bar{p}$$

$$Z_\beta = \frac{(p_1 - p_2) \cdot \sqrt{n}}{\sqrt{(1 + 1/c \cdot \bar{p}\bar{q})}} - Z_\alpha$$

where n = number of exposed subjects or cases

Ex. 7.9. Formulae for calculating the size of a study. For meaning and values of Z_α, Z_β and K, see Ex. 7.10. A formula for 1:1 matched studies is given in Appendix 1, Ex. A1.8

(3) A colleague hopes a new therapy will increase the proportion of patients recovering, from his current 40 per cent to 60 per cent. He sees 100 patients each year whom he would like to enter into a trial. Is it worth it?

Set significance = 0.05, one-sided hence $Z_\alpha = 1.64$; $p_1 = 0.4$, $p_2 = 0.6$, $n = 50$; hence $Z_\beta = 2.04 - 1.64 = 0.40$. From Exhibit 7.10, the power is less than 70 per cent; for more accuracy, looking up the one-sided probability of

CONSTANTS FOR USE IN SAMPLE SIZE FORMULAE

A. Table relating normal deviates to power and to significance level

Power $(1-\beta)$ (%)	Z-value (Normal deviate)	Significance level (α) One-sided	Significance level (α) Two-sided
99.5	2.58	0.005	0.01
99	2.33	0.01	0.02
98	1.96	0.025	0.05
95	1.64	0.05	0.1
90	1.28	0.1	0.2
80	0.84	0.2	0.4
70	0.52	0.3	0.6
50	0.0	0.5	

B. Values of $K = (Z_\alpha + Z_\beta)^2$, for commonly used values of α and β

Significance level: Two-sided value	Power 50%	Power 80%	Power 90%	Power 95%	Significance level: One-sided value
0.1	2.7	6.2	8.6	10.8	0.05
0.05	3.8	7.9	10.5	13.0	0.025
0.02	5.4	10.0	13.0	15.8	0.01
0.01	6.6	11.7	14.9	17.8	0.005

Ex. 7.10. Normal deviates corresponding to frequently used values for significance levels (Z_α) and for power (Z_β); and table of K where $K = (Z_\alpha + Z_\beta)^2$. The value of Z_β is the normal deviate corresponding to the one-sided test for (1 – power)

this value of 0.40 in a table of the normal distribution (statistical Table 4) yields 0.35, that is a power of 1 – 0.35 or 65 per cent. His study would miss a difference of the size given on one occasion out of three, and is too weak. For adequate power, e.g. 80 per cent, he would need 74 patients in each group; for 90 per cent, 103 patients; thus a two year accrual period would be likely to be satisfactory, if all subjects seen could be entered into the study.

(4) In a case–control study, we wish to be able to detect a doubling of risk (odds ratio = 2) associated with a factor which is present in 10 per cent of the normal population from which the control series will be drawn. Hence $p_2 = 0.1$ and p_1 is given by Ex. 7.9 as 0.18; if power = 80 per cent, significance level = 0.05 two-sided, therefore $K = 7.9$, $n = 293$; we need approximately 300 cases and 300 controls. If controls are easily found, we might wish to try a study with, say, 3 controls per case. Keeping the other parameters the same, $p = 0.14$ $q = 0.86$ and $n = 198$; a study design with 200 cases and 600 controls would give similar results to one with 300 cases and 300 controls.

The formulae given here are fairly simple. More complex formulae, tables of results, and applications to a range of study designs may be found in major reference works, for example Pocock (1983) and Meinert (1986) for clinical trials, and Schlesselman (1982) for case–control studies. The justification for presenting only a simple formulation here is that the general reader should use such formulae only as a broad guide. In practice many quantities are unknown when a study is being contemplated; not only the likely difference between the outcomes, but the extent of loss of information by drop-outs or missing data, and the extent to which stratification or other techniques will have to be used which will reduce the power of the study. The main usefulness of these sample size formulae is to indicate the order of magnitude of the number of subjects necessary for a particular study, or conversely the approximate power which is achievable with the numbers available. Such calculations may show that the numbers of patients necessary far exceed those readily available, or conversely that the power of the study is very low, perhaps 50 per cent or less. Such results should be taken to indicate that the study as envisaged is not a worthwhile endeavour and a different approach is necessary, such as moving from a single centre to a multi-centre study, or addressing the question on a different subset of subjects.

It is often helpful to compare the power produced by studies with different numbers of subjects, and to calculate a 'power curve', that is a graph showing the relationship between sample size and power within the other constraints of the study. This will help to choose the most efficient design, that is the one which gives the most information for least cost, in subjects, time, and finances.

The major properties of the formulae are useful guides. The number of patients required is inversely proportional to the square of the difference in outcome rates; in other words if the difference to be detected is halved, the number of subjects required will be four times as large. The biological effect of a factor will be expected to give a certain ratio of outcome events; the difference in numbers corresponding to a fixed ratio will be greater if the frequency of the outcome is higher, at least up to high frequencies. Given that a new intervention reduces mortality by a third, it is easier to detect a difference between 45 and 30 per cent mortality than between 15 and 10 per cent; often a study design can be made more efficient by selecting subjects who have a high risk of the outcome under investigation. There is little room to manoeuvre in terms of significance levels, and one should not be overly tempted to use one-sided significance levels unless these are clearly indicated, and the remaining factor is the relationship between the number of subjects and power. The tabulation in Ex. 7.10 shows that a study with 80 per cent power requires about twice as many subjects as one with 50 per cent power, and a very powerful study with 95 per cent power requires about 60 per cent more subjects than one of 80 per cent power.

The power of a study is increased by increasing the number of subjects in the study, either in the intervention or case group or in the comparison group, or both. When a similar effort is required to enrol a test or a comparison subject, studies with equal numbers in each group are optimal. A slight variation of this may be made on the basis of the projected effects, as the information in the study depends on the number of subjects with the outcome in a cohort study, or the number with the exposure in a case–control study, and slight modifications of the ratio may be made to design a study where the number of outcome events or exposed subjects are likely to be the same. For example, more than half the patients in a trial may be allocated to the new therapy, on the basis of the anticipated benefit yielding equal numbers of deaths in each group. It may be easier to increase the size of the comparison group than of the intervention or case group, because more potential subjects are available, data on them has already been collected, or because the number of exposed subjects or cases is fixed. The power of the study is increased by increasing the number of controls, but this is less effective than increasing both groups. It can be shown from Ex. 7.9 that the power of a study with n subjects in each group can be equalled by one with c controls per test subject, and $n\{1 + (1/c)\}/2$ test subjects; thus an alternative to finding 100 cases and 100 controls is to use, say, two controls per case and find 75 cases and 150 controls. A little arithmetic will show the decreasing benefit of increasing the ratio of controls to cases; unless data for controls are very easy to get, for example by being available on a computer file, it is rarely worth using ratios greater than 5:1.

Dealing with a statistician

When designing a major study, or as an alternative to using the formulae given, statistical help may be requested in regard to sample size. The non-statistical reader should, however, be prepared for the questions which the statistician will ask, which amount in principle to a prediction of the results of the study. In cohort studies and trials, we need to predict the frequency of the outcome in the control group, and the expected frequency of the outcome in the intervention group on the basis of a reasonable prediction of the size of the difference which we regard as important and worth detecting. To arrive at this judgment it is worth thinking in operational terms; if the frequency of the outcome in the comparison series, such as patients treated on conventional therapy, is a certain percent, to what would this have to change before we would wish to employ the new therapy? For a case–control design, the statistician will want to know the likely frequency of exposure in the comparison group, which may be obtained from literature or a pilot study, and the size of the association to be detected, best expressed as the odds ratio. The remaining questions are to define the significance level and the desired power of the study. For the first, there is rarely a good reason to stray from the convention of the five per cent level. The question of one-sided and two-sided tests has been alluded to. As to power, a frequently used starting point is 80 per cent in an exploratory study; in a study to reassess a finding or in other circumstances where it is important not to miss a true association, higher power is desirable.

Ordered exposure variables and tests of trend

Frequently the outcome variable has only two categories, while the exposure or intervention variable may have a number of ordered categories. For example, the incidence of lung cancer, a yes/no outcome variable, may be compared in a number of groups of individuals categorized by different levels of smoking. Or, the survival of a group of patients, a yes/no outcome variable, may be described in terms of groups of patients categorized by different stages of disease.

To compute relative risks, an arbitrary category is chosen as the reference category, and this should logically be the unexposed or minimally exposed category of subjects, although another choice may be made if for example that category is extremely small. The relative risks for each of the other categories of exposure are calculated by comparing each category to this constant reference group. If the categories of exposure represent a logically ordered variable, a reasonable a priori hypothesis may be that the association will show a regular dose–response effect, with increasing (or decreasing) relative risks with increasing levels of exposure. An appropriate statistical method in those circumstances is to use the whole data set and test for a linear dose–response effect. A commonly used test is the trend test developed by Mantel (1963), which in essence comprises a regression test of the odds ratio against a numeric variable representing the ordered categories of exposure (Appendix 1, p 288). Where the exposure categories are defined numerically, such as different measured amounts of smoking, they may be represented by numbers taken as the mid-point of the exposure category, or some variation of it such as its logarithm; otherwise arbitrary values such as 0, 1, 2, etc. are chosen to represent categories which although ordered are not defined in precise quantitative terms. An example would be stage of disease, the ordering reflecting increasing extent of disease on a qualitative scale. These tests yield a chi-squared statistic on 1 d.f. which tests a linear trend in odds ratio over the ordered categories of the exposure variable, and also a chi-squared statistic on $k-2$ d.f., where k is the number of exposure categories, which tests the deviation of the data from the linear trend. The sum of these two statistics will yield approximately the standard chi-squared statistic for homogeneity which has $k-1$ d.f.

In Ex. 7.11, data from the case–control study presented previously in Ex. 6.18 are shown, showing cases (twin births) and controls (singletons) by maternal parity, in four groups. An ordinary or global χ^2 statistic can be calculated for this two by four table; it has 3 degrees of freedom and tests the

TEST FOR TREND IN AN ORDERED VARIABLE

	Degree of exposure (parity of mother)			
	0	1	2	3 +
Cases (twins)	716	582	454	720
Controls (singletons)	1833	1269	853	1003
Odds ratio	1.0 (R)	1.17	1.36	1.84

Global χ^2 statistic, test for homogeneity	= 91.2	d.f. = 3	$P < 0.001$
Trend χ^2 statistic, test for linear trend	= 88.0	d.f. = 1	$P < 0.001$
Residual χ^2 statistic, test for deviations from trend	= 3.2	d.f. = 2	$P = 0.2$

Thus the data are consistent with a linear increase in twinning by parity
However, this analysis takes no account of confounding

Ex. 7.11. Application of a test for trend to an ordered variable. Data from Elwood (1978). Formulae given in Ex. A1.7, p 288

hypothesis of homogeneity—i.e. that the ratio of cases to controls is the same in each category. The result is $\chi^2 = 91.2$, $P < 0.001$ (Statistical Table 2, p 314). This statistic would be the same if the same data were in a different order, for example if the odds ratios with increasing parity were 1.0, 1.84, 1.36, and 1.17 although such an irregular pattern would make a direct effect of parity less plausible. It is more logical to apply a linear trend test; the formula is given in Ex. A1.7, p 288; using scores of 0, 1, 2 and 3 for parity it yields $\chi^2 = 88.0$, d.f. = 1, $P<0.0001$. The deviation from the linear trend is given by the difference between these, giving $\chi^2 = 3.2$, d.f. = 2, $P = 0.2$; this is non-significant.

Such trend tests should be used with caution, as particularly where there are only a few categories of the exposure variable, a trend can be fitted and may be significant even if inspection of the data shows no regular pattern over the ordered exposure categories. The tests are appropriate primarily where there is an a priori hypothesis of an approximately linear relationship between odds ratio and the ordered exposure variable. In such circumstances, the test can be more powerful than the standard chi-squared test for homogeneity in an $n \times 2$ table.

The Mantel trend test can deal easily with stratified data, so that the Mantel–Haenszel estimator of the odds ratio for each category can be calculated after stratification, and the test then assesses a linear trend in these adjusted odds ratios.

The data in Ex. 7.11 are confounded by maternal age; a full table stratified by maternal age was previously shown as Ex. 6.18 (p 109). The appropriate statistical test is a test for trend, after stratification by maternal age, which yields a χ^2 statistic of 22.6, 1 d.f., $P<0.001$. The deviation from the linear trend is non-significant; $\chi^2 = 3.6$, d.f. $= 2$, $P > 0.2$. Thus although the association with parity is reduced by control for maternal age, as shown by the adjusted odds ratios in Ex. 6.18, it is still highly significant.

Assumptions in stratification: interaction

The calculation of a summary measure of odds ratio or relative risk implies that this adequately describes the data, that is that the odds ratios or relative risks in the different strata are similar. This is usually a reasonable a priori assumption, and in studies with only moderate amounts of information the estimates of odds ratio or relative risk based on individual strata will be unlikely to be based on large enough numbers to allow a definitive assessment of their similarity. However, the estimates in each stratum should be examined to recognize any apparent major differences. For example, the odds ratio may be greater than one in some strata and less than one in others, and the summary estimate may disguise important real variation. With an ordered confounder, such as age, there may be a regular trend in the odds ratio estimate over strata of the confounder.

Methods are available which compare the stratum specific values with a measure such as the Mantel–Haenszel summary odds ratio, and test the hypothesis that the summary estimate applies to all strata. A fairly simple test is based on calculating for each subtable the squared difference between the observed log odds ratio (or relative risk) in each table and the summary log odds ratio—which is the expected value—and dividing by the variance of the observed log odds ratio; this gives a measure of the 'goodness of fit' of the model applying the summary odds ratio in each stratum to the observed data. Summing over all subtables gives

$$\chi^2_{(I-1)} = \sum_i \frac{(\ln OR_i - \ln OR_s)^2}{(\text{var} \ln OR_i)}$$

where $\ln OR_i$ and var $\ln OR_i$ are the log odds ratio and its variance for each subtable, and $\ln OR_s$ is the log of the summary odds ratio. Given I subtables the χ^2 has $I - 1$ degrees of freedom. The formulae for the variances in the different study designs are given in Appendix 1. This is a test of the hypothesis that the odds ratios are homogeneous. Other tests can assess a linear trend in the odds ratios over the strata, which may sometimes be more relevant. Further discussion is given by Rothman (1986) and Breslow and Day (1980) pages 142–146. However, substantial numbers of observations are required to detect heterogeneity in stratum specific relative risks.

Exhibit 7.12 shows an example of variation of the odds ratio estimate. In this study 217 patients with in situ carcinoma of the cervix were compared to

INTERACTION IN A STRATIFIED ANALYSIS

A. Full table		Cases	Controls	
All ages:	smokers	130	45	
	non-smokers	87	198	Odds ratio = 6.6
		217	243	χ^2 = 83.1; 95% confidence limits = 4.4, 9.9
B. Subtables by age				
Age 20–29:	smokers	41	6	*OR* = 27.9
	non-smokers	13	53	χ^2 = 49.7; 95% C.L. 11.1, 70.2
Age 30–39:	smokers	66	25	*OR* = 5.9
	non-smokers	37	83	χ^2 = 35.8; 95% C.L. 3.3, 10.6
Age 40 +	smokers	23	14	*OR* = 2.8;
	non-smokers	37	62	χ^2 = 6.7; 95% C.L. 1.3, 5.9

Odds ratio after adjustment for age, Mantel–Haenszel method = 6.3
χ^2 statistic after adjustment for age, one degree of freedom = 82.4
95 per cent confidence limits of adjusted *OR* = 4.2, 9.3

χ^2 for homogeneity on the three subtables = 14.4 d.f. = 2 $P < 0.01$

Ex. 7.12. An example of interaction, defined here as non-homogeneity of the odds ratio in different categories of a third, modifying variable. In this case–control study comparing 217 patients with *in situ* carcinoma of the cervix to 243 population based female controls, a significant association with smoking is seen (Table A); adjustment for confounding by age makes little difference to this result. However, the odds ratios in the three age categories are substantially different, as shown by their confidence limits and by the χ^2 test for homogeneity over the three subtables. Data from Lyon *et al.* (1983). Calculations shown in Appendix 1, Ex. A1.1

243 population based controls. A significant association between the disease and smoking was seen, with an odds ratio of 6.6, which is highly significant (Table A). After subdivision into three categories by age, the Mantel–Haenszel age adjusted odds ratio is 6.3, only slightly reduced compared to the crude odds ratio, and has confidence limits of 4.2 to 9.3. Age is thus not a major confounder, as is expected because frequency matching on age has been done. However, the odds ratios in each of the three strata of age are considerably different, being 27.9, 5.9, and 2.8 in successively older age groups; all of these odds ratios are significantly different from one, but the confidence limits show that the odds ratio in the youngest age group is significantly different from the overall Mantel–Haenszel estimate, and also significantly different from the other odds ratios. The summary estimate of 6.3 is not an adequate description of the relationship of smoking with disease. The chi-squared statistic testing for homogeneity of the odds ratio, calculated as

above, is 14.4 on 2 d.f., $P<0.01$. Further stratification to control for religious affiliation and number of sexual partners reduced all the odds ratios, but the significant variation in odds ratios in different age groups remained.

Interaction

Thus it is good practice to employ a test of homogeneity in stratified analyses. The hypothesis this is testing is that the relative risks in subgroups defined by other variables are constant. Where there are two or more risk factors related to the outcome, the assumption is that the odds ratio or relative risk for each factor will not vary with the value taken by the other factors. The risk in subjects exposed to more than one factor, compared to those with no exposure, will be given by the product of the relative risks for each factor. This multiplicative model is assumed in techniques such as the Mantel–Haenszel estimate of odds ratio, as a summary estimate is calculated on the assumption that it can be applied to the different subgroups in the study. The same model is also assumed in many multivariate analyses, such as those using the logistic regression model which will be described subsequently. The attractiveness of this model in a wide range of medical applications arises both from its mathematical advantages, as it is a relatively simple model, and from the empiric evidence that it appears to apply to a wide range of biomedical applications. The situations where such a model can be tested are those in which two or more strong risk factors related to a particular outcome can be quantified, and subjects with an adequate range of the combinations of categories of these risk factors can be identified and their risks of the outcome assessed. Important examples in medicine which have shown that a multiplicative model appears to be an appropriate description of the natural state of affairs include the joint effect of oral contraceptives and smoking on cardiovascular disease, which was described in Ex. 3.4 page 31; the interactions between several major risk factors for coronary heart disease, as shown in the Framingham study and other major prospective studies (Truett *et al.*, 1967; Pooling Project Research Group, 1978), the interactions between factors relating to several cancers, such as smoking and asbestos exposure in relation to lung cancer (Saracci, 1977), and several others.

There are also some examples where that model does not seem to be appropriate. One relatively simple alternative model, also described in Chapter 3, is an additive model in which the risk of disease in subjects exposed to more than one factor is the sum of the excess risks conferred by each of the factors. Such a model implies that the absolute excess risk associated with one factor will be constant in different categories of other factors. This means that the relative risk or odds ratio must vary. For example, in Ex. 7.12 it has been shown that the odds ratio varies with age. We know, however, that the baseline risk of *in situ* carcinoma of the cervix increases with age over the age range given in non-smokers; therefore it is possible that the decrease in odds ratio with increase in age may reflect a relatively constant attributable risk associated with smoking in different age groups. From this case–control study alone we cannot directly test that hypothesis, although it could be assessed by using information on the absolute risk in different age categories relevant to the same population. The issue of the appropriateness of these different models, and their relevance in both public health and biological terms, has been discussed extensively and the reader is referred to sources such as Rothman (1986), who also has provided some useful measures and tests based on the additive model (Rothman, 1976). The terms 'interaction', 'synergism', or 'antagonism' can all be used in these contexts, but it should by now be clear that they are meaningful only if the underlying model which is regarded as the non-interaction situation is described. Caution in the acceptance and interpretation of interaction is desirable, as it is difficult to detect unless the risk factors concerned have large effects and subjects representing a wide range of categories of the joint distribution of the factors involved are available. In the analysis, it is appropriate not only to show whether a model such as a multiplicative model fits the data, but also that alternative models do not. A study in which both a multiplicative and an additive model have been applied to the same set of data, and their predicted results compared to those observed empirically, is given by Elwood *et al.* (1984).

Statistical tests in matched analysis

As shown in Chapter 6, in a case–control study controls can be chosen to be matched to the cases on certain confounding factors, and this technique will control matching if and only if the appropriate matched analysis is used, based on the matched sets of cases and controls. For matched case–control data with one control per case, the resultant analysis is simple, and the appropriate statistical test is McNemar's chi-squared test (McNemar, 1947), which is shown in Ex. 7.13. Note that for the calculation of both the odds ratio and the statistic, the only contributors are the pairs which are disparate in exposure, that is the pairs where the case was exposed but the control was not, and those where the control was exposed and the case was not. On the null hypothesis the numbers of each of these will be the same.

For a matched case–control study in which a fixed ratio other than one to one is used such as two or three controls per case, formulae for the calculation of odds ratio estimates and statistical tests are given in Appendix 1, p 284. For more complex situations the reader is referred to texts such as Breslow and Day (1980), pages 169 to 187.

Matched cohort studies will not be discussed in detail, as they are less common. The measures of association—relative and attributable risk—are calculated in the same way as for an unmatched cohort study. For statistical tests, the methods for matched case–control data are applicable, although

MATCHED PAIR ANALYSIS

		Controls	
		Outcome positive	Outcome negative
Cases	Outcome positive	31	30 s
	Outcome negative	7 t	52

Odds ratio $= s/t = 30/7 = 4.3$

$$\chi^2 \text{ on 1 d.f.} = \frac{(s-t)^2}{s+t} = \frac{23^2}{37} = 14.3 \quad P < 0.001$$

$$\text{Continuity corrected } \chi^2 = \frac{(|s-t|-1)^2}{s+t} = 13.1 \quad P < 0.001$$

Ex. 7.13. Statistical test for 1:1 matched case-control studies. Note both the odds ratio and χ^2 depend only on the numbers of discordant pairs. Data from Ex. 6.20; Elwood (1981)

usually very similar results are given by analysing the data in the unmatched format, by the formulae given in Ex. A1.2 or A1.3 (p 272).

Statistical tests in multivariate analysis

An introduction to the concept of multivariate analysis in the control of confounding was given in Chapter 6, and a frequently used type of multivariate analysis described, the application of a multiple logistic model. For each dependent variable in this model which represents an exposure factor, the odds ratio can be estimated as the exponential of the coefficient of that variable, if appropriate coding has been used. There are two main ways in which statistical tests are applied to such models. One is to estimate the significance of each coefficient, by taking the ratio of its value to that of its standard error as a standardized normal deviate. The other is to assess the goodness of fit of an entire model to the data set, comparing models by calculating a statistic representing the difference in the log likelihood (a measure of the 'fit' of the model to the data) produced by adding or deleting variables. The log likelihood statistic, or deviance, is a numerical value which indicates the deviation of the fitted model from the data, and the better the model fits the data, the smaller is the statistic. If an exposure variable is added to the model, and that exposure is related to the outcome variable, the value of the log likelihood statistic will decrease. The value of the change in the log likelihood statistic is distributed approximately as a chi-squared statistic, and if K extra variables are entered into the model, the change in the log likelihood can be considered as a chi-squared statistic on K degrees of freedom. This method can be used to assess not only if one extra variable is significant, but if a set of variables, which may represent a number of factors or different categories of one factor, has a significant effect on the fit of the model.

The statistical aspects of the multivariate analysis which was previously presented in Chapter 6 (Ex. 6.21), are shown in Ex. 7.14. In this case–control study involving 83 cases and 83 controls, the overall model with no independent variables fitted has $n - 1$, or 165 d.f. and a deviance of 230.1. The results of fitting variables singly into the model are equivalent to those from cross-tabulations, and show that the two factors, number of moles and sunburn history, fitted singly are each statistically significant. The effect of fitting the two variables, which together represent the number of moles, gives a change in deviance of 38.1 on 2 d.f., $P<0.001$. Similarly for sunburn (one variable) the chi-squared statistic is 13.0 on 1 d.f., $P<0.001$. These chi-squared statistics are the same as those obtained from cross-tabulations (with no continuity correction). The coefficients from the models where only one factor is fitted give the crude odds ratio associated with that variable, and most computer programmes for this analysis produce a standard error estimate of this coefficient, which can be used to calculate confidence limits. In this analysis there were three other relevant factors, and therefore the full model fitted had ten variables representing number of moles, sunburn history, and the three other factors, and this full model had a deviance of 157.7 with $n - 10 - 1 =$ 155 d.f. The results from this full model give coefficients whose exponentials give the odds ratio of each variable, controlled for the presence of all the other variables in the model. The overall effect of a factor represented by a number of variables is best judged by comparing the deviance of the full model with all factors fitted, with that of the model with that one variable removed. This change in deviance shows the effect of that single factor given that all the other factors are included. As shown in Ex. 7.14, the factor of number of moles remains highly significant in the presence of all other factors. For sunburn history, the change in deviance statistic shows that this is no longer significant when the other factors are included in the model. The conclusion in terms of these two variables is that the effect of number of moles on melanoma risk is reduced slightly by control for confounding by the other variables included but remains as a strong and statistically significant association; the association seen with sunburn history in crude data is greatly reduced by controlling for confounding by the other variables, and is no longer statistically significant.

Statistical tests in life table analysis

We deal with statistical tests for life table analyses in Appendix 2, where these methods are explained and an example given. A most useful test, the log-rank test, is again a special application of the Mantel–Haenszel test.

MULTIVARIATE ANALYSIS

Coefficients and standard errors

Factor	Model with only one factor				Model with 10 variables representing 5 factors			
	Coeff†	Std error‡	OR§	95% limits††	Coeff†	Std error‡	OR§	95% limits††
No. of moles (reference = 0)								
1–2	0.6008	0.4107	1.82	0.82–4.08	0.3011	0.4697	1.35	0.54–3.39
3 +	2.830	0.5705	16.95	5.54–51.84	2.5870	0.6095	13.29	4.02–43.89
Sunburn history (reference = none)								
yes	1.150	0.3246	3.16	1.67–5.97	0.4276	0.4207	1.53	0.67–3.50

Deviance statistics

Model	Deviance	d.f.	Change in deviance	d.f.	
No variables	230.1	165	—	—	
Moles only	192.1	163	38.1	2	$P < 0.001$
Sunburn only	217.1	164	13.0	1	$P < 0.001$
Full model	157.7	155	—	—	
Full model less moles	183.4	157	25.7	2	$P < 0.001$
Full model less sunburn	158.9	156	1.2	1	$P < 0.25$

Ex. 7.14. Multivariate analysis. The analysis previously shown in Ex. 6.21 (p 121), fitting a multiple logistic model to data from a case–control study of 83 patients with melanoma and 83 controls. †Coeff = fitted coefficient; ‡Standard error of coefficient; §Odds ratio = exponential (coefficient); ††Limits = exp(coeff. ± 1.96 × std error); Deviance = log likelihood statistic. From Elwood *et al.* (1986)

Issues in the interpretation of results: general

These considerations lead to some general points about the interpretation of published results. First let us consider the situation where the results are reported as 'statistically significant'. To interpret this, we must first consider if the results reported are free from problems of observation bias and of confounding. The statistical significance of the result is in itself no protection against these problems. Perhaps the easiest way to produce highly significant results in an observational study is to use a design which is open to severe observation bias, for example, biased recall between cases and controls in a retrospective study, or an intervention study using a subjective outcome measure made by someone involved in the intervention being assessed. With these issues dealt with, the next is to know whether the statistical methods used are appropriate and correctly applied; where these methods are complex, expert statistical advice may be required at this step.

Multiple testing

A particular problem in interpretation is posed by the issue of multiple testing. The familiar statistical tests such as those which have been described above are designed for hypothesis testing, to be applied to one particular result which has arisen in the course of a study designed to test that association. Where a study produces a large number of associations, such as a study of patient prognosis which assesses 20 factors and uses conventional five per cent significance level tests, we expect at least one of these factors to appear as statistically significant even if none of them in truth is related to the outcome. Greater problems arise in observational studies where very large numbers of factors can be assessed, or in explorations of very large data sets, for example comparisons of all causes of mortality with occupational categories using death registrations and census data, which may involve comparisons of perhaps 100 categories of causes of death with several hundred possible occupations. A further example is in the context of a clinical trial, where the investigators examine the results in the intervention and control groups very frequently during the course of the trial. For these situations special statistical methods have been developed some of which are quite complex. The issue of to what extent the existence of other comparisons should be taken into account when assessing a particular result is one of considerable dispute. It is valuable to distinguish between results which have been produced from a study specifically set up to test that particular hypothesis, and others which have been generated from a study in which a large number of associations have been examined. The latter studies may be considered as having a hypothesis generation function, and the validity of particular results from the study will be uncertain until confirmatory evidence is available from further work. The particular circumstance of clinical trials has been examined in detail and methods are available to allow the continuous assessment of trial data, the so-called sequential trial designs, fully described by Armitage (1975). Methods intermediate between those and a fixed sample size design, allowing the examination of the data at pre-set frequent intervals, have also been developed. A method appropriate for large scale trials is that the investigating group examines and tests the results of the study only after a pre-set number of subjects have been enrolled, or preferably a pre-set number of outcome events have occurred, and a totally independent group examines the data more frequently. This latter monitoring gives an ethical safeguard, as the trial can be stopped if the results are in the direction of showing the new intervention as being detrimental, or extremely beneficial. The criteria for stopping the trial, or 'stopping rules' will involve both statistical and clinical issues, and must be determined before the trial is commenced; further discussion is given in texts on clinical trial design.

Publication bias

We can take this further and consider the more general issue of what can be called publication bias. Just as a particular association may be one of a number tested in a study, one study is merely one part of the universe of all studies being carried on. We will have incomplete knowledge of these studies, and the subset which we know about will not be representative, as the results of the study will influence whether we know about it. In particular, positive and statistically significant results are much more likely to lead to publications and scientific presentations. Peto *et al.* (1977) have considered what may happen in one particular situation, that of clinical trials of new therapies for cancer. Let us suppose that over a given period, there are 120 large clinical trials with several hundred patients involved in each, and 1200 small clinical trials with maybe fifty subjects involved in each (Ex. 7.15). Let us further suppose that the large trials test therapies which have survived some preliminary evaluation, and of the 120 new therapies tested, 20 are actually beneficial. Of these large trials of beneficial therapies, if the power of the trials is 90 per cent, 18 of the 20 will be correctly reported as beneficial. Of the 100 therapies which are not beneficial and are assessed by large trials, five will be expected to show significant results because of the use of a significance level of five per cent. Thus the great majority of the large trials give accurate results and because large trials are major undertakings even the negative results are likely to be reported. Of the 1200 small trials, representing therapies for which less previous work has been done, let us say 100 are beneficial. However the power of the small study to detect these benefits is only say 50 per cent, and therefore there will be 50 correct reports of benefit, and 50 false negative results. Of the 1100 non-beneficial new interventions assessed by small trials, some 55 may have erroneously positive results. These are likely to be published, whereas the 1045 results of small trials which show no

PUBLICATION BIAS

Type of trial	True situation	No. of trials in progress	Numbers with results which show		
			No significant difference	New therapy better	
Large (several hundred patients)	No difference	100	95	5	Significance level 0.05
	New therapy better	20	2	18	Power 90% (optimistic)
Small (Several dozen patients)	No difference	1100	1045	55	Significance level 0.05
	New therapy better	100	50	50	Power 50%

Proportion of trial results which are correct: (no adjustment for publication bias)

large trials showing no difference:	98%
large trials showing a significant difference:	78%
small trials showing no difference:	95%
small trials showing a significant difference:	48%

Ex. 7.15. Publication bias. The problem of judging one result in terms of others, and the issue of publication bias, in that small trials with no significant differences will often not be published. Adapted from Peto *et al*. (1977)

significant difference are likely not to come to our attention. The morals of this story are several. First, perhaps half of the statistically significant benefits reported for new therapies on the basis of small trials may be incorrect, and therefore a consideration of the size and the power of the study is important even when the results of that study are statistically significant. From this we could argue that all results from small studies should be ignored, but that leads to the difficulty that many of the large studies would not be done if it were not for the encouraging results from previous small studies. A wise counsel might be to regard as definitive only the results of large studies, and a useful test is to ask whether the study would have been published if it had shown no benefit of the new intervention.

Interpreting non-significant results

Let us move to the interpretation of the results which are reported as not showing statistical significance. We must consider first the issues of observation bias and confounding, assessing whether there are problems which could make the observed result smaller than the true result; these include the problem of random error. Again we must assess if the statistical methods used are appropriate and correctly applied, although the issue of multiple testing is not important here. The main difficulty in interpreting non-significant results, is to what extent we can interpret the results as showing that there is no difference between the groups being compared. The computation of confidence limits is very useful, as these show the range of values of the association with which the results are compatible. Where limits are not shown in the original material, it is often possible to calculate them using the simple formula given in Ex. 7.8. If the non-significant result is based upon a small study, the confidence limits will be wide, making it clear that we cannot conclude that there is no appreciable difference between the groups being compared. The consideration of confidence limits calculated for two or more studies of the same topic will often show that the studies are not inconsistent, despite the fact that in one the result may be statistically significantly different from the null hypothesis value and in the other study it might not.

Combining results from several studies: overviews

In reviewing available evidence it may be valuable to combine the results of a number of studies, if these address the same issue and use broadly comparable methods. This type of combined analysis, 'overview', or 'meta-analysis', has received great attention and major overviews have been published on several important clinical issues on which no consensus had emerged despite many studies over many years of research. Topics dealt with include the use of beta-blockers to prevent re-infarction (Yusuf *et al.*, 1985), the use of diuretics in pregnancy (Collins, 1985), the value of adjuvant radiotherapy in breast cancer (Cuzick *et al.*, 1987), and an overview of observational studies assessing the association between passive smoking and lung cancer (Wald *et al.*, 1986). A very useful symposium has been reported in *Statistics in Medicine*, April–May 1987.

The issues involved in combined analyses include those of which studies should be included, how the data are to be found, and what statistical methods should be used. Yusuf, Peto and their colleagues have emphasized the need to include all randomized studies of a particular topic, to avoid the publication bias described above. Other authors have tried to introduce various criteria to avoid using results based on poor quality studies.

In regard to statistical methods, one option is to apply the methods described already: the individual studies can be treated as strata in a stratified analysis, and techniques such as that of Mantel–Haenszel used to calculate the best estimate of the overall measure of association, with confidence limits, and a test of homogeneity can be applied to show if the differences between the results of the various studies are statistically significant.

An alternative method has been presented by Peto and colleagues, which is mathematically sound and has the attraction of great simplicity. Briefly, from each trial a summary two by two table is produced in the format already emphasized in Chapter 3; the number of observed events (usually deaths) in the intervention group (O_i) and the number expected (E_i) is found; the value $O_i - E_i$ is then calculated. The variance of $O(V_i)$ is calculated by the methods previously shown (Ex. 7.3). Then, a summary normal deviate statistic can be calculated over i trials as

$$\chi = \frac{\sum_i (O_i - E_i)}{\sqrt{\sum_i V_i}}$$

This is of course the Mantel–Haenszel summary statistic shown earlier (Ex. 7.3). As a measure of effect, the quantity

$$\sum_i (O_i - E_i)$$

is recommended, and it can be shown (Yusuf *et al.*, 1985, appendix) that the summary odds ratio is given by

$$OR_s = \text{exponential} \left\{ \frac{\sum_i (O_i - E_i)}{\sum_i V_i} \right\}$$

An example of the calculations and presentation is given in Ex. 7.16.

In Ex. 7.16, the results of one trial of a beta-blocker used in post-myocardial infarction subjects are shown (Subtables A and B). This study is

OVERVIEWS OF CLINICAL TRIALS

A. Summary of one trial of beta blockers after myocardial infarction

	Deaths/no. randomized		$O-E$	Variance
	Allocated beta blocker	Allocated control		
Julian *et al.* (1982)	64/873	52/583	−5.6	25.65

B. Derivation of above results for one trial

	Deaths	Survivors	Total
Beta blocker	64	809	873
Control	52	531	583
	116	1340	1456

$O = 64 \quad E = 873 \times 116/1456 = 69.6 \quad (O-E) = -5.6$

$V = (873 \times 583 \times 116 \times 1340)/(1456 \times 1456 \times 1455) = 25.65$

For this trial, odds ratio $= \exp[-5.6/25.65] = 0.80$

normal deviate $= -5.6/\sqrt{25.65} = -1.11 \quad P = 0.3$

C. Summary of 15 trials

$\sum_i (O_i - E_i) = -85.1 \quad \sum_i V_i = 330.3$

odds ratio $= \exp(-85.1/330.3) = 0.77$

normal deviate $= -85.1/\sqrt{330.3} = 4.68 \quad P = 0.000003$ (Stat. Table 4, p 318)

Ex. 7.16. Overview of clinical trials. Data from Yusuf *et al.* (1985), who presented data on 15 randomized trials of beta blockers given to patients after myocardial infarction. For each trial, the data were summarized as shown in A. This trial is described in full in Chapter 11. The derivation is shown in B. For the 15 trials, involving 16 348 randomized subjects, the summary results are shown in C

reproduced in full and discussed in Chapter 11; it shows a beneficial effect of the drug therapy compared with a placebo, with an odds ratio of 0.80, but this result is not statistically significant. For the overview, this result is combined with those from 14 other randomized trials; for each the quantities $(O-E)$ and the variance of O are calculated, and these are summed. The total data from the 15 trials give an odds ratio of 0.77, which is highly statistically significant, as shown in Subtable C.

8. The diagnosis of causation

What is more unwise than to mistake uncertainty for certainty, falsehood for truth?
—*Cicero (106–43 BC); De senectute, XIX*

We have now come to the point where we can summarize how to assess whether a given study or set of studies allows us to decide whether a relationship is causal. As was pointed out in Chapter 1, the question of absolute proof is irrelevant. It can be argued that no amount of data on past experience can ever allow us to predict with absolute certainty the outcome of situations in individuals we have not studied, such as future patients. In medicine there are few situations where there is not another factor that could be considered, another study that could be done, or a compromise in the hypothesis which could be suggested. To balance this, however, we have to be able to make judgments in order to make decisions, whether these are decisions about the diagnosis and treatment of an individual patient, or whether they are policy decisions which may affect many people. These decisions must be made by a process of judgment, and that judgment should be based on an objective consideration of the evidence.

In this chapter a scheme for assessing causal relationships in the context of studies in human medicine will be presented. The approach is that the diagnosis of causation depends on the consideration of both causal and non-causal explanations for the associations seen. A reasoned judgment must be reached as to the likelihood of the association seen being produced by causality rather than by any other mechanism. Thus the conclusion as to whether a given association reflects causation is not a simple yes or no, but requires reasoned and probabilistic judgments.

An overall scheme to assess causality is shown in full in Ex. 8.1, and in a shorter aide-memoire form in Ex. 8.2. The questions shown will be dealt with in turn.

Questions 1 to 5: What evidence do we have?

Consider the practical situation with initially one set of evidence, such as a report of a scientific investigation or raw data from our own or others' experience. We must critically evaluate the methods used and the results given, and decide whether a causal relationship seems a likely explanation for the results. The questions to be asked are:

A SCHEME FOR THE ASSESSMENT OF CAUSATION

A. Description of the evidence

1 What was the exposure or intervention?
2 What was the outcome?
3 What was the study design?
4 What was the study population?
5 What was the main result?

B. Internal validity—consideration of non-causal explanations

6 Are the results likely to be affected by observation bias?
7 Are the results likely to be affected by confounding?
8 Are the results likely to be affected by chance variation?

C. Internal validity—consideration of positive features of causation

9 Is there a correct time relationship?
10 Is the relationship strong?
11 Is there a dose–response relationship?
12 Are the results consistent within the study?
13 Is there any specificity within the study?

D. External validity—generalization of the results

14 Can the study results be applied to the eligible population?
15 Can the study results be applied to the source population?
16 Can the study results be applied to other relevant populations?

E. Comparison of the results with other evidence

17 Are the results consistent with other evidence, particularly evidence from studies of similar or more powerful study design?
18 Does the total evidence suggest any specificity?
19 Are the results plausible, in terms of a biological mechanism?
20 If a major effect is shown, is it coherent with the distribution of the exposure and the outcome?

Ex. 8.1. Twenty questions relevant to the assessment of evidence relating to a causal relationship

THE ASSESSMENT OF CAUSATION

A. Description of the evidence
1 Exposure or intervention
2 Outcome
3 Study design
4 Study population
5 Main result

B. Non-causal explanations
6 Observation bias
7 Confounding
8 Chance

C. Positive features
9 Time relationship
10 Strength
11 Dose–response
12 Consistency
13 Specificity

D. Generalizability
14 Eligible population
15 Source population
16 Other populations

E. Comparison with other evidence
17 Consistency
18 Specificity
19 Plausibility
20 Coherence

Ex. 8.2. A scheme for the assessment of causation, in note form

A. Description of the evidence

1. What was the exposure or intervention?
2. What was the outcome?
3. What was the study design?
4. What was the study population?
5. What was the main result?

The first and often overlooked step is to understand for the particular study exactly what relationship is being evaluated, or to put it another way, what hypothesis is being tested. We should be able to reduce every study to a consideration of a relationship between an *exposure* or intervention, and an *outcome*. It is also necessary to categorize the study in terms of the *design* used; comparative studies of individuals will fall into either a survey, a case–control or a cohort design, the latter including observational and intervention studies. As was shown in Chapter 3, understanding which design has been employed shows what type of analysis is appropriate and indicates which methodological issues will be most important. The fourth aspect of the definition of a study is a general definition of the *subjects* studied, in terms of the source populations, the eligibility criteria, and the participation rates of the different groups compared. More than occasionally, describing a published study in this way requires a critical perusal of the methods section rather than simply a glance at the title, because the question which has actually been answered may be somewhat different from the one the investigators would like to have answered.

Having defined the topic of the study, it is very useful to summarize the main result—what is the result in terms of the association between exposure and outcome? This step forces us to distinguish the main result from subsidiary issues, which should be considered only after the main result is dealt with. It should be possible to express the main result in a simple table, and obtain from the paper or calculate ourselves the appropriate measure of association (usually relative risk, odds ratio, or a difference in proportions) and the appropriate test of statistical significance.

B. Internal validity—consideration of non-causal explanations

Having described the study, we assess its internal validity—that is, for the subjects who were studied, does the evidence support a causal relationship between the exposure and the outcome? This assessment is in two parts; first, we consider the three possible non-causal mechanisms which could produce the result seen. The questions are

6. Are the results likely to be affected by observation bias?
7. Are the results likely to be affected by confounding?
8. Are the results likely to be affected by chance variation?

These have been dealt with in detail in Chapters 5, 6, and 7. For each, we need to consider how the main result of the study may be influenced. It is useful to consider each separately, making our assessment of the likelihood of the study result being produced by that mechanism compared with a causal effect. Thus, for a study which shows an association between exposure and outcome, the questions can be summarized as: could the results seen have arisen by observation bias, if there were no true difference between the groups being compared? Do the results show a true difference, but is it due to a confounding factor rather than to the putative causal factor? Do the results show a true difference, but one which has occurred through chance, there being no general association between exposure and outcome? As mentioned previously, while our final assessment will take all these three factors into account, and the problems in a particular study may involve all three, considering each in the extreme case of it alone explaining the results seen will often clarify our judgment. The order of these non-causal explanations is relevant. If there is severe observation bias, no internal manipulation of the data will overcome the problem. If there is confounding, an appropriate data analysis may be able to demonstrate it and control for it—we need to assess if such analysis has been done. The assessment of chance variation should be made on the main result of the study, after considerations of bias and confounding have been dealt with.

C. Internal validity—consideration of positive features of causation

So far we have considered the recognition of a causal relationship only by the exclusion of non-causal explanations, and the new material in this chapter is a consideration of features which when present can be regarded as positive indicators of causality. At this point we will discuss the assessment of these features within a particular study, and later we will discuss them in regard to all available information relevant to the hypothesis under assessment.

The relevant questions are:

9. Is there a correct time relationship?
10. Is the relationship strong?
11. Is there a dose–response relationship?
12. Are the results consistent within the study?
13. Is there any specificity within the study?

Question 9: Time relationship

For a relationship to be causal, the putative exposure must act before the outcome occurs. In a prospective design where exposed and non-exposed subjects are compared, this is established by ensuring that the subjects do not already have the outcome when the study is commenced. The ability to clarify time relationships is obviously weaker in retrospective studies, and care must be taken to avoid considering as possible causal factors events which took place after the outcome had developed. For this reason, in retrospective studies of disease it is best to enrol incident subjects (those who have just had the outcome), to interview subjects fairly rapidly, and to record only information related to events preceding the outcome.

A difficulty in all study designs, but particularly in retrospective studies, is that the occurrence in biological terms of the outcome of interest may precede the recognition and documentation of that outcome by a long and variable time; often some arbitrary assumption about this time is used. For example, in the retrospective study described in Chapter 10, drug histories of case and control subjects were taken from medical records, but only to a time one year prior to clinical diagnosis in the cases, and an equivalent time in the controls.

A similar issue may arise in the definition of exposure. For example, in assessing an association between an occupational exposure and disease, it may be reasonable to define exposure as a minimum of, say, five years in particular occupation. In that event, the follow-up period begins immediately the five year period is completed.

A study may show no association because the time scale is inadequate; a treatment comparison may give irrelevant results if based on a short follow-up, and long term effects of an exposure factor such as radiation or oral contraceptive use will be missed by studies with a short time scale.

Question 10: Strength of the association

A stronger association, that is a larger relative risk, is more likely to reflect a causal relationship. One reason is that as the measured factor gets closer to the biological event on the causal pathway, the relative risks will become larger. The deterministic ideal is that the factor is the necessary and sufficient cause, which gives a risk of zero in the unexposed and 100 per cent in the exposed, and a relative risk of infinity. However, this is a very rare situation in medicine. Suppose that a rare disease is in fact caused totally by exposure to a specific chemical used in the manufacture of photographic film. In sequential studies, we might detect a weak association with employment in a photographic plant, a stronger one with working in the film manufacture process, and a very strong association with the extent of exposure to the particular chemical. We can however argue that a true causal factor may be related to a small increase of risk, as the factor may be one of a number of such factors operating. Consider the role of air pollution in the causation of chronic bronchitis. Where there are few other factors operating to cause the disease, for example in non-smoking subjects who are not exposed to occupational hazards, the role of air pollution may be major, producing a high relative risk which is relatively easy to demonstrate. However, in a heavy smoker, the smoking factor is of such overwhelming importance that the extra risk contributed by atmospheric air pollution will be relatively small; if the attributable risk of air pollution is similar to that in a non-smoker, the relative risk will be small because of the very high base-line risk produced by smoking. This does not alter the causal nature of the relationship, but it does make the strength of the relationship less, and makes it more difficult to demonstrate.

The fact that a relationship is strong does not protect us against certain non-causal relationships. Severe observational bias may produce very strong relationships. For example, if we question mothers who have recently been delivered of defective babies about exposure to drugs in early pregnancy, and compare their responses to those of mothers of healthy babies, we should anticipate that bias in selective recall might be very considerable; if it operated at all there is little reason to assume that the bias it could produce in relative risk would be small; it could quite easily be very large. Similarly, strength does not protect us against confounding caused by closely associated factors. An example of this is the situation where a disease risk may be related to a previous drug exposure, or to the reason for that exposure. There may be a close relationship between the indication and the drug, and therefore if one of them is a true causal factor the association of disease with the other factor will be strong in spite of the fact that it is due only to confounding.

However, if a strong relationship is due to bias, the bias must be large, and so should be relatively easy to identify. If a strong relationship is due to confounding, either the association of the exposure with the confounder must be very close, or the association of the confounder with the outcome must be very strong. For example, the relative risk of lung cancer in heavy smokers compared to non-smokers is in the order of 30. It has been suggested that this relationship is due to confounding by a genetic predisposition to lung cancer, linked to a genetically determined personality trait leading to smoking. If so, that genetic predisposition factor must have a relative risk of about 30 for lung cancer. Even given the difficulties of assessing personality, it should be possible to demonstrate the existence of such a relationship.

Question 11: Dose–response relationship

The consideration of a dose–response relationship is similar to that of strength. The major issue which it does not protect against, is the relationship being due to a confounding factor closely related to the exposure, such as in the drug versus indication for drug situation. In some circumstances the demonstration of a smooth dose–response relationship may be a strong argument against the relationship being due to bias. It could be argued for example that women who use oral contraceptives might be more likely to report certain symptoms simply because they are seen by general practitioners more frequently than are women who do not use oral contraceptives. It is somewhat less likely that there is a close relationship between the oestrogen dose of the oral contraceptive and the frequency of being seen, and therefore if the characteristic under study shows a regular dose response relationship with the oestrogen dosage, it would suggest that this bias was unlikely to be the explanation. We should expect uni-directional dose–effect relationships. Obviously other types of associations, showing a threshold or all-or-none effect, or a complex relationship may in fact be the true situation. However, the general assumption that if a causal relationship holds, the frequency of the outcome should show a uni-directional increase or decrease with increasing exposure, even though the relationship may not be linear, seems very reasonable. So reasonable, that evidence that that is not the case should be considered carefully. For example, the age distribution of Hodgkin's disease does not show the common uni-directional increase of incidence with age as is seen in many other cancers, but instead shows a complex pattern with a peak at younger ages followed by a decrease followed by a further increase. On the general assumption that complex relationships are unlikely, this pattern suggests that there are two distinct diseases, one of which shows the steady increase of incidence with age characteristic of many other cancers, and the second which shows a peak incidence at young ages (MacMahon, 1957). This suggestion that Hodgkin's disease has two distinct sub-types was later confirmed by the demonstration of differences in clinical and pathological features between the previously unseparated types of disease.

Question 12: Consistency of the association

A causal relationship will be expected to apply across a wide range of subjects. If a new pain killer is effective, it is likely to be effective in patients of both sexes and different ages, for a wide variety of causes of pain. In other circumstances, specificity (see below) rather than consistency might be predicted—for example, a hormonal treatment for breast cancer might be expected to work in only post-menopausal patients. If an association within one study is seen to be consistent in different groups of subjects, that may well be regarded as support for causality, particularly if the likely sources of bias and confounding are different in those subgroups. Similarly in reverse: when a new study showing a positive association between the consumption of artificial sweeteners (mainly saccharine) and bladder cancer was published, the association was seen only in males, and in the absence of a biological explanation for that lack of consistency, that fact weakened the case for causality (Howe *et al.*, 1977).

The difficulty with consistency is that very large data sets are required to assess the similarity or otherwise of associations in different subgroups of subjects—the effective sample size is the number of observations in each subset. Even with adequate numbers, the subgroups to be compared need to be defined on a priori grounds, and not merely generated from the analysis. In a large analysis where many subgroups are defined, it is to be expected that some will show different results by chance alone. This has been a major problem in clinical trials: even where no overall benefit of a new treatment is shown, a benefit may be apparent in one subgroup of patients. Such *post hoc* analysis is misleading and best avoided; at the most, such findings should be regarded as new hypotheses which require testing.

Question 13: Specificity of association

It has been argued that a specific association, between one causal factor and one outcome, is good evidence for causality. This may be misleading; some took the view that the fact that smoking was shown to be associated with the occurrence of a number of cancers and other serious diseases and therefore demonstrated non-specificity of action, made the hypothesis of a causal link with lung cancer less likely. In the medical area specificity when it occurs is often contrived by definition. If we define tuberculosis as a clinical disease comprising various signs and symptoms, which is produced by infection by the tubercle bacillus, we end up with a specific association between that disease so defined and the infectious agent. Without that definitional convenience, the associations between infection with tubercle bacillus and chronic meningitis, swollen joints, and lung disease do not appear to be specific.

In many situations, however, demonstration of specificity may be valuable, as it may show that bias or confounding is unlikely to be the explanation for the observations made. For example, consider a retrospective study in which recently delivered mothers are interviewed, which shows that use of a certain drug is much more frequently reported by mothers of infants with cardiac malformations than by mothers of healthy babies. We would have to question whether recall bias is the explanation of that association. If however, mothers of babies with a range of other defects were questioned, and their reported histories of drug use were similar to the mothers of the healthy babies, this would be a strong argument against recall bias being the explanation of the association seen with cardiac disease.

A hospital based study showed that women who had developed endometrial cancer had a higher frequency of past use of oestrogenic drugs than did patients who had cervical cancer (Smith *et al.*, 1975). Endometrial cancer is more common in high socio-economic groups, while cervical cancer is less common. The use of a non-essential drug such as this is likely to be greater in the higher socio-economic groups, so the association seen may be due to confounding. However, patients with ovarian cancer, which has a similar socio-economic distribution to endometrial cancer, were also assessed, and their usage of oestrogen drugs was also much lower than that of the endometrial cancer patients. This makes confounding by socio-economic status a less likely explanation for the association seen.

Specificity may therefore be useful, if we do not make it an absolute criterion, as one causal agent may in truth produce various outcomes, and one outcome may result from various agents. The concept is often useful in study design: as a check on response bias we may deliberately collect information on factors which we expect to be the same in the groups compared, as similar results will indicate a lack of observation bias. We may choose control groups to capitalize on similar effects, as noted above.

Summary of internal validity

By this point, we should be able to decide whether the internal validity of the study is adequate. A positive decision means that we accept the results to be a valid measure of the true association in the subjects studied, and if an association between exposure and outcome is present, we regard it as likely to be due to a causal relationship.

A negative decision means that we decide that one or more of the non-causal explanations is likely to hold; the association seen is due to observation bias, to confounding, or to chance, and we should be able to specify the likely biases or confounding factors.

Often we will be able to eliminate some but not all of the options, and decide for example that the result is likely to be due to causation or to confounding; such a conclusion is very valuable as it makes clear what further information is necessary.

D. External validity—generalization of the results

If the internal validity of the study is very poor, there is no point in proceeding further, for if the study result is not valid even for the subjects studied, its application to other groups of subjects is irrelevant. However, if we conclude that it is a reasonably valid result, and that a causal relationship is a reasonably likely explanation, we need to go on to consider the external validity of the result. The relevant questions are:

14. Can the study results be applied to the eligible population?
15. Can the study results be applied to the source population?
16. Can the study results be applied to other relevant populations?

The relationship between the study participants and the population of eligible subjects should be well documented. Losses due to non-participation have to be considered carefully as they are likely to be non-random, and the reasons for the losses may be related to the exposure or to the outcome. These issues were discussed in Chapter 4.

Beyond this, it is unlikely that the study participants will be a 'representative sample' of a definable source population, and even if they were, we should want to extrapolate the results further, for example to our own community, future patients, and so on. The issue is not whether the subjects studied are 'typical' or 'representative', but whether the *association* between outcome and exposure given by the study participants is likely to apply to other groups. In assessing the applicability of results, we need to be specific about the factors which are likely to affect the association. Most clinical trials are done on patients in teaching hospitals. If a new therapy for breast cancer is shown to be effective in such a trial, we would readily apply the results to patients in a district hospital who had a similar stage and type of tumour and were of similar age, even though the trial patients cannot be said to be 'representative' of district hospital patients in a general or statistical sense. Similarly, women in the United States and in Japan have very different incidence rates of breast cancer, and very different diets; but if a causal relationship exists between saturated fat intake and breast cancer incidence, we should expect to see it in both populations, even though its strength might be modified by the relative importance of other factors. However, other considerations may apply. If we read of a clinical trial of a new drug therapy used for severe depression in a well known teaching centre, we should not apply the results to patients in general practice uncritically; the general practice patients, even with the same diagnosis are likely to be different (for example in the severity and duration of disease) from those in the teaching centre, and the effects of the therapy may well differ in inpatients and in ambulant patients. In general, the difficulties of applying results from one group of subjects to another will be minimal for issues of basic physiology and maximal for effects in which cultural and psycho-social aspects are dominant.

E. Comparison of the results with other evidence

We have now made a critical assessment of the evidence presented by one study. We have assessed the internal validity, and come to a reasoned judgment as to whether the results of the study are consistent with a cause and effect relationship. We have explored the external validity of the study, and come to a decision concerning how far we can generalize the result beyond the subjects who participated in the study.

We can now move to the issue of comparing the result of this particular study with the evidence from other studies and other types of experience. As we did with the evidence from within the study, we shall make these comparisons with specific questions in mind, but before doing that we have to consider what other types of evidence we might have available, and how we give appropriate importance to each of these types.

A hierarchy of evidence

For many practical questions a large amount of evidence is available which comes from different types of studies. In these circumstances it is useful to consider a hierarchy of evidence. Given that the studies are adequately performed within the limitations of the design used, the reliability of the information from them can be ranked in the manner shown in Ex. 8.3.

A HIERARCHY OF EVIDENCE

1. Randomized trials
2. Cohort and case–control studies
3. Other comparative studies
4. Case series, descriptive studies, clinical experience, etc.

Ex. 8.3. A hierarchy of types of evidence relevant to human studies

At the top are randomized intervention trials, if properly performed on adequate numbers of subjects, and of course in the human situation. Evidence from such studies should be given the greatest weight because of the unique advantages of these studies in overcoming the problems of bias and confounding.

Second come observational studies of appropriately selected groups of subjects, that is, cohort and case–control designs. There is logic in placing cohort designs somewhat ahead of case–control designs, as, if well performed, cohort studies should have less observation bias, give clearer evidence of the time relationships of the association, and have a comparison group whose results are more easily interpreted. However, both these observational designs can have severe problems in practice, and a well performed case–control study may be of more value than a poorly performed cohort study.

The third level of evidence comes from studies which compare groups of subjects not chosen specifically for the purpose of the study but representing different population or subject groups. This includes correlation studies of populations in which data on each individual are not assessed separately, and also informal comparisons between patients in different hospitals, patients treated at different time periods, and so on.

In the fourth category there is evidence which is largely anecdotal, based on the unsystematic recollection of personal or group experience (often referred to as 'clinical judgment'), conclusions based on traditional practice, and information derived from other species, *in vitro* testing, basic physiological principles, and other indirect assessments.

This hierarchy is useful in assessing the very large amounts of information which may be available on a particular topic. It is sensible to concentrate on the best possible evidence. If there are randomized trials available on the question, they should be evaluated first, and if they provide strong evidence for or against causality, the results of the other less rigorous types of study may be judged less relevant. On many topics, randomized trial evidence will not be available, and therefore one must look particularly at the results of well performed cohort and case–control studies.

Although such a ranking of different sorts of evidence is frequently used informally and even subconsciously, there are only a few published examples of the systematic use of such a system. One such is the report of a Canadian group of clinicians and academics, which was set up to assess the effectiveness of procedures which had been recommended at various times for inclusion in regular medical examinations for prevention or early diagnosis (Canadian Task Force on the Periodic Health Examination, 1979). The committee concerned itself only with medical effectiveness, not with questions of economic value or social acceptability. They assessed 88 suggested procedures for the general population, including for example testing new born babies for phenylketonuria, routine tests for urinary tract infection in pregnancy, screening of preschool children for hearing impairments, and of adolescents for spinal deformity. Of the 88 situations, evidence from randomized trials was available in only 20 (of these 12 were questions of immunization), for 17 conditions evidence from cohort or case–control studies was available, for 22 only descriptive or uncontrolled observations were available, and for 29 there was nothing other than subjective opinions and 'experience'. The relationship between the type of evidence available and the final decision of the multidisciplinary committee (Ex. 8.4) shows, as we would expect, that the better the quality of evidence the more readily the committee were able to come to a firm recommendation on whether to include or to exclude the procedure as a routine. The situation where a firm recommendation was based on only category three evidence was one with a

EVIDENCE AND DECISION

Best evidence	Recommendation					Total	With firm recommendation
	include			exclude			
	firm	weak	none	weak	firm		
1. Randomized trials	11	0	1	2	6	20	17
2. Cohort, case–control	3	5	1	8	0	17	3
3. Other comparative	1	11	2	8	0	22	1
4. Other types	0	0	29	0	0	29	0
						88	

Ex. 8.4. Evidence and decision. Relationship between decisions of a multidisciplinary group regarding regular health examinations and the best type of evidence available, for 88 procedures for the general population. (Derived from Canadian Task Force on the Periodic Health Examination, 1979)

long clinical tradition—the use of silver nitrate drops in a neonate's eyes to prevent ophthalmia neonatorum.

This report is unusual because rather than only giving the committee's final recommendations it summarizes the type of evidence available for each procedure. This is done both in terms of the hierarchical system of classification of evidence, which is a gross measure of internal validity, and in terms of its applicability to the relevant population, patients in the primary care situation in Canada, giving a measure of external validity.

The reader of this text may well be faced with the problem of compiling a literature review, or coming to a decision on a therapeutic or management issue on which much has been written and no clear consensus is apparent. Each study must be assessed carefully enough to make an assessment of its internal and external validity, as a study which is badly performed is of no value irrespective of its design. In reviewing each piece of available evidence, it will be helpful to record (1) what the results were, (2) what type of evidence they represent, and (3) how applicable the study is to the relevant subjects and circumstances.

Comparisons with other studies

In comparing the results of a particular study with those of other studies, we will ask:

17. Are the results consistent with other evidence, particularly evidence from studies of a similar or more powerful study design?
18. Does the total evidence suggest any specificity?
19. Are the results plausible, in terms of a biological mechanism?
20. If a major effect is shown, is it coherent with the distribution of the exposure and the outcome?

Question 17: Consistency with other studies

This is the most important characteristic used in the judgment that an association is causal. To say that the result is consistent requires that the association has been observed in a number of different studies, each of which individually can be interpreted as showing a causal explanation, and which have enough variation in their methodology and study populations to make it unlikely that the same biases or confounding factors apply in all the studies. Consistency of results between studies, each of which is individually unsatisfactory is of little value, as is consistency between studies all of which suffer from the same design defects. Lack of consistency argues against causality, but care must be taken in its assessment also. The failure to find an association in a study which is limited in its methodology and size so that it has very little power to detect an association if one were present, is of no value. When a new and controversial result is published, weak, badly designed and small studies which show no association are often presented to refute it; these studies have to be examined with the same critical approach as is applied to the original.

Question 18: Specificity

The issues of specificity are those covered already in the context of one study, and relate closely to those of consistency. Whether a difference in results between two studies is interpreted as inconsistency or as specificity depends on whether the difference is anticipated by a hypothesis set up before the comparison is made. If not, but a plausible mechanism can be found or if the difference is itself found consistently, then the hypothesis may be modified to take into account the specificity which has been shown. This creates a new hypothesis which should be assessed by a further independent study.

Thus Paffenbarger *et al.* (1977), after the analysis of a case–control study, showed a positive association between breast cancer and the use of oral contraceptives used before the first pregnancy. This finding, derived from an analysis, gave a new specific hypothesis which has since been assessed, so far with inconsistent results (Pike *et al.*, 1983; McPherson and Drife, 1986).

Question 19: Plausibility

Plausibility refers to the observed association being biologically understandable on the basis of current knowledge concerning its likely mechanisms. The consideration of plausibility is useful, particularly as it may indicate biases or confounding factors which should be considered. The interpretation of the positive association between ice-cream sales and drowning in summer holiday resorts is an example, as a consideration of its plausibility will suggest a confounding factor.

In 1982, a case–control study showed a positive association between exposure to fluorescent light through indoor work and malignant melanoma, a skin tumour (Beral *et al.*, 1982). The result did not seem readily explicable by bias, confounding or chance. The most obvious biological mechanism was given by assuming that fluorescent lights emitted ultraviolet radiation, but one feature of the results was inconsistent with such a mechanism: the subjects with high exposure to fluorescent light showed the excess of cancers on the trunk, rather than on sites which would be normally exposed to indoor lighting such as the upper limbs. To fit this, more complex mechanisms were suggested, such as chemical emissions or immunological effects, but these seemed inherently less plausible.

However, any dramatically new observation may be in advance of current biological thinking and its lack of plausibility may reflect deficiencies in biological knowledge rather than an error in the observation. John Snow effectively prevented cholera in a district of London 25 years before the isolation of the cholera bacillus and the general acceptance of the principle that the disease could be spread by water. Percival Pott demonstrated the causal relationship between exposure to soot and scrotal cancer some 150 years before the relevant carcinogen was isolated and the mechanism further understood. The greatest value of the concept of plausibility is to emphasize that where an association does not match a known biological mechanism, further studies are indicated to clarify this, but these need not necessarily delay appropriate action if the evidence for causality is strong enough. Lists of the expected features in causality often include the concept of analogy, meaning that a relationship is regarded as more acceptable if it is analogous to some other well established relationship, but clearly this concept comes within the overall concept of plausibility.

Question 20: Coherence

An association is regarded as coherent if it fits the general features of the distribution of both the exposure and the outcome under assessment; thus if lung cancer is due to smoking, the frequency of lung cancer in different populations and in different time periods should relate to the frequency of smoking in those populations at relevant earlier time periods. The limitation of this is that it assumes that the exposure and the outcome are the same in these different populations, and it holds only if a high proportion of the outcome is caused by the exposure, and if the frequency of the outcome is fairly high in those exposed. If the factor causes only a small proportion of the total disease, the overwhelming influence of other factors may make the overall pattern inconsistent. Similarly, a comparison of an exposure such as smoking in different countries, or a general category of disease such as lung cancer, may not take sufficient note of differences in types of smoking and in types of lung cancer.

As an example of an argument based on coherence, it was suggested some years ago that neural tube defects were caused by a teratogen in damaged potatoes; in support the high frequency of the defects in Ireland, and the strong association with low social class were quoted, on the argument that these populations had a high consumption of potatoes. However, it was also noted that the condition is fairly common in Taiwan, and there also is more common in the poor, although potato consumption is probably higher in the upper social classes (Emanuel and Sever, 1973).

Summary: assessing causal relationships and making decisions

A general method has now been set forth which should assist the reader to assess written evidence, his or her own experience, and the experience of

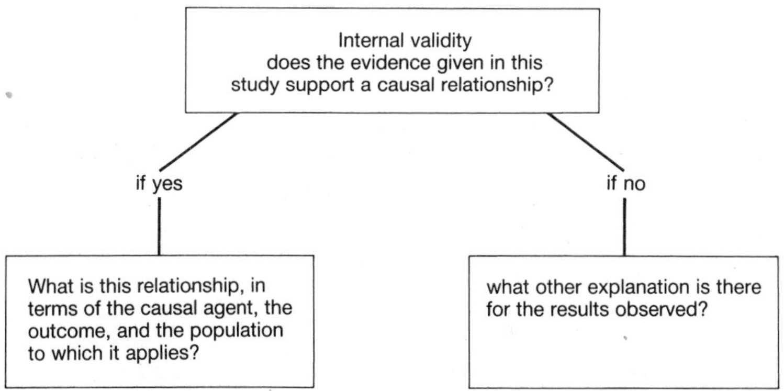

Ex. 8.5. Assessment of causal relationships: the decision process

colleagues. The system is obviously only a framework, and issues specific to each subject will influence the relative importance of different aspects of the process; a minor issue in one subject may be a major issue in others. The entire process can be summed up in the way shown in Ex. 8.5. Presented with new results from a study of a putative causal relationship, the question we must ask is, 'Does the evidence given in this study support a causal relationship?' This involves the assessment of the internal and external validity of the study, and its relationship to other evidence, as expressed in the scheme given in this chapter.

If our judgment is that the evidence does support a causal relationship, we should be able to reinforce this by answering the question, 'What is this relationship, in terms of the causal agent, the outcome, and the population to which it applies?'

If the answer to our question is in the negative, we need to be able to answer the question, 'What other explanation is there for the results observed?' The results we have been presented with do not go away; they are the facts from which we are arguing. If we reject a causal explanation, we must be able to propose an alternative hypothesis. The specification of the alternative hypothesis, or hypotheses, will help us to see the weaknesses in the evidence we have and guide us in how to search for better information.

Further application of these concepts

This volume has concentrated on the assessment of cause and effect relationships, and almost exclusively on evidence provided by studies of groups of individuals. The reader will have realized early on that there are many important relationships which are not necessarily of a cause and effect type, and also that there are other types of data which can be considered. While there is no intention to go into these fully, a few comments on the relevance of the concepts expressed in this approach to these other questions may be helpful.

Associations can be useful even if not causal

If we can establish that an association exists, even if it is not causal, this information may be very valuable. In particular the large and fascinating subject of *diagnosis* is dependent on the reliable demonstration of associations which are not causal associations. We learn to diagnose a condition, to separate subjects with that condition from subjects who do not have that condition, by knowing what features are associated with that condition; whether they are part of the causation of the condition is irrelevant. Diagnostic symptoms, signs, and laboratory measured abnormalities, are usually in fact other features which are produced by the same causal mechanism as produces the disease which we are trying to diagnose. Despite that, many of the principles outlined in this volume are applicable to the study of diagnostic concepts, particularly the issues of observation bias and external validity.

Similarly in the social sciences the emphasis has generally been on exploring associations between factors, for example whether attitudes to health care are different in different social groups, without of necessity considering cause and effect relationships. Often, however, assumptions and judgments about cause and effect relationships lie not far below the surface, and again the principles set forth in this volume should be of assistance in assessing such questions.

Application to studies of populations, and of physiological or biochemical parameters

This book is primarily about studies of individuals, where each contributes one exposure and one outcome event. Causal relationships may often be suggested, and sometimes be assessed, by data comparing different population groups; e.g. routine statistics of disease incidence, morbidity, or case fatality. Such studies yield comparisons between rates of exposure and rates of outcome in populations, without having data showing which individuals within those populations are involved. While such studies are inherently weaker than studies of individuals, they can be analysed in the same way. Most can be considered as cross-sectional surveys or cohort studies. For example, Miller *et al.* (1976) presented a correlation study in which it was shown that populations (Canadian provinces) with more intense programmes of cervical cytology (the exposure) showed a larger decrease in mortality from uterine cancer (the outcome). The analysis of this association is conceptually the same as for a study of individuals: is the association likely to be due to bias, confounding, or chance, and does it show the positive features of causation? The same logical approach can be applied.

Similarly, we have not dealt directly with the other main group of human studies: those where the results are based on series of physiological or biochemical measurements within an individual. Thus, to show the causal relationship between external temperature and peripheral blood flow, measurements could be made in different subjects at different temperatures, but it is much more efficient to compare the same individuals, making a series of measurements of peripheral blood flow while varying the external temperature. The logic of causal inference presented here is totally applicable—bias, confounding and chance must be considered, and the positive indicators of causality sought. Such studies can be considered as matched cohort studies, each group of subjects under one set of conditions being one study cohort.

While the logic can be applied to both descriptive epidemiological and physiological studies, often the outcome and/or exposure factors will be continuous rather than discrete variables, such as temperature, peripheral blood flow, morbidity rate; the statistical methods applicable are those for continuous variables, including Student's t-test, correlation and regression methods, analysis of variance, multiple linear regression, and non-parametric methods such as rank correlation techniques. Such methods are well described in most statistical textbooks.

Application of the scheme in designing a study

This scheme can also be used in the design of studies. A useful general approach to the design of a study is that the investigator should attempt a forward projection in time to the point where the study has been completed and the results have been compiled. It is useful for the investigator to consider all possible types of results; that is, a positive association or one in the direction expected, no association, or a negative one, or one in the opposite direction from that expected. The investigator can then ask the question, given that those results arise: 'How shall I assess this study in terms of its internal and external validity?' or in simpler terms, 'Shall I believe the results that I have obtained?'. A good test of a well designed study is that the investigator will be willing to accept and act on the results, even if they are different from the anticipated result. This is also a useful question to ask colleagues who wish you to be involved in their research. By projecting yourself to the point of assessing the possible results of the study, you as investigator can consider the major issues of bias, confounding and chance variation, and consider methods by which these issues can be recognized and dealt with. You can also consider the desirability of being able to demonstrate strong associations, dose–response effects, specific relationships, and so on. By doing this, you give yourself the opportunity to incorporate into the design of the study the potential for demonstrating such features. The discussion of the study design with colleagues who are prepared to adopt a similar critical approach and who bring to bear specialist knowledge of the issues involved in the study will be a major safeguard against embarking on a study which is inadequately designed.

Introduction to Chapters 9, 10, and 11

The following chapters present examples of the application of the scheme for the assessment of causal relationships to three different types of studies; an observational cohort study, a case–control study, and a randomized trial of medical treatment. The assessment of any study involves issues which are particular to that study, and may demand specific subject matter knowledge. In these chapters the full details of all such particular issues will not be dealt with. The objective is to show that the application of the general system which has been outlined in the previous chapters will give a framework by which the major strengths and weaknesses of any study can be described, so that the reader can then concentrate on the few particular issues which are of critical importance. The studies have been chosen with a number of points in mind. They have all been published in major journals to which most readers should have ready access. They address questions of considerable importance. They are good examples of the use of the research methods which they employ, and the main issues in their interpretation are issues which are found in many other studies. At the time they were first published, their results were new findings. The reader may now have a great deal more information about the topics under consideration from more recent work, but the purpose of this text is not to deal with the whole of the subject matter introduced by these studies, but only to show how the studies themselves can be evaluated.

One way the reader may like to use these chapters is to read the studies quoted and either with or without reference to sections of the previous text, make his or her own assessment of the strengths and weaknesses of the study. The reader may then compare this assessment with the notes which follow, to see if the application of the general method will help to clarify issues which otherwise would have been ignored or confused.

For each study, the text will go through the twenty questions set out in Chapter 8, in enough detail to illustrate the major issues. It is not exhaustive: the reader will be able to add more to each issue. The major aspects of the study may be summarized in exhibits, referred to as Ex. 9.1 and so on, and reference may be made to other parts of this text; where reference is made to the original paper, reproduced here, the tables and figures are indicated by the method of the original: Figure 1, Table 1, etc., and the text by the paragraph numbers inserted in our reproduced version. For each study, a very brief summary of the major points in response to the scheme for assessment of causation is presented as an exhibit.

9. Critical appraisal of a cohort study

This chapter deals with the assessment of the study entitled, 'Neoplasia of the cervix uteri and contraception: a possible adverse effect of the pill', by M.P. Vessey, M. Lawless, K. McPherson, and D. Yeates, published in *The Lancet*, 22 October 1983, pages 930–934. This is reproduced on pages 200–210.

A. Description of the evidence:

1. What was the exposure or intervention?
2. What was the outcome?
3. What was the study design?
4. What was the study population?
5. What was the main result?

The first section of our scheme for the assessment of evidence (Ex. 8.1, p. 164) is noted above, and consists of describing the causal relationship which is being investigated in terms of the exposure and the outcome, and defining the study design and the characteristics of the study population. We then move to summarizing the main result. We could work through each of these five questions in order, but it is more natural to address them all by describing the design of the study and the results.

This is a prospective cohort study, the source population being 17 032 white married women living in England and Scotland, aged between 25 and 39 years, recruited through 17 Family Planning Association Clinics during the period 1968 to 1974 (paragraph 3). The design of this cohort study is shown in Ex. 9.1, and was previously referred to in Chapter 5 (p. 75). For this particular study, a further restriction is that all the subjects were parous (paragraph 4).

The exposed group is defined as 6838 women who were, at entry to the study, currently using oral contraceptives and had been for at least five months, and the control group is defined as the 3154 women who at entry to the study were currently using an interuterine device (IUD), also for at least five months, without prior exposure to an oral contraceptive (paragraph 2). The justification for this choice of control group is noted in the methods section, where it is pointed out that other studies from this group had shown that the incidence of cervical neoplasia in women using a diaphragm is likely to be reduced, and therefore to include them would have given a control

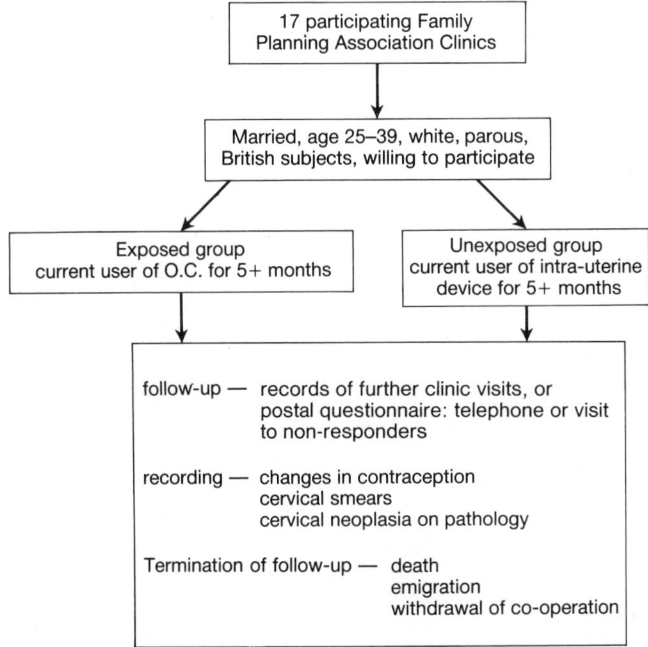

Ex. 9.1. Design of the prospective cohort study of oral contraceptive use, based on Family Planning Clinics, to assess association with cervical neoplasia (Vessey *et al.*, 1983)

group with an abnormally low rate (paragraph 4). The assumption being made therefore is that IUD users have an unmodified incidence of cervical neoplasia.

The outcome under investigation is described in the last paragraph of the methods section, being biopsy proven dysplasia, carcinoma-in-situ, or invasive cancer of the cervix uteri (paragraph 6). The analysis is made complex by the fact that women will change their contraceptive practice over time, and so the analysis is based on total accumulated use of either oral contraceptives or IUDs (paragraph 5). The main results are shown in Ex. 9.2. For each of the three outcomes defined, the observed incidence rates were higher in the oral contraceptive users than in the control group.

B. Internal validity—consideration of non-causal explanations

6. Are the results likely to be affected by observation bias?

The study has shown a higher recorded incidence of cervical neoplasia in the oral contraceptive users than in the comparison group. Our first question is:

CONTRACEPTION AND CERVICAL CANCER

	Oral contraceptive users	Intra-uterine device users
No. of women	6 838	3 154
No. of woman-years of observation	65 101	26 432

	O.C. users		I.U.D. users		
Outcome	No.	Rate/1000 w-yrs	No.	Rate/1000 w-yrs	Relative risk
Dysplasia	50	0.77	14	0.53	1.45
In situ carcinoma	47	0.72	12	0.42	1.71
Invasive cancer	13	0.20	0	0.00	infinity
All outcomes	110	1.69	26	0.98	1.72

Ex. 9.2. Main results from the study of oral contraception and cervical cancer. (Vessey *et al.*, 1983, tables I and IV)

is this difference influenced by observation bias? The extreme case would be that the excess incidence observed is not a true excess, but an artifact. To answer this question appropriately, we have to have some knowledge of the clinical and pathological methods of diagnosing cervical uterine neoplasia, and of the usual operation of diagnostic services in England and Scotland. If we do not have such specialized knowledge, we would wish to discuss this with a gynaecologist or pathologist. It is helpful to emphasize that the main issue is whether there is some systematic *bias* in the observations made in this study, rather than merely random error and inter-observer variation. The outcome used was a pathologically confirmed diagnosis made as part of routine medical care; the diagnoses were not made by pathologists working particularly in regard to this study (paragraph 6). Given that the women lived in various parts of the country, and the diagnoses were made over a long period, it seems on general principles unlikely that there would be systematic differences between the way in which the diagnoses were made or recorded in oral contraceptive users and in users of an IUD. We do not know if the pathologists would have been aware that the women were in this study, or of their contraceptive practice. The relevant question is: would clinical and pathological diagnoses of cervical neoplasia in this country during this time period be influenced by knowledge of the women's use of contraception, particularly whether or not they were using oral contraceptives? This is the specific question which we should ask gynaecologists or pathologists. Our own opinion is that during that period in time it did not seem to be a relevant issue.

If the study were repeated now, after the attention given to this publication, it is more likely that pathologists' diagnoses might be influenced by knowledge of the women's contraceptive history. Some useful information is given by the results in Ex. 9.2, given the knowledge that the milder cervical lesions are open to more inter-observer variation and dispute about their classification. If the difference in incidence between oral contraceptive users and the control group were due to observer bias, we should expect these differences to be most obvious in the milder categories of disease where the definitions are less well accepted. In fact if we had a difference in incidence of dysplasia, but no difference in carcinoma-in-situ or invasive cancer, bias would be one of the most likely explanations. The data show, in terms of relative risk, that the association is maximum for invasive cancer, and becomes weaker for the less extreme forms of disease, which argues against it being due to observer bias. We will accept that there is a certain degree of error, rather than bias, particularly in the diagnosis and recording of the milder abnormalities, but an error component alone will merely act to reduce the apparent difference between the two groups.

That deals with the accuracy of the observations of the pathological outcome. There is a second issue as to whether the two groups have had the same chance of being assessed. If the oral contraceptive users were subjected to clinical and cytological examination more frequently, the chances of detecting a cervical neoplasm would be higher, and this could give a spurious positive association. There is some relevant information. Table II shows that the two groups were similar in terms of cervical smears before study entry. In table III, information on the smear frequency per 1000 women-years is given for the two groups, and shows that within all but the lowest exposure group, the clinical smear frequency was higher in the IUD group. This would suggest that if there were any bias introduced by differences in follow-up procedures, this would produce a higher recorded incidence in the IUD group, the opposite to that found; thus bias in terms of intensity of follow-up does not give an explanation for the observed result. The data in table III apply only to smears done at the FPA clinics; some information is available on smears done elsewhere, which suggests no major difference between the two groups (paragraph 14).

Thus our answer to question 6 is that the result is unlikely to be affected by observation bias.

7. *Are the results likely to be affected by confounding?*

Our approach to this question starts with the definition of confounding: do the oral contraceptive group and the comparison group differ to a substantial extent in terms of factors which themselves would affect the incidence of cervical neoplasia? Again, if we have limited subject matter knowledge, as well as reading this paper we have to learn from other sources what factors seem likely to influence the incidence of cervical neoplasia in a population like this. We could make a list of these factors, and then decide to what extent they have been assessed in this study, and if they are likely to influence its result. Table I of the paper gives comparisons of the oral contraceptive group and the comparison group in terms of several important potential confounding factors. It presents the percentage distribution in each group, without applying any statistical tests. This is appropriate, as it is the size of the difference in the distribution of a confounding factor which is important, and whether the difference is statistically significant is irrelevant. The results of table I, also described in paragraph 7, show that the oral contraceptive users tended to be younger at first pregnancy and at marriage, and to be heavier cigarette smokers; these three differences are in the direction which would lead us to expect an increased risk of cervical neoplasia. However the oral contraceptive users were slightly younger in age at diagnosis, and of marginally higher social class distribution, two factors which would lead us to expect them to have a slightly lower incidence of cervical neoplasia.

General knowledge of the subject area, or even a brief literature review, will reveal however that current thinking suggests that the major risk factors for cervical neoplasia are early age at first intercourse and the number of sexual partners, both of which appear to have stronger relationships than factors like social class or age at marriage, and these factors have not been assessed in this study. If the oral contraceptive group had an earlier age at first intercourse, and a greater average number of sexual partners, it would be expected to have a higher incidence of cervical neoplasia. The authors provide some information, on a small sample of 75 oral contraceptive users and 25 IUD users from the main cohort who had a supplemental interview (paragraph 8); these data show that the oral contraceptive users had a somewhat earlier age at first intercourse, and a slightly higher percentage, 27 compared to 24 per cent had had more than one sexual partner. Although these differences are not large, the difficulty is that this sample is very small, and it is therefore impossible to be sure that the two groups compared in this study do not differ in terms of these important confounders.

A further confounding factor might be the use of other methods of contraception. The use of barrier methods would be expected to lead to a reduction in cervical neoplasia, and table III shows that these methods accounted for a considerably higher percentage of women-years in the oral contraceptive group than in the IUD group; this difference is in the direction of indicating a lower risk of neoplasia in the oral contraceptive users, thus strengthening the observed results.

All the women in each group were white, married and parous, although we are not given information on their parity, nor are we given any information on their distribution in terms of the location of the different recruitment clinics, whether this is different between the two groups, and whether there are any geographic differences in cervical cancer neoplasia, which if present would make geographical distribution a potential confounder.

The next step is to assess what methods have been used in the study to control confounding. In this study the only methods are the restriction criteria of all women being white, married, and parous, and we might suggest that the recruitment system through the Family Planning Association Clinics would lead to some similarity in terms of social class, which is shown in table I. Otherwise, no analytical methods of controlling confounding are used, because the authors concluded that the differences between the oral contraceptive users and the comparison groups were small enough that they thought it reasonable to use direct comparison of the two groups without further control for confounding (paragraph 10).

Our answer therefore to question 7, must be that we accept that the result is likely to be affected by confounding. The main difficulty is that we do not have adequate information on age at first intercourse or number of sexual partners, even though we can be reasonably confident about the comparability of the groups in terms of the other factors which have been assessed. We proceed therefore with the acceptance that one viable alternative hypothesis to causation is that the observed increase in cervical neoplasia in the oral contraceptive users is due to their having different sexual histories.

8. *Are the results likely to be affected by chance variation?*

The statistical results reported in the paper are $P<0.05$ in regard to the difference in incidence of invasive cancer between the groups; $P<0.02$ in regard to the incidence of all grades of cervical cancer; a significant trend relating the incidence rate of all grades to the duration of exposure among pill users (χ^2 for trend $= 8.7$, $P<0.01$), and no such trend in the IUD users (paragraph 16). The statistical methods used are not referenced, but it is possible to reproduce the P-values quoted by comparing the outcome measures for invasive cancer by a Fisher exact test (Ex. A1.4, p. 280), for total cancer by a χ^2 test (Ex. A1.3, p. 276), both based on the data in Ex. 9.2, and for the duration of use information we can apply a trend test (Ex. A1.7, p. 288) to the data given in table IV. If we repeat the tests ourselves we obtain for the comparison of all types of neoplasia a χ^2 value on one degree of freedom of 6.30 ($P = 0.012$, two-sided), from which we can calculate test based confidence limits for the overall risk ratio of 1.72, giving 95 per cent two-sided limits of 1.13 and 2.63. The important issue is that the statistical tests used appear to be appropriate, and therefore we can conclude that chance variation is a very unlikely explanation for the results seen.

In regard to Section B of our system therefore, the study is acceptable in terms of observation bias and chance variation being unlikely explanations of the results, and we proceed with the knowledge that both a causal association and an association due to confounding by another factor, most likely sexual history, are viable hypotheses to explain the results seen.

C. Internal validity—consideration of positive features of causation

9. Is there a correct time relationship?

The time relationship is appropriate, as the neoplasia cases occurred over the extended follow-up from the beginning of the study, and table II shows that the great majority of subjects had a (normal) cervical smear within the year preceding recruitment to the study. We assume that only subjects whose prior smears were normal were admitted to the study, although this is not explicitly stated. To explore the time relationship further, it would be helpful to have information on the relative risk of cervical neoplasia as a function of time since first exposure to oral contraception. This type of analysis is not presented. If such an analysis could be done it might be a considerable help in separating a causal from a confounding relationship. If the association is causal, we would expect that the increased relative risk would not be apparent shortly after first use of oral contraception, but would only become apparent after a reasonable time interval. On the other hand if the association is due to confounding, there is no reason why the relative risk estimate should vary with time since first use of oral contraception. However such an analysis would be difficult to perform even in a study of this size, because time since first use of oral contraception will be closely related to total duration of exposure to oral contraception, and will also increase along with ageing of the cohort. An appropriate analysis would have to be able to assess the relationship of relative risk to time since first use of oral contraception, controlling for total duration of use and for age.

10. Is the relationship strong?

We have already noted that the overall association for all types of neoplasia gives a relative risk of 1.72, with confidence limits of 1.13 to 2.63. This is not a particularly strong association. Perusal of the literature linking factors like early age at first intercourse and number of sexual partners to cervical neoplasia produces relative risks in excess of this, in the range of two to five, and therefore it is conceivable that a relative risk of 1.72 could be produced by confounding by such factors. For invasive cancer alone the relative risk is infinite, but this is based on rather small numbers.

11. Is there a dose–response relationship?

There is a clear and statistically significant dose–response relationship between the incidence of all types of neoplasia and the duration of use of oral contraceptives (figure). This is one of the main features of the results which is quite impressive and consistent with a causal relationship. The relevant question is to what extent this dose–response relationship helps us to decide between the main competing hypotheses of causation and confounding. If we admit that oral contraceptive users may differ from non-users in terms of sexual history factors which are related to cervical neoplasia, it is also conceivable that users of oral contraceptives for a longer time, who may largely be women who started using the pill at an earlier age, may have a more extreme distribution of these sexual history factors, and therefore the dose response relationship could also be consistent with this confounding effect. We might wonder if the absence of a similar relationship in the IUD users is an effective counter-argument to this point, but it is not clear that it is, as the social and sexual activity characteristics of IUD users are likely to be considerably different from those of oral contraceptive users.

12. Are the results consistent within the study?

There is little that can be said on this point in this particular study, the only opportunity for consistency being the relationships with different pathological grades of cervical neoplasia, which has been remarked on already.

13. Is there any specificity within the study?

There is no information presented in the analysis which allows us to assess any specificity. An aspect of specificity which, if available, might greatly help the interpretation is mentioned in paragraph 17, in that the authors attempted to determine whether cervical neoplasia was associated with a specific component of oral contraception, in terms of the hormone involved, the dose, or the brand. If a specific association were shown which was coherent with other knowledge, for example the increased risk being particularly determined by the oestrogen dose of the contraceptive, that would be a very powerful argument for causality, primarily because it is unlikely that the users of a certain type of oral contraceptive would differ from the users of another type in regard to the main potential confounding factors such as sexual history. Therefore a specific relationship with one particular type of oral contraception would be unlikely to be due to confounding. The authors state that, 'no significant findings were obtained'; unfortunately it is not very clear what this means. If it means that it was impossible to make a clear decision as to whether the relative risks for different types of oral contraceptive differed then we are no further on. If it means that the data and the analysis employed were powerful enough to detect such a difference if one existed, and the results were that the different types of oral contraception gave the same association with cervical neoplasia, this would favour confounding rather than the causality hypothesis. Given the limited number of outcome observations, it is unlikely that a powerful analysis could be done, and we will assume that the authors mean that no firm conclusion can be reached on whether such specificity exists.

Conclusions in regard to internal validity

We have now worked through the first three sections in the scheme of assessment of evidence, which puts us in a position to make a judgment about the internal validity of the study, that is the extent to which the observed results are likely to reflect a causal relationship within the study participants. Our conclusion is that there are two reasonable explanations for the results seen; (1) that they reflect a causal relationship between oral contraception and cervical neoplasia, and (2) that the observed results are due to confounding, in particular that the oral contraceptive users are likely to have had earlier sexual intercourse, a greater number of sexual partners, and other related factors which put them at higher risk of cervical neoplasia. We now proceed, with that conclusion in mind, to consider the external validity of the study.

D. External validity—generalization of the results

14. Can the study results be applied to the eligible population?

The eligible population consists of all the women fulfilling the eligibility criteria of being white, married, parous and aged 25 to 39, who could have been recruited through the Family Planning Clinics chosen in the time period stated. We are given, at least in this paper, no information about how the original cohort of 17 032 women were recruited within the clinics, and to what extent they were representative or otherwise of the entire eligible population. A reference is given to an earlier study which described these methods more fully, and if we take the trouble to refer to it, it merely states that these women were recruited as volunteers who were willing to and likely to fulfil the follow-up criteria. However the issue of selectivity applies equally to the oral contraceptive users and the IUD users, and should not therefore introduce any differences or confounding between the two groups. The second issue in regard to the eligible population, is whether all women who originally participated in the study actually provided data for the analysis, and in a long term prospective cohort study like this we would expect some losses to follow-up. The methods section tells us that the annual loss rate for reasons other than emigration or death is only about 0.3 per cent, and this is reassuring (paragraph 3). It would be more helpful to have a direct statement giving the number of subjects who started this study, to compare with the number of subjects included in these results. Again, previous reports from this group are helpful, and confirm that the losses to follow-up for any reason appear to be small, and therefore are unlikely to make the final study participants unrepresentative of the original eligible population.

15. Can the study results be applied to the source population?

This is a more difficult question, as it is up to us to define the source population, as this is not obvious from the study. We must first accept the time and place restraints of the study; the study was performed on women recruited in England and Scotland during the period 1968 to 1974. This is very important as it is relevant to the definition of the exposure; the oral contraception being investigated comprises methods which were used by women in England and Scotland during that time period. Many of the women used higher oestrogen doses than are used currently (paragraph 18).

Are the women involved in the study likely to be representative of British women using oral contraception during that time period? To answer this we would need to know the characteristics of the Family Planning Clinics in which the women were recruited, and how their clientele were chosen. That would require some further reading of the references in this paper and other work, and would lead us to suggest that these clinics catered primarily for stable middle class women. This can be confirmed by comparing the social class distribution shown in table I to general population figures. It is reinforced by the criteria that the women had to be married and stable enough to allow follow-up through these clinics. We would therefore be cautious in applying the findings of this study to different populations, for example particularly disadvantaged, or promiscuous women. However the crucial issue is not whether the study participants are a representative sample of British users of oral contraception, but whether the association seen—the increased risk observed in oral contraceptive users compared to IUD users—can be applied outside the confines of the study. We need to consider therefore the characteristics of the control group. This group share the selection characteristics of the oral contraceptive users, and also the follow-up procedures. We should expect from these selection characteristics, and also from the regular cervical cytology carried out on this group, that the incidence rate of cervical neoplasia in the control group might be below that of women in general in that country and time period. This in fact is so; no cases of invasive cancer occurred in the IUD group, while three to four would be expected on the basis of national rates (paragraph 21). While this deficiency is within the bounds of chance variation, it is also consistent with our observations about the selection of the subjects. Thus we would conclude that the results are likely to be applicable to British women using the types of oral contraception prevalent at that time, and to women sharing the main characteristics of the study group, which are a middle or upper social class and a stable lifestyle.

16. Can the study results be applied to other relevant populations?

To answer this question, we have to assess to what extent the exposure, oral contraceptive use, and the outcome, cervical neoplasia, are likely to vary between different populations. On an international basis, the types and dosages of oral contraceptives, and the sociological characteristics of those who use them, will vary considerably, and these results might not apply to other types of oral contraception. In regard to cervical neoplasia, the range of incidence rates in different societies is very large. It is reasonable to suppose, unless we have specific evidence to the contrary, that a causal association between oral contraception and cervical neoplasia will hold irrespective of the influence of other factors, although its importance will vary with the background incidence rate. As against this there are considerable differences between various cancers and hormonally related diseases in different racial groups, and the relationship between oral contraceptive use and cervical neoplasia might be truly different in different racial groups; that must remain an open question until we have some direct evidence.

We can now review the issues of external validity. Although there are, as there always will be, considerable limitations in the assurances we can give that the results will be applicable to other populations, it is relevant to ask the other question, which is: is there any evidence that the results would *not* be applicable to other populations? and it is reasonable to accept that these results are likely to apply to other groups of women. The major limitation is in the exposure assessed in this study; oral contraceptives used in other societies or at other time periods may be considerably different from those used by the participants in this study.

E. Comparison of the results with other evidence

We have gone about as far as we can in assessing this particular paper. Further discussion will take into account other relevant information. The interested reader should go to the literature for an up to date review which would put this paper in the context of contemporary knowledge. It is not appropriate to the aim of this book to consider such issues here, and the information would be out of date by the time the reader sees it. We can usefully consider the other evidence available at the time of publication of this paper. We can also use our assessment of the paper to identify the particular questions which need to be answered by other work.

17. Are the results consistent with other evidence, particularly evidence from studies of similar or more powerful study design?

The study design used here is a powerful one. For a topic such as this, the scientifically ideal method of assessment, a large scale randomized trial comparing women on oral contraception with similar women using no contraception or using other methods, is impossible for practical and ethical reasons. A randomized trial to compare one particular type of oral contraception with another type could be set up, but no such study has been done on anything like the scale required to be relevant to this question. A large scale prospective cohort study with good follow-up is therefore the best method of assessing the question. Two other such cohort studies are referred to (paragraph 22); one gave results consistent with those of this paper but open to the same confounding; in the other a rather different outcome, the rate of progression of cervical dysplasia to carcinoma-in-situ, was reported as being greater in women using a particular oral contraceptive than in women using IUD's.

The other powerful method of assessing this type of association is a case–control study comparing women with cervical neoplasia with unaffected controls. Several such case–control studies are noted in paragraph 22; two of these showed a positive association and three showed no association. As the authors of this paper point out, these studies are only relevant if they had adequate power to detect a positive association if one was truly present, and this requires an adequate number of subjects who have had extensive exposure to oral contraception. The current authors suggest that the negative case–control studies did not have such power, as they had insufficient long term users of oral contraceptives in the study.

18. Does the total evidence suggest any specificity?

The most relevant issue here would be the question of the relationship to a specific type or dose of oral contraceptive, and the other evidence is as lacking on this point as the current paper. One could also include under this heading the rather naive suggestion that perhaps women who use oral contraceptives are overly diagnosed with almost anything, and there is a nonspecific over-diagnosis or over-reporting effect. This could be adequately argued against by referring to other results from this study and from other cohort studies showing a lack of association between oral contraceptive use and many other outcomes, and even a protective effect against some other conditions such as benign breast lesions.

19. Are the results plausible, in terms of a biological mechanism?

There is a short comment on this issue in paragraph 25, stating that there is some experimental evidence that cervical tissues are known to be responsive to contraceptive steriods, and noting again the study suggesting an increase in progression rate from cervical dysplasia.

20. If a major effect is shown, is it coherent with the distribution of the exposure and the outcome?

One can discuss whether the current study, if it reflects causality, gives a major effect. On the one hand, the overall relative risk of 1.72 is not particularly high, and there are many other factors which have strong influences on the incidence of cervical neoplasia. On the other, the exposure under consideration is very widespread, and therefore the attributable risk may be considerable. To assess this question one would need to know for the particular population involved what proportion of women from different age groups had had the length of exposure to oral contraception which is associated with increased risk in this study. A coherent effect would be shown by a rise in the incidence of cervical neoplasia in populations in which a substantial proportion of women had had extensive exposure to oral contraception. The authors point out that the reported increase in the incidence of the disease in younger women in England and Wales over the decade prior to 1983 would be consistent with such an effect (paragraph 24). However there are many other relevant factors, and this argument of coherence does not add greatly to our overall judgment.

Conclusions

After working through all these points, we are left with two reasonable hypotheses which would explain the observations seen (Ex. 9.3). One is that they do reflect a causal relationship, and the other is that the association is due to confounding, most likely by aspects of sexual history. We would also conclude that the association seen is likely to be applicable to other populations exposed to the same types of oral contraception as were used in this study, although the same alternative hypothesis would apply.

Implications

The results are therefore consistent with a causal relationship, but as the alternative hypothesis of confounding is also likely we cannot make a firm conclusion concerning a causal relationship. Because of this, taking action to

ASSESSMENT OF A COHORT STUDY

Oral contraception and cervical cancer: Vessey *et al.*, 1983.

A. Description of evidence

1	Exposure	oral contraceptives, as used in the UK from 1968. Controls: users of IUD's.
2	Outcome	cervical dysplasia, carcinoma-in-situ, and invasive cancer
3	Design	prospective cohort study
4	Study population	white, married, parous women aged 25–39, recruited from Family Planning Association clinics in England and Wales, 1968–74
5	Main result	higher incidence of each outcome in oral contraceptive users: overall relative risk 1.72

B. Non-causal explanations

6	Observation bias	observations not blind, but bias unlikely
7	Confounding	likely—sexual history factors not controlled
8	Chance	unlikely; 95 per cent confidence limits for overall association 1.13–2.63

C. Positive features of causation

9	Time relationship	correct
10	Strength	only moderate—weaker than associations of outcome with some potential confounders
11	Dose–response	present in regard to length of use of oral contraceptives
12	Consistency	excess seen for each grade of outcome.
13	Specificity	not assessed

Summary of internal validity: most likely explanations are causality, or confounding by sexual history factors.

D. External validity

14	To the eligible population	high validity—very few losses to follow-up
15	To the source population	study participants are volunteers, not typical of all women in source population, and likely to vary systematically from the general population: but the association seen is likely to apply widely, for the same definitions of exposure and of outcome
16	To other populations	

E. Other evidence

17	Consistency	consistent with the, limited, other relevant evidence
18	Specificity	no information
19	Plausibility	acceptable, on limited evidence
20	Coherence	association not strong enough to make this crucial: coherence with some limited evidence

Summary of external validity: if result is valid, it is likely to apply to other women using the types of oral contraceptive common in this study.

Ex. 9.3. Assessment of causality in a cohort study of oral contraception and cervical cancer (Vessey *et al.*, 1983)

advise women to avoid oral contraception or to change their type of oral contraception, or taking action to influence the availability or use of these drugs would not be appropriate. We can use this result to increase the priority given to other opportunities to assess this possible causal relationship, particularly studies which can deal with the main alternative explanation, that of confounding by sexual history factors. We should ask if it is possible to investigate sexual history in the participants in this study to a much greater extent than has already been done; for example it might be possible to mount a case-control study within this cohort, taking the observed cases of cervical neoplasia and a random sample of unaffected women, and obtaining further details of the relevant confounders from them.

Clinical investigations and animal experimental work investigating the relationship between oral contraceptives and the biology of the cervical epithelium are also relevant. It is important to look for opportunities to perform studies like this one in populations using those oral contraceptives which are in widespread use currently.

Although we cannot state that the association seen is causal, we have come to the conclusion that it is real. We therefore conclude that women with extensive use of oral contraception are at higher risk of cervical neoplasia, whether that higher risk is due to a causal effect of oral contraception, or due to the association between long term oral contraceptive use and other factors which confer an increased risk. It is therefore appropriate to ensure a high degree of surveillance by cervical smears for long term oral contraceptive users, so a practical recommendation can be made that women who have used oral contraceptives for perhaps more than five years should be assessed to see if they have had regular cervical smears. It is useful to realize that we can be much firmer about this recommendation than any recommendation concerning changes in oral contraceptive practice, because this recommendation holds whether the association seen is causal or due to confounding, whereas any recommendation about changing oral contraceptive practices is appropriate only if the association is causal. The authors' final paragraph sets forth this conclusion.

Follow-up to this study

The reader will find it interesting and constructive to look at the follow-up of the scientific issues. This can conveniently be done by a literature search, or by using the Scientific Citations Index, as well as from informal reading of subsequent journals. Several points were raised in correspondence to *The Lancet*, and the authors' reply on 10 December 1983 is of interest (Vessey *et al.*, 1983a). It gives further information on the possible confounding effects of sexual history factors. The authors state that they had considered trying to obtain this information on a larger sample of women in the cohort but had found that this detailed investigation caused some resentment and could, if extended, have jeopardized the cooperation necessary for the main prospective study. They show that within the small group on which they had data, there was no association between duration of oral contraceptive use and early intercourse or multiple sexual partners. They also show for the whole cohort that adjustment by stratification for age at first marriage, age at first term pregnancy and cigarette smoking made no substantial difference to the variation of incidence of cervical neoplasia with duration of oral contraceptive use. These points are helpful, but the lack of data on sexual history for the whole cohort remains the major limitation of the study. At the time of writing (1987) two important subsequent studies have been published. A very large study, which in the main analysis compared 699 women with invasive cervical cancer to 3913 hospital controls, was carried out in collaborating centres in twelve countries (WHO Collaborative Study, 1985). This study was restricted to invasive cancer and was based mainly in the developing world, and the patients represent a mixture of races. Discrepancies between the results and those of the study we have examined in detail might be expected from those differences alone. However, because it is a case–control study using extensive interviews, more information is available on potential confounding factors such as age at first sexual relations, number of sexual relationships, and history of vaginal discharge. The relative risk for ever use of oral contraceptives was 1.4, with confidence limits of 1.2 to 1.7 after adjustments for age and centre only. However adjustment for the sexual history factors and for history of cervical smears reduced this to 1.2, with confidence limits of 1.0 and 1.4. The relationship between risk and duration of use of oral contraceptives was assessed, and showed a dose–response relationship even in the adjusted data, the risk with over 8 years' use being 1.6, with 95 per cent limits of 1.0 to 2.6. The assessment of the internal validity of this study leads to rather similar conclusions to that of the prospective study, in that bias appears not to be a major problem, chance variation is quite a likely explanation as shown by the confidence limits, and although some aspects of confounding were dealt with, there is still a considerable likelihood of residual confounding. The information collected on sexual history seems likely to be incomplete and no information was available on some other possible confounders such as smoking. The authors of this case–control study come to a similar conclusion as the authors of the prospective cohort study, that the results suggest either a causal relationship with a low relative risk or reflect residual confounding.

Brinton *et al.* (1986) compared 479 women with invasive cervical cancer, identified in five major cities in the USA, with 789 controls selected from the community by a random digit dialling technique: that is, using random phone numbers to enquire about eligible subjects and then attempting to enrol them as controls. Eligible cases and controls were then visited at home for interviews; the interviewers carried sets of photographs of all oral contraceptive preparations ever marketed in the USA. A slightly lower proportion of case subjects than of controls had ever used oral contraceptives, giving an odds ratio of 0.8. However, there was strong negative confounding by the interval since the last cervical smear had been taken: oral contraceptive users were much more likely to have had a recent smear, and this was associated with a 5 to 6 fold decrease in the risk of cervical cancer. This was controlled both by multivariate analysis and by stratification: from the latter analysis it was shown that within each stratum of time since last cervical smear, the case subjects reported oral contraceptive use more frequently than did the controls. Multivariate analysis also took into account several other confounders, such as education, number of sexual partners, age at first intercourse, and history of genital infection; adjusting for all these, and for age and ethnic origin, gave an odds ratio for ever use of oral contraceptives of 1.5 with 95 per cent confidence limits of 1.1 to 2.1. This result is consistent with those from the other studies. Again, a positive trend in risk with increasing duration of use was seen. This study is the best of those available in its power to assess the confounding effects of other variables, and its results favour a causal relationship rather than one secondary to associations with any of the major accepted risk factors for cervical cancer. However, even with this study, confounding cannot be excluded, and the mechanism for the increased risk is still unclear.

NEOPLASIA OF THE CERVIX UTERI AND CONTRACEPTION: A POSSIBLE ADVERSE EFFECT OF THE PILL

M. P. Vessey M. Lawless
K. McPherson D. Yeates

University Department of Community Medicine and General Practice, Radcliffe Infirmary, Oxford OX2 6HE

Reproduced from *The Lancet* **2**, 930–934, 1983

Summary

1. The incidence of biopsy-proven cervical neoplasia during a 10-year follow-up was determined in 6838 parous women who entered the Oxford-Family Planning Association contraceptive study while using oral contraceptives and 3154 parous women who entered the study while using an intrauterine device (IUD). Risk factors for cervical

neoplasia, continuation of attendance at family planning clinics, and frequency of examination by cervical cytology were similar in the two groups. All 13 cases of invasive cancer occurred in women in the oral contraceptive group; 9 had more than 6 years' use of the pill. Both carcinoma-in-situ and dysplasia also occurred more frequently in the oral contraceptive group than in the IUD group, and when the two conditions were considered together there was a trend in incidence with duration of oral contraceptive use. The incidence for all three forms of neoplasia combined rose from 0.9 per 1000 woman-years in those with up to 2 years' pill use to 2.2 per 1000 woman-years in those with more than 8 years' pill use. Amongst IUD users, there was no such trend in incidence with duration of use: the rate fluctuated around 1.0 per 1000 woman-years. The great majority of cases of invasive cancer were detected by means of cervical smears and were treated while the disease was still curable. Long-term users of oral contraceptives should have regular cervical cytological examination.

Introduction

2. In 1978, we reported some results from the Oxford-Family Planning Association (Oxford-FPA) contraceptive study which suggested that use of a diaphragm might offer protection against cervical neoplasia.[1] We also noted that all 6 women in the study in whom invasive cancer of the cervix had developed at that time had been using oral contraceptives. Since then, we have kept the accumulating data under scrutiny and we now present an analysis in which the incidence of cervical neoplasia in 6838 parous women who entered the study while using oral contraceptives is compared with that in 3154 parous women who entered the study while using an intrauterine device (IUD).

Methods

3. The methods used in the Oxford-FPA contraceptive study have been described in detail elsewhere.[2] In brief, 17 032 White married women, aged 25–39 years, were recruited at 17 family planning clinics in England and Scotland during the period 1968–74. At entry, each of these women had to be either a current user of oral contraceptives of at least 5 months' standing or a current user of a diaphragm or an IUD of at least 5 months' standing without prior exposure to the pill. These women are being followed up at the clinics or, when necessary, by post, telephone, or home visiting. The annual lapse-rate for reasons other than emigration or death is only about 0.3%. Information

collected about each woman during follow-up is coordinated at each clinic by a research assistant and includes details of pregnancies and their outcome, changes in contraceptive practices, results of smears taken at the clinic and reasons for referral to hospital as an outpatient or an inpatient. Hospital discharge diagnoses are confirmed by obtaining copies of discharge letters or summaries. A copy of the histological report is also requested for any patient with a neoplastic condition.

4. The object of the present analysis was to see whether or not there was a correlation between the duration of use of oral contraceptives and the incidence of cervical neoplasia. Accordingly, we decided to focus our attention on women entering the study while using the pill. We judged that women using a diaphragm would be unsatisfactory as a comparison group in view of the relatively low incidence of cervical neoplasia among them,[1] and instead we decided to use for this purpose the women entering the study while using an IUD. In our previous report[1] we had found the standardised incidence of cervical neoplasia in the IUD entry group to be similar to that in the oral contraceptive entry group. Since only a handful of IUD users were nulliparous at recruitment, we were obliged to limit our analysis (both of oral contraceptive users and IUD users) to parous subjects. Data for nulliparous women who developed invasive cancer are, however, included for completeness in table V. [Table V is not reproduced here.]
5. Our approach to the analysis was to compute woman-years of observation in the oral contraceptive and IUD entry groups within five duration-of-use categories (up to 24 months, 25–48 months, 49–72 months, 73–96 months, 97 months or more). Women entered the analysis at the point dictated by the duration of use of the relevant method before entry to the study (for example, a woman recruited to the investigation after 58 months use of an IUD began to contribute woman-years of observation in the third duration-of-use group). Women left the analysis when any of the following events occurred: (a) hysterectomy, (b) histologically confirmed diagnosis of cervical neoplasia, (c) end of follow-up, and (d) loss to follow-up. In addition, women in the IUD entry group left the analysis if they switched to oral contraception. From the above it will be apparent that the analysis is concerned not with continuous use of the method, but rather with total accumulated use. Thus a woman stopping oral contraception permanently after accumulating 78 months of pill use would continue to contribute woman-years of observation to the fourth duration-of-use group indefinitely.
6. "Cervical neoplasia" in the present analysis includes biopsy proven dysplasia, carcinoma-in-situ, and invasive cancer. These diagnoses represent the individual opinions of many local histopathologists rather

than that of one "reference" histopathologist and must, therefore, be treated with some caution. It should be noted, however, that women using oral contraceptives and IUDs were recruited at each of the 17 participating clinics and that there is no reason to suspect that any one histopathologist would have received a disproportionate amount of the material from women using a particular contraceptive method.

Subjects

7. Women in the two contraceptive groups were quite closely comparable with respect to factors known to predict the risk of cervical neoplasia in the Oxford-FPA study[1] (table I). The oral contraceptive users were slightly younger at marriage and at first term pregnancy, and were slightly heavier cigarette smokers than the IUD users. But the IUD users

Table I. Comparison of women in the two contraceptive groups at entry to study

Attribute	**Oral contraceptive group (6838) (%)**	**IUD group (3154) (%)**
Age (years):		
25–29	42	35
30–34	35	39
35–39	23	26
Age at first term pregnancy (yr):		
15–19	15	11
20–24	59	57
25–29	23	27
30–	3	4
Age at marriage (yr):		
15–19	30	26
20–24	61	63
25–29	8	10
30–	1	1
*Social class of husband:**		
I–II	34	33
III	54	53
IV–V	12	14
Cigarettes smoked (per day):		
None ever	50	57
Ex-smoker	12	11
1–4	5	6
5–14	15	14
15–	18	12

*Registrar General's classification.

were slightly older and of marginally lower social class than the pill users.

8. Unfortunately, data about age at first intercourse and number of sexual partners are not collected routinely in the Oxford-FPA study. In 1977, however, a sample of 75 women who had entered the study while using the pill and 25 women who had entered the study while using an IUD were interviewed and inquiries were made about their sexual histories.[1] 8% of both groups reported first having sexual intercourse at age 17 years or less while an additional 30% of pill users and 20% of IUD users stated that they first experienced intercourse at 18 or 19 years of age. In addition, 27% of pill users and 24% of IUD users indicated that they had had more than one sexual partner.
9. At the time of recruitment to the study, a record was made for each woman of the date of the most recent smear to be taken at the family planning clinic. The pattern was almost identical for pill users and IUD users (table II).

Table II. Most recent clinic smear before recruitment to study

Smear	Oral group(%)	IUD group (%)
Within 12 mo of admission	72	75
Within 13–24 mo of admission	14	14
More than 24 mo before admission	6	5
No smear recorded	8	6
Total	100	100

10. As a result of these analyses, we concluded that it was reasonable to proceed to direct comparisons between the oral contraceptive and IUD entry groups.

Results

Comparability of Study Groups during Follow-up

11. Some information about the comparability of the two study groups during the follow-up period is summarised in table III. In examining the figures, it is important to bear in mind the exact way in which the analyses were conducted (see Methods).
12. Within the five total duration-of-use groups, the ages of the oral and IUD users were, as expected, very much the same. Rates of attendance at the family planning clinics were also closely similar, but clinic

Table III. Comparability of two contraceptive groups during follow-up

Attribute	Contraceptive group	Total duration of contraceptive use* (mo)				
		– 24	25–48	49–72	73–96	79 +
Woman-years of observation	Oral	5772	13071	15346	12745	18167
	IUD	2429	4899	5535	4879	8690
Mean age of women (yr)	Oral	33.6	34.3	35.5	36.8	39.3
	IUD	33.7	34.3	35.7	37.3	40.3
Percentage of women-years accumulated while subject still attending clinic (at least one contact/yr)	Oral	50.3	50.6	49.3	48.3	44.9
	IUD	53.4	54.0	49.8	46.5	45.4
Clinic smear frequency per 1000 woman-years	Oral	320	304	304	299	287
	IUD	305	368	359	348	333
Percentage of woman-years accumulated while using:						
Oral contraceptives	Oral	40.0	46.3	49.3	52.7	50.9
	IUD	—	—	—	—	—
IUD	Oral	8.0	8.2	6.6	5.5	5.0
	IUD	56.0	69.2	73.4	77.3	86.1
Barrier method	Oral	17.7	14.0	12.1	11.6	12.2
	IUD	9.7	5.7	5.3	3.1	3.4
Vasectomy	Oral	11.8	12.2	15.3	14.7	14.1
	IUD	9.2	10.2	9.0	9.1	3.7
Other or no method	Oral	22.5	19.3	16.7	15.5	17.8
	IUD	25.1	14.9	12.3	10.5	6.8

*Oral contraceptives for oral group, IUD's for IUD group.

cervical smear rates were slightly higher in the IUD group than in the oral contraceptive group. In interpreting the data on use of other methods of birth control, it should be remembered that there is evidence that occlusive methods[1] and vasectomy[3] may offer some protection against cervical neoplasia. Such methods were used more frequently by those in the oral contraceptive group than by those in the IUD group.

13. Women with long durations of oral contraceptive use were slightly more likely to be heavy smokers and to have married and have had their first term pregnancy at an early age than women with short durations of use. Similar small differences were, however, also apparent in the IUD group.

14. Data about smears taken outside the family planning clinics are not routinely collected during the Oxford-FPA study, but some information was available for the small samples of pill and IUD users referred to earlier. Smear examinations were not often performed outside the clinic and the rates for oral contraceptive users and IUD users were much the same (123 and 114 per 1000 woman-years of observation, respectively).

15. As a result of these analyses, we concluded that the two study groups remained closely comparable during follow-up but that, if anything, rates of cervical neoplasia might be expected to be slightly higher in the IUD group because cervical smears and the use of non-occlusive methods of birth control were both a little more frequent in this group.

Incidence of Cervical Neoplasia

16. All 13 cases of invasive cancer occurred in the oral contraceptive group ($p<0.05$) while, in addition, there was evidence of a positive correlation between the risk of this condition and length of exposure to the pill (table IV). Both carcinoma-in-situ and dysplasia also had higher overall incidences in the oral contraceptive group than in the IUD group, although neither difference reached statistical significance. There was no indication of any trend in the incidence of carcinoma-in-situ with duration of oral contraceptive use, but there was such a trend for dysplasia and for the two conditions combined. The aggregated data for all forms of cervical neoplasia provided considerable evidence for an association with oral contraceptive use. Not only was the overall incidence nearly 75% higher in the pill group than in the IUD group ($p<0.02$), but there was also a statistically significant regression of the rate on duration of exposure amongst the pill users (χ_1^2 trend = 8.7, $p<0.01$, see accompanying figure) with no suggestion of such an association amongst the IUD users (χ_1^2 trend = 1.1, NS).

17. We attempted to determine whether cervical neoplasia was associated with a specific oestrogen or progestogen, with any particular dose of

Table IV. Incidence* of biopsy-proven cervical neoplasia in two contraceptive groups in relation to total duration of use

Type of neoplasia	Contraceptive group	Total duration of contraceptive use (mo)					
		– 24	25–48	49–72	73–96	97–	Total
Invasive cancer	Oral	0.17(1)	0.00(0)	0.20(3)	0.24(3)	0.33(6)	0.20(13)
	IUD	0.00(0)	0.00(0)	0.00(0)	0.00(0)	0.00(0)	0.00(0)
Carcinoma-in-situ	Oral	0.52(3)	0.92(12)	0.52(8)	0.55(7)	0.94(17)	0.72(47)
	IUD	0.82(2)	0.41(2)	0.18(1)	0.61(3)	0.46(4)	0.45(12)
Cervical dysplasia	Oral	0.17(1)	0.15(2)	0.91(14)	1.26(16)	0.94(17)	0.77(50)
	IUD	0.82(2)	0.61(3)	0.72(4)	0.61(3)	0.23(2)	0.53(14)
Total—preinvasive neoplasia	Oral	0.69(4)	1.07(14)	1.43(22)	1.81(23)	1.88(34)	1.49(97)
	IUD	1.64(4)	1.02(5)	0.90(5)	1.22(6)	0.69(6)	0.98(26)
Grand total	Oral	0.86(5)	1.07(14)	1.63(25)	2.05(26)	2.21(40)	1.69(110)
	IUD	1.64(4)	1.02(5)	0.90(5)	1.22(6)	0.69(6)	0.98(26)
Woman-years of observation	Oral	5772	13071	15346	12745	18167	65101
	IUD	2429	4899	5535	4879	8690	26432

*Results are given as rates per 1000 woman-years with numbers of affected women in parentheses.

oestrogen, or with a brand of oral contraceptive, by comparing the pills used by the affected women with those used by comparable control groups of unaffected women. No significant findings were obtained.

18. It should be noted that a high proportion of the oral contraceptive use in our study relates to products containing 50 μg oestrogen or more.

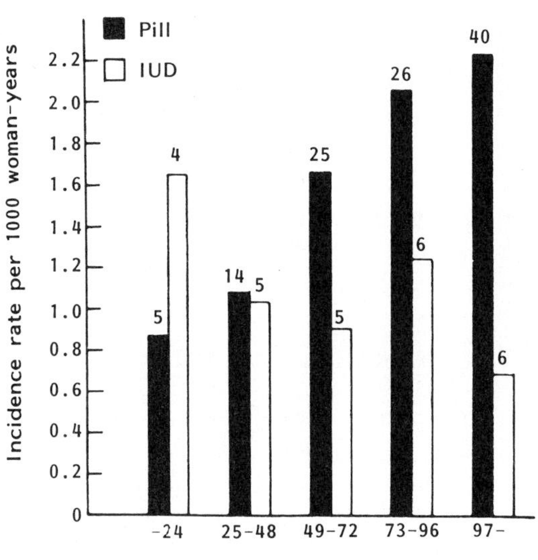

Fig. I. Incidence of cervical neoplasia (preinvasive and invasive) by total duration of contraceptive use

Discussion

19. Studies attempting to relate the risk of neoplasia of the cervix uteri to the use of different contraceptive methods are beset by many difficulties.[4] First, it is extremely difficult to identify groups of women for comparison who have the same intrinsic risk of the disease. Secondly, women tend to change contraceptive methods fairly frequently and this can easily blur the contrasts under investigation. Thirdly, since almost all preinvasive lesions and many invasive ones are detected by cervical cytology, any substantial difference in the pattern of smear examinations between the groups being compared may easily lead to incorrect conclusions being drawn. Fourthly, histopathologists vary greatly in their interpretation and classification of preinvasive lesions of the cervix and this can lead to serious bias if any one pathologist

receives a disproportionate amount of material from women using a particular contraceptive method.

20. We believe that we have dealt as adequately as possible with each of these difficulties and, accordingly, we regard our findings, especially those for invasive cancer of the cervix, as disturbing (although not, of course, conclusive). Not only are the overall incidences of invasive cancer, carcinoma-in-situ, and dysplasia higher in the oral contraceptive group than in the IUD group, but, more importantly, the data for invasive cancer and for the two types of preinvasive lesion combined indicate a relation between the risk of neoplasia and duration of oral contraceptive use. By contrast, there is no suggestion of any such relation amongst the IUD users. We have been unable to find any association between a particular type of oral contraceptive and increased risk.

21. We were a little surprised at the absence of any cases of invasive cancer in the IUD group, but we estimate that, at the national rates, only about 3 or 4 would have been expected. The observed deficiency could, therefore, have occurred by chance. Alternatively, cervical cytology may have been particularly effective at preventing the occurrence of invasive disease in the IUD users.

22. A large number of epidemiological studies concerned with oral contraception and the risk of cervical neoplasia have been published. Most have been well reviewed by a World Health Organisation Scientific Group.[5] Of the case–control studies, those by Worth and Boyes,[6] Thomas,[7] and Boyce *et al.*[8] indicated no relation, while those by Ory *et al.*[9] and Harris *et al.*[10] showed a positive association between risk and duration of use. The negative studies included very few long-term users of oral contraceptives; no association between exposure to the pill and the risk of cervical neoplasia would have been apparent in our study if the data had been restricted to women with up to 48 months' (or even up to 72 months') use of oral contraceptives. Other cohort studies of cervical neoplasia and the pill have tended to produce positive results. Thus in the Walnut Creek study a statistically significant association between the incidence of carcinoma-in-situ and duration of pill use was reported,[11] although it was subsequently suggested that this result was largely attributable to confounding by differences in sexual activity, both between users and non-users of oral contraceptives and among women with different durations of oral contraceptive use.[12] Again, in a large cohort study conducted in Los Angeles, rates of progression from cervical dysplasia to carcinoma-in-situ were much higher in women using 'Ovulen' than in women using IUDs.[13]

23. Studies of the possible relation between IUD use and cervical neoplasia are few. They have been reviewed by Edelman *et al.*[14] who have concluded that there is no evidence of any increased risk.

24. Death rates from cancer of the cervix and incidences for invasive cervical cancer and for carcinoma-in-situ have been rising steadily in women up to 34 years of age in England and Wales during the past decade.[15] It has generally been considered that these trends are attributable to changes in sexual behaviour, but the possibility that prolonged oral contraceptive use is also making a contribution should be borne in mind.

25. It is uncertain by what mechanism oral contraceptives might have an unfavourable influence on the risk of cervical neoplasia, but cervical tissues are known to be responsive to the influence of contraceptive steroids.[16,17] Furthermore, if oral contraceptives do indeed speed up the "transit time" from cervical dysplasia to more serious neoplastic lesions, as described by Stern *et al.*,[13] this might explain why we have observed a substantial relation between pill use and invasive cancer.

26. We conclude that our data offer considerable support to the view that long-term oral contraceptive use may increase the risk of cervical neoplasia. We cannot, however, be sure that our results are not attributable to some subtle influence of confounding, perhaps by sexual factors—indeed, it is unlikely that any observational study will ever be able to provide conclusive results. We nonetheless recommend that women who have accumulated more than, say, 4 years of oral contraceptive use should regularly have cervical smears. The data shown in table V suggest that this procedure should enable serious disease to be detected and treated while it is curable.

[Acknowledgements and references omitted]

Reproduced by permission of the publishers and the first author, to whom thanks are given.

10. Critical appraisal of a case-control study

The paper for discussion is, 'Increased risk of endometrial carcinoma among users of conjugated estrogens', by H.K. Ziel and W.D. Finkle, *New England Journal of Medicine*, 4 December 1975, **293**, 1167–1170. This is reproduced on pages 223–229.

A. Description of the evidence

1. What was the exposure or intervention?
2. What was the outcome?
3. What was the study design?
4. What was the study population?
5. What was the main result?

The exposure is the use of conjugated estrogenic† drugs, as recorded in medical records up to one year before the date of diagnosis of the cases, or the equivalent time for the controls. The outcome is the pathologically confirmed diagnosis of endometrial adenocarcinoma or adenoacanthoma. The design is an individually matched retrospective case-control study. The case subjects were diagnosed at the Kaiser Permanente Medical Center between 1 July 1970 and 31 December 1974, and were reported to its tumour registry. For each case, two controls were chosen from the membership files of the health plan which operates this hospital, matched for birth date within one year, area of residence by postal code, duration of health plan membership, and possession of an intact uterus. The main result of the study: estrogen use was recorded in 57 per cent of cases and in 15 per cent of controls, giving an odds ratio of 7.6 for 'ever use' (Table 1 (p 223), paragraph 7).

We proceed first to assess the internal validity of this result.

B. Internal validity—consideration of non-causal explanations

6. Are the results likely to be affected by observation bias?

Being a case-control study, the major problems relate to the assessment of exposure. Assessment of disease status is straightforward; for the cases this

† In keeping with the original, we shall use the American spelling.

was a pathologically confirmed diagnosis with little chance of inaccuracy; it is possible that some of the control subjects had undiagnosed endometrial adenocarcinoma, but this would result only in a reduction of the observed risk ratio.

The information on estrogen use is based on a medical record review done in a blind fashion. One clerk obtained the records for each set of cases and controls, and concealed all information recorded after a reference date one year before the date of diagnosis for the case, and a corresponding date for the controls. A different clerk abstracted the information from each record, without knowing if the record belonged to a case or a control (paragraph 6). Further information on the quality of the medical records would be helpful, in particular any independent assessment of the completeness and accuracy of drug recording. There could be substantial under-reporting of drug usage, as drugs might have been used which were not prescribed within this particular health plan, or were not recorded; also, some drugs prescribed may not have been used. Such errors, if randomly distributed amongst all subjects, would serve only to reduce the observed association. The crucial question is whether there is any likelihood of estrogen use being more completely recorded in those subjects who later were diagnosed as having endometrial cancer, than in the control subjects. The blindness of the abstraction, and the exclusion of any material relating to the period one year before diagnosis provides some protection. Could other factors affect this? Endometrial cancer is more common in the higher socio-economic groups; might such patients have more completely recorded drug histories? This seems unlikely as all the study participants used the same health care system. Is it possible that patients who eventually were diagnosed with endometrial cancer had a more frequent history of gynaecological and related problems, resulting not only in a greater prescribing of these drugs but also a greater recording of such prescribing? Paragraphs 13 to 15 show that for parity, obesity, and age at menopause, the data were more complete for the cases than for the controls; could the information on estrogens also be more complete? Counter-arguments are that no excess was seen for several other drugs, an indication for the use of estrogens was recorded more frequently in the controls, (paragraph 17), and that the association was very strong (see below). It seems unwise to accept totally results based on review of one medical record, without independent verification, and the issue of observation bias cannot be dismissed.

7. Are the results likely to be affected by confounding?

The subjects were matched by age, area of residence (which probably gives some measure of socio-economic matching), and by duration of health plan membership: a matched analysis has been performed. Potential confounding factors are those which are related to the incidence of endometrial cancer, and also to the use of estrogenic drugs. The existing literature on endometrial cancer is reviewed in the paper; at the time the paper was written there were several recognized risk factors, such as high parity, obesity, and late age at menopause. For each of these, the authors have used information from the medical records to assess the confounding effect by stratified analysis. However there are substantial missing data on each of these topics. Rather than presenting unconfounded odds ratio estimates obtained from the stratified analysis, the authors have used a less familiar technique in calculating the 'confounding risk ratio', which is a measure of the extent to which the association is produced by confounding (paragraphs 13 to 15). An explanation of this method is given at the end of this chapter. For each of the three factors of parity, obesity, and age at menopause, the confounding effect is very minor. However, this analysis is limited by the completeness and the detail of the data on these factors. No other confounding factors are dealt with. We would need to review the literature on endometrial cancer to see whether any important factors have been omitted. One such is racial origin, which is not mentioned. No other factors have been shown to have major associations. Some protection against the observed association being due to confounding by other risk factors for endometrial cancer is given by the strength of the association; the odds ratio is high compared to the odds ratios of 1.5 to 3 usually quoted for factors such as parity or obesity.

At the time this paper was published there was little written on the factors related to estrogen use. Of prime importance is the indication for estrogen usage, and as with any drug association we must consider whether the observed association with the drug could be disguising a true association with the indication for the drug. This is difficult, as the indications for the use of conjugated estrogens are unclear, and must reflect psychological and social factors as well as medical ones. The most frequently recorded indication was hot flashes (paragraph 17). If the case patients used more estrogenic drugs, and if the indications for their use were the same, this implies that the case subjects suffered from hot flashes more frequently than did the controls, suffered from them more severely, sought treatment more readily, or for some other reason were given these drugs as treatment more readily. There is thus a competing hypothesis that endometrial cancer could be related to hot flashes. Further discussion of this will come when evidence from outside the study is considered. A further possibility is that cases might have a high usage of drugs in general; this however can be dismissed as the cases were recorded as using diazepam, reserpine and thyroid drugs *less* commonly than were the controls (paragraph 17).

Thus we have protection against confounding by most of the major known risk factors for endometrial carcinoma. There is, however, a viable alternative hypothesis to causation: that the disease is related not to the use of these drugs but to the indications for their use.

8. Are the results likely to be affected by chance variation?

The estimated odds ratio is 7.6, and the associated *P*-value is less than 10^{-8}, giving 95 per cent two-sided confidence limits of 4.3 and 13.4 (paragraph 7 and footnote). Thus chance variation can be excluded. The methods used in the statistical analysis are a little different from those presented in this text; a note on them is given at the end of this chapter. Some publications will use more complex methods than those described in this book, which may have particular advantages for that study. The results should however not be greatly different from those obtained by the methods described here. The reader might like to apply the methods for analysis of a matched case-control study which are presented in Appendix I (Ex.A1.6, p. 286). These give an odds ratio of 8.2, and an associated χ^2 statistic of 48.8.

Summary: non-causal explanations

Thus of the three non-causal explanations, we can effectively exclude chance, but must proceed bearing in mind the possibilities of observation bias, and of confounding, particularly by the indication for the drug usage.

C. Internal validity—consideration of positive features of causation

9. Is there a correct time relationship?

This study, as is common with case control studies, is fairly weak in regard to time relationships. The method of data collection has the important feature of excluding any information recorded in the year before clinical diagnosis, and we can therefore conclude that the drugs assessed were prescribed before the endometrial cancer was diagnosed. But could the disease or its precursor have been present even earlier, and have produced symptoms which led to the prescription for the drugs? We do not know if any of the case subjects had previous tests (e.g. a curettage) which would have detected the disease or a related state such as hyperplasia. The time relationship is not clear; no data for risk by time since first use of estrogens are given. As it is unlikely that the records go back many years, we assume that the risk is seen only a few years from first exposure. This appears inconsistent with a cancer initiator action, which typically takes decades; if the risk is causal, it shows a short term action.

10. Is the association strong?

The relationship is strong, the odds ratio of 7.6 being very high. This odds ratio is greater than those associated with even extremes of parity, obesity, late menopause and other recognized risk factors for endometrial carcinoma, making it unlikely that this association could be produced by confounding by such factors. However it is no protection against the association being due to the indication for the drug rather than the usage of the drug, as the association between these two may be very close. To assess its relevance for observation bias, it is useful to go to the raw data which shows that estrogens were recorded for 57 per cent of the case subjects compared to 15 per cent of the controls. Thus for the association to be totally due to observation bias would require for example that estrogen use was always recorded for the case subjects, but recorded on only about 25 per cent of occasions for the controls; this seems implausible. Thus the strength of the association protects against some aspects of confounding and against observation bias, but not against what is emerging as the chief competing hypothesis, an association with the indication rather than the drug prescribed.

11. Is there a dose–response relationship?

Information on this is likely to be limited by the completeness of the records, but the data in Table 2 show the odds ratio increasing from shorter to longer exposures. While the odds ratios for each exposure category are significantly different to the unexposed, a test for trend is not included. This dose response is not very helpful—it could occur if the relationship were produced by confounding by the indication for the drug, or even from observation bias. Information on the relationship between risk and time since first use or since last use might be of more help, but is not given.

12. Are the results consistent within the study?
and
13. Is there any specificity within the study?

There is little information on consistency or specificity reported. The most useful subgroups would be patients with different indications for the use of the drugs, but such a distinction would probably need a special study rather than one using routine medical records. Subgrouping by different specific estrogenic preparations would also help; there is no information on the precise preparations used. An association with a particular drug is more convincing if there is no association seen with other drugs used for the same indications.

Conclusions in regard to internal validity

The second part of our assessment of internal validity has therefore not been particularly helpful, and this is often the situation in assessing a relatively small study. Larger studies give more opportunity to assess consistency between subgroups, dose–response relationships, and so on. The assessment of internal validity therefore depends on the comparison of the causal hypothesis with the alternatives of bias and confounding. The main alternative hypothesis which has emerged is that the association is not due to the drug itself, but due to the symptoms for which the drug has been prescribed, which might be caused by the developing carcinoma, or be indications of an altered physiological state produced by mechanisms akin to those producing the tumour. To assess this alternative we need information from other studies, as will be seen.

D. External validity—generalization of the results

14. Can the study results be applied to the eligible population?

The eligible population are the members of the Kaiser Foundation Health Plan, and there is little problem applying the results to them. If we accept that they would all attend this medical centre, and that the tumour registry is efficient, all patients with a histological diagnosis during the stated time period were included, and medical records on all of them were obtained. The control subjects, apart from the appropriate matching criteria, seem to be representative of unaffected members of the plan, with the limitation that they include women only with an intact uterus. This is an appropriate criterion, both on the argument that women without a uterus are not at risk of developing endometrial cancer and are therefore not eligible as cases, and also because women who have had their uterus removed may be different in terms of estrogen usage.

15. Can the study results be applied to the source population?

The source and eligible populations in this study are essentially the same.

16. Can the study results be applied to other relevant populations?

The study was done on members of the Kaiser Foundation Health Plan diagnosed in 1970 to 1974 in Los Angeles. Are members of this health plan different to women in Los Angeles in general? Further information would be required, but we might assume that plan members are likely to be fairly affluent, stable subjects, who can afford a comprehensive prepaid health plan. No information is given on racial origin. However, the representativeness of the subjects in the study is not the most important issue. The main question is, is the *association* seen likely to apply to other women? If the true relationship is between the drug and the disease, the finding is likely to be widely applicable. In other populations, the value of the odds ratio may be considerably different, depending on the usual dosage and length of time the drugs are used. If the true association is with a specific type of drug, the association may not be seen in societies where other types are used. Even if the association is consistent, its importance will depend on the type, frequency and dosage of the drugs used and on the level of background incidence of endometrial cancer, produced by other factors. In this study population, a strong association is seen with a drug used frequently—in 15 per cent of controls; the attributable proportion in those exposed is 87 per cent, and in the population is 50 per cent—if causal, estrogens are the main cause of the disease. (These calculations are shown at the end of this chapter.)

E. Comparison of the results with other evidence

17. Are the results consistent with other evidence, particularly evidence from studies of similar or more powerful study design?

This study was chosen because it was one of the first studies to suggest this association. In the same issue of the same journal another case–control study, from Seattle, was published, showing a similar association, and this strengthens the credibility of these results (Smith *et al.*, 1975). If this other study is assessed, bearing in mind the conclusion we have reached on this study, that the association is likely to be either causal or be due to an association between the indication for the drug and endometrial cancer, we should find that the same limitation applies to the interpretation of that study. Thus, at the time of publication there was no great consistency, but because of the importance of the association suggested, these two papers were followed reasonably rapidly by many other studies.

18. Does the total evidence suggest any specificity?

Again, at the time this paper was published there was no relevant information. However the future development of the issue does show an interesting example of specificity, in that many other studies confirmed the association in the United States, where conjugated estrogens were used widely, whereas studies in several other countries did not suggest any problem, because the use of conjugated estrogens was much less. It appears that patients who would be treated with conjugated estrogens in the United States, would be treated in Europe with a mixture of estrogens and progestogens, and this combination does not appear to confer a marked increased risk of endometrial carcinoma. The issue of specificity in terms of disease is also important; if these drugs increase endometrial cancer by an estrogenic action, they might produce an increase in other hormonally related conditions, such as breast cancer, and considerable research has been done on this also.

19. Are the results plausible, in terms of a biological mechanism?

The authors review epidemiological and experimental evidence that estrogens may produce endometrial cancer, and the association seems biologically acceptable (paragraphs 2,21,22). The time issue is relevant. Classical cancer producing factors produce tumours only many years after exposure, but this association does not fit this pattern. Hormones in general are not initiators of cancer, but appear experimentally to act as cancer promotors, and this action would be consistent with a short term effect.

20. If a major effect is shown, is it coherent with the distribution of the exposure and the outcome?

This study does show a major effect, and the authors calculate that in this population approximately 50 per cent of endometrial cancer was caused by these drugs, if the association they have shown is causal. They also point out that the usage of these drugs quadrupled between 1962 and 1973, and therefore one would expect a noticeable increase in the incidence of endometrial carcinoma in the United States to have occurred. They review the literature available at that time, which did not show any such increase, but point out that an increase might be disguised by an increase in the prevalence of hysterectomy for non-cancer reasons in American women (paragraphs 18,19). In fact subsequent work published some months later, using rather better information, did show a substantial rise in the incidence of endometrial cancer in the United States, and there is even evidence some years later that the impact of this and other studies resulted in a reduction in the prescribing of these drugs, and a fairly rapid reduction in the incidence of this tumour (Weiss *et al.*, 1976; Austin and Roe, 1982). As well as the time relationship, we would expect the excess incidence to occur in geographical areas, and in social groups, in which the usage of these estrogenic drugs was maximum, and the difference between American and European experience in this regard has already been mentioned.

Coherence is the item on which the two major hypotheses can be separated. If the association with the drug is merely indicating a true association with symptoms, the rapid rise in use of the drugs will not affect the incidence rate, while a direct effect of the magnitude given will have doubled the previous incidence in this population. Thus, given the size of the effect, there should be a close association between the use of these drugs and the incidence of endometrial cancer in terms of time, place and person. If the real relationship is with the indication, no such associations will be found. The subsequently shown concordance of drug usage and disease between countries, social groups and over time is therefore crucial.

Conclusions

Our major conclusions are that the study shows a large and important association, which seems most likely to be due to one of two mechanisms; either a causal relationship between the use of these particular drugs and the development of endometrial cancer, or an association between the indications for those drugs and an increased risk of endometrial cancer. There are other possibilities, that the result reflects other confounding factors, or that it is produced by observation bias in regard to the medical records on which the data on estrogen exposure were based, but these seem somewhat less likely. We have also concluded that if the association is real, it is likely to apply to other women who are exposed to these same agents, and therefore be of substantial practical importance (Ex.10.1).

ASSESSMENT OF A CASE-CONTROL STUDY

Endometrial cancer and estrogenic drugs: Zeil and Finkle (1985)

A. Description of evidence		
1	Exposure	conjugated estrogens; use in period up to 1 year before diagnosis; assessed from medical records
2	Outcome	endometrial cancer; adenocarcinoma, adenoacanthoma
3	Design	case-control study
4	Study population	cases—all those diagnosed at Kaiser Permanante Medical Center, Los Angeles, July 1970–Dec.1974; $n = 94$ controls—from L.A. members of Kaiser plan, matched for age, residence, length of membership; two per case.
5	Main result	Odds ratio = 7.6; 95 per cent confidence limits = 4.3 to 13.4; strong positive association of estrogen use with endometrial cancer
B. Non-causal explanations		
6	Observation bias	possible—recording of drug use might be more complete on cases, despite protection of blind abstraction and avoiding period immediately before diagnosis
7	Confounding	major risk factors for endometrial cancer controlled by matching or stratification. Most likely non-causal hypothesis is an association with the indications for drug usage
8	Chance	can be excluded
C. Features consistent with causation		
9	Time relationship	drug usage at least 1 year before clinical diagnosis. But it is possible that preclinical or precursor state might have existed prior to diagnosis

Ex. 10.1. *Continued*

Ex. 10.1. *Continued*

10	Strength	strong association—protects against many alternative hypotheses but not helpful if the true association is with the indication for the drug
11	Dose response	seen with total duration of exposure
12	Consistency	information not available
13	Specificity	information not available
D.	*External validity*	
14	Eligible population	no difficulties in applying results
15	Source population	same as eligible
16	Other populations	while frequency and mode of usage may vary, association, if causal, is likey to be widely applicable. Studies in other populations may help distinguish causal hypothesis from hypothesis of an association with the indication for the drug, and indicate which particular drugs are involved
E.	*Comparison with other evidence*	
17	Consistency	one other case-control study at time of publication. Further support later. No strong support for competing hypothesis of the association being with indications for the drug
18	Specificity	evidence for specificity to unconjugated estrogens used alone emerged later
19	Plausibility	time relationship makes a long term cancer initiator action unlikely. A short term, promoter action is plausible and supported by some experimental work
20	Coherence	shown by later work. Evidence of incidence rate of endometrial cancer rising with use of estrogenic drugs and later falling is strong evidence against the competing hypothesis of the association being with the indication

Ex. 10.1. Summary of assessment of the case-control study of endometrial cancer by Zeil and Finkle (1975)

Thus, in assessing priorities for further investigation and for critical reading of subsequent results, we shall look particularly for studies which will differentiate between a direct effect of the drug and an effect of the indications for the drug. One piece of evidence which has already been noted is the secular variation in the incidence of the disease. Studies in other countries, where women presumably have the same sort of symptoms but may be treated differently, are helpful. Other than that, we look for studies which use more reliable methods of assessing drug exposure, perhaps medical records supplemented by independent reviews or direct interviews, even though recall bias may then become an issue. Prospective studies of users of these drugs would be useful, and the ultimate would be a trial in which women regarded as eligible for treatment with conjugated estrogens were randomized either to receive such treatment or to receive a non-estrogen alternative. However, to mount such a study would be extremely difficult in terms of the number of women required, and also might be regarded as unethical. Randomized trials which have been set up to look at the short term effects of estrogens, such as the relief of symptoms, are unlikely to be large enough to look at the issue of cancer production.

The subsequent history of this particular issue is complex and interesting, and some useful reviews are available, e.g. Thomas and Chu (1986) and one by the senior author of this paper, Ziel (1982). In brief, the association seen in this study was confirmed by many other case–control studies. Various alternative hypotheses were put forward to explain the results of this and other similar studies: for example, that estrogens merely made evident a cancer which would have remained undiagnosed or that endometrial hyperplasia was misdiagnosed as cancer. These were shown to be untenable by further case–control studies, which also dealt with most of the methodological issues raised in our discussion of this paper: examples are the studies of Antunes *et al.* (1979) and Shapiro *et al.* (1980). Prospective studies of women treated with estrogens for breast cancer or for gonadal agenesis also showed an increased risk of endometrial cancer. Sequential oral contraceptives are associated with an increased risk of endometrial cancer, while combined oral contraceptives may give a reduction in risk (Centres for Disease Control, 1983).

Supplementary note: The analysis used in the paper by Zeil and Finkle

Main analysis

The basic data for this matched case–control study with two controls per case is given in Table 1. The formula shown in Appendix I (Ex. A1.6, p. 286) gives an odds ratio of 8.2. This is somewhat different from the maximum likelihood point estimate calculated by the authors by a more complicated iterative procedure, which is 7.6, and such disparity is to be expected with these relatively small numbers. The chi-squared statistic, calculated by the variant of the Mantel–Haenszel procedure given in Ex. A1.6 is 48.8, identical to that given in the paper. A chi statistic of 6.98 ($\sqrt{48.8}$) is out of the range of most conventional tables; Statistical Table 3 (p. 316) gives the corresponding two-sided *P*-value as $< 10^{-9}$.

The odds ratio calculated from an unmatched analysis can also be derived from Table 1, which gives a value of 7.4; the difference between this and the result of the matched paired analysis is small. In Table 2, where small numbers are subdivided by duration of exposure, unmatched analyses are used, and the appropriate chi-squared statistic can be derived by the usual formula for case–control studies given in Ex. A1.1 (p. 268).

The test based confidence limits calculated in the paper use the method we have shown in Ex. A1.1, incorporating the maximum likelihood point estimate of odds ratio derived by the authors and the chi statistic of 6.98.

Control of confounding

Briefly, the confounding risk ratio (Miettinen, 1972) is the odds ratio linking exposure to outcome which is produced by the confounder; it can be thought of as the risk ratio which would be observed in the absence of any direct association. If there is no confounding, it will be 1.0; if the crude association is totally due to confounding the confounding risk ratio will equal the crude risk ratio. The crude risk ratio R_{cd}, the confounding risk ratio R_{cf}, and the unconfounded or standardized risk ratio R_s, are simply related as:

$$R_{cd} = R_{cf}\, R_s$$

Thus controlling for parity (paragraph 13) gives a crude odds ratio (*OR*) for estrogens and endometrial cancer of 6.71 (different from the risk for the whole study because of the missing data), and a confounding *OR* of 1.18 (showing very little confounding). An unconfounded *OR* can be derived as 6.71/1.18 = 5.69. The authors also calculate a 'confounding effect' relating the extent of confounding to the size of the unconfounded risk ratio giving (1.18–1)/(5.69–1) = 4 per cent.

Attributable risk

Given the overall odds ratio of 7.6 and the proportion of controls exposed, $p = 15$ per cent (Table 1), the attributable proportion (= 'etiological fraction') in those exposed = $(OR - 1)/OR$ = 87 per cent; the attributable proportion in the population = $p(OR - 1)/\{p(OR - 1) + 1\}$ = 50 per cent (see Ex. 3.2, p. 27).

Table 1. History of conjugated-estrogen use among 94 patients with endometrial cancer and 188 matched* control subjects

Distribution of triples by use of conjugated estrogens

Patients' use of conjugated estrogens	Controls' use of conjugated estrogens: Both	One	Neither	Totals
Used	1	16	37	54
Did not use	0	11	29	40
Totals	1	27	66	94

	Used conjugated estrogens		Did not use conjugated estrogens		Totals
Exposure rates:	No.	%	No.	%	
Patients	54	(57)	40	(43)	94
Controls	29	(15)	159	(85)	188

*The matching criteria were age, area of residence, duration of Health Plan membership, and potential for development of uterine cancer.

Table 2. Duration of conjugated-estrogens use* by patients with endometrial cancer and by control subjects, with risk-ratio analysis: point estimate ($\widehat{RR}$), 95 per cent one-sided lower confidence bound ($\underline{RR}$), and chi-square test statistic (χ_1^2).

Group	Duration of exposure (yr): Unknown	≥7	5.0–6.9	1.0–4.9	<1	Non-exposed	Totals
Patients (No.)	14	14	9	14	3	40	94
Controls (No.)	6	4	5	10	4	159	188
$\widehat{RR}$	9.3	13.9	7.2	5.6		(1.0)†	
($\underline{RR}$)	4.2	6.0	2.8	2.7			
χ_1^2	22	26	12	15			
P	$<10^{-5}$	$<10^{-5}$	<.01	<.01			

*Duration of use for both patients and controls was defined by difference in years between date of most recent prescription for conjugated estrogens and date of first such prescription given in record. If a first prescription date was given, but subsequent prescription dates were absent, a statement in the record, such as "conjugated estrogens for 5 year" was acceptable as a statement of duration. If a first prescription date was given, but subsequent dates were absent and no summary of conjugated estrogens use was in the record, the duration of use was defined as unknown.
†By definition.

INCREASED RISK OF ENDOMETRIAL CARCINOMA AMONG USERS OF CONJUGATED ESTROGENS

Harry K. Ziel and William D. Finkel

Department of Obstetrics and Gynecology, Kaiser Permanente Medical Center, Los Angeles and the Department of Medical Economics, Kaiser Foundation Health Plan, Southern California Region

Reproduced from *The New England Journal of Medicine*, **293**, No. 23, 1167–1170, 1975

Abstract

1. The possibility that the use of conjugated estrogens increases the risk of endometrial carcinoma was investigated in patients and a twofold age-matched control series from the same population. Conjugated estrogens (principally sodium estrone sulfate) use was recorded for 57 per cent of 94 patients with endometrial carcinoma, and for 15 per cent of controls. The corresponding point estimate of the (instantaneous) risk ratio was 7.6 with a one-sided 95 per cent lower confidence limit of 4.7. The risk-ratio estimate increased with duration of exposure: from 5.6 for 1 to 4.9 years' exposure to 13.9 for seven or more years. The estimated proportion of cases related to conjugated estrogens, the etiologic fraction, was 50 per cent with a one-sided 95 per cent lower confidence limit of 41 per cent. These data suggest that conjugated estrogens have an etiologic role in endometrial carcinoma. (*New Engl. J. Med.* 293: 1167–1170, 1975).

2. Between 1962 and 1973, dollar sales of estrogen quadrupled in the United States.[1,2] Conjugated estrogens (Premarin, Ayerst Laboratories) containing principally sodium estrone sulfate constituted the vast majority of the quantity supplied. A recent series of articles by Siiteri and his colleagues[3-5] has suggested that the estrone form of estrogen might be associated with the development of endometrial cancer. Siiteri's theory is consistent with previous data from animal experiments indicating carcinogenicity of estrogen.[6-9] In addition, MacMahon[10] cites clinical and epidemiologic evidence that exogenous estrogen increases the risk of the development of endometrial cancer.
3. The present work addresses the relation of estrogen to endometrial cancer using the case–control approach. Members of the Kaiser Foundation Health Plan with endometrial cancer who were reported to the tumor registry of the Kaiser Permanente Medical Center, Los Angeles, were compared with control subjects selected from the same Health

Plan population and matched for age, duration of Health Plan membership, and area of residence.

Subjects and methods

Patients

4. Between July 1, 1970, and December 31, 1974, the diagnosis of endometrial cancer was made in 94 patients at the Kaiser Permanente Medical Center, Los Angeles, and reported to its tumor registry. The criterion for the definition of endometrial cancer was a pathological diagnosis of endometrial adenocarcinoma or adenoacanthoma; mixed Müllerian sarcoma and choriocarcinoma were excluded.

Control Subjects

5. Control subjects were selected in the following way. The membership files of the Southern California Kaiser Foundation Health Plan population were reviewed, and all members in the vicinity of the Los Angeles facility whose record designations ended in arbitrarily selected numbers were identified and listed. From the list, two control subjects were selected for each patient and matched for birth date within one year, area of residence by postal zip code, duration of Health Plan membership (each control subject had been a member at least as long as the associated patient), and potential for the development of endometrial cancer by the control subject's having an intact uterus. The patient and the two control subjects thus constituted a matched triple.

Record Review

6. The data source for the 94 matched triples was the clinic record. To avoid information bias that could result from the more probing clinical history taking after identification of the cancer, the following procedure was employed for each matched triple. A medical-records clerk requested all three records from the record room and reviewed those of the control subjects to determine whether they had an intact uterus. Subjects without an intact uterus were replaced by selection of others from the original list. The clerk determined the date of diagnosis for each patient, and then the date one year before that diagnosis (the reference date). The clerk concealed all information in the record after the reference date. For control subjects, information recorded during the same period was similarly concealed. The record was then given to an abstractor, who filled out the abstract form without knowing whether the record was that of a patient or a control.

Results

7. For any given triple, there were six possible combinations of conjugated-estrogen use: all three were users; the patient and one of the control subjects were users; and so forth. The observed frequencies for each of the six possible combinations for each of the 94 triples are shown in Table 1. These data were used to estimate the risk ratio associated with the use of conjugated estrogens and the etiologic fraction (the proportion of cases due to conjugated estrogens). The (maximum-likelihood) point estimate of the relative risk ($\hat{RR}$) is 7.6.[11]* The significance test statistic (χ_1^2) is 49 ($P << 10^{-8}$).[12] The approximate 95 per cent one-sided lower confidence limit of the risk ratio ($\underline{RR}$) is 4.7.[13] The point estimate of the etiologic fraction ($\hat{EF}$) is 50 per cent.[14] For this parameter, Miettinen's proposed (test-based) computation[15] of the 95 per cent one-sided lower confidence limit ($\underline{EF}$) yields 41 per cent.†
8. Data on the relation of risk ratio to duration of exposure are given in Table 2. Even with only 1.0 to 4.9 years of use, the point estimate is 5.6, with a corresponding 95 per cent one-sided confidence limit of 2.7. For uses of less than one year's duration, the data are too scanty to be informative.‡
(Tables 1 and 2 are reproduced on p. 223).

Discussion

9. The apparent association between conjugated estrogens use the development of endometrial cancer requires consideration of several explanations other than causality.
10. Information bias, particularly bias in ascertaining the use of conjugated estrogens, is an unlikely explanation. The history of such use was ascertained from pre-existing records, which covered at least as many

*The computations for the point estimate and significance test were performed according to Miettinen, 1970[11] *and* 1969[12] respectively. The 95 per cent confidence interval[13] was computed according to: $(\underline{RR}, \overline{RR}) = \hat{RR}^{1 \pm Z_{1-\alpha}/\chi} = 7.6^{1 \pm 1.96/6.98} = (4.3, 13.4)$.

†The point estimate of EF was calculated by $\hat{EF} = [(\hat{RR} - 1)/\hat{RR}]$ (exposure rate of the cases).[14] The 95 per cent confidence interval was calculated by:
$(\underline{EF}, \overline{EF}) = 1 - (1 - \hat{EF})^{1 \pm Z_{1-\alpha}/\chi} = 1 - (1-0.50)^{1 \pm 1.96/6.98} = (0.39, 0.59)$.

‡Data were also recorded on the use of conjugated estrogens by control subjects who had been excluded from the study because of hysterectomy or radiation therapy to the uterus. If the restrictive criterion of an intact uterus in the control subjects had not been applied, the estimated relative risk and etiologic fraction would have been 4.9 and 46 per cent respectively.

years of care for the controls as for the patients. The original notations on the record, and the subsequent notations used to determine duration of use of conjugated estrogens, were made at least one year before detection of the cancer. Moreover, the method of record abstraction was expressly designed to eliminate bias in the process of extracting data.

11. As for selection bias, the ascertainment of subjects (patients and controls) does not appear to have depended directly upon use of conjugated estrogens. The vast majority of cases are reported to the cancer registry, regardless of whether the patient used conjugated estrogens, and the controls were selected from a defined population by a procedure that precluded selection on the basis of a history of such use.
12. Among various potential confounding factors, age, duration of Health Plan membership, and area of residence were controlled by (matching and) stratification. Among other known correlates of risk of development of endometrial cancer,[10] parity, excessive weight, and age at menopause deserve consideration.
13. In the present data, the risk of endometrial cancer of nulliparas was estimated to be 1.5 times that of parous women, and their rate of conjugated-estrogens use was also somewhat higher. However, the estimate of the confounding risk ratio[16] from subjects with parity recorded (90 per cent of patients and 84 per cent of controls) was as low as 1.18. This small ratio, together with an overall crude risk ratio of 6.7, implies a confounding effect of only $(1.18-1)/[(6.71/1.18)-1] = 4$ per cent.
14. To estimate the confounding risk ratio and confounding effect for subjects with height and weight recorded, Quetelet's index (Wt/Ht^2) was employed. The risk of endometrial cancer for the patients in the upper third of the weight index was estimated to be twice that for patients in the lower two thirds, and their use of conjugated estrogens was also slightly higher. Data could be obtained from 89 per cent of the patients and 80 per cent of the controls; the confounding risk ratio, crude risk ratio, and confounding effect were estimated as 1.1, 5.7, and 2 per cent respectively.
15. The analogous calculations for confounding by the risk factor "age at menopause" were as follows. The risk ratio for endometrial cancer for subjects with an age at menopause of 51 years or more versus those with an age at menopause below 51 was estimated to be 1.3, and the rate of conjugated-estrogens use was slightly lower in the former age group. On the basis of data obtained from 90 per cent of the case records and 70 per cent of the control records, the confounding risk ratio, crude risk ratio, and confounding effect were estimated as 1.08, 5.6, and 2 per cent, respectively.
16. From these considerations, it is apparent that the observed association

between conjugated-estrogens use and the development of endometrial cancer cannot be explained to any appreciable extent by confounding due to age, parity, excessive weight, or age at menopause. It is possible, of course, that there could be a major confounding effect by other, unknown factors that lead to the development of endometrial cancer.

17. As an overall check on the validity of the method, data were also collected on the use of diazepam (Valium), reserpine, and thyroid drugs by both patients and controls. The point estimates of the risk ratio were 0.7, 0.5, and 0.9, respectively. All these estimates are small in comparison with the estimated risk ratio of 7.6 that was found for conjugated estrogens. In addition, data were collected on the indications given in the record for prescribing conjugated estrogens. Where an indication was recorded (for 54 per cent of patients and 72 per cent of controls), it was "hot flashes" for 72 per cent of patients and 71 per cent of controls, indicating that the reasons for prescribing this drug were similar for patients and controls. Chance is an extremely unlikely explanation, considering the magnitude of the P value.

18. Causal explanation of the association involves the difficulty of explaining why an association of this magnitude has remained undetected until now. Estrogens have been used extensively only during the last decade or two,[1,2] and if the results of this study are generalizable to all postmenopausal women, there should have been an appreciable increase in the occurrence of endometrial cancer. Specifically, the present data imply that the etiologic fraction for conjugated estrogens has a point estimate as high as 50 per cent, with a 95 per cent one-sided lower confidence limit of 41 per cent. A 50 per cent etiologic fraction would correspond to a 100 per cent increase in the incidence of this cancer. Whether an increase of this order of magnitude has occurred in regions of high estrogen use, such as the one in which this study was conducted, is difficult to assess, but no such increase is believed to have occurred. Analysis of the Second and Third National Cancer Surveys suggests that the incidence of endometrial cancer did not increase appreciably in the United States between 1947 and 1971.[17] The same conclusion holds for England, Wales, and Canada.[18]

19. Those surveys, however, are affected by a major bias. The incidence rates are in reference to the total female population, whereas the rates should be expressed in reference to women at risk.[18] For the 1950's, the frequency of hysterectomy must be surmised from incidental sources, which suggest that 10 to 15 per cent of postmenopausal women had undergone hysterectomy.[19-22] MacMahon and Worcester[23] and Hammond[24] provide evidence of increased prevalence of hysterectomy in this age group during the early 1960s. Recent national survey data show much higher frequencies and continued increase in the rate of hysterectomy. By 1968, the prevalence of hysterectomy among American women at the age of 60 years was 31 per cent[25]; in the period

from 1968–1973, the incidence rate in women 15 years of age or older rose from 6.8 per 1000 woman-years[26] to 8.6 per 1000 woman-years.[27] It is apparent, therefore, that the incidence rate of the development of endometrial cancer for women at risk (those with an intact uterus) has increased dramatically during the past decade or so.

20. Another difficulty in employing the 1969 and 1971 Third Survey to assess the impact of use of conjugated estrogens on the incidence of endometrial cancer is that the survey may have been performed too early for this purpose. The Kaiser Permanente Medical Center's tumor-registry data are not particularly helpful in settling the question of increase in the incidence of endometrial cancer, owing to uncertainty about the completeness of reporting over time, particularly before 1971. However, the data do indicate a significant increase (uncorrected for hysterectomy) in 1972 to 1974.
21. Causal interpretation of the association between conjugated-estrogens use and the development of endometrial cancer has some biologic credibility. Carcinogenicity of estrogens has been demonstrated in laboratory animals at various sites,[6–9] including the endometrium.[9] In addition, the cases of endometrial cancer observed in surgically castrated women or in girls with ovarian dysgenesis exceed the expected number,[28–33] and these women receive replacement estrogen therapy. Moreover, endometrial cancer has been found to be associated with high estrogen-producing granulosa-theca ovarian tumours.[34–36]
22. Recently, Siiteri *et al.*[3–5] have suggested a theory of hormone conversion that implies a higher level of estrone in women in whom endometrial cancer develops than in those in whom it does not. They found rates of conversion of androstenedione to estrone two to three times as high in women with endometrial cancer or hyperplasia (a precursor of endometrial carcinoma[37,38]) as in women without such cancer. Confirming Siiteri's findings, Schindler and his associates[36] discovered that adipose tissues of patients with endometrial cancer converted androstenedione to estrone nearly four times as fast as those of subjects without cancer.
23. The evidence for a connection between the use of conjugated estrogens and the development of endometrial cancer seems rather persuasive. Caution is urged, however, in view of the absence of data both from similar epidemiologic studies in other populations and from follow-up studies. Such information is necessary before policy conclusions can be drawn. Further studies are necessary to evaluate the possible relation between the use of other estrogens and endometrial cancer.

[Acknowledgements and references omitted]

Reproduced by permission of the publishers and the first author, to whom thanks are given.

11. Critical appraisal of a randomized trial

The third of our critical assessments deals with a multicentre randomized clinical trial, 'Controlled trial of sotalol for one year after myocardial infarction' by Julian, D.G., Prescott, R.J., Jackson, F.S. and Szekely, P. *The Lancet*, May 22 1982, 1142–1147. This is reproduced on pages 243–255.

A. Description of the evidence

1. What was the exposure or intervention?
2. What was the outcome?
3. What was the study design?
4. What was the study population?
5. What was the main result?

The issue addressed here is whether the use of sotalol, a beta adrenergic receptor blocking agent, in patients who have had an acute myocardial infarction, will reduce their chances of death or reinfarction. The intervention therefore is the prescription of sotalol 320 mg once daily, compared to a placebo (paragraph 2). Three outcomes were assessed during 12 months from the first infarction: the primary one was death from any cause; re-infarction was also assessed, divided into 'confirmed' and 'suspected' infarctions. Information on strokes and angina is also given. The study design is a randomized intervention trial, using 19 hospitals in northern England, one in London and one in Scotland.

The study population, as is usual in clinical trials, is specified in detail and is quite restricted. Eligible patients in the participating hospitals were aged between 30 and 69 years, had had an acute myocardial infarction 5 to 14 days previously, and gave their consent to the study. Patients were recruited between January 1st 1978 and August 31st 1980. Paragraphs 6 to 8 give the criteria for the diagnosis of myocardial infarction and the exclusion criteria, a considerable list of items of past history and current clinical state. Nine other groups of drugs were not permitted during the study; this applied to both intervention and comparison groups.

The main results, expressed in the summary, are a reduction in overall mortality which is not statistically significant, a reduction in definite myocardial reinfarction which is statistically significant, and a reduction in total reinfarctions which is not significant. The results, expressed as simple two by

RANDOMIZED TRIAL OF SOTALOL: MAIN RESULTS

Outcome 1: total mortality (table VII)

Intervention	Deaths	Survivors	Total patients	Death rate (%)
Sotalol	64	809	873	7.3
Placebo	52	531	583	8.9

Relative risk sotalol:placebo = 0.81 95% C.L. 0.55 – 1.19 (paragraph 23)
Risk difference sotalol–placebo = – 1.6%
Log-rank test χ^2 = 1.1 P = 0.3 (paragraph 23)

Outcome 2: confirmed reinfarctions (table VIII)

Intervention	Confirmed reinfarction		Total patients	Death rate (%)
	Yes	No		
Sotalol	29	844	873	3.3
Placebo	33	550	583	5.7

Relative risk = 0.59 (from above table, although it would be better from log-rank analysis)
Log-rank test χ^2 = 4.7 P = 0.03 (fig. 3)
95% C.L. for relative risk, test based on this χ value of $\sqrt{4.7}$ = 2.17 = 0.37 to 0.95.

Outcome 3: total reinfarctions (table VIII)

Intervention	Total reinfarction		Total patients	Death rate (%)
	Yes	No		
Sotalol	37	836	873	4.2
Placebo	38	545	583	6.5

Relative risk = 0.65
χ^2 = 3.3 P = 0.07 (both from above table; log-rank analysis would be preferable)
95% C.L. (test based) = 0.42 to 1.01

Ex. 11.1. Main results of randomized trial of sotalol (Julian *et al.*, 1982)

two tables, are shown in Ex. 11.1; as three outcome measures were used, three tables can be constructed. At this point we note that for each outcome there is a protective effect of sotalol; we will examine the statistical issues in due course.

We note that of patients fulfilling the general eligibility criteria, 45 per cent were actually randomized, and of the 1456 randomized, 125 in fact violated the protocol but were maintained in the analysis (paragraphs 16, 18). Further, 25 per cent of patients randomized to sotalol and 21 per cent of those randomized to placebo were withdrawn from treatment during the one year follow-up period (paragraph 20). These subjects were also maintained in the analysis, which was therefore done on an intention-to-treat basis.

B. Internal validity—consideration of non-causal explanations

6. Are the results likely to be affected by observation bias?

Let us accept that there is no likelihood of observation bias in terms of total mortality, merely assessing whether each subject was alive or dead. Such bias could occur only if there were substantial losses even to this follow-up assessment, and we are assured that death or survival was confirmed for all subjects (paragraph 13). In terms of any other measure in a clinical trial, more care is needed, and it is required in this study in regard to reinfarction. The criteria of reinfarction were the same as the criteria for the original infarct, plus necropsy evidence; such information was obtained from hospitals and general practitioners, and then verified by the consultants to the study (paragraphs 13, 14). It is not clear if any blind review of objective data was performed, and one would hope that the assessment of reinfarction was made on each subject before the coding for the trial was broken and therefore with the consultants being unaware of which patients were on sotalol.

In fact loss of blindness might well have occurred because of some of the recognized effects of sotalol, such as a substantial decrease in heart rate (table III), and therefore it seems possible that the assessments of reinfarction were not made blind. Further information on these points would be helpful.

Reinfarctions were divided into confirmed and suspected (table VIII), and the criteria for the latter are not clear; these are presumably reinfarctions reported by hospitals or general practitioners which were not confirmed by the consultants; whether this was because the steps needed for confirmation could not be taken or whether the results were equivocal is not specified. However, the association between treatment and confirmed reinfarction is slightly stronger than that for all reinfarctions (Ex. 11.1). It is worth looking at the absolute difference in the number of reinfarctions. There were 37 total reinfarctions in the sotalol group of which 29 were confirmed; if the experience had been identical to that of the placebo group one would have expected 57 in total, and 50 confirmed; the difference between those observed and those expected on the placebo experience is therefore quite substantial in absolute terms, and there would have to be a very major observation bias to produce the results seen. Observation bias therefore seems unlikely to affect the results of this study.

As always, there is the possibility of some random error, but that would act only to reduce the observed association. It is reasonable to proceed by accepting the observations of death and at least confirmed reinfarction as valid.

7. Are the results likely to be affected by confounding?

Control of confounding in this study was achieved of course by the randomization process, and the numbers of subjects in the study. The characteristics of the groups obtained by randomization are set out in table II, showing percentage distributions in regard to a range of factors which would be expected to relate to the risks of reinfarction and death. There are differences which appear relevant; the intervention group has fewer males and a higher proportion with a history of angina, but the distribution in terms of the other factors seems very similar. Where differences persists on a possible confounding factor which has been recorded, further analysis can be undertaken by stratification or multivariate analysis. In this study multivariate analysis was performed using linear logistic models and the authors concluded that the inclusion of the factors given in table II produced no difference in the main results (paragraph 17); this is what one would expect from the similarity of the two groups, as shown in table II. The groups are of unequal size (60 per cent to sotalol, 40 per cent to placebo); this is a design decision on the logic that if sotalol reduces the death and reinfarction rates, the number of such events in the two groups will be approximately equal, which will maximize statistical efficiency.

The protection against confounding is given by the fact that the analysis is done on an intention to treat basis, that is the group randomized to sotalol is compared to the group randomized to placebo. This point has been discussed in Chapter 6 (p 101). In this study, substantial numbers of subjects were found not to fulfil the eligibility criteria after randomization, or were withdrawn from treatment, or had sotalol or another beta-blocker prescribed openly; this is summarized in Ex. 11.2. The total number of subjects who had

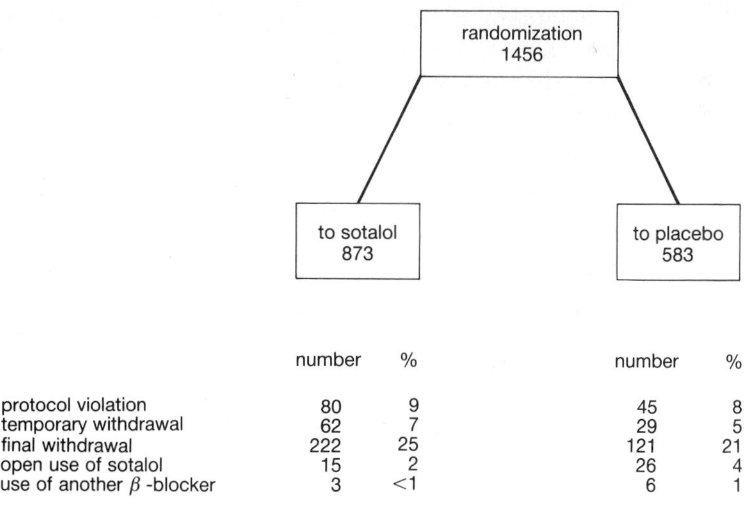

	to sotalol number	%	to placebo number	%
protocol violation	80	9	45	8
temporary withdrawal	62	7	29	5
final withdrawal	222	25	121	21
open use of sotalol	15	2	26	4
use of another β -blocker	3	<1	6	1

compliance estimated 78 per cent by blood test

Ex. 11.2. Subsequent course of subjects randomized. Some subjects may appear in more than one category (Julian *et al.*, 1982)

no known protocol violation cannot be calculated exactly, as there is some overlap between these categories, but ignoring this gives approximately 491 patients on sotalol (56 per cent of original group) and 356 on placebo (61 per cent of the original group). However, any comparison other than that performed—comparing the groups as originally randomized—loses the value of the randomization. For example, comparing only those subjects who remained on sotalol with those remaining on placebo is dangerous, as these groups are likely to be substantially different in terms of factors recorded as potential confounders, and also factors which are much more difficult to record such as other aspects of lifestyle, social and medical support, and other features which might well be related to prognosis. Thus, the correct use of the intention-to-treat analysis is of great importance as it is the only way in which the advantages of the randomized study in terms of confounder control are realized. It also means that the study results reflect a management based trial, that is they compare the results expected if sotalol is offered as treatment after myocardial infarction compared with no treatment.

Thus because the study is reasonably large, the groups compared were obtained by randomization, and the data on recorded factors suggest no major differences between the groups, confounding is unlikely to have a major influence on the results.

8. *Are the results likely to be affected by chance variation?*

The statistical results given in the paper are summarized in Ex. 11.1. For each of the three end-points, mortality, confirmed reinfarctions, and total reinfarctions, a simple table can be created as shown in tables VII and VIII of the paper. However, the more precise analysis uses actuarial methods and the log-rank test, as described in Appendix 2 (p. 295); these results are shown in figures 1 and 3 of the paper. The one year mortality rates were 8.9 per cent on placebo and 7.3 per cent on sotalol. The log-rank test gave a chi-squared statistic of 1.1, and a P-value of 0.3; so a difference as large or larger than that observed would be expected to occur in 30 per cent of trials if the true situation were that the two groups had the same prognosis. The results are also expressed in terms of the relative risk, which is given as 0.81, with confidence limits of 0.55 to 1.19 (paragraph 23). Thus the results are consistent with the mortality rate of patients on the new drug being as low as 55 per cent of the rate in patients on the placebo, but also with the mortality rate with the new intervention being 19 per cent higher than that with the placebo.

The other outcome measure was reinfarctions, and these were also assessed by a log-rank analysis, during which patients who died without a reinfarction were treated as censored, as described in Appendix 2. For confirmed reinfarctions, the relative risk, from the table, is 0.59 and the log-rank χ^2 statistic is 4.7 ($P = 0.03$); confidence limits are not given in the paper but the test based limits can be calculated as 0.37 to 0.95. There is thus a 41 per cent decrease in confirmed reinfarctions, which is statistically significant. A comparison of total reinfarctions, including those suspected but not confirmed, gives a smaller difference which is not quite significant, the *P*-value being 0.07.

In assessing chance variation we need to assess not only whether the appropriate test has been done, but whether it has been done at the appropriate time, as in clinical trials the issues of multiple testing, and perhaps publication of results or termination of studies on the basis of one of a series of tests, is a very relevant issue. In regard to this study, like so many other published randomized trials it is unfortunate that we are not given a clearer idea of what decisions were made when the trial was initiated. Presumably some sample size and time calculations were carried out, and it would be interesting to know if this analysis, based on one year's follow-up and the occurrence of some 110 deaths, was an analysis defined in the original protocol. If so, the statistical tests used can be taken at their face value. Unfortunately in many clinical trials, no decision as to when the trial is to be analysed is taken, nor is any logical monitoring or continuous assessment programme set up. This may allow the investigators to examine the results frequently and, even unconsciously, select for presentation an analysis chosen because at that point in time the results appear impressive.

Thus we cannot exclude chance variation in this study. The difference in mortality, which is the more important end-point, is consistent with chance variation, and the difference in reinfarction rate is very close to the conventional 0.05 significance level, particularly given the uncertainty of the definition, and the question of whether only confirmed or all reinfarctions should be counted.

C. Internal validity—consideration of positive features of causation

9. Is there a correct time relationship?

This is not a problem in an intervention study: the outcomes follow the randomization. Note that, to preserve the value of randomization as discussed above, we employ criteria which are somewhat illogical in terms of timing. Patient follow-up starts from randomization, so a death occurring in a patient randomized to sotalol even before he receives any is attributed to the sotalol group; similarly with a death occurring long after the treatment was stopped. The pattern of outcome occurrence may be examined to see if there is an indication of time-specificity (paragraph 23, fig. 1), as long as this is treated as a subsidiary issue to the main analysis. The short follow-up period (one year) does not allow us to make conclusions about what might happen later.

10. Is the relationship strong?

The value of a strong relationship in an observational study is largely because bias or confounding should be readily detected. In a randomized trial, such issues can be dealt with firmly, so the strength of the relationship is less crucial to internal validity, although still helpful. In practical terms, the associations seen here are strong enough to warrant importance, if the results are valid.

11. Is there a dose–response relationship?

This is not a relevant question, as a fixed dose of the drug was used. In some randomized trials more than one dose of drug is used, and consideration of dose response may be relevant. One might be tempted to deal under this heading with the question of did the patients who took the drug according to the protocol rather than dropped out, have a better survival, as of course one would expect that they would do on the basis of a pharmacological drug action. However, as mentioned already, this is a very dangerous area, as patients who stay on the drug are likely to be very different from patients who do not in regard to many characteristics. An example of this has been given (Ex. 6.14, p. 103) from a study on lipid lowering agents, which showed that patients who took the active drug according to protocol had a much better survival than those who did not, but that a virtually identical difference in survival was seen between patients who maintained their placebo drug and patients who did not.

12. Are the results consistent within the study?

This is often a relevant issue in clinical trials, as one wishes to know whether the active drug produces an improvement particularly in some groups of patients, but again is a very difficult issue to look at unless the trial is specifically designed to answer questions about subgroups of patients from the beginning. The use of *post hoc* analysis looking at subgroups of patients defined after the event is a procedure which is open both to the problems of multiple comparisons and comparisons between non-randomized groups. Such analyses are appropriately avoided in this paper.

13. Is there any specificity within the study?

The specificity involved would be that expected by the pharmacological action of the drug, in that one would expect to see a reduction in cardiovascular events and cardiovascular related deaths, but would not expect to see differences in other causes of death or other major morbidity. Deaths from other causes are in fact listed but were too few to allow any analysis (two in each group). There was an excess of strokes in the sotalol group, 15 (1.7 per cent) versus 6 (1.0 per cent) in the placebo group; but this is likely to be due to chance (paragraph 25). The timing of the cardiovascular deaths was also examined, and it is conceivable that the drug would act specifically early or late after the first infarct, and while again such comparisons are open to the problems of *post hoc* interpretation they could give valuable leads for other work (paragraph 23).

Conclusions in regard to internal validity

We expect a large scale randomized trial to lead to firm conclusions about internal validity. We can dismiss with considerable certainty observation bias and confounding as explanations of the differences seen. However, and again characteristic of randomized trials, the remaining issue is that of chance variation, and despite the fact that in this trial 3234 patients were assessed and 1456 randomized, the mortality results are based on 64 deaths in one group and 52 in the other, and we cannot be confident that the difference seen is not due to chance variation. In terms of reinfarctions, the numbers are again small, a total of 37 in one group and 38 in the other, and the differences are again on the borderline of conventional statistical significance.

In summary: this trial shows that the use of sotalol rather than placebo in post-infarction patients has been followed by reductions at one year of 19 per cent in mortality, 41 per cent in confirmed reinfarctions, and 35 per cent in total reinfarctions. Confounding and bias are unlikely to affect these results; they may reflect a true drug effect, but chance variation is a possibility, the *P*-values being 0.3 for total mortality, and 0.03 and 0.07 for confirmed and total reinfarctions.

D. External validity—generalization of the results

14. Can the study results be applied to the eligible population?

The eligible population comprises all those patients fulfilling the eligibility criteria, which are fairly strict. There were 136 eligible patients not randomized (paragraph 16): thus 91 per cent were randomized. Given those criteria, the relevant issue is whether losses occurred after randomization. We are assured that death or survival was confirmed for every patient at the completion of the study, and therefore the mortality data can be applied directly to the eligible population. It is not clear whether there were any losses to follow-up in terms of reinfarction, and one would assume that these were also small. In applying the results, we need again to emphasize that the results show the difference between subjects randomized to the active drug and those randomized to the placebo, as many subjects were withdrawn (Ex. 11.2). This gives us some practical indication of the likely difficulties there would be in maintaining compliance to sotalol, or (from the placebo results) to any drug. If the results are due to the effectiveness of the drug, but in routine clinical practice the compliance rate was lower than that seen here, the beneficial effect would also be lower. Similarly, if by changes in management technique or changes in the drug, the active component could be given with higher compliance, a larger beneficial effect would result.

15. Can the study results be applied to the source population?

We can define the source population in this study as those who were considered for inclusion, and therefore as the patients who would be considered for treatment in a practical clinical situation. These were defined as patients between the ages of 30 and 69 who had survived for five days after an acute infarction (paragraph 4), and this study included only 45 per cent of such subjects. This is important in terms of the clinical application of the results, and it is obviously an over-simplification to say that these results can be applied to post-infarction patients. The contra-indications expressed in this study should be accepted in terms of applying the results, unless and until there is further evidence as to how they relate to the efficacy or safety of the drug.

We need to review the eligibility and exclusion criteria to clarify how the results can be applied: we would note for example that the study excluded 'women of childbearing potential', and those with defined cardiac or respiratory signs, but also a group with undefined cardiac or non-cardiac conditions serious enough to reduce the prognosis.

16. Can the study results be applied to other relevant populations?

We should see little difficulty in applying the results in terms of time and space, given that the diagnostic criteria used in this study are reasonably consistent with those used in normal clinical practice. If the results of this study reflect a causal relationship with the intervention, it seems likely that such a relationship will hold in similar patients seen in other areas of the United Kingdom, and even in similar patients elsewhere in the world, at the current time and into the future. We would hesitate to apply the results to any groups in which the natural history of myocardial infarction might be substantially different; this might include patients with concomitant clinical conditions even if these are not listed in the eligibility criteria, and perhaps patients of different races or in totally different environments. A relevant issue is whether the results apply to patients outside the age range of 30 to 69 chosen for this study, and the practical answer is to assess whether the patients' age is sufficiently outside that range for it to be likely that the natural history of their condition would be greatly affected. A similar relevant issue is that of consistency, in that whereas the results give the overall effect of the treatment in all the patients randomized, it does not necessarily follow that the same effect holds within subgroups, for instance within female subjects. However, unless there is evidence that it does not, or other grounds to suspect that it would be substantially different, it seems to be reasonable to assume consistency of the results.

In keeping with the overall emphasis on assessing the main result of the study, the question of generalizability in terms of the main result, that is in terms of the efficacy of the drug, has been considered. In terms of applying these results in clinical practice, we also have to assess the generalizability of the side effects and compliance achieved in the study. For instance, a reluctance to use the drug on patients who are somewhat older than the age range given in this study might be based on the argument not that efficacy might be different, but that the side effects and ability to tolerate the drug might be considerably different. Similar considerations apply to the facilities for follow-up and monitoring of patients in a clinical situation, and in terms of clinical applications of the results we have to look closely at the follow-up techniques and assessments made in this study to see whether they can be translated into routine clinical practice.

E. Comparison of these results with other evidence

17. Are the results consistent with other evidence, particularly evidence from studies of similar or more powerful study design?

This issue is addressed to some extent in the study, in that in the discussion (paragraphs 28, 29) the results of randomized trials of similar pharmacological agents are reviewed. It is argued that the overall effects of all these trials are consistent with a decrease in mortality of 20 to 25 per cent, even though most of the other trials individually show non-significant results. This issue is very relevant, given our overall conclusion so far, which is that the main counter-hypothesis to a causal effect of the drug is that the results reflects chance variation. It is therefore logical to combine the results from trials if we can assume that the agents and protocols used are basically similar, and to use an overview or meta-analysis to try to deal with the main competing hypothesis, that of chance variation. In regard to the use of beta blockers after myocardial infarction, such an analysis has been done and presented by Yusuf *et al.* (1985), and is a good example of this technique; results are shown in Ex. 7.16 (p 162). In that paper the authors make a good case for the value of combined analyses of trials which are methodologically and clinically similar but suffer from the problem of inadequate numbers, and also make some interesting comments about the generalizability of results from such trials.

18. Does the total evidence suggest any specificity?

The assessment of specificity within the one trial was limited because of small numbers; another of the values of meta-analysis is that it may provide the very large numbers of observations needed to make reliable assessments of specificity. If, for example, there is a difference in efficacy of a drug like this between male and female patients, we should need to see such a difference consistently over a number of trials before accepting it as real. There is no major specificity suggested.

19. Are the results plausible in terms of the biological mechanism?

This is rarely of prime importance in clinical trials; usually the issue of a biological mechanism has been answered before the trial is initiated, and that certainly applies to the role of beta blocking agents.

20. If a major effect is shown, is it coherent with the distribution of exposure and the outcome?

Again, the question as set is not directly related to clinical trials. However, with a modification it becomes the issue of: if the results show a true effect, is the effect substantial enough in absolute terms to be clinically important? Such analyses may have to include economic issues. In this particular study, one could summarize the results in terms such as these, on the assumption that if treated with placebo the sotalol patients would have had the same outcome as the placebo patients. The initiation of treatment in 873 patients has resulted in a reduction in the number of deaths in one year from an expected number of 78 to an observed of 64, that is a reduction of 14, and has also resulted in a reduction in confirmed reinfarctions of 20. We could go further and calculate the costs in person-time and financial terms of the drugs and any extra medical care necessary to achieve this objective. We shall come ultimately to a judgment value, and may wish to compare the cost of these benefits with those of other interventions used in medicine or in other aspects of life. For instance, in the treatment of mild hypertension, the British randomized trial showed no difference in mortality but a reduction in strokes, but the report pointed out that it was necessary to treat 850 mildly hypertensive patients for a year to prevent one stroke (Medical Research Council Working Party, 1985). In comparison, the results of the sotalol study seem encouraging. However, such issues relating effects to resources need fuller discussion than can be given here.

Summary of external validity

The eligibility criteria limit the results to under half of all patients who might be considered for such treatment, largely on specific clinical grounds but also by excluding some general groups such as women of child bearing potential and patients outside the age range 30–69 years. The disease is common, and the diagnostic criteria, other care given, and follow-up procedures are likely to be similar to those in use in other developed countries, so that the results, if valid, have wide applicability.

Conclusions (Ex. 11.3)

In summary, this study illustrates both the strengths and weaknesses of randomized trials. The strengths are that one can with reasonable confidence exclude confounding and observation bias as explanations for the results seen. The main weakness is that despite the enormous effort involved, the study is still limited in terms of size, and the main result is within the range which could be produced purely by chance variation. Also, as is typical of randomized trials, there were strict eligibility criteria for the subjects, and therefore we have to be careful about the generalizability of the results from the subjects actually involved in the study. The eligibility criteria are clearly set out and could be reproduced in clinical practice, and we are told what proportion of the source population were eventually entered into the trial, information which is all too often not recorded.

Subsequent development

Yusuf *et al.* (1985) reviewed 65 trials of beta blockers, and concluded that, 'long term beta blockade for perhaps a year or so following discharge after a myocardial infarct is now of proven value, and for many such patients mortality reductions of about 25 per cent can be achieved'. This huge review thus suggests that the reduction in mortality seen in the study we have reviewed—19 per cent—is close to the truth. Further trials have assessed the earlier use of beta blockers, and include a remarkable trial of 16 027 patients (ISIS-1 Collaborative Group, 1986). In 1984, a survey of British cardiologists showed that the majority prescribed beta blockers in post-infarct patients, although it seemed unlikely that general practitioners also did (Baber *et al.*, 1984). But the issue of management of heart disease is wider than that of beta blockers; Evans (1986) has reviewed other approaches as well, and questions whether the efforts concentrated on these drugs have directed attention away from other management approaches, such as smoking cessation, antiplatelet agents or aspirin.

ASSESSMENT OF A RANDOMIZED TRIAL

Sotalol after myocardial infarction: Julian *et al.* (1982).

A. Description of evidence	
1 Intervention	sotalol 320 mg daily, compared to placebo
2 Outcome	at 12 months: death, reinfarction
3 Design	randomized clinical trial
4 Study population	entered 5–14 days after myocardial infarct; age 30–69 years; various exclusions; England and Scotland, 1978–80
5 Main result	Mortality reduced by 19%, confirmed reinfarctions reduced by 41%, total reinfarctions reduced by 35%
B. Non-causal explanations	
6 Observation bias	death—no bias; reinfarctions—possible but unlikely to be major
7 Confounding	no serious confounding
8 Chance	a likely competing hypothesis particularly for mortality (*P*-value for the observed result = 0.3); less likely for reinfarctions but cannot be dismissed (*P*-value for total reinfarctions 0.07, confirmed reinfarctions 0.03)
C. Positive features of causation	
9 Time relationship	correct
10 Strength	adequate
11 Dose response	not applicable
12 Consistency	not assessed
13 Specificity	information too limited

Summary of internal validity: fairly high: result most likely shows causation; chance variation the main alternative hypothesis.

D. External validity	
14 To the eligible population	no major problem
15 To the source population	many exclusions: 45% of relevant patients randomized: this restricts generalizability
16 To other populations	acceptable in time and place to a reasonable extent; in terms of age and exclusion criteria, unknown
E. Other evidence	
17 Consistency	consistent with other trials of beta blockers
18 Specificity	none apparent
19 Plausibility	given
20 Coherence	not directly relevant. Effect of intervention appears substantial

Summary of external validity: if result is valid, it is of major importance.

Ex. 11.3. Assessment of causality in a randomized trial of sotalol in patients with myocardial infarction, by Julian *et al.* (1982)

CONTROLLED TRIAL OF SOTALOL FOR ONE YEAR AFTER MYOCARDIAL INFARCTION*

D.G. JULIAN R.J. PRESCOTT
F.S. JACKSON P. SZEKELY

Department of Cardiology, Freeman Hospital, Newcastle upon Tyne NE7 7DN; and Medical Computing and Statistics Unit, University of Edinburgh

Reproduced from *The Lancet*, **1**, 1142–1147, 1982

Summary

1. In a multicentre double-blind randomised study, the effect of sotalol 320 mg once daily was compared with that of placebo in patients surviving an acute myocardial infarction. Treatment was started 5–14 days after infarction in 1456 patients (60% being randomised to sotalol, and 40% to placebo) who represented 45% of those evaluated for entry. Patients were followed for 12 months. The mortality rate was 7.3% (64 patients) in the sotalol group and and 8.9% (52 patients) in the placebo group. The mortality was 18% lower in the sotalol than in the placebo group, but this difference was not statistically significant. The rate of definite myocardial reinfarction was 41% lower in the sotalol group than in the placebo group ($p < 0.05$). Although the differences in mortality were not significant, this trial supports the evidence that, in the year after myocardial infarction, beta adrenoceptor blocking drugs reduce mortality by 20–25%.

Introduction

2. For more than a decade there has been interest in the long-term use of beta adrenoceptor blocking drugs to improve prognosis after recovery from myocardial infarction. Because earlier studies gave equivocal results[1-6] several further trials were begun in the late 1970s, of which three have lately been reported.[7-9] In 1978 we started a multicentre trial with sotalol. This drug was selected because, in addition to beta adrenoceptor blockade, it has the advantage of a long half-life permitting once-daily dosage, and, uniquely for a beta blocking drug, class 3 antiarrhythmic action (prolongation of the action potential). This report concerns 1456 patients who were randomised to sotalol ('Sotacor', 'Sotalex', Bristol-Myers Company, International

Division) 320 mg daily or placebo, all of whom were followed for 12 months.

Materials and methods

3. Physicians in all the general hospitals administered by the Northern Region of England Health Authority (population served 3.1 million) were invited to collaborate in the multicentre trial. Staff of 19 out of the 23 hospitals agreed to take part; in addition, 2 hospitals outside the region (Victoria Hospital, Kirkcaldy, Scotland, and St George's Hospital, London) participated. The trial was planned to correspond as far as possible with the earlier Multicentre International Study of practolol,[6] while at the same time eliminating some of the drawbacks of that trial.
4. All patients between the ages of 30 and 69 years who had survived for five days after the onset of an acute myocardial infarction were considered for inclusion in the study. A record was kept of all such patients whether or not they were ultimately included. The nature and purpose of the trial was first explained to the patient and consent for inclusion obtained; the general practitioner was subsequently informed. The design of the trial was approved by the ethical committees of the participating hospitals.
5. Randomization was undertaken separately for each centre in blocks of ten, each block containing six allocations to sotalol and four to placebo. The time of randomization was determined as that when the next available numbered package was opened and the first dose given to the patient.

Patient recruitment and evaluation

6. Recruitment started on Jan. 1, 1978, and ended on Aug. 31, 1980. Patients were considered for inclusion in the trial if acute myocardial infarction had occurred 5–14 days previously. The diagnosis of acute myocardial infarction was based on the presence of any two of the following three criteria: (1) a typical history of chest pain of longer than 15 min duration and other clinical features of myocardial infarction; (2) electrocardiographic (ECG) changes as defined in the *W.H.O. Technical Report Series* no. 168, categories 1A (a–e); (3) raised serum enzyme levels greater than (*a*) twice the upper limit of normal of serum aspartate aminotransferase (AST) or lactate dehydrogenase (LDH), (*b*) three times the upper limit of normal of creatine phosphokinase (CPK). The upper limit of normal of these enzymes was defined by each hospital laboratory.

7. Patients were excluded from the trial for the following reasons: heart block of greater than first degree; heart rate less than 54 per min; women of childbearing potential, history of asthma or obstructive airways disease; insulin-dependent diabetes; clinical evidence of heart failure at the 12th post-infarction day; systolic blood-pressure persistently less than 100 mm Hg; positive antinuclear factor; other cardiac or non-cardiac conditions thought to be serious enough to worsen the short-term prognosis; and lack of cooperation by the patient or inability to follow up the patient for psychological or geographical reasons. If the patient was considered eligible for the study, tablets containing sotalol (320 mg) or placebo were administered once daily. Administration of the following drugs was not permitted according to the protocol of the study: quinidine, procainamide, diphenylhydantoin, mexiletine, disopyramide, monoamine oxidase inhibitors, tricyclic antidepressant drugs, adrenoceptor blocking agents, clacium antagonists.
8. Patients previously on a beta adrenoceptor blocking agent were entered only if they had been off this therapy for at least 5 days.
9. In patients in whom anginal symptoms could not be controlled by regulation of physical activity and treatment with trinitrin, and/or long-acting nitrates, additional open administration of sotalol was permissible, irrespective of the randomized study medication. Table I shows the number of patients excluded and the reasons for exclusion.

Table I. Entry to the study and reasons for exclusion

	No.	**(%)***
Patients considered for entry to study	3234	
Excluded from study	1778	(55%)
Beta blockers contraindicated	750	(23%)
Psychological reasons or refusal	250	(8%)
Severe extra-cardiac condition	210	(6%)
Receiving beta blockers	197	(6%)
On antiarrhythmic drugs	182	(6%)
Omitted in error	136	(4%)
Geographical reasons	53	(2%)
Randomized	1456	(45%)

*All percentages are expressed in relation to the 3234 patients considered for entry.

Follow-up

10. Patients still on trial medication returned for follow-up examination at 1 month, 3 months, 6 months, and 1 year. At each visit a full history was taken and the examination included a 12-lead ECG and a 30 s lead 2

strip. At 6 months and 12 months, routine blood and biochemical tests were done; antinuclear factor was tested for and a chest X-ray was taken. At follow-up clinics patients returned unused tablets for counting. As part of the 6-month review blood sotalol levels were measured, by a modification of the method of Sundquist *et al.*[10]

11. At each visit, patients were asked about any suspected adverse effects, and specific inquiry was made about rashes and eye symptoms. At the 6-month follow-up they completed a detailed questionnaire including 27 questions about symptoms and possible side-effects.
12. The medication was halved or temporarily discontinued if heart failure or a systolic blood-pressure under 100 mm Hg developed, and in the event of other suspected serious side-effects, the medication was halved or temporarily stopped. Initially the drug was reduced or discontinued when heart rates were less than 50 per min, but subsequently bradycardia in itself was not an indication for discontinuation. The medication was not restarted if any of the above events was not speedily controlled. If reinfarction was suspected and beta-blockade was not thought to be contraindicated, the medication was continued. In other case it was withdrawn temporarily or finally. Another reason for withdrawal of medication was development of a positive antinuclear factor.

End-point evaluation

13. The primary end-point of the study was death evaluated on an "intention to treat" basis. All patients who were randomized have been included, whether or not the allocated regimen had been discontinued. Information on deaths and reinfarctions was obtained from hospitals and general practitioners, and each event was verified by the consultants. Death or survival was confirmed for each patient at the completion of the study.
14. The criteria for reinfarction were the same as those for the initial infarction except that, when a patient died, necropsy evidence of recent infarction was accepted even in the absence of clinical or definite electrocardiographic features. Deaths were subcategorised by time from the onset of fresh symptoms into deaths within 24 h and those occurring subsequently. Those dying within 24 h were further subcategorized into those less than 1 h, those between 1 and 24 h, and those uncertain but within 24 h.

[Description of data handling details omitted]

Statistical methods

15. Standard methods were used for comparison of the two treatment

groups for all variables except survival, where the logrank test was applied. In addition, linear logistic models were fitted to investigate which variables affected the survival at one year. In calculation of the cumulative rates of reinfarction (fig. 2) the usual life-table methods were employed, with those patients who died without reinfarction being treated as "lost to follow-up" from the time of death.

Results

16. 3234 patients with acute myocardial infarction were considered for inclusion in the study. 1778 of these were not included because they fulfilled the criteria for exclusion or (in 136 cases) because they were inadvertently not identified as being suitable. 1456 patients were included in the study and were randomized—873 (60%) to the active treatment group and 583 (40%) to the placebo group.

Comparability of treatment groups

17. Table II shows the major characteristics of the 1456 patients randomized. The randomization resulted in broadly comparable groups with the largest differences occurring in the distribution of sex, previous angina, and left bundle branch block (LBBB). The main purpose of assessing comparability is to ensure that the analysis of outcome will not be affected by any differences. When linear logistic models were fitted, the conclusion regarding the effect of treatment on survival was unaffected by the inclusion of other variables.

Protocol violations

18. 125 patients, 80 on sotalol and 45 on placebo, did not fully satisfy the trial protocol. The distribution of reasons was similar in the two groups. Being outside the period of 5–14 days post-infarct (72 patients) was the most common reason. A further 20 patients received drugs not allowed in the protocol; 17 did not satisfy the criteria for myocardial infarction; 10 had a low heart rate; 5 were aged 70 or more; and 1 was an insulin-dependent diabetic. Despite the violation of the protocol these patients are included in the analysis since the violation was detected after randomization.

Compliance

19. Attempts were made to assess compliance in three ways. Firstly, the number of tablets returned at each visit was counted. Owing to an

Table II. Characteristics of 456 patients before randomization

Characteristics	**Percentages within categories**	
	Placebo	**Sotalol**
Sex Male	83	77
Female	17	23
Clinical history:		
Previous infarction	15	15
Angina	23	28
Hypertension	12	13
Smoking	65	64
Therapy before infarct:		
Beta blockers	11	13
Diuretics	9	8
Digitalis	2	2
Risk factors during acute phase:		
Heart failure	21	22
Cardiothoracic ratio >0.5	36	38
Lowest systolic Bl' <100 mm Hg	28	27
Atrial fibrillation or flutter	5	6
Other arrhythmias in acute stage:		
Supraventricular tachycardia	2	3
Ventricular tachycardia	5	5
Ventricular fibrillation	3	3
Second and third degree heart block	3	4
LBBB	3	1
RBBB	4	2
Site of infarct:		
Inferior	40	42
Anterior	44	42
Other/uncertain	17	17
	Mean ± SD	
Age (yr)	55.2 ± 7.9	55.4 ± 7.9
Interval from infarction to randomization (days)	8.2 ± 2.6	8.3 ± 2.6
Lowest recorded systolic BP after infarct (mm Hg)	104.6 ± 16.5	101.5 ± 15.6
Systolic BP at randomization (mm Hg)	122.4 ± 15.1	123.2 ± 15.6
Heart rate at randomization	77.3 ± 11.0	76.4 ± 11.2
Cardiothoracic ratio	0.47 ± 0.13	0.47 ± 0.11

ambiguity in the form design which led to the date being recorded unreliably, this method of determining compliance proved unsuccessful. Secondly, blood samples were taken from 1165 patients (692 sotalol, 473 placebo) still taking trial medication at the six month follow-up, 78% of the sotalol group and 4% of the placebo group had concentrations above 1.0 μg/ml (the level above which assays are

Table III. Heart rate during follow-up

Time (mo.)	Heart rate mean ± SD	
	Placebo	**Sotalol**
At entry	77.3 ± 11.0	76.4 ± 11.2
1	76.3 ± 13.9	59.6 ± 10.3
3	74.3 ± 12.9	58.7 ± 9.5
6	73.3 ± 12.8	58.3 ± 8.7
12	73.3 ± 12.8	59.8 ± 9.7

reliable) and the results in the placebo group correspond to the proportion receiving sotalol openly. Finally, the heart rate was considered to provide evidence of compliance; among the patients still on trial medication the resting heart rate was 15 beats/min less in those allocated to sotalol than in those allocated to placebo (table III).

Adverse reactions and withdrawal

20. 25% of the patients randomized to receive sotalol and 21% of those randomized to placebo were withdrawn from treatment during the

Table IV. Main reasons for discontinuation of study medication in 873 patients treated with sotalol and 583 patients treated with placebo

Reason	Temporary		Final	
	Placebo	**Sotalol**	**Placebo**	**Sotalol**
Angina pectoris	1 (0.2%)	3 (0.3%)	13 (2.2%)	16 (1.8%)
Reinfarction	4 (0.7%)	7 (0.8%)	6 (1.0%)	8 (0.9%)
Possible reinfarction	2 (0.3%)	0 (0.0%)	1 (0.2%)	0 (0.0%)
Heart failure	2 (0.3%)	8 (0.9%)	22 (3.8%)	23 (2.6%)
Hypotension	0 (0.0%)	2 (0.2%)	4 (0.7%)	18 (2.1%)
Bradycardia	0 (0.0%)	18 (2.1%)	0 (0.0%)	38 (4.4%)
Resistant hypertension	0 (0.0%)	0 (0.0%)	4 (0.7%)	1 (0.1%)
Arrhythmia	1 (0.2%)	1 (0.1%)	8 (1.4%)	12 (1.4%)
Adverse reaction	2 (0.3%)	4 (0.5%)	4 (0.7%)	23 (2.6%)
Other (total)	17 (2.9%)	19 (2.2%)	59 (10.1%)	83 (9.5%)
Including:				
Non-compliance	3 (0.5%)	2 (0.2%)	18 (3.1%)	25 (2.9%)
Criteria insufficient	0 (0.0%)	0 (0.0%)	8 (1.4%)	10 (1.1%)
Use of contraindicated drug	0 (0.0%)	0 (0.0%)	6 (1.0%)	6 (0.7%)
Doctor's discretion	1 (0.2%)	1 (0.1%)	4 (0.7%)	4 (0.5%)
Ran out of tablets	5 (0.9%)	5 (0.6%)	1 (0.2%)	1 (0.1%)
Total discontinuations	29 (5.0%)	62 (7.1%)	121 (20.8%)	222 (25.4%)

Table V. Percentage patients reporting possible adverse reactions

Category	**Percentage of patients with adverse reaction (no. of final withdrawals)**	
	Placebo ($n = 583$)	**Sotalol ($n = 873$)**
Dizziness	2.6	7.0 (2) $p < 0.001$
Depression	0.5	2.4 $p < 0.05$
Other central nervous system	12.0 (1)	14.0 (6)
Nausea	0.5 (1)	2.2 (1) $p < 0.05$
Other gastrointestinal	7.0	8.1 (1)
Dermatological	6.0 (2)	5.3 (3)
Cardiovascular	5.3	5.6 (2)
Coldness	3.3	5.5
Ophthalmic	2.9	5.6 (3) $p < 0.05$
Respiratory	4.5 (1)	4.4 (4)
Musculoskeletal	3.3	2.7
Genitourinary	1.0	1.3 (2)
Miscellaneous	2.7	2.9
Any adverse reaction	36.4 (4)*	41.6 (23)*

*The number of individual adverse reactions does not add up to these totals since some patients had multiple reactions.

1-year follow-up. Also, the tablets were withdrawn temporarily from 7% of sotalol patients and 5% of placebo patients for reasons given in table IV. The excess of withdrawals in the sotalol group was due to hypotension, bradycardia, and adverse reactions. 18 patients were taken off trial medication after it was realised that they did not satisfy fully the criteria for trial entry. However, since they had been randomised they are included in the analysis.

21. The adverse reactions leading to withdrawal are specified in table V which lists all adverse reactions recorded throughout follow-up. For this purpose all occurrences reported by the patient are deemed adverse reactions even if the physician did not record them as such. Dizziness, nausea, and depression, though not common, were significantly more common in the patients treated with sotalol. Also, ophthalmic reactions were significantly more common overall with sotalol, though no single adverse reaction in this category was significantly more common than with placebo. The severity of symptoms was not recorded, but persistence of any symptoms from one follow-up examination to the next was extremely uncommon. The detailed questionnaire administered at the 6-month follow-up showed only one statistically significant difference between the two treatment groups, cold extremities being reported by 34% of patients receiving sotalol compared with 25% of those on placebo (table VI).

Table VI. Patients' responses to specific inquiries at 6 month follow-up*

	Placebo	**Sotalol**
Feels well	89%	87%
Shortness of breath on exertion	43%	48%
Shortness of breath in night	4%	4%
Swelling of ankles	4%	7%
Chest pain	42%	41%
Faintness or giddiness	16%	17%
Nausea	6%	7%
Vomiting	2%	3%
Cough	17%	18%
Headaches	11%	13%
Tiredness	37%	42%
Weakness	14%	16%
Cold extremities	25%	34%
Pain in legs on walking	11%	11%
Loss of sexual desire	17%	19%
Failure of erection	12%	15%
Failure of ejaculation	9%	9%
Change in dreaming	6%	6%
Gritty eyes	7%	10%

*Major findings from original list of 27 questions.

Open use of sotalol

22. 26 (4.5%) patients randomized to placebo were given sotalol in addition to the trial medication for uncontrolled angina. A further 6 patients in this group (1.0%) received a beta-blocker other than sotalol, in violation of the trial protocol. In the group randomized to sotalol the corresponding figures were 15 (1.7%) and 3 (0.3%).

Outcome

23. *Survival.*—The mortality rates of 8.9% on placebo and 7.3% on sotalol do not differ significantly (logrank test: $\chi^2 = 1.1$, $p = 0.3$) (fig. 1). This conclusion did not change when the linear logistic analysis, which allows for the effect of other variables on survival, was performed. However, the direction and magnitude of the observed treatment difference is consistent with that observed in other secondary prevention trials of beta-blockers. The observed relative risk of patients on sotalol compared with placebo is 0.81, 95% confidence limits 0.55–1.19. The causes of death and the timing from onset of symptoms are shown in table VII. The variables found to affect survival significantly were the expected ones of age, site of infarct, pulmonary

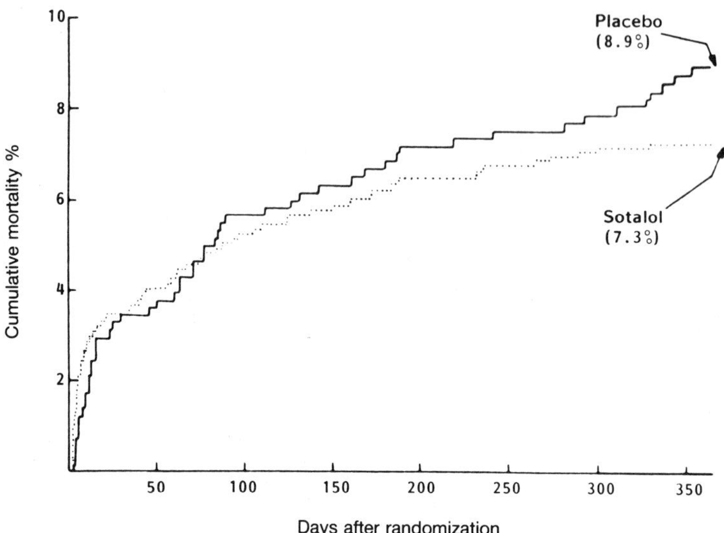

Fig. 1. Cumulative mortality in 873 patients randomized to receive sotalol and 583 patients randomized to receive placebo, all followed-up for 1 year

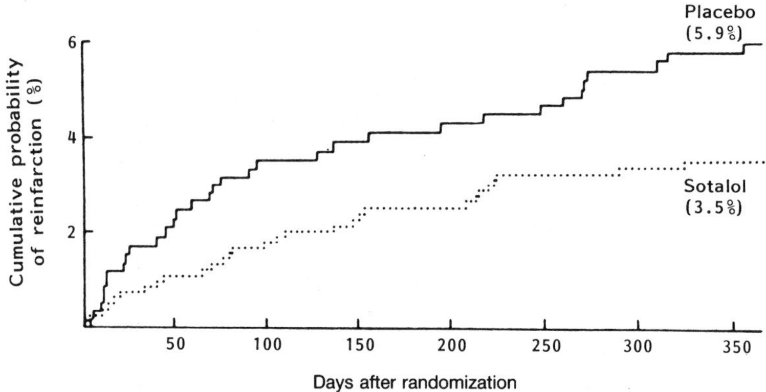

Fig. 2. Cumulative probability of reinfarction in 873 patients randomized to receive sotalol and 583 patients randomized to receive placebo
Logrank test: $\chi^2 = 4.7$, $p < 0.05$.

Table VII. Analysis of mortality

	No. of patients	
	Placebo ($n = 583$)	**Sotalol ($n = 873$)**
Cause of death:		
Cardiovascular	50 (8.6%)	62 (7.1%)
Non-cardiovascular		
(suicide, carcinoma of rectum,	—	2
carcinoma of oesophagus)	1	—
Cause not known	1	—
Total	52 (8.9%)	64 (7.3%)
Timing of cardiovascular deaths:		
Deaths within 24 h of symptoms		
<1 h	14 (2.4%)	25 (2.9%)
1–24 h	13 (2.2%)	16 (1.8%)
Uncertain	11 (1.9%)	7 (0.8%)
Total	38 (6.5%)	48 (5.5%)
Deaths after 24 h	11 (1.9%)	13 (1.5%)
Interval unknown	1	1
Concurrent use of study medication:		
Medication in use	35 (67%)	51 (80%)
Medication discontinued	17 (33%)	13 (20%)

congestion, cardiothoracic ratio, heart rate at entry, previous angina, and LBBB and RBBB. As indicated in fig. 1, the mortality in the first week of treatment was relatively high in those receiving sotalol, with an apparent benefit to the sotalol group later on in the follow-up period. There was no indication of any special clinical features in those patients who died soon after randomization, and indeed no statistical significance can be claimed for the apparently different mortality patterns in the two groups.

24. *Reinfarction.*—The rate of confirmed reinfarction was 5.7% in controls and 3.3% in the sotalol group. This difference is statistically significant at the 5% level, but with inclusion of possible but unconfirmed reinfarctions the difference narrows slightly and the level of significance falls to 7% (table VIII). Fig. 2 shows the cumulative rate of confirmed reinfarctions in the two treatment groups.

25. *Strokes.*—There was no statistically significant difference in the incidence of strokes between the groups. In the sotalol group there were 11 confirmed non-fatal strokes, 2 suspected non-fatal strokes, and 2 fatal strokes (1.7% overall). The corresponding numbers in the placebo group were 3,2, and 1 (1.0%).

Table VIII. Reinfractions

	No. of patients	
	Placebo ($n = 583$)	**Sotalol ($n = 873$)**
Confirmed reinfarctions:		
Non-fatal	22 (3.8%)	24* (2.7%)
Fatal	11 (1.9%)	5 (0.6%)
Total	33 (5.7%)	29 (3.3%)
		$x^2 = 4.1, p < 0.05$
Suspected reinfarctions:		
Non-fatal	3 (0.5%)	0 (0.0%)
Fatal	2 (0.3%)	10* (1.1%)
Total	5 (0.9%)	10 (1.1%)
Confirmed or suspected	38 (6.5%)	37 (4.2%)
		$x^2 = 3.3, p = 0.07$

*2 patients had both a confirmed non-fatal reinfarction and a suspected fatal reinfarction.

26. *Angina.*—Throughout the period of follow-up the prevalence of angina ranged from 25% to 33% and did not differ between the treatment groups.

Discussion

27. In this study, the mortality in those treated with sotalol was 7.3%–i.e., 18% less than that in the placebo group (8.9%). This difference was not statistically significant (p = 0.3). When the material was further studied for various risk factors, no special group emerged which seemed to benefit in a statistically significant way from sotalol. The incidence of definite myocardial reinfarction in the sotalol group was significantly less than in the placebo-treated group ($p < 0.05$); but when suspected reinfarctions were also considered the level of significance fell, since deaths suspected to be due to reinfarction could be confirmed less frequently in the sotalol group.
28. Although two recently reported studies[7,8] showed statistically significant benefits from the use of beta adrenoceptor blocking drugs, several previous trials were inconclusive. The differing results from the various trials has excited much controversy and speculation. It is important to recognise that when 95% confidence limits for these studies are reviewed, all the reported studies overlap and would be consistent with a benefit from all beta-blockers of 20–25%.

[Further detailed comparisons with other trials omitted]

29. The differences in the trials might, at least in part, be accounted for by the characteristics of the individual drugs. In most respects, timolol, propranolol, and sotalol are similar; all lack partial agonist activity and cardioselectivity. Sotalol differs importantly in having a clearly demonstrable class 3 antiarrhythmic effect which might be expected to reduce the risk of sudden death rather than reinfarction, but this did not prove to be the case. Indeed, there was a significant reduction of confirmed reinfarctions in this study. In reviewing all the trials in which beta adrenoceptor blocking drugs have been started more than 48 h after the onset of acute myocardial infarction, we see no clear evidence that any special characteristics of any beta-blocker are advantageous. The differences which have emerged may be explained by chance, the dosage chosen, the duration of the study, and the number and selection of patients. A reasonable conclusion is that, in those for whom they are not contraindicated, beta-blockers reduce mortality in the year after myocardial infarction by 20–25%.
[Acknowledgements and references omitted]

Reproduced by permission of the publishers and the first author, to whom thanks are given.

References

American Journal of Epidemiology (1978). Symposium on CHD prevention trials. *Am. J. Epidemiol.* **108**, 85–111.

Antunes, C.M.F., Stolley, P.D., Rosenshein, N.B., Davies J.L., Tonascia, J.A., Brown, C., Burnett, L., Rutledge, A., Pokempner, M. and Garcia, R. (1979). Endometrial cancer and estrogen use. Report of a large case-control study. *New Engl. J. Med.* **300**, 9–13.

Armitage, P. (1955). Test for linear trend in proportions and frequencies. *Biometrics* **11**, 375–86.

Armitage, P. (1971). *Statistical methods in medical research.* Blackwell Scientific, Oxford.

Armitage, P. (1975). *Sequential medical trials* (2nd edn). Blackwell Scientific, Oxford.

Arnold, F.A. Jr., Dean, H.T., Jay, P. and Knutson, J.W. (1956). Effect of fluoridated public water supplies on dental caries prevalence: tenth year of the Grand Rapids-Muskegon study. *Public Health Rep.* **71**, 652–8.

Austin, D.F. and Roe, K.M. (1982). The decreasing incidence of endometrial cancer: public health implications. *Am. J. Public Health* **72**, 65–8.

Baber, N.S., Julian, D.G., Lewis, J.A. and Rose, G. (1984). Beta blockers after myocardial infarction: have trials changed practice? *Br. med. J.* **289**, 1431–2.

Beral, V., Evans, S., Shaw, H. and Milton, G. (1982). Malignant melanoma and exposure to fluorescent lighting at work. *Lancet* **2**, 290–3.

Breslow, N.E. and Day, N.E. (1980). Statistical methods in cancer research. Vol. 1—The analysis of case-control studies. *IARC Scientific Publications No. 32*, Lyon.

Brinton, L.A., Huggins, G.R., Lehman, H.F., Mallin, K., Savitz, D.A., Trapido, E., Rosenthal, J. and Hoover, R. (1986). Long-term use of oral contraceptives and risk of invasive cervical cancer. *Int. J. Cancer* **38**, 339–44.

Buck, G. and Donner, A. (1982). The design of controlled experiments in the evaluation of non-therapeutic interventions. *J. chron. Dis.* **35**, 531–8.

Canadian Task Force on the Periodic Health Examination (1979). The periodic health examination. *Can. Med. Assn. J.* **121**, 1193–1254.

Carter, C.O., David, P.A. and Laurence, K.M. (1968). A family study of major central nervous system malformations in South Wales. *J. Med. Genet.* **5**, 81–106.

Cederlof, R., Friberg, L., Jonsson, E. and Kaij, L. (1966). Respiratory symptoms and 'angina pectoris' in twins with reference to smoking habits. An epidemiological study with mailed questionnaire. *Archiv. Env. Health (Chicago)* **13**, 726–37.

Centers for Disease Control Cancer and Steroid Hormone Study (1983). Oral contraceptive use and the risk of endometrial cancer. *J. Am. med. Assn.* **249**, 1600–4.

Charig, C.R., Webb, D.R., Payne, S.R. and Wickham, J.E.A. (1986). Comparison of treatment of renal calculi by open surgery, percutaneous nephrolithotomy, and extracorporeal shockwave lithotripsy. *Br. J. Med.* **292**, 877–882.

Charlton, A. (1984). Children's coughs related to parental smoking. *Br. med. J.* **288**, 1647–9.

Chisholm, E.M., de Dombal, F.T. and Giles, G.R. (1985). Validation of a self administered questionnaire to elicit gastrointestinal symptoms. *Br. med. J.* **290**, 1795–6.

Cohen, J. (1960). A coefficient of agreement for nominal scales. *Educ. psychol. Meas.* **20**, 37–46.

Coldman, A.J. and Elwood, J.M. (1979). Examining survival data. *Can. Med. Assoc. J.* **121**, 1065–71.

Cole, P., Mack, T., Rothman, K., Henderson, B. and Newell, G. (1973). Tonsillectomy and Hodgkin's Disease. *New Engl. J. Med.* **288**, 634–5.

Collette, H.J.A., Day, N.E., Rombach, J.J. and de Waard, F. (1984). Evaluation of screening for breast cancer in a non-randomised study (the DOM project) by means of a case-control study. *Lancet* **1**, 1224–6.

Collins, R., Yusuf, S. and Peto, R. (1985). Overview of randomized trials of diuretics in pregnancy. *Br. med. J.* **290**, 17–23.

Coronary Drug Project Research Group (1980). Influence of adherence to treatment and response of cholesterol on mortality in the coronary drug project. *New Engl. J. Med.* **303**, 1038–41.

Cox, D.R. (1972). Regression models and life tables. *J. R. Stat. Soc.* **34**, 187–220.

Cuzick, J., Stewart, H., Peto, R., Baum, M., Fisher, B., Host, H., Lythgoe, J.P., Ribeiro, G., Scheurlen, H. and Wallgren, A. (1987). Overview of randomized trials of postoperative adjuvant radiotherapy in breast cancer. *Cancer Treatment Reports* **71**, 15–29.

Dawber, T.R. (1980). *The Framingham Study.* Harvard University Press, Cambridge.

Doll, R. and Hill, A.B. (1950). Smoking and carcinoma of the lung. *Br. med. J.* **ii**, 739–48.

Doll, R. and Hill, A.B. (1952). A study of the aetiology of carcinoma of the lung. *Br. med. J.* **ii**, 1271–86.

Doll, R. and Hill, A.B. (1964). Mortality in relation to smoking: Ten years' observations of British doctors. *Br. med. J.* **i**, 1399–1410.

Doll, R. and Peto, R. (1976). Mortality in relation to smoking: 20 years' observations on male British doctors. *Br. med. J.* **ii**, 1525–36.

Doll, R., Gray, R., Hafner, B. and Peto, R. (1980). Mortality in relation to smoking: 22 years' observations on female British doctors. *Br. med. J.* **280**, 967–71.

Elwood, J.M. (1978). Maternal and environmental factors affecting twin births in Canadian cities. *Br. J. obstet. Gynaecol.* **85**, 351–8.

Elwood, J.M. (1981). Wood exposure and smoking; association with cancer of the nasal cavity and paranasal sinuses in British Columbia. *Can. Med. Assn. J.* **124**, 1573–7.

Elwood, J.M., Raman, S. and Mousseau, G. (1978). Reproductive history in the mothers of anencephalics. *J. chron. Dis.* **31**, 473–81.

Elwood, J.M., Williamson, C. and Stapleton, P.J. (1986). Malignant melanoma in relation to moles, pigmentation, and exposure to fluorescent and other lighting sources. *Br. J. Cancer* **53**, 65–74.

Elwood, J.M., Gallagher, R.P., Davison, J. and Hill. G.B. (1985). Sunburn, suntan and the risk of cutaneous malignant melanoma—The Western Canada Melanoma Study. *Br. J. Cancer* **51**, 543–9.

Elwood, J.M., Pearson, J.C.G., Skippen, D.H. and Jackson, S.M. (1984). Alcohol, smoking, social and occupational factors in the aetiology of cancer of the oral cavity, pharynx and larynx. *Int. J. Cancer* **34**, 603–12.

Emanuel, I. and Sever, L.E. (1973). Questions concerning the possible association of potatoes and neural-tube defects, and an alternative hypothesis relating to maternal growth and development. *Teratology* **8**, 325–32.

Evans, A.E. (1986). Secondary prevention after myocardial infarction. *Lancet* **2**, 150–1.

Farquhar, J.W. (1978). The community-based model of lifestyle intervention trials. *Am. J. Epidemiol.* **108**, 103–11.

Farquhar, J.W., Maccoby, N., Wood, P.D., Alexander, J.K., Breitrose, H., Brown, B.W.Jr., Haskell, W.L., McAlister, A.J., Meyer, A.J., Nash, J.D. and Stern, M.P. (1977). Community education for cardiovascular health. *Lancet* **1**, 1192–5.

Fentiman, I.S., Cuzick, J., Mills, R.R. and Hayward, J.L. (1984). Which patients are cured of breast cancer? *Br. med. J.* **289**, 1108–11.

Fisher, G.H. (1965). *The new form statistical tables* (2nd edn.) Hodder and Stoughton, Sevenoaks, (formerly University of London Press, London).

Fisher, R.A. and Yates, F. (1963). *Statistical tables for biological, agricultural and medical research* (1974 printing). Longman, London.

Fleiss, J.L. (1973). *Statistical methods for rates and proportions*. Wiley, New York.

Gillies, P., Elwood, J.M., Pearson, J.C.G. and Cust, G. (1987). An adolescent smoking survey in Trent, and its contribution to health promotion. *Health Education J.* **46**, 19–22.

Godolphin, W., Elwood, J.M. and Spinelli, J. (1981). Estrogen receptor quantitation and staging as complementary prognostic indicators in breast cancer: a study of 583 patients. *Int. J. Cancer* **28**, 677–83.

Gordon T., Castelli, W.P., Hjortland, M.C., Kannel, W.B. and Dawber, T.R. (1977). Predicting coronary heart disease in middle-aged and older persons: The Framingham Study. *J. Am. med. Assn.* **238**, 497–9.

Hennekens, C.H., Speizer, F.E., Rosner, B., Bain, C.J., Belanger C. and Peto R. (1979). Use of permanent hair dyes and cancer among registered nurses. *Lancet* **1**, 1390–3.

Herbst, A.L., Ulfelder, H. and Poskanzer, D.C. (1971). Adenocarcinoma of the vagina: association of maternal stilbestrol therapy with tumor appearance in young females. *New Engl. J. Med.* **284**, 878–81.

Herbst, A.L., Cole, P., Colton, T., Robboy, S.J. and Scully, R.E. (1977). Age-incidence and risk of diethylstilbestrol-related clear cell adenocarcinoma of the vagina and cervix. *Am. J. obstet. Gynecol.* **128**, 43–50.

Hill, J.D., Hampton, J.R. and Mitchell, J.R.A. (1978). A randomised trial of home-versus-hospital management for patients with suspected myocardial infarction. *Lancet* **1**, 837–41.

Howe, G.R., Burch, J.D., Miller, A.B., Morrison, B., Gordon, P., Weldon, L., Chambers, L.W., Fodor, G. and Winsor, G.M. (1977). Artificial sweeteners and human bladder cancer. *Lancet* **2**, 578–81.

ISIS–1 Collaborative Group (1986). Randomised trial of intravenous atenolol among 16 027 cases of suspected acute myocardial infarction. *Lancet* **2**, 57–66.

Johnson, S.K. and Johnson, R.E. (1972). Tonsillectomy history in Hodgkin's Disease. *New Engl. J. Med.* **287**, 1122–5.

Julian, D.G., Prescott, R.J., Jackson, F.S. and Szekeley, P. (1982). Controlled trial of sotalol for one year after myocardial infarction. *Lancet* **1**, 1142–7.

Kalbfleisch, J.D. and Prentice, R.L. (1980). *The statistical analysis of failure time data*. Wiley, New York.

Kleinbaum, D.G., Kupper, L.L. and Morgenstern, H. (1982). *Epidemiological Research*. Lifetime Learning Publications, Belmont, California.

Lyon, J.L., Gardner, J.W., West, D.W., Stanish, W.M. and Hebertson, R.M. (1983). Smoking and carcinoma in situ of the uterine cervix. *Am. J. Public Health* **73**, 558–62.

MacGregor, J.E., Moss, S.M., Parkin, D.M. and Day, N.E. (1985). A case-control study of cervical cancer screening in north east Scotland. *Br. med. J.* **290**, 1543–6.

MacMahon, B. (1957). Epidemiological evidence on the nature of Hodgkin's disease. *Cancer* **10**, 1045–54.

McNemar, Q. (1947). Note on the sampling of the difference between corrected proportions or percentages. *Psychometrika* **12**, 153–7.

McPherson, K. and Drife, J.O. (1986). The pill and breast cancer: why the uncertainty? Editorial. *Br. med. J.* **293**, 709–10.

Mantel, N. (1966). Evaluation of survival data and two new rank order statistics arising in its consideration. *Cancer Chemother. Rep.* **50**, 163–70.

Mantel, N. (1963). Chi-square tests with one degree of freedom: extension of the Mantel–Haenszel procedure. *J. Am. Stat. Assoc.* **58**, 690–700.

Mantel, N. and Haenszel W. (1959). Statistical aspects of the analysis of data from retrospective studies of disease. *J. Natl. Cancer Inst.* **22**, 719–48.

Medical Research Council (1948). Streptomycin treatment of pulmonary tuberculosis. *Br. med. J.* ii, 769–82.

Medical Research Council Working Party (1985). MRC trial of treatment of mild hypertension: principal results. *Br. med. J.* **291**, 97–104.

Meinert, C.L. (1986). *Clinical Trials: Design, conduct and analysis*. Oxford University Press, New York.

Miettinen, O.S. (1970). Estimation of relative risk from individually matched series. *Biometrics* **26**, 75–86.

Miettinen, O.S. (1972). Components of the crude risk ratio. *Am. J. Epidemiol.* **96**, 168–72.

Miettinen, O.S. (1976). Estimability and estimation in case-referent studies. *Am. J. Epidemiol.* **103**, 226–35.

Miller, A.B., Lindsay, J. and Hill, G.B. (1976). Mortality from cancer of the uterus in Canada and its relationship to screening for cancer of the cervix. *Int. J. Cancer* **17**, 602–12.

Miller, A.B., Klaassen, D.J., Boyes, D.A., Dodds, D.J., Gerulath, A., Kirk, M.E., Levitt, M., Pearson, J.C.G. and Wall, C. (1980). Combination v. sequential therapy with melphalan, 5-fluorouracil and methotrexate for advanced ovarian cancer. *Can. Med. Assoc. J.* **123**, 365–71.

Moser, C. and Kalton, G. (1979). *Survey methods in social investigations*. Heinemann, London.

Multiple Risk Factor Intervention Trial Research Group (1982). Multiple Risk Factor Intervention Trial—risk factor changes and mortality results. *J. Am. Med. Assoc.* **248**, 1465–77.

Neri Serneri, G.G., Rovelli, F., Gensini, G.F., Pirelli, S., Carnovali, M. and Fortini, A. (1987). Effectiveness of low-dose heparin in prevention of myocardial reinfarction. *Lancet* **1**, 937–42.

Odenheimer, D.J., Zunzunegui M.V., King, M.C., Shipler, C.P. and Friedman G.D. (1984). Risk factors for benign breast disease: a case-control study of discordant twins. *Am. J. Epidemiol.* **120**, 565–71.

O'Muircheartaigh, C.A. and Marckwardt, A.M. (1980). *An assessment of the reliability of World Fertility Survey data.* World Fertility Survey Conference, London.

Paffenbarger, R.S. and Hale, W.E. (1975). Work activity and coronary heart mortality. *New Engl. J. Med.* **292**, 545–50.

Paffenbarger, R.S., Fasal, E., Simmons, M.E. and Kambert, J.B. (1977). Cancer risk as related to use of oral contraceptives during the fertile years. *Cancer* **39**, 1887–91.

Paul, C., Skegg, D.C.G., Spears, G.F.S. and Kaldor, J.M. (1986). Oral contraceptives and breast cancer: a national study. *Br. med. J.* **293**, 723–6.

Peto, R., Pike, M.C., Armitage, P., Breslow, N.E., Cox, D.R., Howard, S.V., Mantel, N., McPherson, K., Peto, J. and Smith P.G. (1977). Design and analysis of randomized clinical trials requiring prolonged observation of each patient. II. Analysis and examples. *Br. J. Cancer* **35**, 1–39.

Pike, M.C. and Morrow, R.H. (1970). Statistical analysis of patient-control studies in epidemiology. Factor under investigation an all-or-none variable. *Br. J. prev. soc. Med.* **24**, 42–4.

Pike, M.C., Henderson, B.E., Krailo, M.D., Duke, A. and Roy, S. (1983). Breast cancer in young women and use of oral contraceptives: possible modifying effect of formulation and age at use. *Lancet* **2**, 926–30.

Pocock, S.J. (1983). *Clinical Trials. A practical approach.* Wiley, Chichester.

Pooling Project Research Group (1978). Relationship of blood pressure, serum cholesterol, smoking habit, relative weight and E.C.G. abnormalities to incidence of major coronary events: final report of the pooling project. *J. chron. Dis.* **31**, 201–306.

Puska, P., Salonen, J.T., Nissinen, A., Tuomilehto, J., Vartiainen, E., Korhonen, H., Tanskanen, A., Ronnquist, P., Koskela, K. and Huttunen, J. (1983). Change in risk factors for coronary heart disease during 10 years of a community intervention programme (North Karelia project). *Br. med. J.* **287**, 1840–4.

Rothman, K.J. (1976). The estimation of synergy or antagonism. *Amer. J. Epidemiol.* **103**, 506–11.

Rothman, K.J. (1986). *Modern Epidemiology.* Little, Brown and Co., Boston.

Rothman, K.J. and Boice, J.D. (1982). *Epidemiologic analysis with a programmable calculator* (2nd edn). Epidemiology Resources Inc. Brookline, MA.

Royal College of General Practitioners (1974). *Oral contraceptives and health. An interim report from the Oral Contraception Study of the Royal College of General Practitioners.* Pitman Medical, London.

Royal College of General Practitioners' Oral Contraception Study. (1977). Mortality among oral contraceptive users. *Lancet* **2**, 727–31.

Sackett, D.L. and Gent, M. (1979). Controversy in counting and attributing events in clinical trials. *New Engl. J. Med.* **301**, 1410–2.

Sackett, D.L., Haynes, R.B. and Tugwell, P. (1985). *Clinical Epidemiology: a basic science for clinical medicine.* Little, Brown and Co., Boston.

Saracci, R. (1977). Asbestos and lung cancer: an analysis of the epidemiological evidence on the asbestos-smoking interaction. *Int. J. Cancer* **20**, 323-31.

Saral, R., Burns, W.H., Laskin, O.L., Santos, G.W. and Lietman, P.S. (1981). Acyclovir prophylaxis of herpes-simplex-virus infections. *New Engl. J. Med.* **305**, 63-7.

Schlesselman, J.J. (1982). *Case-control studies: design, conduct, analysis.* Oxford University Press, Oxford.

Schull, W.J. and Cobb, S. (1969). The intrafamilial transmission of rheumatoid arthritis III. The lack of support for a genetic hypothesis. *J. chron. Dis.* **22**, 217-22.

Shapiro, S., Kaufman, D.W., Slone, D., Rosenberg, L., Miettinen, O.S., Stolley, P.D., Rosenshein, N.B., Watring, W.G., Leavitt, T. and Knapp R.C. (1980). Recent and past use of conjugated estrogens in relation to adenocarcinoma of the endometrium. *New Engl. J. Med.* **303**, 485-9.

Shapiro, S., Venet, W., Strax, P., Venet, L. and Roeser R. (1982). Ten to fourteen year effect of screening on breast cancer mortality. *J. Natl. Cancer Inst.* **49**, 349-55.

Shapiro, S., Slone, D., Hartz, S.C., Rosenberg, L., Siskind, V., Monson, R.R., Mitchell, A.A., Heinonen, O.P., Idanpaan-Heikkila, J., Haro, S. and Saxen, L. (1976). Anticonvulsants and parental epilepsy in the development of birth defects. *Lancet* **1**, 272-5.

Shrout, P.E., Spitzer, R.L. and Fleiss, J.L. (1987). Quantification of agreement in psychiatric diagnosis revisited. *Arch. Gen. Psychiatry* **44**, 172-7.

Smith, D.C., Prentice, R., Thompson, D.J. and Herrmann, W.L. (1975). Association of exogenous estrogen and endometrial carcinoma. *New Engl. J. Med.* **293**, 1164-7.

Statistics in Medicine (1987). Proceedings of the workshop on methodological issues in overviews of randomized clinical trials. *Statistics in Medicine* **6**, 217-409.

Susser, M. (1977). Judgment and causal inference: criteria in epidemiologic studies. *Am. J. Epidemiol.* **105**, 1-15.

Taylor, K.M., Margolese, R.G. and Soskolne, C.L. (1984). Physicians' reasons for not entering eligible patients in a randomised clinical trial of surgery for breast cancer. *New Engl. J. Med.* **310**, 1363-7.

Thomas, D.B. and Chu, J. (1986). Nutritional and endocrine factors in reproductive organ cancers: opportunities for primary prevention. *J. chron. Dis.* **39**, 1031-50.

Truett, J., Cornfield, J. and Kannel, W.B. (1967). A multivariate analysis of the risk of coronary heart disease in Framingham. *J. chron. Dis.* **20**, 511-24.

University Group Diabetes Program (1970). A study of the effects of hypoglycemic agents on vascular complications in patients with adult-onset diabetes. II: mortality results. *Diabetes* **19**, (suppl.2), 785-830.

Vecchio, T.J. (1966). Predictive value of a single diagnostic test in unselected populations. *New Engl. J. Med.* **274**, 1171-3.

Veronesi, U., Saccozzi, R., Del Vecchio, M., Banfi, A., Clemente, C., De Lena, M., Gallus, G., Greco, M., Luini, A., Marubini, E., Muscolino, G., Rilke, F., Salvadori, B., Zecchini, A. and Zucali, R. (1981). Comparing radical mastectomy with quadrantectomy, axillary dissection, and radiotherapy in patients with small cancers of the breast. *New Engl. J. Med.* **305**, 6-11.

Vessey, M.P. (1971). Some methodological problems in the investigation of rare adverse reactions to oral contraceptives. *Am. J. Epidemiol.* **94**, 202-9.

Vessey, M.P. and Doll, R. (1969). Investigation of relation between use of oral contraceptives and thromboembolic disease. A further report. *Br. med. J.* **ii**, 651–7.

Vessey, M.P., Johnson, B. and Donnelly, J. (1974). Reliability of reporting by women taking part in a prospective contraceptive study. *Br. J. prev. soc. Med.* **28**, 104–7.

Vessey, M.P., Doll, R., Peto, R., Johnson, B. and Wiggins, P. (1976). A long-term follow-up study of women using different methods of contraception—an interim report. *J. biosoc. Sci.* **8**, 373–427.

Vessey, M.P., Lawless, M., McPherson, K. and Yeates, D. (1983). Neoplasia of the cervix uteri and contraception: a possible adverse effect of the pill. *Lancet* **2**, 930–4.

Vessey, M.P., Lawless, M., McPherson, K. and Yeates, D. (1983a). Oral contraceptives and cervical cancer (letter). *Lancet* **2**, 1358–9.

Wakabayashi, T., Kato. H., Ikeda, T. and Schull, W.J. (1983). Studies of the mortality of A-bomb survivors. Report 7, Part III. Incidence of cancer in 1959–78, based on the tumour registry, Nagasaki. *Radiation Res.* **93**, 112–146.

Wald, N.J., Nanchahal, K., Thompson, S.G. and Cuckle, H.S. (1986). Does breathing other people's tobacco smoke cause lung cancer? *Br. med. J.* **293**, 1217–22.

Wald, N.J., Cuckle, H.S., Boreham, J., Brett, R., Stirrat, G.M., Bennett, M.J., Turnbull, A.C., Solymar, M., Jones, N., Bobrow, M. and Evans, C.J. (1979). Antenatal screening in Oxford for fetal neural tube defects. *Br. J. Obst. Gynaecol* **86**, 91–100.

Weiss, N.S., Szekely, D.R. and Austin, D.F. (1976). Increasing incidence of endometrial cancer in the United States. *New Engl. J. Med.* **294**, 1259–62.

WHO Collaborative study of neoplasia and steroid contraceptives (1985). Invasive cervical cancer and combined oral contraceptives. *Br. med. J.* **290**, 961–5.

Woolf, B. (1955). On estimating the relationship between blood group and disease. *Ann. Human Genet.* **19**, 251–3.

Yusuf, S., Peto, R., Lewis, J., Collins, R. and Sleight, P. (1985). Beta blockade during and after myocardial infarction: an overview of the randomized trials. *Prog. cardiovasc. Diseases* **27**, 335–71.

Ziel, H.K. and Finkle, W.D. (1975). Increased risk of endometrial carcinoma among users of conjugated estrogens. *New Engl. J. Med.* **293**, 1167–70.

Ziel, H.K. (1982). Estrogen's role in endometrial cancer. *J. Obstet. Gynecol.* **60**, 509–15.

Appendix 1
Statistical formulae

Summary of calculations of measures of association and of statistical tests, for the main study designs discussed; and reference tables for sample size calculation.

Introduction

Appendix 1: Statistical formulae

Introduction

In this appendix, we set out some commonly used formulae which are useful for the analysis of data from the types of study covered in this text. The formulae, together with the relevant sections of the text and the statistical tables in Appendix 3, will enable the reader to analyse most studies where the factors involved are discrete rather than continuous variables. Of course, major or crucial analyses should not be done without consideration of alternative methods and discussion with colleagues, including those more skilled in statistical and epidemiological methods.

The formulae we have chosen to present are primarily those derived from the work of Mantel and Haenszel. These formulae involve approximations which are appropriate if the numbers of observations available are adequate: in a two-by-two table each expected value should be greater than five. For the formulae used to produce summary risk estimates and test statistics after confounder control by stratification, it is the total number of observations which is relevant; the formulae can be applied even if some strata have few observations. The statistics used to test whether an odds ratio or attributable risk estimate is constant over several strata *do* depend upon having reasonable numbers of observations within each stratum.

The one exception in this Appendix to the limitation of small numbers is the test for a two-by-two table presented in Ex. A1.4. This gives the reader one exact method which makes no assumptions about the number of observations available, which can be applied to simple tables with small numbers. For all the other designs considered, more precise formulae ('exact' tests) are also available, but these will usually give similar results except where the numbers of observations are small.

The sources of the formulae are given with each table. There are many texts which discuss these and related formulae in detail, describe the situations in which more complex formulae may be appropriate, and provide information on them. Amongst the sources to which we have made frequent reference are *Modern Epidemiology* by K.J. Rothman (1986), and *Statistical Methods in Cancer Research, Volume I: the analysis of case control studies* by N.E. Breslow and N.E. Day (1980) published for the International Agency for Research on Cancer. A volume on the analysis of cohort studies is due to be published by the IARC and will undoubtedly be another very useful reference. Other appropriate references are available, but many require more mathematical sophistication than the ones noted above.

The reader is warned to be cautious about the notation employed by different authors, as sources differ from each other and may well differ from the notation used here. It is important in taking formulae from any source to check the notation used for the basic table on which the formulation is based.

Ex. A1.1. Case–control studies. Unmatched

1. *Format of table*

	Cases (affected)	Controls (unaffected)	Total
Exposed	a	b	N_1
Unexposed	c	d	N_0
Total	M_1	M_0	T

2. *Risks*

Odds ratio, $OR = \dfrac{a}{b} \Big/ \dfrac{c}{d} = \dfrac{ad}{bc}$.

3. *Statistical tests*

Observed exposed cases $= a$
Expected value of a $= E = N_1M_1/T$
Variance of a $= V = N_1N_0M_1M_0/T^2(T-1)$

3A Chi-square statistic, χ^2, with 1 degree of freedom $= \dfrac{(a - E)^2}{V} =$

$$= \frac{(a - N_1M_1/T)^2}{\dfrac{(N_1N_0M_1M_0)}{\{T^2(T-1)\}}}$$

3B χ statistic, or Normal deviate $= \chi = \sqrt{\chi^2}$.

3C Continuity correction: reduce absolute value of numerator by $\frac{1}{2}$ before squaring; i.e. replace numerator by $(|a-E| - \frac{1}{2})^2$, $|a-E|$ means the absolute value of $(a-E)$, irrespective of being positive or negative.

4. *Confidence limits (C.L.)*

y% limits for logarithm of odds ratio $= \ln OR \pm Zy(\text{dev} \ln OR)$, where
Zy = appropriate Normal deviate (see Ex. A3.1) and dev ln OR = standard deviation of ln OR

4A Test based formula: dev ln $OR = (\ln OR)/\chi$
hence y% limits for ln OR $= \ln OR \pm Zy(\text{dev} \ln OR)$
$= \ln OR(1 \pm Zy/\chi)$
and y% limits for OR $= \exp[\ln OR(1 \pm Zy/\chi)]$.

4B Alternative formula: dev ln $OR = \sqrt{\left(\dfrac{1}{a} + \dfrac{1}{b} + \dfrac{1}{c} + \dfrac{1}{d}\right)}$.

Worked example

Data from the case-control study shown in Ex. 7.12 (p 151); association between cervical carcinoma and smoking.

1. Crude table:

	Cases	Controls	Total
Smokers	130	45	175
Non-smokers	87	198	285
Total	217	243	460

2. Odds ratio = (130 × 198)/(45 × 87) = 6.57

3A, B Statistical test:

a = 130 E = 175 × 217/460 = 82.55

V = (175 × 285 × 243 × 217)/(460 × 460 × 459) = 27.08

χ^2 = $(130 - 82.55)^2/27.08$ = 83.14 $\chi = \sqrt{83.14} = 9.12$

d.f. = 1 $P < 0.000\,001$ (Statistical Table 1).

3C With continuity correction χ^2 = 81.4

4A 95% confidence limits for OR = exp[ln 6.57 (1 ± 1.96/9.12)]
= 4.4, 9.8

4B or, by formula 4B: dev ln OR = $\sqrt{(1/130 + 1/45 + 1/87 + 1/198)}$
= 0.216

and 95% c.l. = exp[ln 6.57 ± (1.96 × 0.216)]
= 4.3, 10.0

5. *Stratified analysis over I subtables of above format, values a_i etc.*

5A Summary odds ratio $= OR_s = \dfrac{\sum_i a_i d_i / T_i}{\sum_i b_i c_i / T_i}$

5B Summary χ^2 statistic, 1 d.f. $= \dfrac{\left(\sum_i a_i - \sum_i E_i\right)^2}{\sum_i V_i}$

Each term analogous to 3 above.

5C Continuity correction: reduce absolute value of numerator by $\frac{1}{2}$ before squaring.

5D Test based confidence limits as in 4 above, using summary *OR* and summary χ statistic.

5E Test of homogeneity $= \sum_i \dfrac{(\ln OR_i - \ln OR_s)^2}{(\text{var} \ln OR_i)}$ where variance of ln OR_i = square of standard deviations given in 4A, 4B above. Gives a χ^2 on I − 1 degrees of freedom.

Sources:		
	3A, 5A, 5B	Mantel and Haenszel (1959)
	4A, 5D	Miettinen (1976)
	4B	Wolff (1955)
	5E	Rothman (1986)

5. Stratified analysis:

Data are shown in Ex. 7.12 (p 151). Totals in the three sub-tables are 113, 211, 136.

5A Summary $OR = \dfrac{(41 \times 53/113) + (66 \times 83/211) + (23 \times 62/136)}{(6 \times 13/113) + (25 \times 37/211) + (14 \times 37/136)}$
$= 6.27$

5B Summary χ^2: calculate for each sub-table a_i, E_i, V_i; and sum each of these.

	a_i	E_i	V_i
Sub-table 1	41	22.46	6.91
2	66	44.42	12.99
3	23	16.32	6.69
Sum	130	83.20	26.59

$\chi^2 = (130 - 83.2)^2/26.59 = 82.4 \quad \chi = \sqrt{82.4} = 9.08$

5C χ^2 with continuity correction $= 80.6$
d.f. $= 1$ $\quad P < 0.000\,001$ (Statistical Table 1).

5D 95% confidence limits for summary $OR = \exp\{\ln 6.27(1 \pm 1.96/9.08)\}$
$= 4.2, 9.3$

5E Test of homogeneity: calculate for each table OR_i, and χ^2 (from a_i, E_i and V_i above); hence dev ln OR_i = ln OR_i/χ; or use formula 4B to obtain dev ln OR_i

	OR_i	χ^2	dev ln OR_i (test based) = ln OR_i/χ	dev ln OR_i (formula 4B)
Sub-table 1	27.86	49.74	0.472	0.536
2	5.92	35.85	0.297	0.307
3	2.75	6.67	0.392	0.398

Hence test of homogeneity = sum of $\{(\ln OR_i - \ln OR_s)^2/\text{var} \ln OR_i\}$
where var ln OR_i = dev ln OR_i^2 and $OR_s = 6.27$
or, equivalently, test = sum of $\{\ln(OR_i/OR_s)/\text{dev} \ln OR_i\}^2$

using test based deviations $\chi^2 = (9.98 + 0.04 + 4.42) = 14.4 \quad P < 0.001$
using formula 4B $\quad \chi^2 = (7.74 + 0.04 + 4.29) = 12.1$
$0.001 < P < 0.01$

d.f. = 2, P-values from Statistical Table 2. The odds ratios vary significantly.

Ex. A1.2. Cohort studies, count data

1. *Format of table*

	Affected	Unaffected	Total	Risk
Exposed	a	b	N_1	$a/N_1 = r_e$
Unexposed	c	d	N_0	$c/N_0 = r_0$
Total	M_1	M_0	T	

2. *Risks*

Relative risk $= r_e/r_0$ Odds ratio $= \dfrac{ad}{bc}$ Attributable risk $= r_e - r_0$

3. *Statistical tests*

Observed exposed cases $= a$
Expected value of $a = E = N_1M_1/T$
Variance of $a = V = N_1N_0M_1M_0/T^2(T-1)$

3A Chi-square statistic, χ^2, with 1 degree of freedom $= \dfrac{(a-E)^2}{V} =$

$$= \frac{(a - N_1M_1/T)^2}{\dfrac{(N_1N_0M_1M_0)}{\{T^2(T-1)\}}}$$

3B χ statistic, or Normal deviate $= \chi = \sqrt{\chi^2}$.

3C Continuity correction: reduce absolute value of numerator by $\frac{1}{2}$ before squaring; i.e. replace numerator by $(|a-E| - \frac{1}{2})^2$; $|a-E|$ means the absolute value of $(a-E)$, irrespective of being positive or negative.

4. *Confidence limits (C.L.)*

(i) for logarithm of RR
$= \ln RR \pm Zy$ dev $\ln RR$

(ii) for logarithm of OR; analogous to RR, hence
$= \ln OR \pm Zy$ dev $\ln OR$

(iii) for attributable risk
$= AR \pm Zy$ dev AR

where Zy = appropriate Normal deviate (see Ex. A3.1) and dev = standard deviation.

Worked example

Data from the prospective cohort study of pregnancy shown in Ex. 3.2 (p 27); association between maternal epilepsy and malformation in infants.

1. Crude table:

	Malformed	Not malformed	Total	Prevalence of malformation (%)
Exposed—epilepsy	32	273	305	10.49
Unexposed—no epilepsy	3216	46 761	49 977	6.43
Total	3248	47 034	50 282	

2. Relative risk = 1.63 Odds ratio = 1.70 Attributable risk = 4.06%

3A Statistical test:

$a = 32 \quad E = 305 \times 3248/50\,282 = 19.70$

$V = (305 \times 49\,977 \times 47\,034 \times 3248)/(50\,282 \times 50\,282 \times 50\,281)$

$= 18.32$

3B $\chi^2 = (a - E)^2/V = 8.26 \qquad \chi = \sqrt{\chi^2} = 2.87$

d.f. = 1 $\quad P < 0.01$ (Statistical Table 1).

3C With continuity correction $\chi^2 = 7.60$.

4A Test based formulae

(i) Relative risk

$$\text{dev}\ \ln RR = \ln RR/\chi$$
$$y\%\ \text{limits} = \ln RR \pm Zy\ \text{dev}\ \ln RR = \ln RR(1 \pm Zy/\chi)$$
$$y\%\ \text{limits for}\ RR = \exp[\ln RR(1 \pm Zy/\chi)]$$

(ii) Odds ratio: for ln OR, analogous to ln RR

(iii) Attributable risk

$$\text{dev}\ AR = AR/\chi$$
$$y\%\ \text{limits} = AR \pm Zy\ \text{dev}\ AR = AR(1 \pm Zy/\chi)$$

4B Alternative formulae

(i) $$\text{dev}\ \ln RR = \sqrt{\left(\frac{b}{aN_1} + \frac{d}{cN_0}\right)}$$

(ii) $$\text{dev}\ \ln OR = \sqrt{\left(\frac{1}{a} + \frac{1}{b} + \frac{1}{c} + \frac{1}{d}\right)}$$

(iii) $$\text{dev}\ AR = \sqrt{\left(\frac{ab}{N_1^3} + \frac{cd}{N_0^3}\right)}$$

5. *Stratified analysis*

5A Risks

(i) Summary RR_s

$$\frac{\sum_i a_i N_{0i}/T_i}{\sum_i c_i N_{1i}/T_i}$$

(ii) Summary OR_s

$$\frac{\sum_i a_i d_i/T_i}{\sum_i b_i c_i/T_i}$$

(iii) Summary AR_s

$$\frac{\sum_i w_i AR_i}{\sum_i w_i}$$

where $w_i = 1/(\text{dev}\ AR_i)^2$

5B Summary χ^2 statistic on 1 d.f. $= \dfrac{\left(\sum_i a_i - \sum_i E_i\right)^2}{\sum_i V_i}$

Each term analogous to 3 above.

5C Continuity correction: reduce absolute value of numerator by $\frac{1}{2}$ before squaring.

5D Test based confidence limits as in 4 above, using summary estimates and summary χ statistic.

(continued p. 275)

4A Confidence limits: 95% two-sided, test based

for RR = exp[ln 1.63 (1 ± 1.96/2.87)] = 1.17, 2.28

for OR = exp[ln 1.70 (1 ± 1.96/2.87)] = 1.18, 2.44

for AR = 4.06 (1 ± 1.96/2.87) = 1.29, 6.83%

4B Using formulae in 4B:

for RR, dev ln RR = 0.168; limits = exp(ln RR ± 1.96 × dev ln RR) = 1.17, 2.27

for OR, dev ln OR = 0.188; limits = exp(ln OR ± 1.96 × dev ln OR) = 1.18, 2.46

for AR, dev AR = 1.758%; limits = AR ± 1.96 × dev AR = 0.61, 7.51%

5. Stratified analysis:

Analogous to Ex. A1.1. If the above data were one stratum of a stratified table, the weight w_i for use in formula 5A(iii) would be $1/(\text{dev } AR_i)^2 = 1/(0.0176)^2$.

5E Tests of homogeneity; χ^2 on $I - i$ degrees of freedom; variances are squares of standard deviations given in 4.

Relative risk

$$\sum_i \frac{(\ln RR_i - \ln RR_s)^2}{\text{var } RR_i}$$

Attributable risk

$$\sum_i \frac{(AR_i - AR_s)^2}{\text{var } AR_i}$$

Sources:	
3A, 5A, 5B	Mantel and Haenszel (1959), Rothman (1986)
4A, 5D	Miettinen (1976)
4B	Rothman (1986), Wolff (1955)
5E	Rothman (1986)

Ex. A1.3. Cohort studies, person-time data

1. *Format of table*

	Affected	Person-time	Risk
Exposed	a	N_1	$a/N_1 = r_e$
Unexposed	c	N_0	$c/N_0 = r_0$
Total	M_1	T	

2. *Risks*

Relative risk $= r_e/r_0$ Attributable risk $= r_e - r_0$

3. *Statistical tests*

Observed exposed cases $= a$
Expected value of a $= E = N_1M_1/T$
Variance of a $= V = N_1N_0M_1/T^2$

3A Chi-square statistic, χ^2 with 1 degree of freedom $= \dfrac{(a - E)^2}{V} =$

$$= \frac{(a - N_1M_1/T)^2}{(N_1N_0M_1)/T^2}$$

3B χ statistic, or Normal deviate $= \chi = \sqrt{\chi^2}$.

3C Continuity correction: reduce absolute value of numerator by $\frac{1}{2}$ before squaring; i.e. replace numerator by $(|a - E| - \frac{1}{2})^2$, $|a - E|$ means the absolute value of $(a - E)$, irrespective of being positive or negative.

4. *Confidence limits (C.L.)*

(i) for logarithm of RR
$= \ln RR \pm Zy \text{ dev} \ln RR$

(ii) for attributable risk
$= AR \pm Zy \text{ dev } AR$

where Zy = appropriate Normal deviate (Ex. A3.1) and dev = standard deviation.

4A Test based formulae:

dev $\ln RR \doteq \ln RR/\chi$
y% limits $= \ln RR \pm Zy \text{ dev} \ln RR$
$= \ln RR(1 \pm Zy/\chi)$
y% limits for $RR = \exp\{\ln RR(1 \pm Zy/\chi)\}$

dev $AR = AR/\chi$
y% limits $= AR \pm Zy \text{ dev } AR$
$= AR(1 \pm Zy/\chi)$

Worked example

Data from the prospective cohort study shown in Ex. 6.7 (p 91); association between exercise and coronary heart disease mortality.

1. Crude table:

	Deaths	Man-years	Rate/10 000
Light or moderate exercise	532	65 000	81.85
Heavy exercise	66	27 700	23.83
Total	598	92 700	

2. Relative risk = 81.85/23.83 = 3.43
   Attributable risk = 81.85 − 23.83 = 58.02/10 000 man-years.

3A Statistical test:
$a = 532 \quad E = 65\,000 \times 598/92\,700 = 419.31$
$V = 65\,000 \times 27\,700 \times 598/92\,700^2 = 125.30$

3B $\chi^2 = (a-E)^2/V = 101.35 \qquad \chi = \sqrt{101.35} = 10.07$
d.f. = 1 $\quad P < 0.000\,001$ (Statistical Table 1).

3C With continuity correction $\chi^2 = 100.45$

4A Confidence limits, 95% two-sided; test based
for $RR = \exp[\ln 3.43\ (1 \pm 1.96/10.07)] = 2.70, 4.36$
for $AR = 58.0\ (1 \pm 1.96/10.07) = 46.7, 69.3$

4B Alternative formulae

$$\text{dev} \ln RR = \sqrt{\left(\frac{1}{a} + \frac{1}{c}\right)} \qquad \text{dev } AR = \sqrt{\left(\frac{a}{N_1^2} + \frac{c}{N_0^2}\right)}$$

5. *Stratified analysis over I subtables of above format, values a_i etc*

5A

Summary relative risk, RR_s

$$= \frac{\sum_i a_i N_{0i}/T_i}{\sum_i c_i N_{1i}/T_i}$$

Summary attributable risk, AR_s

$$= \frac{\sum_i w_i AR_i}{\sum w_i}$$

$$w_i = 1/(\text{dev } AR_i)^2$$

5B Summary χ^2 statistic $= \dfrac{\left(\sum_i a_i - \sum_i E_i\right)^2}{\sum_i V_i}$

Each term analogous to 3 above.

5C Continuity correction: reduce absolute value of numerator by $\frac{1}{2}$ before squaring.

5D Test based confidence limits as in 4 above, using summary estimates and summary χ statistic.

5E Tests of homogeneity; χ^2 on $I - i$ degrees of freedom; variances are squares of standard deviations given in 4.

Relative risk

$$= \sum_i \frac{(\ln RR_i - \ln RR_s)^2}{\text{var } RR_i}$$

Attributable risk

$$= \sum_i \frac{(AR_i - AR_s)^2}{\text{var } AR_i}$$

Odds ratio: analogous to relative risk.

Sources: 3A Derived from Mantel and Haenszel (1959), by Rothman & Boice (1982) and Rothman (1986).
5B Mantel and Haenszel (1959)
4A, 5D Miettinen (1976)
4B, 5E Rothman (1986)

4B Using formulae 4B

dev ln RR = 0.131 95% limits = exp{ln 3.43 ± (1.96 × 0.131)} = 2.66, 4.43

dev AR = 4.60/10 000 95% limits = 58.0 ± (1.96 × 4.60) = 49.0, 67.0

5. Stratified analysis. Analogous to Ex. A1.1

Ex. A1.4. Cohort (count data) or case–control, with small numbers; exact test for a fourfold table

1. *Format of table*

	Affected	Unaffected	Total
Exposed	a	b	N_1
Unexposed	c	d	N_0
Total	M_1	M_0	T

2. *Risks*

As in table A1.2; the small numbers make no difference.

3. *Statistical test*

$$\text{Probability of a particular table occurring} = \frac{N_1!N_0!M_1!M_0!}{T!a!b!c!d!}.$$

To calculate one sided probability of a or a more extreme value: if a is greater than expected, i.e. $a > N_1M_1/T$, calculate quantity above for each value of a from observed value to the maximum, given when $a = N_1$ or $a = M_1$; sum these values. If a is less than expected, calculate for values of a down to zero. For two sided tests, the one sided value is usually doubled.

! represents a factorial; e.g. 5! is $5 \times 4 \times 3 \times 2 \times 1$.

Sources: This test was developed independently in the 1930's by RA Fisher, JO Irwin and F Yates.
Exact confidence limits and stratified analysis will not be presented; see, for example, Breslow and Day (1980) and Rothman (1986)

Worked example

Saral, Burns, Laskin *et al.* (1981) performed a double-blind randomized trial of the drug acyclovir, compared to placebo, as prophylaxis against herpes simplex infection in twenty bone marrow transplant recipients who were seropositive for herpes simplex before randomization; the outcome was development of active herpes simplex infection.

1. Table of results:

	Infection	No infection	Total
Acyclovir	0	10	10
Placebo	7	3	10
Total	7	13	20

2. Risk: the relative risk and odds ratio are both zero.

3. Statistical test:

probability of this set of data, given the null hypothesis

$$P = \frac{10!\ 10!\ 13!\ 7!}{20!\ 0!\ 10!\ 7!\ 3!}$$

$$= \frac{10!\ 13!}{20!\ \ 3!} \quad (0! = 1)$$

$$= \frac{10 \times 9 \times 8 \times 7 \times 6 \times 5 \times 4}{20 \times 19 \times 18 \times 17 \times 16 \times 15 \times 14}$$

$$= 0.0015$$

This is the one-sided P-value; the two-sided value of $P = 0.003$.

As the result obtained was an extreme one, only one calculation is necessary. Otherwise, further calculations are needed. For example, suppose there had been two infections in the acyclovir group compared to seven in the placebo. To assess significance, we add the probability of the observed table to the probability of more extreme results with the same marginal totals: the observed table is:

	Infection	No infection	Total
Acyclovir	2	8	10
Placebo	7	3	10
Total	9	11	20

$$P = \frac{10!\ 10!\ 11!\ 9!}{20!\ 2!\ 8!\ 7!\ 3!} = 0.032$$

More extreme results, given that a is less than its expected value, are $a = 1$ and $a = 0$ with the same marginal totals:

Worked example. *Continued*

	Infection	No infection	Total	
Acyclovir	1	9	10	$P = 0.0027$
Placebo	8	2	10	
Total	9	11	20	

	Infection	No infection	Total	
Acyclovir	0	10	10	$P = 0.00006$
Placebo	9	1	10	
Total	9	11	20	

giving the final P-value (one-sided) of $0.032 + 0.0027 + 0.00006 = 0.035$ or (two-sided) $= 0.07$

Ex. A1.5. Case–control, 1:1 matching

1. *Format of table: numbers of pairs*

		Controls	
		Exposed	Unexposed
Cases	Exposed	u	s
	Unexposed	t	v

2. *Risks*

Odds ratio $= s/t$

3A *Statistical tests*

$$\chi^2 \text{ statistic on 1 d.f.} = \frac{(s-t)^2}{(s+t)}$$

3B χ statistic, or Normal deviate $= \sqrt{\chi^2}$.

3C Continuity correction: reduce absolute value of numerator by 1 before squaring; it becomes $(|s-t|-1)^2$.

4. *Confidence limits*

Test based limits can be based on the χ statistic by the methods shown in Table A1.1.

Sources: McNemar (1947). Stratified analysis of matched data is not frequently performed, matched multivariate models being more useful: see Breslow and Day (1980).

Worked example

Data from the case–control study shown in Ex. 6.20 (p 114) and Ex. 7.13 (p 154); association between nasal cancer and smoking.

1. Table:

		Controls	
		Smokers	Non-smokers
Cases	Smokers	31	30
	Non-smokers	7	52

2. Odds ratio $= 30/7 = 4.29$

3A, B χ^2 statistic $= (30-7)^2/(30+7) = 14.30 \quad \chi = \sqrt{14.30} = 3.78$

3C With continuity correction, $\chi^2 = 13.1$.

4. 95% confidence limits for OR, test based $= \exp\{\ln 4.29\,(1 \pm 1.96/3.78)\}$
$= 2.0, 9.1$

Ex. A1.6. Case–control studies, fixed 1:*m* matching

1. *Format of table: numbers of pairs*

Cases	No. of controls exposed (maximum $= M$)					
	0	1	2	...	m	...
Exposed	a_0	a_1	a_2	...	a_m	...
Unexposed	c_0	c_1	c_2	...	c_m	...

The pairs of sets (a_{m-1}, c_m) form the basis for the calculations. The values a_m (sets where all are exposed) and c_0 (sets where none is exposed) do not contribute.

2. *Risks*

$$\text{Odds ratio} = \frac{\sum_{m=1}^{M} (M+1-m)a_{m-1}}{\sum_{m=1}^{M} mc_m}$$

$$= \frac{Ma_0 + (M-1)a_1 + (M-2)a_2 + \ldots + a_{M-1}}{c_1 + 2c_2 + 3c_3 + \ldots + Mc_M}$$

3. *Statistical tests*

$$\chi^2 \text{ statistic on 1 d.f.} = \frac{\left\{\sum_{m=1}^{M} (M+1-m)a_{m-1} - \sum_{m=1}^{M} mc_m\right\}^2}{\sum_{m=1}^{M} (a_{m-1} + c_m)m(M+1-m)}$$

For the continuity correction, reduce the absolute value of the numerator by $\frac{1}{2}(M+1)$ before squaring.

4. *Confidence limits*

Test based limits may be based on the χ statistic by the method shown in Table A1.1.

Sources: 2. Based on Mantel and Haenszel (1959)
3. Mantel and Haenszel (1959), Miettinen (1970), Pike & Morrow (1970)
For more complex matched designs, see Breslow and Day (1980), pp 169–187.

Worked example

Data from Collette *et al.* (1984); a 1:3 matched case–control study assessing the value of screening for breast cancer by physical examination and xero-mammography. The cases were women from the defined population who had died from breast cancer; the controls were age-matched women randomly selected from this population.

1. Table:

	No. of matched controls screened (m)			
	0	1	2	3
Cases: screened	1	4	3	1
unscreened	11	10	12	4

Here $M = 3$; summations are from $m = 1$ to $m = 3$.

2. Odds ratio $= \dfrac{(3 \times 1) + (2 \times 4) + (1 \times 3)}{(1 \times 10) + (2 \times 12) + (3 \times 4)}$
$= 14/46 = 0.30$

3. χ^2 statistic $= \dfrac{(14 - 46)^2}{(11 \times 1 \times 3) + (16 \times 2 \times 2) + (7 \times 3 \times 1)}$
$= 1024/118$
$= 8.68 \qquad \chi = 2.95$
With continuity correction, $\chi^2 = 7.63$

4. 95% confidence limits for *OR* (test based) $= \exp[\ln 0.30\,(1 \pm 1.96/2.95)]$
$= 0.13, 0.67$

Ex. A1.7. Cohort (count data) or case–control studies: test for trend

1. *Format of table*

		Cases (affected)	Controls (unaffected)	Total	Score
Exposure level	0 (referent)	c	d	N_0	x_0
	1	a_1	b_1	N_1	x_1
	2	a_2	b_2	N_2	x_2
	3 . . . k	a_k	b_k	N_k	x_k
Total		M_1	M_0	T	

2. *Risks*

$$\text{Odds ratio for exposure level } k = \frac{a_k d}{b_k c} = \frac{a_k}{b_k} \Big/ \frac{c}{d}.$$

3. *Statistical tests*

3A For each level k against the referent level: tests and confidence limits as in Table A1.1.

Heterogeneity χ^2 for the table above, on $k - 1$ degrees of freedom

$$= (T-1)\left(\frac{1}{M_1} + \frac{1}{M_0}\right) \sum_k \frac{(a_k - E_k)^2}{N_k}$$

where E_k = expected value of $a_k = N_k M_1 / T$.

This test assesses whether the odd ratios, or more directly the proportions of cases, in the various exposure levels are consistent with the overall value—it does not take into account the order of the levels of exposure.

3B Test for trend from regression of the values $a_k - E_k$ on the score x_k; χ^2 on 1 d.f.

$$= \frac{T^2(T-1)\left\{\sum_k x_k(a_k - E_k)\right\}^2}{M_1 M_0 \left\{T \sum_k x_k^2 N_k - \left(\sum_k x_k N_k\right)^2\right\}}.$$

For a continuity correction, if x_k scores are one unit apart, replace

$$\left\{\sum_k x_k(a_k - E_k)\right\}^2 \text{ by } \left\{\left|\sum_k x_k(a_k - E_k)\right| - \frac{1}{2}\right\}^2.$$

Worked example

Data from a case–control study relating twinning to maternal parity (Ex. 7.11, p 149).

1. Table and elements of calculations:

Category	Cases	Controls	Total	Score	Odds ratio	E	$(a-E)$
Parity 0	716	1833	2549	0	1.0(R)	848.07	− 132.07
1	582	1269	1851	1	1.17	615.84	− 33.84
2	454	853	1307	2	1.36	434.85	19.15
3 +	720	1003	1723	3	1.84	573.25	146.75
Total	2472	4958	7430				

2. Risks:
Given above: e.g. for parity 2 odds ratio = (454 × 1833)/(853 × 716)
= 1.36

3A Global or heterogeneity χ^2. For each level $E_k = N_k M_1/T$
e.g. for parity 2, $E_2 = 1307 \times 2472/7430 = 434.85$

$$\chi^2 = 7429 \left(\frac{1}{2472} + \frac{1}{4958}\right)\left(\frac{(716-848.07)^2}{2549} + \text{etc. for each level}\right)$$

= 91.16 d.f. = 3 $P < 0.001$ (Statistical Table 2).

3B Test for trend:

$$\chi^2 = \frac{7430^2 \times 7429(-33.84 + 2 \times 19.15 + 3 \times 146.75)^2}{2472 \times 4958\{7430(1851 + 4 \times 1307 + 9 \times 1723) - (1851 + 2 \times 1307 + 3 \times 1723)^2\}}$$

$$= \frac{7430^2 \times 7429 \times 444.71^2}{2472 \times 4958(7430 \times 22\,586 - 9634^2)}$$

= 88.24 With continuity correction, $\chi^2 = 88.04$

d.f. = 1 $P < 0.000\,001$ (Statistical Table 1).

3C An approximate test of departure from the linear trend is given by the difference between the heterogeneity and the trend χ^2 statistics, on $k - 2$ degrees of freedom: this tests the adequacy of the linear trend in describing the data.

4. *Stratified analysis*

The trend statistic above can be generalised to a stratified analysis over I subtables of the format above, but the formula is tedious for hand calculation; see Breslow and Day (1980) pp 148–150, Rothman (1986) pp 346–348.

The stratified χ^2 statistic on 1 d.f. is

$$= \frac{\left\{\sum_k x_k \left(\sum_i a_{ki} - \sum_i E_{ki}\right)\right\}^2}{\sum_i \frac{M_{0i}}{T_i - 1}\left\{\sum_k x_k^2 E_{ki} - \frac{1}{M_{1i}}\left(\sum_k x_k E_{ki}\right)^2\right\}}.$$

where $E_{ki} = N_{ki}M_{1i}/T_i$.

Sources: 3A: Armitage (1971)
3B Mantel (1963)
The one stratum test is the same as the test for trend in proportions by Armitage (1955).
All are reviewed by Breslow and Day (1980) and by Rothman (1986).

3C Test for departure from linear trend:
$\chi^2 = 91.2 - 88.2 = 3.0$ d.f. $= 2$ $P > 0.2$ (Statistical Table 2).

Ex. A1.8. Formulae for sample size determination

1. *Unmatched studies, equal groups*

basic formula $$n = \frac{(p_1q_1 + p_2q_2) \cdot K}{(p_1 - p_2)^2}$$

approximately equivalent to $$n = \frac{2\bar{p}\bar{q} \cdot K}{(p_1 - p_2)^2}$$

to calculate power $$Z_\beta = \frac{(p_1 - p_2) \cdot \sqrt{n}}{\sqrt{(p_1q_1 + p_2q_2)}} - Z_\alpha$$

case–control studies, given OR and p_2, then $$p_1 = \frac{p_2 \cdot OR}{1 + p_2(OR - 1)}$$

2. *Multiple controls per case*

given c controls per case: n = no. of cases or exposed subjects,
cn = no. of controls.

$$n = \frac{(1 + 1/c) \cdot \bar{p}\bar{q} \cdot K}{(p_1 - p_2)^2}$$

$$Z_\beta = \frac{(p_1 - p_2) \cdot \sqrt{n}}{\sqrt{\{(1 + 1/c) \cdot \bar{p}\bar{q}\}}} - Z_\alpha$$

3. *1:1 matched studies*

$$M = \left[\frac{Z_\alpha/2 + Z_\beta\sqrt{\{H(1 - H)\}}}{H - 0.5}\right]^2 \Big/ (p_2q_1 + p_1q_2)$$

where $H = \dfrac{OR}{1 + OR}$ $\quad OR$ = odds ratio

and M = number of matched pairs.

Notation

n = number of subjects in each group
p_1 = probability of outcome in group 1 $q_1 = 1 - p_2$
p_2 = probability of outcome in group 2 $q_2 = 1 - p_2$
$\bar{p}$ = probability of outcome in whole study group $\bar{q} = 1 - \bar{p}$
K = constant dependent on significance level and power $= (Z_\alpha + Z_\beta)^2$
See Ex. A1.9
Z_α = normal deviate corresponding to significance level See Ex. A1.9
Z_β = normal deviate corresponding to power See Ex. A1.9

c = number of controls per case
M = number of matched pairs.

Sources: various, including Schlesselman (1982) and Pocock (1983), both of whom give more detail. A very detailed review is given by Meinert (1986).

Worked examples

See text pages 143–145.

Ex. A1.9. Constants for use in sample size formulae

A. Table relating normal deviates to power and to significance level

Power $(1-\beta)$ (%)	Z-value (Normal deviate)	Significance level (α) One-sided	Two-sided
99.5	2.58	0.005	0.01
99	2.33	0.01	0.02
98	1.96	0.025	0.05
95	1.64	0.05	0.1
90	1.28	0.1	0.2
80	0.84	0.2	0.4
70	0.52	0.3	0.6
50	0.0	0.5	

B. Values of $K = (Z_\alpha + Z_\beta)^2$, *for commonly used values of* α *and* β

Significance level: Two-sided value	Power 50%	80%	90%	95%	Significance level: One-sided value
0.1	2.7	6.2	8.6	10.8	0.05
0.05	3.8	7.9	10.5	13.0	0.025
0.02	5.4	10.0	13.0	15.8	0.01
0.01	6.6	11.7	14.9	17.8	0.005

Normal deviates corresponding to frequently used values for significance levels (Z_α) and for power (Z_β); and table of K where $K = (Z_\alpha + Z_\beta)^2$. The value of Z_β is the normal deviate corresponding to the one-sided test for (1 – power).

Appendix 2
Lifetable methods

Appendix 2: Lifetable methods

Introduction

This section offers a description of lifetable methods of analysis. These are applicable to cohort type studies where the risk varies with the time interval since first exposure to the causal factor or intervention, and where the period of follow-up varies for different individuals in the study. These methods are commonly used in clinical trials as both these situations are likely to apply, and are also applicable to epidemiological cohort studies. We shall describe the method of calculation of outcome risks using lifetable methods, which is comparable to the calculation of basic results from other methods of analysis shown in Chapter 3. The control of confounding in doing these analyses, analogous to the issues discussed for other analytical designs in Chapter 6, is discussed, as also are some appropriate statistical tests, which represent yet another application of the general Mantel–Haenszel statistic applied to other studies in Chapter 7. The general issues of bias, confounding and so on are of course relevant to all cohort type studies. This section is partly based on a review article (Coldman and Elwood, 1979).

In the cohort designs discussed in section 3, we dealt with two formats of results. For cohort designs in which individuals are observed throughout the period of the study, the analysis consists of a comparison of the proportions of individuals affected in the exposed and unexposed groups; an example is the study of outcomes of pregnancy, where once the pregnancy is completed we can unequivocally assign each individual to outcome positive or outcome negative categories (for example Ex. 3.1, p 26).

The second situation was where the period of follow-up of individuals varies, and therefore the number of outcome events must be related to the number of person-years of experience during which an event could occur, the person-time type of analysis (Ex. 3.3, p 30). In this type of analysis, we make an important assumption that the risk of the outcome is constant over the whole of the person-time experience, and therefore groups of subjects with different follow-up periods can be adequately compared by looking only at the total person-time experience and the number of events occurring. In many situations this is manifestly not true. For example, for patients started on medical treatment in hospital for an acute myocardial infarction, the risk of death is maximum at the time the treatment is started and then decreases rapidly. If we try to compare two different methods of treating patients with acute myocardial infarction, and compare 50 patients who have been followed up for one year each, with 600 patients who have been followed up for one month each, the total person-time experience of each group is the same. However, we should expect the measured death rates, as deaths per unit person-time, to be much higher in the second group because it is measuring only death rates during the first month after diagnosis, which are likey to be much higher than death rates during the subsequent 11 months. To reduce this problem we use methods which divide the follow-up period into small sections, and assess the probability of an outcome event happening in each small section of the follow-up period. Because such methods have been most widely used in assessing survival after diagnosis or treatment, these methods are often referred to as survival curve methods. However they can be applied to any non-recurrent outcome event in a group of subjects, such as death, onset of a complication, onset of recovery, return to work, or discharge from hospital. The results can be expressed either as the proportion of patients at different times who have not undergone the event, as is seen in a survival curve, or as a proportion of patients who have undergone the event, which gives a cumulative incidence curve. Exhibit A2.1 shows a survival curve for a group of patients with breast cancer, showing the proportion of the original group who are still alive at various points from the date of diagnosis; thus at three years after diagnosis, 68 per cent of patients are still alive. The same data could be plotted to show the cumulative incidence of death; at three years, 32 per cent have died.

To construct such a curve, we need to know for each individual in the study, the starting date of the period of observation, the finishing date of this period, and the outcome for that individual. The starting date in a clinical situation may be defined as the date of diagnosis, the date of first treatment,

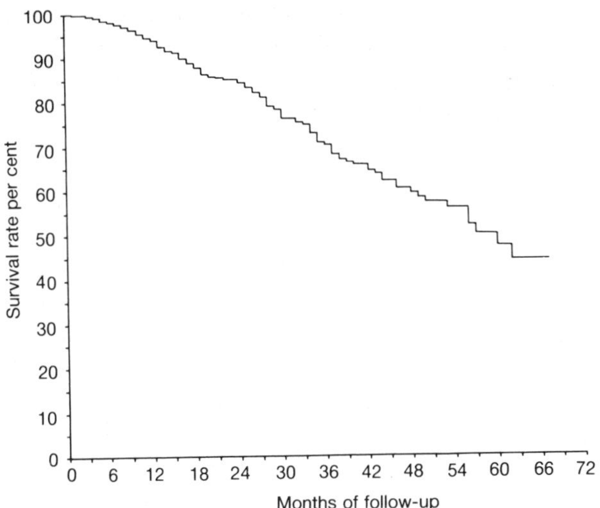

Ex. A2.1. Survival of 596 patients with breast cancer, from date of confirmed diagnosis, calculated by the product limit method. For this graph, only deaths from breast cancer were counted; the few other deaths were not, the observations being censored at that point

or in a randomized study the date of randomization. In an epidemiological cohort study the starting date may be the date of first exposure to the causal agent under investigation, such as working in a particular job or using a drug.

In a simple example assessing survival in a group of patients, the survival curve is simply the proportion surviving at various points in time. The 'curve' has, in fact, a step-type pattern: if we start with ten patients the survival rate is 100 per cent until one dies, then it remains at 90 per cent until another dies, and so on. As the number of patients enrolled in the study increases, each step gets smaller and the curve appears smoother. Usually we do not know all the dates of death, as some patients will still be alive at the time of analysis and others may have been lost to follow-up, so that their current status will be unknown. The observations on these patients are said to be *censored*. Censoring also occurs if the particular end point under study is precluded by

SURVIVAL DATA

Patient no.	Survival time, (months)†	Treatment group
14	1	A
12	1	A
13	3 +	A
4	4	A
7	6	A
2	9 +	B
9	11 +	A
8	11 +	B
19	12	A
20	13	B
1	15	A
3	16	B
15	22	B
5	22 +	A
10	23	A
6	23	B
16	25 +	B
11	32 +	B
17	32 +	B
18	41	B

†The + indicates a censored observation

Ex. A2.2. Hypothetical survival data, arranged in order of increasing survival time, for a clinical trial with ten patients in each of two treatment groups

Note: as emphasized in Chapter 7, we do not recommend trials of this size: this is for explanation only

another event: for example, if we wish to count only deaths from a certain cause, other deaths produce censored observations. We shall describe two commonly used methods for constructing a survival curve: the product-limit method (also known as the Kaplan–Meier estimate) and the actuarial or life-table method.

The product-limit method

Consider the data in Ex. A2.2, which shows survival times for twenty patients, and at this point ignore the treatment designation. The data show survival time in months, calculated from the date of diagnosis to the date of death, arranged with the patients in order of increasing survival time. Eight patients are still alive or have been lost to follow-up. For them, we have used the date of the last follow-up assessment, but indicate that their survival times are censored. The product-limit method is based on two simple concepts. First, patients with censored observations are included in the total number of patients at risk of death only up to the time of their censoring. Second, we use a simple application of probability theory in calculating that the chance of surviving two months equals the probability of surviving the first month multiplied by the probability of surviving the second, and so on with subsequent months.

The calculations are shown in Ex. A2.3. Two deaths occurred in the first month, so that the probability of surviving that month was 18/20 or 0.9, and the survival at one month, that is at the end of the first month, was 0.9. During the second month no deaths occurred and during the third month there was one censored observation but still no deaths, so that the cumulative survival by the end of the third month was $0.9 \times 1 \times 1 = 0.9$. During the fourth month one death occurred; because only 17 patients were under follow-up at the time the probability of survival was 16/17 or 0.94, and the cumulative survival at the end of the fourth month was $0.94 \times 0.9 = 0.85$. The survival curve changes only when a death occurs, hence a calculation need be made only when this happens. Each relevant interval ends therefore when one or more deaths occur. The resultant step type curve is shown in Ex. A2.4.

The estimation of survival by this method not only allows for censoring, but gives an efficient estimate since in each section of the follow-up period the information available on all subjects observed during that interval is used. The adjustment made for censored observations assumes that they are censored randomly; that is, we assume that the patients whose data are censored at a certain time have a subsequent course similar to that of the patients remaining under follow-up. If this is not so, bias will result; for example, if those lost to follow-up do worse than those followed, perhaps because very ill patients no longer attend for treatment, the calculated

SURVIVAL CURVE CALCULATION

Interval i	Interval between deaths (months)	No. of deaths at end of interval d_i	No. of patients alive immediately prior to end of interval n_i	Probability of surviving interval $P_i = 1 - (d_i/n_i)$	Value of survival curve subsequent to interval $S_i = S_{i-1} \times P_i$	Standard error of survival curve
0	0	—	—	1.0000	1.0000	—
1	0–1	2	20	0.9000	0.9000	0.0671
2	1–4	1	17	0.9412	0.8471	0.0814
3	4–6	1	16	0.9375	0.7941	0.0919
4	6–12	1	12	0.9167	0.7279	0.1054
5	12–13	1	11	0.9091	0.6618	0.1147
6	13–15	1	10	0.9000	0.5956	0.1209
7	15–16	1	9	0.8889	0.5294	0.1242
8	16–22	1	8	0.8750	0.4632	0.1251
9	22–23	2	6	0.6667	0.3088	0.1221
10	23–41	1	1	0.0000	0.0000	

Ex. A2.3. Calculation of product limit estimate of survival curve from data in Ex. A2.2. Formula for standard error given on p 301

survival curve will over-estimate the actual survival which would be correctly calculated if full information were available. The product-limit method gives the survival curve that is the most likely estimate, in statistical terminology the 'maximum likelihood' estimate of the true survival curve.

The actuarial or lifetable method

Because hand calculation of the product limit estimate is tedious with a large set of data, the actuarial or lifetable method may be used. This gives an approximation to the product-limit estimate, with the number of calculations being reduced by grouping the data into suitable intervals of follow-up, such as one year or three months. Calculations for the data used in Ex. A2.2, with a six month interval, are shown in Ex. A2.5. For each time interval we calculate the probability of surviving that interval, which is given as one minus the probability of dying during that time interval. The probability of dying is given by the number of deaths during the interval divided by the number of patients under follow-up during that interval. This denominator is estimated as the number of patients alive at the beginning of the interval, minus one half of the number whose data are censored during the interval. We are making the assumption that if patients are censored during an interval, their

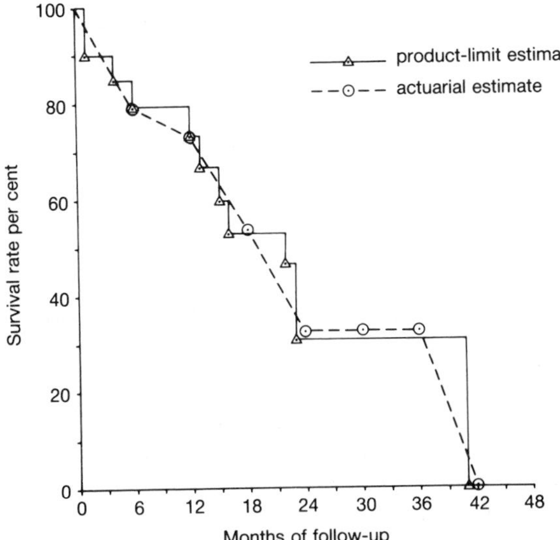

Ex. A2.4. Survival curves for the data shown in Ex. A2.2. The step pattern is the product-limit survival curve calculated in Ex. A2.3; the dotted line is the actuarial curve calculated in Ex. A2.5

follow-up experience is approximately half of that interval. The cumulative probability of survival is calculated, as with the product limit method, as the product of the probability of survival over each of the intervals up to that point. The resultant survival curve is shown in Ex. A2.4.

Survival curves are usually shown with an arithmetic horizontal scale, and either an arithmetic or a logarithmic vertical scale. If the risk of death during each section of the follow-up period is in fact the same, a survival curve with an arithmetic vertical scale will show an exponential decreasing curve, while one with a logarithmic scale will show a straight line. Product limit estimates, being actual calculations of survival rate at every event, are best shown by stepped patterns, while actuarial estimates are an approximation and can be reasonably shown as a series of points connected by straight lines. The intervals chosen for actuarial calculation need not be of equal length and are often chosen on a convenient arbitrary basis, such as annual intervals; but they should be short enough to keep the number of censored observations in any interval relatively small.

Accuracy of estimates

The standard error of the survival rate S_i at the end of a given interval, is given by

$$\text{SE} = S_i \sqrt{\left(\sum_i \frac{1 - P_i}{n_i P_i} \right)}$$

where the summation $\sum_i$ is over all the intervals up to and including the last interval i. This formula is applicable to both product limit and actuarial calculations and while approximate is adequate for most purposes (Ex. A2.3). In the usual way, the 95 per cent two-sided confidence limits are given as the estimate $S_i \pm 1.96 \times$ standard error.

ACTUARIAL SURVIVAL

Interval (months)	Patients alive at start r_i	Patients censored c_i	Patients 'at risk' $n_i = r_i - \frac{1}{2}c_i$	Deaths during interval d_i	Probability of surviving interval $P_i = 1 - (d_i/n_i)$	Survival curve estimate $S_i = S_{i-1} \times P_i$
0– 6	20	1	19.5	4	0.7949	0.7949
7–12	15	3	13.5	1	0.9259	0.7360
13–18	11	0	11.0	3	0.7273	0.5353
19–24	8	1	7.5	3	0.6000	0.3212
25–30	4	1	3.5	0	1.0	0.3212
30–36	3	2	2.0	0	1.0	0.3212
37–42	1	0	1.0	1	0.0	0.0

Ex. A2.5. Calculation of actuarial estimate of survival curve from the data in Ex. A2.2, using 6-month intervals. This example is to show the method; the actuarial method is not advisable with such small numbers, but is useful with large sets of data

Differences between groups

Frequently we wish to assess whether an apparent difference in the survival experiences of two (or more) groups of subjects is likely to be due to chance variation or to represent a real difference in survival. A comparison between two curves could be made by selecting one arbitrary point in time and comparing the survival at that point, using a simple two-by-two table of deaths versus survivors at that point, or using the formula given above for the standard error. Such a comparison is unsatisfactory as the results will depend on the particular time point used. An alternative is to find a mathematical formula which will describe the form of the survival curve adequately and compare the relevant parameters of the formula: these methods are called parametric, as the shape of the curve is assumed: for example, in some situations there may be a simple linear relationship between the logarithm of the survival rate and time. Such methods are clearly dependent on the validity of the parametric model chosen.

To avoid both these difficulties, a non-parametric test is often used. Such a test compares the order in which the outcome events occur in each group of subjects, without reference to the precise timing. The tests thus evaluate the whole curve, but make no assumptions about the shape of the curve.

The log-rank test

Although there are several different non-parametric tests, one method has emerged in recent years which is simple and at the same time powerful and appropriate over a wide range of circumstances (Mantel, 1966; Peto *et al.*, 1977). This is the log-rank test, and it will come as no surprise to the reader that this is an application of the Mantel–Haenszel test which is discussed in other contexts in Chapter 7. The test is sometimes known as the Mantel or Mantel–Haenszel test. At each point in time at which a death occurs, a two by two table showing the number of deaths and the total number of subjects under follow-up is created, as shown in Ex. A2.6. For each such table, the observed deaths in one group, the expected deaths, and the variance of the expected number are calculated in the same way as was shown in Chapter 7 and Ex. A1.1. These quantities are summed over all tables, and the Mantel–Haenszel statistic derived from the summations. The calculation for the data given in Ex. A2.1, comparing the two treatment groups, is shown in Ex. A2.7.

LOG-RANK STATISTIC

For each time interval i:

	Deaths at end of interval i	Subjects still alive at end of interval i	Subjects alive immediately prior to end of interval i
'Exposed'	a_i	b_i	N_{1i}
'Unexposed'	c_i	d_i	N_{0i}
Total	M_{1i}	M_{0i}	T_i

$$\text{Log-rank statistic} = \frac{\left(\sum_i a_i - \sum_i E_i\right)^2}{\sum_i V_i}$$

Where $E_i = N_{1i}M_{1i}/T_i$

and $V_i = N_{1i}N_{0i}M_{1i}M_{0i}/T_i^2(T_i - 1)$

Ex. A2.6. The log-rank statistic. For each time interval, ending when one or more deaths occurs, a two by two table is created which has usual format; compare Ex. A1.1. The log-rank statistic is calculated as the stratified Mantel–Haenszel statistic, summing over all time intervals, and yields a χ^2 statistic on 1 degree of freedom

CALCULATION OF LOG-RANK STATISTIC

Interval i	Interval between deaths (months)	No. of deaths at end of interval		No. of patients alive immediately prior to end of interval		Expected deaths E_i	Variance V_i
		Group A a_i	Both groups M_{1i}	Group A N_{1i}	Both groups T_i		
1	0–1	2	2	10	20	1.0000	0.4737
2	1–4	1	1	7	17	0.4118	0.2422
3	4–6	1	1	6	16	0.3750	0.2344
4	6–12	1	1	4	12	0.3333	0.2222
5	12–13	0	1	3	11	0.2727	0.1983
6	13–15	1	1	3	10	0.3000	0.2100
7	15–16	0	1	2	9	0.2222	0.1728
8	16–22	0	1	2	8	0.2500	0.1875
9	22–23	1	2	1	6	0.3333	0.2222
10	23–41	0	1	0	1	0.0000	0.0000
		$\sum a_i = 7$				$\sum_i E_i = 3.4983$	$\sum_i V_i = 2.1634$

Ex. A2.7. Calculation of log-rank statistic from the data in Ex. A2.2. The quantities a_i, E_i, and V_i are calculated for each time period i; a time period ends when a death occurs, or two or more deaths occur together. Calculation is shown in Ex. A2.6

$$\text{The log-rank } \chi^2 \text{ statistic} = \frac{\left(\sum_i a_i - \sum_i E_i\right)^2}{\sum_i V_i}$$

$$= (7 - 3.4983)^2/2.1634$$

$$= 5.6679$$

hence probability $P = 0.019$

$$\text{Equivalently, the log-rank } \chi = \left(\sum_i a_i - \sum_i E_i\right) \Big/ \sqrt{\sum_i V_i}$$

$$= 2.381$$

The log-rank test calculations also produce for each group the observed to expected ratio $\Sigma_i\, a_i \,/\, \Sigma_i\, E_i$, which relates the number of deaths observed during the follow-up period with the number expected on the null hypothesis that the survival curve for that group would be the same as that for the combined data. A subgroup of patients with a mortality rate higher than the whole group will have an observed to expected ratio greater than one.

Several exposure categories

The log-rank method can be expanded to look at a number of different categories of subjects, which might correspond to graded severities of disease, stages of disease, dose regimens of treatment, and so on. Comparison between the curves can be based on either an overall chi-squared statistic, with $(n-1)$ degrees of freedom where n is the number of groups compared, which assesses the total variation from the null hypothesis that survival is the same in each group, or by a trend statistic on 1 degree of freedom which assesses the linear component of a trend in difference in survival experience over the ordered groups.

Thus, Ex. A2.8 shows a further analysis of the survival of the patients whose overall survival was shown in Ex. A2.1. The patients have been divided into four groups in terms of the measurement of estrogen receptor (ER) concentration in the tumour removed at operation. The graph shows that the survival is better for those with a higher concentration of estrogen receptors. The log-rank analysis for the four groups gives an overall

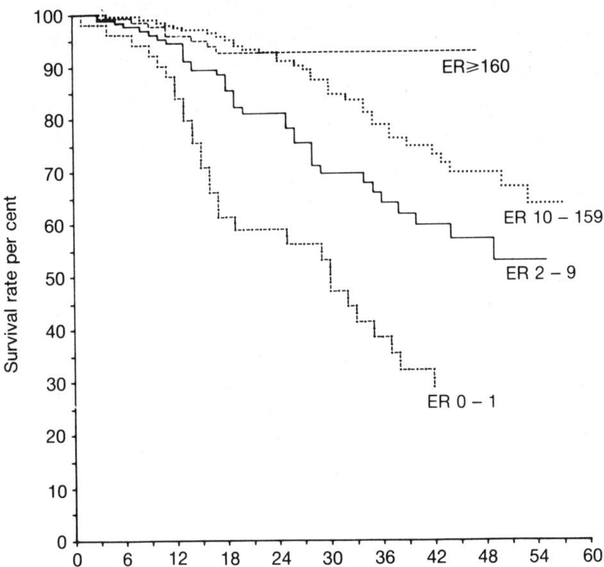

Ex. A2.8. Survival curves for 583 breast cancer patients (those shown in Ex. A2.1, less 13 with incomplete data), divided into four groups on the quantity of estrogen receptor (ER) in the breast tumour, measured in femtomoles per milligram. Derived from Godolphin *et al.* (1981)

chi-squared of 60.4 on 3 degrees of freedom ($P < 0.0001$), and the trend statistic, assessing whether survival changes in a linear fashion with a change in receptor concentration, gives a chi-squared of 48.6 on 1 degree of freedom ($P < 0.0001$).

Control for confounding

The log-rank method of analysis, being derived from the Mantel–Haenszel statistical method, can be easily adapted to the consideration of confounding variables. The logic is the same as that with the simpler types of data analysis already discussed, in that the experience of the groups to be compared is examined within categories of the confounding factor, by generating survival curves for the groups to be compared for each sub-category of the confounder. The log-rank statistic allows summarization of the data over levels of the confounding factor, giving an overall observed to expected ratio, and an overall chi-squared statistic which assesses the difference between the groups being compared after control for the confounder. For example, the data shown in Ex. A2.8 show that survival in breast cancer patients is related to estrogen receptor concentration. It is important to know if this effect is independent of the effect of other prognostic factors such as staging. A stratified analysis in which the effect of estrogen receptor status was assessed within clinical stage categories, and the log-rank statistic calculated over the strata, was therefore done. This showed that the observed to expected ratios were little changed, that for subjects with the highest receptor concentration being 0.44 before control for clinical stage and 0.45 after such control, and the trend statistic was 48.6 before controlling for stage and 47.3 after. This shows that the prognostic effect of estrogen receptor quantity is independent of clinical stage (Godolphin *et al.*, 1981).

Multivariate analysis

Beyond this type of analysis, multivariate methods can be applied to survival data. Such methods are similar in principle to the logistic regression model described in Chapter 7. Methods which can deal with a multivariate analysis and the complexity of censored survival data are of course complex, and specialist statistical and programming advice is required; a highly regarded text has been published by Kalbfleisch and Prentice (1980). A powerful method with wide applicability is the proportional hazards model developed by Cox (1972). This model allows the survival curve to take any form: that is, the hazard function, or instantaneous mortality rate, is allowed to vary with the time since the start of follow-up. However, it is assumed that the relative effect of any factor on the hazard function will be constant over time. Thus, if the hazard function at time t in the referent group of subjects is expressed as $\lambda_{0,t}$, the function for subjects with a factor x_1 is given by

$$\lambda_{1,t} = \lambda_{0,t} \cdot \exp b_1 x_1$$
$$\text{or } \ln \lambda_{1,t} = \ln \lambda_{0,t} + b_1 x_1$$

where b_1 is the coefficient related to x_1. If x_1 has the values 0 or 1, the exponential of b_1 will be the ratio $\lambda_{1,t}/\lambda_{0,t}$, that is, the ratio of the hazard function, which is a relative risk. With multiple factors, the model becomes

$$\lambda_{k,t} = \lambda_{0,t} \cdot \exp(b_1 x_1 + b_2 x_2 + \ldots + b_k x_k)$$

where $\lambda_{k,t}$ is the hazard function at time t for subjects with covariates (x_1, x_2 . . . x_k.). In a survival analysis, a positive coefficient means an increase in x gives a higher hazard function, that is a higher death rate, a poorer survival. Thus using such a model, one can test whether a factor is related to survival after adjusting for confounding factors.

Appendix 3
Statistical tables

Appendix 3: Statistical tables

In this appendix, a set of six statistical tables is presented, each with a 'user's guide' and examples. Statistical Tables 1 and 2 should suffice for almost all purposes; 3, 4, 5 and 6 add further detail.

Tables 1–4 are taken from tables I, II, and VIII4 of Fisher and Yates: *Statistical tables for biological, agricultural and medical research*, published by Longman Group Ltd, London (previously published by Oliver and Boyd Ltd, Edinburgh, and by permission of the authors and publishers. Tables 5 and 6 are derived from *The new form statistical tables* by G.H. Fisher, published by Hodder and Stoughton, Sevenoaks, 2nd edition, 1965, by permission of the author and publishers.

Statistical Table 1. Table of probabilities (*P*-values) and corresponding values of χ^2 on 1 d.f., standardized normal deviate 2-sided, and 1-sided

***P*-value**	χ^2 **1 d.f.**	**Normal deviate 2-sided**	**Normal deviate 1-sided**
0.000 001	23.9	4.89	4.75
0.000 01	19.51	4.42	4.27
0.000 1	15.14	3.89	3.72
0.001	**10.83**	**3.29**	**3.09**
0.01	**6.63**	**2.58**	**2.33**
0.02	5.41	2.33	2.05
0.03	4.71	2.17	1.88
0.04	4.22	2.05	1.75
0.05	**3.84**	**1.96**	**1.64**
0.06	3.54	1.88	1.55
0.07	3.28	1.81	1.48
0.08	3.06	1.75	1.41
0.09	2.87	1.70	1.34
0.10	**2.71**	**1.64**	**1.28**
0.11	2.55	1.60	1.23
0.12	2.42	1.55	1.18
0.13	2.29	1.51	1.13
0.14	2.18	1.48	1.08
0.15	2.07	1.44	1.04
0.16	1.97	1.41	0.99
0.17	1.88	1.37	0.95
0.18	1.80	1.34	0.92
0.19	1.72	1.31	0.88
0.20	**1.64**	**1.28**	**0.84**
0.25	1.32	1.15	0.68
0.3	1.07	1.04	0.52
0.35	0.87	0.93	0.39
0.4	0.71	0.84	0.25
0.45	0.57	0.76	0.13
0.5	0.45	0.67	0.0
0.6	0.27	0.52	
0.7	0.15	0.39	
0.8	0.06	0.25	
0.9	0.02	0.13	

Statistical Table 1. Table of probabilities (*P*-values) and corresponding values of χ^2 on 1 degree of freedom, standardized normal deviate two-sided; and standardized normal deviate, one-sided

The values tabulated

1. The chi-square χ^2 statistic on one degree of freedom. For any other number of degrees of freedom, use Statistical Table 2.

The table gives the probability of the given χ^2 or a larger value under the null hypothesis.

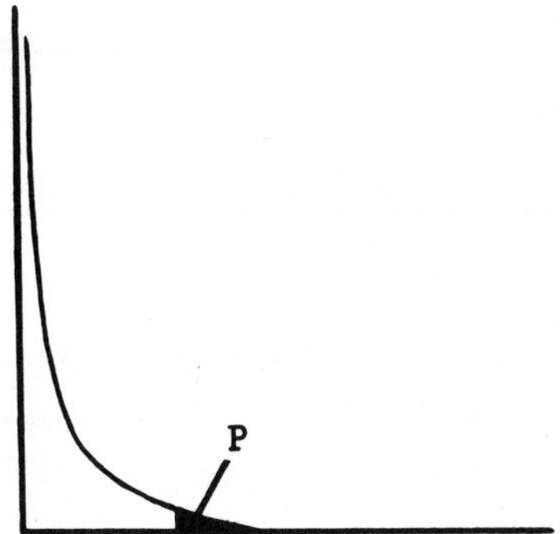

Although this is a one tail probability on a χ^2 distribution, because the χ^2 distribution is given by a normal deviate squared, this gives a two-sided test; assessing a variable x^2 using a χ^2 distribution is equivalent to assessing x using a normal distribution and a two-sided test.

2. The standardized normal deviate (often called Z or chi) using a two-sided test.

The probability given is that of the given value $\pm Z$ or a more extreme value of either sign, under the null hypothesis.

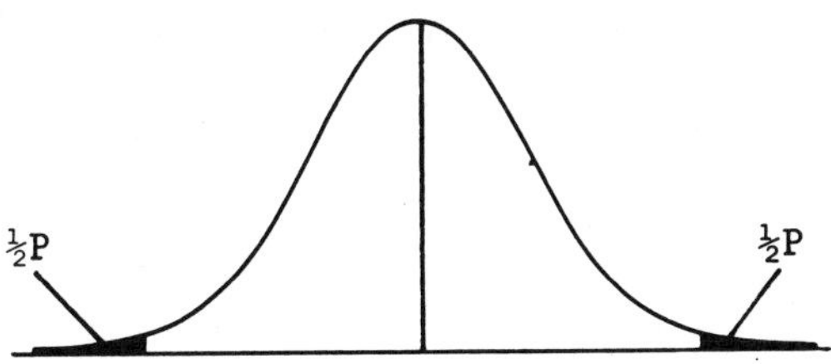

3. The standardized normal deviate (often called Z or chi), using a one-sided test. The probability given is that of the given value Z or a more extreme value of the same sign.

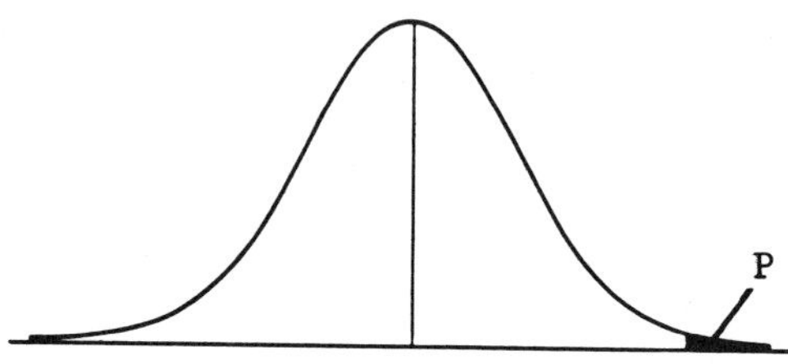

Relationships between these

1. For a given value of P, the corresponding $\chi^2_{(1)}$ value is equal to the two-sided standardized normal deviate squared.

e.g. for $P = 0.05$ $\chi^2 = 3.84$ $Z = 1.96 = \sqrt{3.84}$

2. For a given normal deviate, the two-sided probability is twice the one-sided.

e.g. for $Z = 1.96$, two-sided probability $= 0.05$, one-sided $= 0.025$

How to use the tables

1. Be sure you know which statistic you wish to use!

2. To find the value of a statistic corresponding to a given P value:
look down the table to find the P-value or the nearest to it;
read off the corresponding statistic.

Examples: What $\chi^2_{(1)}$ value corresponds to $P = 0.05$? Result: 3.84
What one-sided deviate corresponds to $P = 0.01$? Result: 2.33

3. To find the P-value corresponding to a given statistic:
find the correct column;
look down the table to find the given value or the nearest to it;
read off the corresponding P-value.

Examples: What P-value corresponds to $\chi^2_{(1)} = 7.4$? Result between 0.001 and 0.01; can be written $0.001 < P < 0.01$
What P-value corresponds to a one-sided test giving a deviate of 1.04? Result: 0.15

Statistical Table 2. Table of probability values (horizontal axis) corresponding to χ^2 statistics (body of table) for degrees of freedom from 1 to 30 (vertical axis)

Degrees of freedom	**Probability value**										
f	**0.90**	**0.80**	**0.70**	**0.50**	**0.30**	**0.20**	**0.10**	**0.05**	**0.02**	**0.01**	**0.001**
1	0.0158	0.0642	0.148	0.455	1.074	1.642	2.706	3.841	5.412	6.635	10.827
2	0.211	0.446	0.713	1.386	2.408	3.219	4.605	5.991	7.824	9.210	13.815
3	0.584	1.005	1.424	2.366	3.665	4.642	6.251	7.815	9.837	11.345	16.266
4	1.064	1.649	2.195	3.357	4.878	5.989	7.779	9.488	11.668	13.277	18.467
5	1.610	2.343	3.000	4.351	6.064	7.289	9.236	11.070	13.388	15.086	20.515
6	2.204	3.070	3.828	5.348	7.231	8.558	10.645	12.592	15.033	16.812	22.457
7	2.833	3.822	4.671	6.346	8.383	9.803	12.017	14.067	16.622	18.475	24.322
8	3.490	4.594	5.527	7.344	9.524	11.030	13.362	15.507	18.168	20.090	26.125
9	4.168	5.380	6.393	8.343	10.656	12.242	14.684	16.919	19.679	21.666	27.877
10	4.865	6.179	7.267	9.342	11.781	13.442	15.987	18.307	21.161	23.209	29.588
11	5.578	6.989	8.148	10.341	12.899	14.631	17.275	19.675	22.618	24.725	31.264
12	6.304	7.807	9.034	11.340	14.011	15.812	18.549	21.026	24.054	26.217	32.909
13	7.042	8.634	9.926	12.340	15.119	16.985	19.812	22.362	25.472	27.688	34.528
14	7.790	9.467	10.821	13.339	16.222	18.151	21.064	23.685	26.873	29.141	36.123
15	8.547	10.307	11.721	14.339	17.322	19.311	22.307	24.996	28.259	30.578	37.697
16	9.312	11.152	12.624	15.338	18.418	20.465	23.542	26.296	29.633	32.000	39.252
17	10.085	12.002	13.531	16.338	19.511	21.615	24.769	27.587	30.995	33.409	40.790
18	10.865	12.857	14.440	17.338	20.601	22.760	25.989	28.869	32.346	34.805	42.312
19	11.651	13.716	15.352	18.338	21.689	23.900	27.204	30.144	33.687	36.191	43.820
20	12.443	14.578	16.266	19.337	22.775	25.038	28.412	31.410	35.020	37.566	45.315
21	13.240	15.445	17.182	20.337	23.858	26.171	29.615	32.671	36.343	38.932	46.797
22	14.041	16.314	18.101	21.337	24.939	27.301	30.813	33.924	37.659	40.289	48.268
23	14.848	17.187	19.021	22.337	26.018	28.429	32.007	35.172	38.968	41.638	49.728
24	15.659	18.062	19.943	23.337	27.096	29.553	33.196	36.415	40.270	42.980	51.179
25	16.473	18.940	20.867	24.337	28.172	30.675	34.382	37.652	41.566	44.314	52.620
26	17.292	19.820	21.792	25.336	29.246	31.795	35.563	38.885	42.856	45.642	54.052
27	18.114	20.703	22.719	26.336	30.319	32.912	36.741	40.113	44.140	46.963	55.476
28	18.939	21.588	23.647	27.336	31.391	34.027	37.916	41.337	45.419	48.278	56.893
29	19.768	22.475	24.577	28.336	32.461	35.139	39.087	42.557	46.693	49.588	58.302
30	20.599	23.364	25.508	29.336	33.530	36.250	40.256	43.773	47.962	50.892	59.703

For larger values of degrees of freedom (f)

calculate $Z = \sqrt{2\chi^2} - \sqrt{(2f-1)}$

Z is a standardized normal deviate, for which the one-sided probability (obtained from Statistical Tables 1 or 4) corresponds to the P-value of χ^2.

Adapted from Fisher and Yates (1963) with permission of the publishers.

Statistical Table 2. Table of probability values (horizontal axis) corresponding to χ^2 statistics (body of table) for degrees of freedom from 1 to 30 (vertical axis)

The values tabulated

The values in the body of the table are the values of χ^2 with the given number of degrees of freedom (f) which correspond to probabilities from 0.9 to 0.001 given on the horizontal axis.

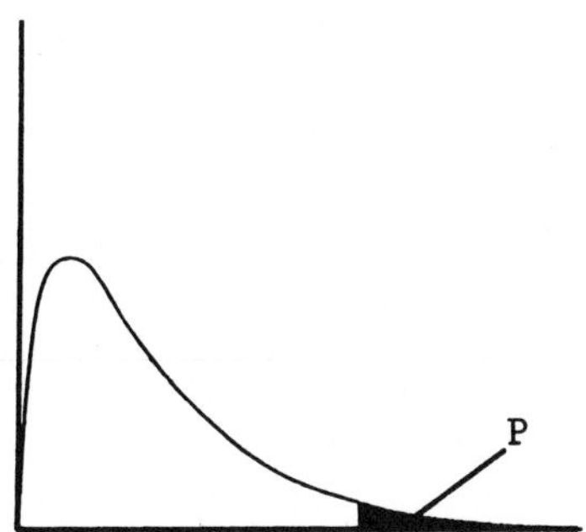

How to use this table

1. To find the probability corresponding to a given χ^2:
find the row for the appropriate number of degrees of freedom
find the χ^2 value or those nearest to it
read off the P-value from the top of the table: interpret this as a two-sided test

e.g. d.f. = 14 $\chi^2 = 25.4$ P is between 0.02 and 0.05; $0.02 < P < 0.05$
d.f. = 27 $\chi^2 = 21.2$ P is between 0.8 and 0.7; $0.7 < P < 0.8$
d.f. = 6 $\chi^2 = 37.4$ P is less than 0.001; $P < 0.001$
d.f. = 22 $\chi^2 = 7.4$ P is greater than 0.9; $P > 0.9$

2. To find χ^2 corresponding to a given P-value and number of degrees of freedom: read the P-value on the horizontal axis, the degrees of freedom on the vertical:

e.g. for $P = 0.05$ at 21 d.f. $\chi^2 = 32.671$
for $P = 0.01$ at 8 d.f. $\chi^2 = 20.090$

3. For higher degrees of freedom: use the formula shown. It is reasonably accurate with substantial numbers of degrees of freedom:

e.g. for $f = 25$ and $\chi^2 = 34.4$
$Z = \sqrt{(2 \times 34.4)} - \sqrt{(2 \times 25 - 1)} = 1.29$

probability from statistical table 4 = 0.0985; compared to 0.10 from this table
for $f = 60$ and $\chi^2 = 79.0$ $Z = 1.66$ and $P = 0.0485$

Statistical Table 3. Two-sided probabilities *P* (axes) corresponding to values of the standardized normal deviate (body of table)—a more detailed table

3(a) Values from 0.01 to 0.99

		P: second decimal									
	P	**0.00**	**0.01**	**0.02**	**0.03**	**0.04**	**0.05**	**0.06**	**0.07**	**0.08**	**0.09**
P:	0.0	∞	2.576	2.326	2.170	2.054	1.960	1.881	1.812	1.751	1.695
first	0.1	1.645	1.598	1.555	1.514	1.476	1.440	1.405	1.372	1.341	1.311
decimal	0.2	1.282	1.254	1.227	1.200	1.175	1.150	1.126	1.103	1.080	1.058
	0.3	1.036	1.015	0.994	0.974	0.954	0.935	0.915	0.896	0.878	0.860
	0.4	0.842	0.824	0.806	0.789	0.772	0.755	0.739	0.722	0.706	0.690
	0.5	0.674	0.659	0.643	0.628	0.613	0.598	0.583	0.568	0.553	0.539
	0.6	0.524	0.510	0.496	0.482	0.468	0.454	0.440	0.426	0.412	0.399
	0.7	0.385	0.372	0.358	0.345	0.332	0.319	0.305	0.292	0.279	0.266
	0.8	0.253	0.240	0.228	0.215	0.202	0.189	0.176	0.164	0.151	0.138
	0.9	0.126	0.113	0.100	0.088	0.075	0.063	0.050	0.038	0.025	0.013

3(b) P-values from 10^{-3} to 10^{-9}

P	10^{-3}	10^{-4}	10^{-5}	10^{-6}	10^{-7}	10^{-8}	10^{-9}
	0.001	**0.0001**	**0.000 01**	**0.000 001**	**0.000 000 1**	**0.000 000 01**	**0.000 000 001**
deviate	3.291	3.891	4.417	4.892	5.327	5.731	6.109

Adapted from Fisher and Yates (1963), with permission of the publishers

Statistical Table 3. Two-sided probabilities P (axes) corresponding to values of the standardized normal deviate (body of table)—a more detailed table

The values tabulated

This table is more detailed than Statistical Table 1, and gives for two-sided probability values from 0.000 000 001 to 0.99 (on the axes) the corresponding standardized normal deviate (in the body of the table).

The P-value corresponds to the area shaded:

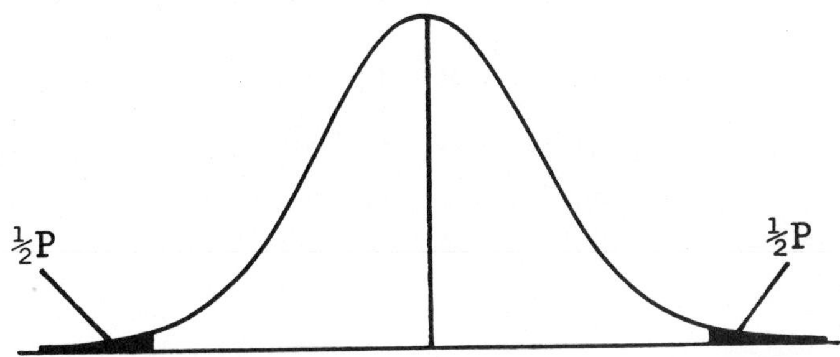

How to use this table

1. To find the standardized normal deviate corresponding to a given two-sided P-value:
look up the P-value using first the vertical and then the horizontal axis, and read off the normal deviate

e.g. for $P = 0.07$ $Z = 1.812$
for $P = 0.72$ $Z = 0.358$
for $P = 0.0001$ $Z = 3.891$

2. To find the two-sided P-value corresponding to a given standardized normal deviate:
look up the deviate in the body of the table; read the P-value from the axis

e.g. for $Z = 0.426$ $P = 0.67$
for $Z = 2.5$ P is between 0.02 and 0.01; $0.01 < P < 0.02$
for $Z = 4.7$ P is between 10^{-5} and 10^{-6}

3. For one-sided P-values, use Statistical Table 4.

4. This table can be used also for χ^2 statistics on ONE degree of freedom by using $\sqrt{\chi^2}$ as the normal deviate

e.g. $\chi^2_{(1)}$ of 3.2 $\sqrt{\chi^2} = 1.79$ $0.07 < P < 0.08$

For χ^2 with more than one degree of freedom, use Statistical Table 2.

Statistical Table 4. Standardized normal deviate (axes) and corresponding one-sided probability value (body of table)—a very detailed table

	Z	**Decimal place indicator**	**Deviate: second decimal** 0	1	2	3	4	5	6	7	8	9
Deviate:	0.0	0.	500	496	492	488	484	480	476	472	468	464
first	0.1		460	456	452	448	444	440	436	433	429	425
decimal	0.2		421	417	413	409	405	401	397	394	390	386
	0.3		382	378	374	371	367	363	359	356	352	348
	0.4		345	341	337	334	330	326	323	319	316	312
	0.5		309	305	302	298	295	291	288	284	281	278
	0.6		274	271	268	264	261	258	255	251	248	245
	0.7		242	239	236	233	230	227	224	221	218	215
	0.8		212	209	206	203	200	198	195	192	189	187
	0.9		184	181	179	176	174	171	169	166	164	161
	1.0		159	156	154	152	149	147	145	142	140	138
	1.1		136	134	131	129	127	125	123	121	119	117
	1.2		115	113	111	109	107	106	104	102	100	^{0}985
	1.3	0.0	968	951	934	918	901	885	869	853	838	823
	1.4		808	793	778	764	749	735	721	708	694	681
	1.5		668	655	643	630	618	606	594	582	571	559
	1.6		548	537	526	516	505	495	485	475	465	455
	1.7		446	436	427	418	409	401	392	384	375	367
	1.8		359	351	344	336	329	322	314	307	301	294
	1.9		287	281	274	268	262	256	250	244	239	233
	2.0		228	222	217	212	207	202	197	192	188	183
	2.1		179	174	170	166	162	158	154	150	146	143
	2.2		139	136	132	129	125	122	119	116	113	110
	2.3		107	104	102	^{0}990	^{0}964	^{0}939	^{0}914	^{0}889	^{0}866	^{0}842
	2.4	0.0^2	820	798	776	755	734	714	695	676	657	639
	2.5		621	604	587	570	554	539	523	508	494	480
	2.6		466	453	440	427	415	402	391	379	368	357
	2.7		347	336	326	317	307	298	289	280	272	264
	2.8		256	248	240	233	226	219	212	205	199	193
	2.9		187	181	175	169	164	159	154	149	144	139
	3.0		135	131	126	122	118	114	111	107	104	100
	3.1	0.0^3	968	935	904	874	845	816	789	762	736	711
	3.2		687	664	641	619	598	577	557	538	519	501
	3.3		483	466	450	434	419	404	390	376	362	349
	3.4		337	325	313	302	291	280	270	260	251	242

Statistical Table 4. *Continued*

Statistical Table 4. Standardized normal deviate (axes) and corresponding one-sided probability value (body of table)—a very detailed table

The values tabulated

This is a very detailed table relating the standardized normal deviate from 0.00 to 4.99 to the corresponding one-sided *P*-value.

The *P*-value corresponds to the area tabulated:

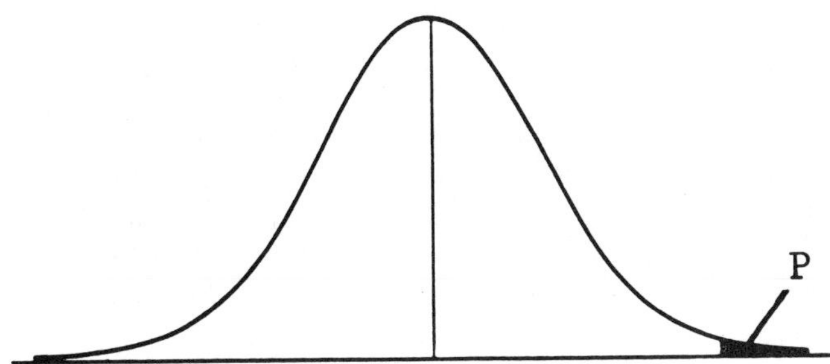

How to use this table

1. To find the one-sided *P*-value for a given standardized normal deviate: look up the deviate using the vertial and then the horizontal axes; read off the *P*-value, using the decimal place indicator in the first column:

e.g. $Z = 2.14$ $P = 0.0162$
$Z = 4.87$ $P = 0.000\,000\,558 = 0.558 \times 10^{-6}$

Be careful about the decimal place.

2. To find a two-sided *P*-value: double the one-sided value

e.g. $Z = 1.23$ one-sided $P = 0.109$ two-sided $P = 0.218$

3. To find the standardized normal deviate corresponding to a given one-sided *P*-value: look up the *P*-value in the body of the table, using the decimal place indicator in the first column; read the normal deviate from the axes:

e.g. $P = 0.42$ $Z \doteq 0.20$
$P = 0.02$ $Z \doteq 2.05$
$P = 0.0005$ $Z \doteq 3.29$

4. To find the normal deviate corresponding to a given two-sided *P* value: divide the *P*-value by 2; look this up as described above.

e.g. two-sided $P = 0.01$ one-sided $= 0.005$ $Z \doteq 2.58$
two-sided $P = 0.008$ one-sided $= 0.004$ $Z \doteq 2.65$

5. To find the two-sided *P*-value corresponding to a given χ^2 on one degree of freedom: take $\sqrt{\chi^2}$; use this normal deviate to look up *P*-value; double this *P*-value

e.g. $\chi^2 = 9.0$ $\sqrt{\chi^2} = 3.0$ $P_{(1)} = 0.00135$ $P_{(2)} = 0.00270$
$\chi^2 = 22.4$ $\sqrt{\chi^2} = 4.73$ $P_{(1)} = 0.112 \times 10^{-5}$ $P_{(2)} = 0.224 \times 10^{-5}$

Statistical Table 4. *Continued*

Z	Decimal place indicator	Deviate: second decimal									
		0	1	2	3	4	5	6	7	8	9
3.5		233	224	216	208	200	193	185	178	172	165
3.6		159	153	147	142	136	131	126	121	117	112
3.7		108	104	$^{0}996$	$^{0}957$	$^{0}920$	$^{0}884$	$^{0}850$	$^{0}816$	$^{0}784$	$^{0}753$
3.8	0.0^4	723	695	667	641	615	591	567	544	522	501
3.9		481	461	443	425	407	391	375	359	345	330
4.0		317	304	291	279	267	256	245	235	225	216
4.1		207	198	189	181	174	166	159	152	146	139
4.2		133	128	122	117	112	107	102	$^{0}977$	$^{0}934$	$^{0}893$
4.3	0.0^5	854	816	780	746	712	681	650	621	593	567
4.4		541	517	494	471	450	429	410	391	373	356
4.5		340	324	309	295	281	268	256	244	232	222
4.6		211	201	192	183	174	166	158	151	143	137
4.7		130	124	118	112	107	102	$^{0}968$	$^{0}921$	$^{0}876$	$^{0}834$
4.8	0.0^6	793	755	718	683	649	617	587	558	530	504
4.9		479	455	433	411	391	371	352	335	318	302

Adapted from Fisher and Yates (1963), with permission of the publishers

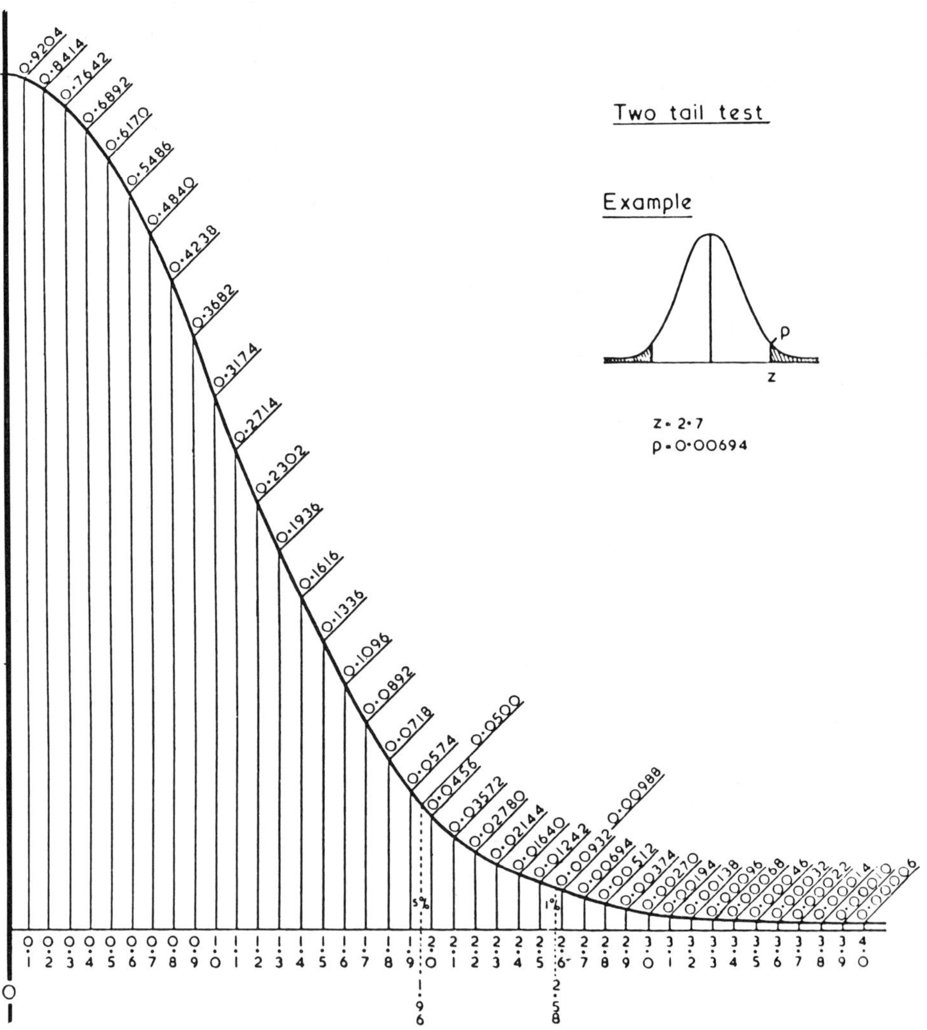
Two tail test
Example
p
z
z = 2·7
p = 0·00694
0·9204
0·8414
0·7642
0·6892
0·6170
0·5486
0·4840
0·4238
0·3682
0·3174
0·2714
0·2302
0·1936
0·1616
0·1336
0·1096
0·0892
0·0718
0·0574
0·0500
0·0456
0·03572
0·02780
0·02144
0·01640
0·01242
0·00988
0·00932
0·00694
0·00512
0·00374
0·00270
0·00194
0·00138
0·00096
0·00068
0·00046
0·00032
0·00022
0·00014
0·00010
0·00006
5%
1%

Statistical Table 5. Diagram of the standard normal distribution showing two-sided probabilities

This diagram is adapted from GH Fisher (1965). The standard normal distribution, that is, with mean = 0 and standard deviation = 1, is drawn to scale with the standardized normal deviate given in units of 0.1 standard deviations. The probability of a deviate Z being drawn from this distribution is given by the proportion of the area of the curve which lies outside the vertical ordinate for Z, and the equivalent ordinate for $-Z$; this is the two-sided P-value.

These probabilities are given for each ordinate. Statistical Table 6 shows a similar diagram for a one-sided test.

This diagram should help readers to understand the meaning of statistical tables; it can be used instead of a table to obtain two-sided P-values from normal deviates, and vice versa.

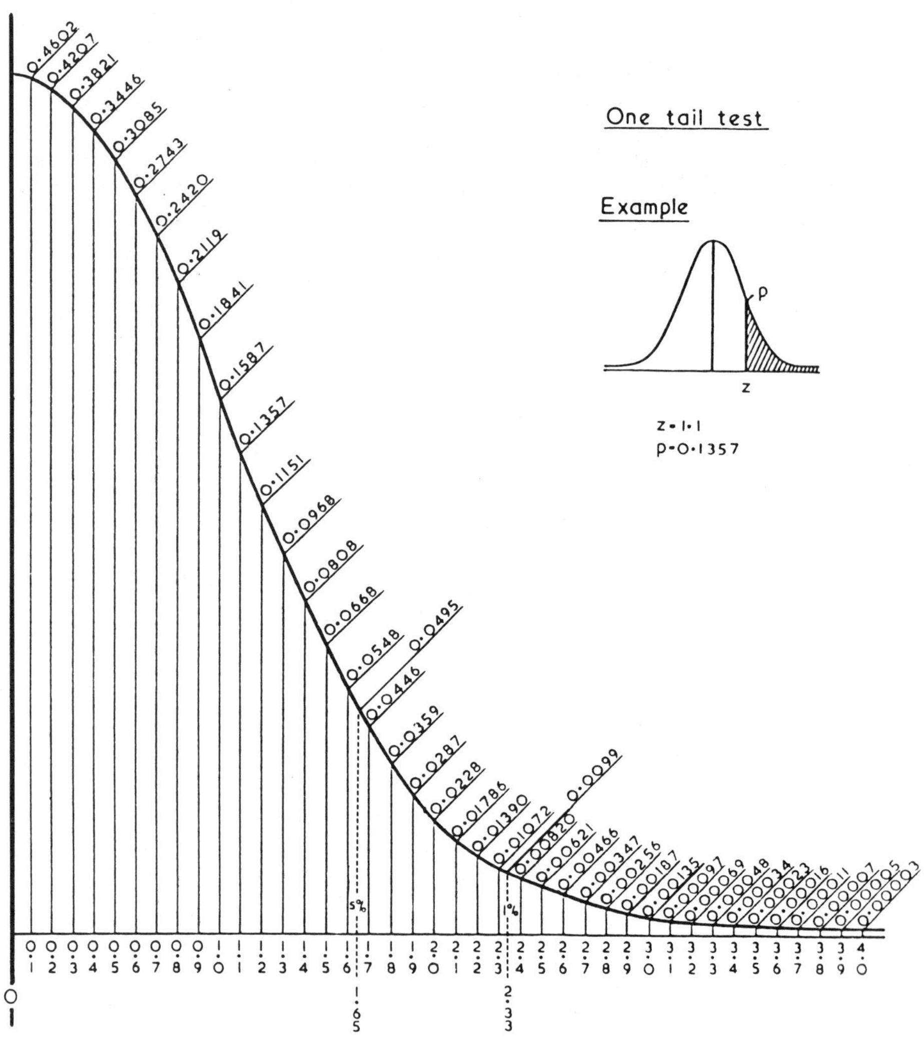
One tail test
Example
p
z
z = 1·1
p = 0·1357
5%
1%
0·4602
0·4207
0·3821
0·3446
0·3085
0·2743
0·2420
0·2119
0·1841
0·1587
0·1357
0·1151
0·0968
0·0808
0·0668
0·0548
0·0495
0·0446
0·0359
0·0287
0·0228
0·01786
0·01390
0·01072
0·0099
0·00820
0·00621
0·00466
0·00347
0·00256
0·00187
0·00135
0·00097
0·00069
0·00048
0·00034
0·00023
0·00016
0·00011
0·00007
0·00005
0·00003
0·1 0·2 0·3 0·4 0·5 0·6 0·7 0·8 0·9 1·0 1·1 1·2 1·3 1·4 1·5 1·6 1·7 1·8 1·9 2·0 2·1 2·2 2·3 2·4 2·5 2·6 2·7 2·8 2·9 3·0 3·1 3·2 3·3 3·4 3·5 3·6 3·7 3·8 3·9 4·0
0·1
1·65
2·33

Statistical Table 6. Diagram of the standard normal distribution showing one-sided probabilities

This diagram is adapted from GH Fisher (1965). The standard normal distribution, that is, with mean = 0 and standard deviation = 1, is drawn to scale with the standardized normal deviate given in units of 0.1 standard deviations. The probability of a deviate of *Z* being drawn from this distribution is given by the proportion of the area of the curve which lies outside the vertical ordinate for *Z*. If *Z* is positive, only the area outside the $+Z$ ordinate is relevant: hence the *P*-value is one-sided. If *Z* is negative, the relevant area is in the other tail of the curve, but as the curve is symmetrical that need not be shown.

These probabilities are given for each ordinate. Statistical Table 5 shows a similar diagram for a two-sided test.

This diagram should help readers to understand the meaning of statistical tables; it can be used instead of a table to obtain one-sided *P*-values from normal deviates, and vice versa.

Index